MW00954739

CALIFORNIA
Life and Health Insurance

License Exam Prep
Updated Yearly

Study Guide Includes State Law Supplement and 3 Complete Practice Tests

Previously published under ISBN 9781654245733 as *(2020 Edition) California Life, Accident and Health Insurance Agent License Exam Study Guide with 3 Complete Practice Exams: General Lines – Life, Accident, Health and Annuities*

Leland Chant

This edition contains the most thorough and accurate information available at printing time. Due to the dynamic nature of insurance licensing, examination content outlines constantly change, and this edition may not feature this new or revised content.

This study guide provides complete and reliable information regarding the covered subject matter. The publisher is not engaged in providing accounting, legal, or other professional services. If such assistance is required, seek the services of a competent professional.

If you find errors or incorrect information in this publication or have any questions or comments, please email us at brightideapublishers@gmail.com.

CONTENTS

INTRODUCTION

Thank you for choosing Bright Idea Publishers. You are preparing to pass the California Life, Accident and Health or Sickness Examination using the content found in this book. We've developed our state-specific prep books based on the exam content outlines published by testing providers in each state (e.g., Pearson VUE, PSI Exams, Prometric). Leland Chant, who has over two decades of experience in the Insurance industry, provides the most up-to-date information that educates test-takers in a streamlined manner. Our number one goal is to prepare you for the actual exam and to help you pass the test on the first attempt.

Study Pointers

- The author presents the information in each chapter based on the exam subject matter outlines provided by the state of California. This material covers only the information you need to learn for the exam.
- Be sure to take notes. This best practice will help you be proactive and engage in the learning process to solidify these insurance concepts.
- Create an outline or "hint" sheet. This best practice will help you complete a full review at the end of each chapter or the end of the book.
- Review the Exam Index section later in this Introduction to identify how every chapter corresponds to the actual exam. Test questions are associated with each chapter to help focus your study efforts accordingly.
- Every so often, take a break from studying. If you have been hitting it hard, but feel like you're having trouble retaining the information, try taking a few days off to recharge your mind.
- Keep the information fresh by studying until the day of your exam. When you cannot take the exam immediately after finishing the book, you should begin the study and review process again. It is always better to delay taking the exam than to be unprepared while taking it.
- Practice exam answers include the page number to the corresponding section of the book. This feature will help streamline the studying process!

Test Taking Pointers

- Be sure to get a whole night's sleep, and don't study right before you take the exam. This best practice will allow you to be well-rested and alert when arriving at the testing center.
- Carefully read the test tutorial and be sure to follow the instructions. Depending on your state, test providers may divide the exam into multiple parts. In this case, you may not be able to go back to review your answers once you have completed the section.
- Be calm and feel at ease. Breathe deeply and remember it is just an exam. If you prepare, the correct answers will become clear if you put in the time.
- Read every question and all the answer choices carefully, but do so quickly. Try not to linger on any one question.
- If a particular question has you stumped, you can mark it for review and move on to the next question. Sometimes you may answer a question later in the exam, which may jog your memory.
- Answer every question!
- Try to understand what the question is asking. Don't allow unfamiliar terms to throw you off since test builders mostly use them as examples or distracters. Read the question multiple times if necessary.
- Rule out incorrect answers. Each answer you exclude increases your chance of selecting the correct one.
- Trust your first answer. If you studied thoroughly, you know the material. Listen to your gut instinct and try not to overthink the question.
- Keywords such as NEVER, ALWAYS, EVERY, EXCEPT, ALL, or NOT may change the meaning of a question. Be sure to pay extra attention to them.
- Every question is multiple choice, and they are commonly either direct questions, incomplete sentences, or "all of the following EXCEPT."
- Remember that being a little nervous is not a bad thing. Most people perform better when they know the heat is on.
- Most importantly, RELAX! If you put in the work and if you put in the time, the results will be there.

Setting Expectations

Before taking your state exam, you must know the material and be familiar with testing procedures and the testing center environment.

Each state provides a candidate handbook or bulletin containing important information about specific testing procedures:

- Scheduling or rescheduling exams;
- Required identification;
- Arriving at the testing center; and
- Items prohibited in the testing center.

Test-takers should read the Candidate Information Bulletin (CIB) in preparation for their exam. This handbook is on the California Department of Insurance (CDI) website and their state testing provider's (PSI Exams) website.

The Exam	• It will test your knowledge and includes questions about various concepts and laws. • Test questions are designed to evaluate your basic understanding and retention of the material in this book. • Verify specific forms of identification required for your state exam by reviewing the candidate's handbook or bulletin or calling the testing center.
The Testing Center	• Be sure to arrive at least 30 minutes before your scheduled exam. • You are not allowed to take personal items like cell phones or study materials into the testing center. Some testing centers will provide lockers. • Food, drinks, or gum are not allowed inside the testing center. • Have your identification ready when you check in at the front desk. • Adjust the seat height and computer monitor as needed to feel comfortable. • Before beginning a computer-based exam, you will have a chance to take a tutorial to help you learn how to mark and review answers. • Remain focused and do not get distracted by others around you. Other test-takers may enter and leave the room while taking your exam.
Taking the Exam	• Most testing centers will provide scratch paper and a pencil to write down challenging questions during the exam. • When you review marked questions, go over the rest of the questions to ensure you didn't overlook any familiar concepts or terms that change what the question is asking.

Exam Index

The Exam Index will help you focus your studying. According to each chapter, all three practice tests include the number of questions. You will most certainly benefit when taking the actual exam by concentrating your efforts.

California Life, Accident and Health or Sickness Examination
150 Questions (plus five to ten non-scored experimental questions)
Time Limit: 3 hours 15 minutes
Passing Score: 60%

CHAPTER	# OF QUESTIONS
General Insurance	**40**
Basic Insurance Concepts and Principles	16
Contract Law	10
The Insurance Marketplace	14
Life Insurance	**49**
Life Insurance – Basics	8
Types of Life Policies	10
Annuities	8
Life Insurance and Annuities – Policy Replacement/Cancellation	4
The Individual Life Insurance Contract	10
Taxation of Life Insurance and Annuities	3
Group Life Insurance Plans	2
Social Security Disability Program	1
Individual Underwriting, Pricing, and Claims	3
Life Policy Riders	**4**
General Concepts of Medical and Disability Insurance	**4**
Medical Expense Insurance	**45**
Individual Insurance	14
Group Medical Expense Insurance	8
Patient Protection and Affordable Care Act (PPACA)	8
Senior Health Products	15
Disability Income Insurance	**4**
Long-Term Care Insurance	**4**

Experimental Questions – In addition to the number of exam questions specified, the testing provider may administer five to ten "experimental" questions to examinees during the examinations. These questions are not scored, and the time to answer them is added to the total time allowed. Administrating such non-scored experimental items is a critical step in developing future licensing examinations.

CHAPTER 1:
Basic Insurance Concepts and Principles

Before you learn about specific policies and their provisions, you will first need to understand some basic concepts and terms associated with the insurance industry. This chapter discusses ideas that make it easier for you to learn the rest of the content in this book, so you need to master these concepts before moving on to the next chapter.

- Insurance
- Definition and Types of Risk
- Perils and Hazards
- Law of Large Numbers
- Loss Exposure
- Adverse Selection
- Risk Situations that Present the Possibility of Loss
- Risk Management Techniques
- Ideally Insurable Risks
- Insurable Events
- Insurable Interest
- Indemnity
- Utmost Good Faith

Insurance

Insurance is a transfer of loss or risk from a business entity or a person to an insurance provider, which then spreads the costs of unexpected losses to many people. If there were no insurance, the cost of a loss would have to be incurred solely by the person who suffered the loss.

In the eyes of the law, a person is a legal entity that acts on behalf of itself. People accept legal and civil responsibility for their actions and make contracts in their own name. Individual human beings, partnerships, corporations, associations, and trusts are included in the definition of a person.

Insurance is a contract in which one individual undertakes to indemnify another individual against damage, loss, or liability arising from an unknown event (Cal. Ins. Code Section 22).

In broader terms, insurance is the legal agreement, or contract, in which the two parties agree to the limits of the indemnification. The parties also agree to the contract's terms and conditions and the consideration (things of value) that will be exchanged.

Definition and Types of Risk

Risk is the uncertainty or likelihood that a loss occurs. There are two types of risk – pure risk and speculative risk, only one of which can be insured.

- *Pure risk* applies to circumstances that can only result in no change or a loss. There is no chance for financial gain. Pure risk is the only kind of risk that insurance companies accept.
- *Speculative risk* includes the opportunity for either gain or loss. Gambling is an example of speculative risk, and insurance companies cannot insure these types of risk.

It is crucial to note that insurance providers can only insure *pure risks*.

Perils and Hazards

In an insurance policy, *perils* are the insured against *causes of loss* that insurance providers will cover.

- *Life insurance* insures against the financial loss caused by the untimely death of an insured;
- *Health insurance* insures against the loss of income or medical expenses caused by the insured's accidental injury or sickness;
- *Property insurance* insures against (covers) the loss of physical property or the loss of its ability to produce income; and
- *Casualty insurance* insures against the resulting liabilities from the loss or damage of property.

Hazards are circumstances or settings that increase the likelihood of an insured loss. Conditions such as congested traffic or slippery floors are hazards and may increase the odds of a loss occurring. Insurers categorize hazards according to physical, moral, or morale hazards.

Physical hazards arise from the risk's structural, material, or operational features, separate from those managing or owning it.

Moral hazards deal with any applicant who lies on an insurance application or submits fraudulent claims against an insurer.

Morale hazards refer to an increase in the danger presented by a risk, stemming from the insured's apathy towards loss because of the presence of insurance. (e.g., "I have no intention of fixing this. If it breaks, my insurance policy will pay to have it replaced.")

Legal hazards describe an array of legal or regulatory conditions that affect an insurer's ability to collect premiums comparable in value with the loss exposure the insurer must bear.

Law of Large Numbers

The foundation of insurance is sharing risk between a large pool of people (a homogenous group) with a similar exposure to loss. The *law of large numbers* states that the actual losses will be more predictable among a *larger* group of people having a similar loss exposure. This law forms the basis for the statistical prediction of loss which insurers use to calculate insurance rates.

Example 1.1 – When an insurance company issues a policy on a 35-year-old male, the company cannot know or accurately predict when he will die. However, the law of large numbers examines a large group of similar risks, which in this case are 35-year-old males of similar lifestyles and health conditions. It makes conclusions based on the statistics of past losses. The law of large numbers gives the insurer a general idea about the predicted time of death for these insureds and sets the premiums accordingly. It is important to note that as the number of individuals in a risk pool increases, future losses become more predictable.

Loss Exposure

Exposure is a unit of measure used in calculating insurance coverage rates. In life insurance, the following factors are considered in calculating rates:

- The age of the insured;
- Sex;
- Occupation; and
- Medical history.

A large number of units with the same or similar exposure to loss are known as *homogeneous*. Sharing risk between a sizeable homogeneous group with a similar loss exposure constitutes the basis of insurance.

A profitable distribution of exposures (or spreading of risk) takes place when poor risks are balanced with preferred risks, with "standard" or "average" risks in the middle. This way of distributing risks protects the insurance provider from adverse selection, which is one of the most critical concepts of insurance.

Adverse Selection

Insurers strive to protect themselves from *adverse selection*, which refers to insuring risks more prone to losses than the average risk. Poorer risks seek insurance or file claims to a greater extent than better risks.

Insurance companies can refuse or restrict coverage for bad risks or charge them a higher rate for insurance coverage to protect themselves from adverse selection.

Risk Situations that Present the Possibility of Loss

When establishing an insurance program, insureds must first recognize their exposure to loss. They must also acknowledge the probability of how likely it is that a loss will occur and how "big" the loss might be. Because of the severity of the possible loss, certain risks will demand attention above others.

For example, a person who handles power tools when engaged in the hobby of carpentry is exposed to the possibility of injuring their hand. If the person is a heart surgeon, this would be considered a critical risk of financial loss because the injury may prevent them from performing their job. However, when the individual is a television announcer, the loss of hand function may be considered a less significant risk.

Exposures to potential losses should be classified into appropriate groups and ranked in the order of their importance:

- *Critical risks* include every exposure in which the potential losses are of the magnitude that would result in the financial ruination of the insured, their business, or their family;
- *Important risks* include loss exposures which would lead the person to significant lifestyle changes or a change in their profession; and
- *Unimportant risks* include those exposures in which the potential losses could be absorbed by current income or assets without imposing unnecessary lifestyle changes or financial strain.

In deciding to establish an insurance program, it is prudent to apply the following common-sense principles:

- Consider the odds;
- Don't risk more than you can afford to lose; and
- Don't risk a lot for a little.

Risk Management Techniques

Sharing – *Sharing* is a way of dealing with risk for a group of individuals or businesses with the same or similar loss exposure to share the losses within that group. A reciprocal exchange of insurance is a formal arrangement for risk-sharing.

Transfer – The most effective approach to handling risk is to *transfer* it so that another party bears the loss. Insurance is the most accepted means of transferring risk from a person or group to an insurance company. Though buying insurance will not remove the risk of illness or death, it relieves the insured of the financial losses accompanying these risks.

There are numerous ways to transfer risk, including holding harmless agreements and other contractual agreements. Still, the most common and safest method is to buy insurance coverage.

Avoidance – *Avoidance* is one of the methods of dealing with risk, which means removing exposure to a loss. For instance, if a person wants to avoid the risk of dying in a motorcycle crash, they may choose never to ride a motorcycle. Risk avoidance can be effective, but it is hardly practical.

Retention – An insured's planned assumption of risk through self-insurance, co-payments, or deductibles is known as risk *retention*. Self-insurance is when the insured accepts responsibility for the loss before the insurance provider pays. The aim of retention is

1. To decrease expenses and improve cash flow;
2. To increase control of claim settlements and claim reserving; and
3. To finance losses that cannot be insured.

Reduction – Since risk usually cannot be avoided entirely, we often try to reduce the likelihood or severity of a loss. *Reduction* includes having an annual health exam to detect health problems early, installing smoke detectors in a home, or perhaps even changing one's lifestyle.

Ideally Insurable Risks

Even though insurance is one of the most effective ways to handle risks, insurers cannot cover every risk. As previously stated, insurance companies will only insure pure risks or those only involving a chance of loss without a chance of gain. However, not all pure risks are insurable. Certain elements or characteristics must exist before a pure risk can be insured.

The loss has to be due to chance (accidental). For a risk to be considered insurable, it must involve a possibility of loss that the insured cannot control.

The loss must be definite and measurable. An insurable risk must involve losses with an exact time, place, cause, and amount. An insurance provider must determine the benefit amount and when it will pay the benefit. Since an insurance policy is a legal contract, it helps if the conditions are as exact as possible.

The loss must be statistically predictable. This characteristic allows insurance companies to estimate the severity and average frequency of future losses and to set appropriate premiums. Using morbidity and mortality tables in life and health insurance allows the insurance provider to project losses based on statistics.

The loss cannot be catastrophic. Insurance companies will not insure a risk that exposes them to catastrophic losses that would exceed certain limits. Usually, insurance policies exclude coverage for losses from wars or nuclear events. No statistical data exists that would allow for developing rates necessary to cover these events should they occur.

The loss exposure to be insured has to involve large homogenous units of exposure. A sufficiently large pool of insureds with similar risks must be grouped into classes so the insurance company can predict losses using the law of large numbers. This large group allows insurers to accurately predict the average severity and frequency of future losses and set appropriate premiums.

The insurance must not be mandatory. Insurers are not required to issue a policy to every applicant applying for coverage. An insurer must be able to require insureds to meet specific underwriting guidelines.

Insurable Events

If a likely future event could result in loss or liability to an individual, it may be insurable (Cal. Ins. Code Section 250). These insurable events may never happen, but insurance policies can provide protection when those times do occur.

Losses become more *insurable* when they become more *predictable*. If a loss is *more unpredictable*, it becomes *less insurable*. For instance, a person cannot insure gambling losses or lottery outcomes because of unpredictability.

The law does not address a limit as to the level of loss that may be insured against; it only clarifies the type of event that can be insured. The contract designates the level of loss to be indemnified (repaid).

Insurable Interest

The policy owner needs to face the possibility of losing money or something of value in the event of a loss to buy insurance. This concept is known as *insurable interest*. In life insurance, insurable interest must exist between the policy owner and the insured *at the time of application*. However, once the insurer issues a life insurance policy, it must pay the policy benefit, whether or not an insurable interest exists.

A valid insurable interest can exist between the policy owner and the insured when the policy is insuring any of the following:

1. The policy owner's life;
2. The life of a family member like a spouse or a close blood relative; or
3. The life of a key employee, business partner, or someone who has a financial obligation to the policy owner, like a debtor to a creditor.

Beneficiaries do not require insurable interest. Since the beneficiary's well-being depends on the insured, and the beneficiary's life is not the one being insured, the beneficiary does not have to show an insurable interest.

Indemnity

Sometimes referred to as reimbursement, *indemnity* is a provision in an insurance contract that states that in the event of loss, a beneficiary or an insured is allowed to collect only to the extent of the financial loss. The insured cannot be entitled to gain financially because of an insurance contract. Insurance aims to restore an insured following a loss but not let a beneficiary or insured profit from the loss.

Example of Life and Health Insurance – Karen has a $20,000 health insurance policy. After being hospitalized, her medical expenses totaled $15,000. The insurance policy only will reimburse Karen for the amount of the loss ($15,000) and not for the total amount of insurance ($20,000).

Example of Property and Casualty Insurance – Karen has a $200,000 homeowners insurance policy. After the destruction of her house, her cost to rebuild the home totaled $150,000. The insurance policy will only reimburse Karen for the amount of the loss ($150,000) and not for the total amount of insurance ($200,000).

Utmost Good Faith

The principle of *utmost good faith* implies that there will be no concealment, misrepresentation, or fraud between the parties. As it pertains to insurance policies, both the insurance company and the insured must be able to rely on the other for relevant information. The insured is expected to provide accurate information on the insurance application. The insurance company must clearly and truthfully describe policy features and benefits and not conceal or mislead the insured.

Chapter Review

This chapter explained the basic insurance concepts and principles you need to know. Let's review them:

BASIC INSURANCE PRINCIPLES	
Insurance	• Insurance transfers loss or risk from a business entity or a person to an insurance provider, which then spreads the costs of unexpected losses to many individuals

Types of Risk	• Uncertainty regarding financial loss
	• Two types of risks:
	   o *Pure* – insurable because it only involves the chance of loss
	   o *Speculative* – not insurable because it involves the chance of gain

Perils and Hazards	• Hazards give rise to a peril; there are three kinds of hazards:
	   o *Physical* – a physical condition
	   o *Moral* – a tendency toward increased risk
	   o *Morale* – an indifference to loss

Law of Large Numbers	• Larger numbers of individuals with a similar exposure to loss are more predictive of future losses

Loss Exposure	• A unit of measure used to calculate rates charged for insurance coverage
	• Factors considered in calculating rates:
	   o The insured's age
	   o Sex
	   o Occupation; and
	   o Medical history

Adverse Selection	• Insurers strive to protect themselves from adverse selection, which refers to the insuring of risks that are more prone to losses than the average risk
Risk Situations	• *Critical risks* – every exposure in which the potential losses are of the magnitude that would result in the financial ruination of the insured, their business, or their family; • *Important risks* – loss exposures which would lead the person to major lifestyle changes or a change in profession; and • *Unimportant risks* – those exposures in which the potential losses could be absorbed by current income or current assets without imposing unnecessary lifestyle changes or financial strain

Ideally Insurable Risks	• Certain elements or characteristics must exist before a pure risk can be insured:
	   o The loss must be due to chance (accidental)
	   o The loss must be definite and measurable
	   o The loss cannot be catastrophic
	   o The loss exposure to be insured has to involve large homogenous units of exposure
	   o The insurance must not be mandatory

BASIC INSURANCE PRINCIPLES *(Continued)*	
Risk Management Techniques	• *Sharing* – a way of dealing with risk for a group of individuals or businesses with the same or similar exposure to loss in order to share the losses that happen within that group • *Transfer* – the most effective approach to handling risk is to transfer it so that another party bears the loss • Avoidance – one of the methods of dealing with risk, which means removing exposure to a loss • *Retention* – the planned assumption of risk by an insured through the use of self-insurance, co-payments, or deductibles • *Reduction* – reducing the likelihood or severity of a loss (e.g., having an annual health exam to detect health problems early, or installing smoke detectors)
Insurable Events	• If a likely future event could result in loss or liability to an individual, it may be insurable • Losses become more insurable when they become more predictable • If a loss is more unpredictable, it becomes less insurable

Insurance Interest	• A valid insurable interest can exist between the policy owner and the insured when the policy insures:
	  o The policy owner's life
	  o The life of a family member like a spouse or a close blood relative; or
	  o The life of a key employee, business partner, or someone who has a financial obligation to the policy owner, like a debtor to a creditor

Indemnity	• Often referred to as reimbursement • Insureds or beneficiaries are allowed to collect to the extent of financial loss • An insured cannot gain financially from a loss
Utmost Good Faith	• This principle implies that there will be no concealment, misrepresentation, or fraud between the parties

CHAPTER 2:
Contract Law

This chapter will explain some essential concepts relevant to insurance contract law. First, you will learn about an insurance contract's special characteristics and the required elements to be included in all contracts. Next, you will focus on legal definitions and concepts for every insurance policy. This chapter contains several key insurance terms; be sure you understand them without referring to the text.

- Contract Law vs. Tort Law
- Four Elements of a Contract
- Special Characteristics of an Insurance Contract
- Legal Terms
- Rescission
- Six Specifications for Insurance Policies
- Insurance Terms

Contract Law vs. Tort Law

Insurance allows risk to be transferred from the insured to the insurer through a contractual arrangement where the insurer promises to pay an agreed-upon amount or indemnify the insured in the event of the specified loss. This promise is in consideration of premiums paid by the insured and their promise to abide by the contract provisions. The insurance policy is the instrument through which this risk transfer is achieved.

Much of the law that shaped the formal structure of insurance and influenced its content comes from the general *law of contracts*. However, because of the many unique facets of insurance transactions, the general law of contracts needed to be modified to fit the insurance requirements.

A *tort* is a civil, private, non-contractual wrong which can be remedied through legal action. A tort can either be unintentional or intentional. Insurance usually will only respond to unintentional torts (losses other than those deliberate acts by an insured intended to cause damage or loss).

An *intentional tort* involves deliberate acts that cause harm to another person irrespective of whether the offending party intended to hurt the injured party. Breach of contract is not considered an intentional tort.

An *unintentional tort* is a consequence of acting without care. This action is commonly referred to as negligence.

Four Elements of a Contract

Contracts are defined as legally enforceable agreements between two or more parties. A contract must contain certain essential elements to be enforceable by law or legally binding. The four elements of a contract are:

- Agreement (offer and acceptance);
- Consideration;
- Competent parties; and
- Legal purpose

Agreement (Offer and Acceptance) – There has to be a definite offer by one party. The other party must accept this offer in its exact terms. Concerning insurance, the applicant usually makes the *offer* when applying. *Acceptance* occurs when an insurance provider's underwriter approves the application and issues a policy.

Consideration – The binding force in any contract is known as *consideration*. Consideration is when each party gives something of value to the other. The consideration on the insured's part is the premium payment and the representations provided in the application. The consideration on the insurance provider's part is the promise to pay if a loss occurs.

Competent Parties – In the eyes of the law, the *parties to a contract* must be able to enter into a contract willfully. Usually, this requires that both parties be mentally competent to comprehend the contract, of legal age, and not under the influence of alcohol or drugs.

Legal Purpose – The contract must have a *legal* purpose and not be against public policy. To ensure the legal purpose of a life insurance policy, for example, it must have both consent and insurable interest. A contract without a legal purpose is void and is not enforceable by any party.

Special Characteristics of an Insurance Contract

Contract of Adhesion – One of the parties to the agreement (the insurer) drafts a *contract of adhesion*. It is either accepted or rejected by the other party (the insured). Insurance companies do not write policies through contract negotiations, and an insured has no input regarding its provisions. Insurers also offer contracts on a "take it or leave it" basis by an insurance provider.

Conditional Contract – Before each party fulfills its obligations, a *conditional contract* requires that the policy owner and insurance company meet certain conditions to execute the agreement. The insured must pay the premium and provide proof of loss for the insurer to cover a claim.

Aleatory Contract – Insurance contracts are *aleatory*. In other words, the parties to the agreement are involved in an unequal exchange of amounts or values. Premiums paid by the insured are small compared to the amount the insurance provider will pay in a loss.

Example of Life and Health Insurance – Chad purchases a life insurance policy for $50,000. His monthly premium is $50. If Chad only had the policy for two months, he only paid $100 in insurance premiums. If he unexpectedly dies, his beneficiary will receive $50,000. A $100 contribution on the insured's part in exchange for a $50,000 benefit from the insurance provider illustrates an aleatory contract.

Example of Property and Casualty Insurance – Chad purchases a homeowner's insurance policy for $50,000. His monthly premium is $50. If Chad only had the policy for two months, he only paid $100 in insurance premiums. If a covered peril unexpectedly destroyed the home, Chad would receive $50,000. A $100 contribution on the insured's part in exchange for a $50,000 benefit from the insurance provider demonstrates an aleatory contract.

Unilateral Contract – In a *unilateral contract*, only one of the parties to the agreement must do anything according to the law. The insured makes no lawfully binding promises. Regardless, an insurance carrier must legally pay for losses covered by an in-force policy.

Personal Contract – In general, insurance contracts are *personal* contracts because they are between individuals and insurers. Insurance companies have a right to decide with whom they will not do business. The insured cannot be changed to another person without the insurer's written consent, nor can the policy owner transfer the contract to anyone else without approval from the insurance provider. Life insurance is an exception to this rule. A policy owner can assign or transfer policy ownership to another person; however, the policy owner must still notify the insurance provider in writing.

Legal Terms

Insurance Policy – The *insurance policy* is the written instrument that sets forth a contract of insurance (Cal. Ins. Code Section 380).

Concealment – *Concealment* is the legal term for intentionally withholding information of a material fact that is crucial in the decision-making process (Cal. Ins. Code Sections 333 and 339). For insurance purposes, concealment occurs when the applicant intentionally withholds information that will result in an imprecise underwriting decision. Concealment may void a policy.

Concealment is the failure to disclose known facts. An injured party is entitled to void the policy regardless of whether the concealment was intentional or unintentional. Every party should reasonably expect the other party to act in good faith without attempting to conceal or deceive the other. Neither party of the contract is legally bound to provide any information regarding their judgment, opinions, or matters in question. The right to rescind the policy is allowable for either party's intentional and fraudulent omission.

The following information is not required to be communicated in a contract:

- Known information;
- Information that should be known;
- Information that the other party waives;
- Information that is not material to the risk and excluded by a warranty;
- Information that is not material to the risk and excepted from insurance; and
- Information based on personal judgment.

Warranty – A *warranty* is a statement guaranteed to be true and becomes a part of the contract. A particular format of words is not necessary to create a warranty (Cal. Ins. Code Sections 440 through 445 and 447). Warranties can either be *implied* or *expressed*. An implied warranty is an unspoken or unwritten guarantee based on the circumstances of a transaction. Statements in a policy are express warranties. Every express warranty becomes part of the insurance contract.

The warranty is created at or before the execution of the policy and will be included in the policy. The warranty is not limited by time. Therefore, it can relate to the past, the present, the future, or any combination of these time frames. Violating a material warranty by either party entitles the other to *rescind* the policy.

Furthermore, the breach of an immaterial (unimportant) provision does not void the policy unless specified by the policy itself. Also, it will be taken as a warranty that such an act or omission will occur if the policy contains a statement implying an intention to affect the risk.

Representations and Misrepresentations – *Representations* are statements believed to be true to the best of one's knowledge; however, they are not guaranteed to be true (Cal. Ins. Code Sections 350 through 361). For insurance purposes, representations are the answers an insured provides to the questions on an insurance application.

A representation cannot qualify an express provision in an insurance contract, but it could qualify an *implied warranty* (Cal. Ins. Code Section 354).

Untrue statements on an insurance application are considered *misrepresentations* and can void the contract (Cal. Ins. Code Sections 780 through 784). A *material misrepresentation* is a statement that would alter the insurer's underwriting decision if discovered. Additionally, if material misrepresentations are intentional, they are considered fraudulent.

It is worth noting that representations may be *withdrawn* or *changed* before the policy implementation but not after. A misrepresentation relevant to underwriting the level of risk is grounds to void a contract. However, an insurer must conclude that the information was given under false pretenses with the intent to commit fraud and was material in deciding to enter into the contract.

Any individual violating this provision is guilty of a misdemeanor punishable by a maximum fine of $25,000, imprisonment in a county jail for no longer than one year, or by both a fine and imprisonment. If the loss to the victim exceeds $10,000, the penalty should not exceed three times the amount of the loss. In addition, the Commissioner can suspend the agent's license for a maximum period of three years.

Materiality – The concept of *materiality* states that all parties to a contract are entitled to all necessary information to decide on the nature or quality of the contract (Cal. Ins. Code Section 334). Materiality is determined by the "reasonable and probable influence of the facts" on the party needing them to make an informed decision, whether they are the insured or the insurer. The "injured" party may be entitled to rescind the contract if a failure to disclose material information occurs.

The weight of *disadvantages* on either party is of paramount importance. Disadvantages are always material information. All contracts have disadvantages for both parties, but they may not be compelling when deciding whether to accept the contract. Insurance companies are allowed to know material information about prospective insureds, such as: Have they been diagnosed or treated for heart disease, cancer, or diabetes? Have they ever been hospitalized? Have they ever been convicted of a felony? Do they fly an aircraft?

The materiality of a concealment establishes the importance of a misrepresentation. For example, if an insured deliberately conceals information about a recent stroke, this would have a more significant impact than if the insured individual had misrepresented their age by five years.

Insureds, however, are allowed to know the contract's disadvantages, which include the following: cash value surrender charges, length of term, increase in premium at the end of the period, internal expenses and fees, a substandard rating, or principal exclusions like war, terrorism, aviation, and suicide, for example. Producers must share disadvantages with the prospect instead of only sharing the advantages of the contract.

Rescission

Intentional or unintentional concealment entitles an injured party to rescind a contract (Cal. Ins. Code Section 331). The revocation of a contract is known as *rescission*.

Injured parties are *permitted to rescind the contract* if any of the following occurs:

- A false material representation in which rescission becomes effective from the time the representation turns out to be false;
- Concealment, irrespective of whether it is intentional;
- Negligence of a material warranty or other material provisions contained in a policy.

Six Specifications for Insurance Policies

Every contract of insurance must identify the following six specific elements (Cal. Ins. Code Section 381):

1. The parties involved in the contract;
2. The property or individuals being insured;
3. If the insured is not the owner, a statement of the insurable interest that exists;
4. The risks insured against;
5. The period during which the policy will continue or be in force; and
6. The stated monthly, quarterly, semi-annual, or annual premium. If it can only be determined at the expiration or termination of the contract, a statement of the method by which the insurer will calculate a premium rate and total premium.

It is worth noting that the financial rating of an insurer does not have to be specified in an insurance policy.

Insurance Terms

Application – The *application* is a printed form of questions about a prospective policy owner and the desired insurance coverage and limits. This form is also called the "app." It provides the underwriter with information for rejecting or accepting the applicant and rating the desired policy. Some policies include the application as part of the policy. Misrepresentations in the application could void a policy.

Contract – A *contract* is a written agreement that puts the insurance into effect and is legally enforceable.

Rider – *Riders* are written modifications attached to a policy that provide benefits not included in the original policy. Riders sometimes require an additional premium, but they also help tailor a policy to meet the insured's specific needs. Insurers classify riders according to their primary purpose.

Cancellation – *Cancellation* refers to terminating an insurance policy or bond before it expires by either the insurer or the insured. Cancellation provisions require insurance providers to notify insureds in advance (typically 30 days) of canceling a policy. These provisions also specify how the insurer will return unearned premiums.

Lapse – *Lapse* refers to terminating an insurance policy due to the insured's failure to pay the premium.

Grace Period – A *grace period* is a time after the premium due date that the policy owner has to pay the premium before the policy lapses (usually 30 or 31 days). The grace period protects the policy owner against an unintentional policy lapse. If a policy owner dies during this period, the death benefit is payable; however, insurers will deduct any unpaid premiums from the death benefit.

Reinstatement – *Reinstatement* is a provision that allows policy owners to reinstate a lapsed policy. If the policy owner reinstates their policy, they must provide evidence of insurability. The policy owner must also pay all back premiums with interest and could be required to repay any outstanding loans and interest.

Rate – A *rate* is a unit of cost multiplied by an exposure base to calculate an insurance premium. Insurance rates are the money insurers require to cover losses and expenses and provide a profit to the insurance company for a single unit of exposure.

Premium – *Premiums* are the amount of money an insurance company charges for providing the coverage described in the policy. Policy owners pay this periodic insurance payment to keep an insurance policy in force.

Earned Premium – An *earned premium* is the premium portion that applies to the part of the policy that has expired. Although insurance premiums are frequently paid in advance, insurance providers typically "earn" the premium at an even rate throughout the policy's term.

Unearned Premium – An *unearned premium* is the premium portion the insurance company has not yet "earned" because the policy term still has time before it expires. The unearned premium portion already paid is kept in the unearned premium reserve.

Chapter Review

This chapter explained the concepts relevant to insurance contract law. Let's review some of the key points:

CONTRACT LAW	
Four Elements of a Legal Contract	<ul><li>*Agreement* – offer and acceptance</li><li>*Consideration* – premiums and representations on the part of the policy owner; payment of claims on the part of the insurance provider</li><li>*Competent parties* – must be of legal age, have sound mental capacity, and not under the influence of alcohol or drugs</li><li>*Legal purpose* – the contract must be for a lawful reason, not against public policy</li></ul>
Special Characteristics of Insurance Contracts	<ul><li>*Adhesion* – one party prepares the contract; the other party must accept it as is</li><li>*Aleatory* – an exchange of unequal amounts</li><li>*Conditional* – certain conditions must be met</li><li>*Unilateral* – only one of the parties to the contract is legally bound to do anything</li><li>*Personal* – insurance contracts are between individuals and insurers</li></ul>
Legal Terms	<ul><li>*Insurance Policy* – the written instrument that sets forth a contract of insurance</li><li>*Concealment* – intentionally withholding information of a material fact that is crucial in the decision-making process</li><li>*Warranty* – a statement guaranteed to be true that becomes a part of the contract</li><li>*Representations* – statements believed to be true to the best of one's knowledge; however, they are not guaranteed to be true</li><li>*Misrepresentations* – untrue statements on an insurance application</li><li>*Materiality* – all parties to a contract are entitled to all necessary information to decide on the nature or quality of the contract</li></ul>
Rescission	<ul><li>Injured parties are permitted to rescind the contract if any of the following occurs:<ul><li>A false material representation in which rescission becomes effective from the time the representation turns out to be false;</li><li>Concealment, irrespective of whether it is intentional;</li><li>Negligence of a material warranty or other material provisions contained in a policy</li></ul></li></ul>
Six Specifications for Insurance Policies	<ul><li>Every contract of insurance must identify these six specific elements:<ul><li>The parties involved in the contract;</li><li>The property or individuals being insured;</li><li>If the insured is not the owner, a statement of the insurable interest that exists;</li><li>The risks insured against;</li><li>The period during which the policy will continue or be in force; and</li><li>The stated monthly, quarterly, semi-annual, or annual premium. If it can only be determined at the expiration or termination of the contract, a statement of the method by which the insurer will calculate a premium rate and total premium</li></ul></li><li>The financial rating of an insurance company does not have to be specified in an insurance policy</li></ul>

CHAPTER 3:
The Insurance Marketplace

This chapter begins with an overview of marketing distribution systems. It then focuses on producers, describing their licensing and education requirements, duties and authorities, and code of ethics. This chapter also explores the different types and qualifications of insurance providers. Finally, you will learn about market regulations for rate making, sales, underwriting, and claims handling. Be sure to pay close attention to the regulations regarding unfair trade practices and fair claims settlement practices.

- Distributions Systems
- Producers
- Insurers
- Market Regulation – General
- Fair Claims Settlement Practices Regulations

Distribution Systems

Agency

A *producer* is a legal entity. Producers can be either a person or corporation that acts on behalf of, or in place of, its principal. In insurance, the producer is the agent, and the principal is the insurance provider.

An insurance agent must first establish a licensing relationship with the state or states where the agent wishes to conduct business. This requirement entails meeting educational standards and passing required tests for the type of insurance sold. This licensing relationship is separate from and can exist without any agent or insurance provider relationship being established.

The *independent agent* has contracts with more than one insurance provider, which puts them in an enhanced position to provide clients with a wide range of product options. When it comes time to renew a policy, the independent agent is said to *own the renewal or the expiration*. In other words, the independent agent can move the client to a different insurance provider for the renewal. These agents should only do this to the client's advantage. An ethical challenge facing the independent agent is to avoid moving clients to earn new or higher commissions.

The *exclusive* or *captive*, or *career agent* chooses to have a contract with one insurance company. An agent can choose this when they find the insurance provider's products to be of extraordinary quality and applicability and feel no need to have other insurer relationships. An agent may also make this choice because the insurance provider only allows its products to be sold through its exclusive agents.

Depending on the viewer, exclusivity can appear to be positive or negative. Positively, the agent can market a product that would otherwise be unavailable to the client. Negatively, the agent cannot search throughout the insurance industry to find a product that will benefit the client.

Direct Response

The mass marketing of insurance products through mail and print media advertisements, solicitations, or television and radio is known as direct response marketing. The policies provided are usually low in benefits and low in premiums. The term *direct response* means the necessity of the potential client to take the initiative and respond to the advertisement through a telephone or mail contact with the insurer as directed in the ad.

Producers

Legal Relationships

Agents – An agent or producer is a person licensed to solicit, negotiate, or sell insurance contracts on behalf of the *principal (insurer)*. Individuals soliciting insurance on behalf of an insurer, taking or transmitting an insurance application or policy, examining any risk or loss, or receiving, collecting, or transmitting premiums are the insurer's agents. The insurance provider typically compensates agents by commissions, paying the agent a percentage of the premium.

The *law of agency* defines the relationship between the principal and the agent or producer. This relationship includes the acts of the agent or producer within the scope of authority deemed to be the acts of the insurer.

According to the *law of agency*:

- An agent represents the insurance provider, not the insured;
- Any knowledge of the agent is assumed to be knowledge of the insurance provider;
- If the agent is working within the boundaries of their contract, the insurance provider is fully responsible; and
- When the insured provides payment to the agent, it is the same as submitting a payment to the insurance provider.

The agent is responsible for accurately completing an insurance application, submitting the application to the insurance provider for underwriting, and delivering the policy to the policyholder.

Insurer as Principal – When applying the law of agency, the insurance provider is the *principal*. The acts of agents or producers acting within the scope of their authority are the acts of the insurance provider.

Producer and Insurer Relationship – An agent or producer will always represent the insurance provider, not the insured. Concerning an insurance contract, any knowledge of the agent is presumed to be knowledge of the insurer. If the agent works within the boundaries of their contract, the insurance provider is fully responsible.

The *agent* is responsible to the insurance provider when completing insurance applications, submitting the application to the insurance provider for underwriting, and when issued, delivering the policy to the policyholder and explaining the contract. In addition, if the insured submits a payment to the agent, it is the same as submitting a payment to the insurance provider.

Responsibilities to the Applicant and the Insured – Even though producers act on behalf of the insurance company, they are legally required to treat insureds and applicants ethically. Since an agent handles the funds of the insured and the insurance provider, they have a *fiduciary responsibility*. An individual in a position of trust is called a *fiduciary*. More specifically, it is illegal for insurance agents to commingle premiums collected from the applicants with their own personal funds.

Authority and Powers of Producers – The agency contract specifies a producer's authority within their insurance company. Contractually, only those actions for which the producer is authorized can bind the principal (insurance provider). In reality, an agent's authority is a lot broader. There are three agent authority types: express, implied, and apparent.

Express – *Express authority* is the authority that is written into the contract. It is the authority a principal intends to grant to a producer through the producer's contract.

Implied – *Implied authority* is the authority that is not expressed or written into the contract but which the producer is assumed to have to conduct insurance business for the principal. Implied authority is incidental to and derives from express authority because not every single authority of a producer can be listed in the written contract.

For example, suppose the agency contract does not explicitly authorize the producer to collect premiums and remit them to the insurance provider. However, the agent routinely does so during the solicitation and delivery of policies. In that situation, the producer has the implied authority to collect and remit premiums.

Apparent – *Apparent authority*, also called perceived authority, is the assumption or appearance of authority based on the principal's words, actions, or deeds or due to circumstances the principal created. For example, suppose a producer uses the insurance provider's stationery when soliciting coverage. In that case, an applicant could believe the producer is authorized to transact insurance on behalf of that insurer.

Definition of "Transact"

When an individual performs any of the following actions, they are *transacting insurance* (Cal. Ins. Code Sections 35, 1631, and 1633). Transacting insurance includes:

- Solicitation of insurance;
- Negotiations before the execution of a contract;
- The actual execution of a contract; and
- Any later transactions that arise from the operation of the contract.

Except for individuals who receive non-commission compensation from their employer for these actions, any other individual who receives payment for "transacting insurance" must be licensed as an agent or broker. It is a *misdemeanor* to transact insurance without a license. This misdemeanor carries a maximum fine of $50,000 or imprisonment in a county jail for one year or both.

Prohibited Actions – No person can perform the activities of an insurance broker or agent without holding the appropriate valid licenses described in the Insurance Code. These activities include soliciting, negotiating, and executing insurance contracts (Cal. Ins. Code Section 1631).

Any person who acts, offers to act, or assumes to act in any way that would require a license, but does not hold a valid license, is guilty of a *misdemeanor*. A misdemeanor conviction in California can result in a maximum fine of $50,000, imprisonment in county jail for up to one year, or both (Cal. Ins. Code Section 1633).

Written Consent Regarding Interstate Commerce

It is fraudulent for anyone engaged in the insurance business to deliberately make any oral or written statement with the intent to deceive. *Unlawful insurance fraud* includes false statements or omissions of material fact, false information and statements made on an insurance application, and malicious statements regarding the financial condition of an insurance company.

Anyone engaged in insurance whose activities affect interstate commerce and who intentionally makes false material statements can be imprisoned for up to ten years, fined, or both. If the activity jeopardized the security of the accompanied insurance provider, the sentence could be extended up to *15 years*. Anyone acting as an agent, officer, director, or another insurance employee caught embezzling funds will be subject to the imprisonment and fines previously described. However, if the embezzlement was in an amount that is *less than $5,000*, prison time could be reduced to one year.

Federal law makes it illegal for anyone convicted of a crime involving breach of trust, dishonesty, or a violation of the Violent Crime Control and Law Enforcement Act of 1994 to work in the insurance business affecting interstate commerce without written consent from an insurance regulatory official (Commissioner of Insurance, Director of Insurance, etc.) This requirement is known as a 1033 waiver. The consent from the official has to specify that it is granted for the purpose of 18 U.S.C. 1033. Anyone convicted of a felony involving breach of trust or dishonesty, who also transacts insurance, will be imprisoned for up to five years, fined, or both.

Anyone who engages in conduct that violates Section 1033 can be subject to a civil penalty of not more than $50,000 for each violation or the amount of payment received from the prohibited conduct, whichever is greater.

Section 1034: Civil Penalties and Injunctions – According to this section, the *Attorney General* can bring a civil action in the appropriate United States district court against any individual who engages in conduct constituting an offense under section 1033 and, upon evidence of such conduct, the individual will be subject to a civil penalty of not more than $50,000 for each violation, or the amount of payment which the individual offered or received for the prohibited conduct, whichever is greater.

Suppose the Attorney General has reason to believe that an individual is engaged in conduct constituting an offense under section 1033. In that circumstance, the Attorney General can petition an appropriate United States district court for an order prohibiting that individual from engaging in such conduct. The court can issue an order barring that individual from engaging in such conduct if the court discovers that the conduct constitutes such an offense.

Types of Licensees

The California Insurance Code defines a variety of specific licenses which can be issued to qualified individuals:

- Property and casualty broker-agent;
- Life-only agent (formerly life agent);
- Accident and health or sickness agent (formerly life agent);
- Life and accident and health or sickness agent;
- Personal lines agent; and
- Surplus lines broker.

Agents vs. Brokers – *Agents legally represent the insurer*, not their clients. An agent's actions are considered to be made on behalf of the insurance company, not the insured. With brokers, however, this is reversed. *Brokers legally represent their clients*, not insurers. They negotiate contracts of insurance on behalf of their clients.

The broker represents and is expected to act in the client's best interests, not those of the insurance provider. Although a broker could receive compensation from an insurer for a transaction, typically, the broker gets a fee for their services directly from the client. It could be unethical for a broker to accept a commission from the insurance provider and a fee from the client.

Insurance Agents and Insurance Brokers – An *insurance agent* in this state refers to a person authorized to transact all classes of insurance on behalf of an admitted insurance provider *other than life, health, or disability insurance.*

Insurance brokers are licensees who, for compensation and on behalf of an individual other than an insurance company, transact insurance other than life, accident and health or sickness, or disability. It is worth noting that there is *no such license* as a "life broker" or "health broker." However, an individual can be life licensed as an independent, acting in the capacity of a broker.

A *life licensee* is authorized to act as a life agent on behalf of a life insurance provider or a disability insurance provider. These individuals transact life insurance, accident and health or sickness insurance, or a combination of life and accident and health or sickness insurance.

A *property and casualty licensee* (formerly fire and casualty licensee) can be authorized to transact any of the following insurance coverages:

- Automobile insurance;
- Residential property (including earthquake and flood);
- Personal watercraft;
- Inland marine insurance; and
- Umbrella or excess liability insurance.

In California, *life-only agents* are authorized only to transact insurance on human lives, including the following benefits:

- Annuities;
- Endowments;
- Death or dismemberment by accident; and
- Disability income.

Accident and health or sickness agents can transact the following types of insurance:

- Bodily injury;
- Sickness;
- Accidental death;
- Disability income; and
- 24-hour coverage.

A *personal lines agent* can only transact personal automobile, residential property, inland marine for personal property, and umbrella or excess liability lines of insurance.

A *limited lines automobile insurance agent* is authorized to transact auto insurance, including automobile physical damage coverage, liability coverage, and collision coverage.

A *surplus lines broker* is authorized to transact insurance with a non-admitted insurer only if a specific class of insurance cannot be obtained from admitted insurers after proof of a diligent search.

Except for a surplus lines broker, regardless of the type of license held, agents or brokers cannot advertise or transact insurance on behalf of a non-admitted insurance provider or aid a non-admitted insurance provider in any way to transact insurance in California.

Life and Disability Analysts – A *life and disability analyst* is any individual who accepts a fee or other compensation from any individual or source other than an insurer for the following: advising or offering to advise an insured, beneficiary, or another individual who has an interest in a life or disability insurance contract about their benefits, rights, or any other aspect of the contract. Under California law, a life and disability analyst must be appropriately licensed.

To be licensed as a life and disability insurance analyst, an individual must be a state resident, competent and knowledgeable on insurance, and have a good business and general reputation. The candidate must take a pre-licensing examination no more than *12 months* before applying for this type of license.

An organization can also hold a license to act as a life and disability insurance analyst if it has an eligible natural person named under an organizational license.

The following eligibility requirements for life and disability analysts include:

- Be a California state resident;
- Pass the license exam within 12 months of the license issue;
- Have a good business and general reputation;
- Have extensive knowledge of life and disability insurance;
- Not be associated with any business that has failed in its fiduciary duty toward any other individual;
- Not attempt to avoid or prevent the operation of insurance laws by being licensed; and
- Not be an employee of an insurer.

In addition to these requirements, before applying for a life and disability insurance analyst license, an individual must have been *licensed as a life and accident and health insurance agent for at least five years*.

Life and disability analysts are not allowed to charge a fee for any services unless they have a signed, written agreement with the party being charged. This agreement must include a statement of the charges or the basis on which charges will be made. They are not allowed to receive a fee from a client for any service generally associated with soliciting or transacting insurance. These individuals also cannot receive fees from clients for any service for which the analyst receives compensation from an insurer.

The written agreement must disclose the services that life and disability analysts will provide and that the same information and services can be available directly from the insurer for free. When the analyst is licensed as a life-only agent, the agreement must inform the client of this fact and that the analyst receives commissions from selling insurance products.

Life Agent vs. Life Analyst – A primary difference between a life agent and a life analyst is how each receives payment. An *analyst* is not paid a commission directly or indirectly by an insurance provider for any insurance transacted by an analyst. On the other hand, an *agent* acts on behalf of an insurance provider and receives commissions for insurance transactions.

Another distinction is that an analyst's principal goal is advising an insured, beneficiary, or another person about their rights, benefits, or any other aspect of the insurance contract. An agent transacts insurance business and creates binding contracts.

Certified Insurance Agent – A *certified insurance agent* is certified by the Exchange to transact in the individual and Small Business Health Options Program (SHOP) Exchanges. Under the health reform law in California, Covered California is the state's Health Benefit Exchange. Certified Insurance Agents assist enrollees with the following: completing the application, tracking their process, helping evaluate individuals' health care needs and budget considerations to recommend a plan that works best for each enrollee, and providing additional assistance on an ongoing basis, among other services.

A certified insurance agent must be a natural person in good standing with a valid license to transact in accident and health insurance. Currently, certified insurance agents are required to be *recertified every five years*.

Life Settlement Brokers – A *life settlement broker* is an individual who, for payment, solicits, negotiates, or offers to negotiate life settlement contracts. Life settlement brokers represent only the policy owners and have a fiduciary duty to the owners to act in their best interest and according to their instructions.

Life settlement brokers do not include licensed life settlement providers or their representatives, accountants, attorneys, or financial planners. These individuals would not receive a commission when completing a life settlement contract but charge a fee for their services, irrespective of whether or not ownership of the policy is transferred.

A *life settlement producer* is an individual licensed as a resident or nonresident insurance agent who is qualified to transact life settlements.

A *life settlement* is a financial transaction where a life insurance policy owner sells a policy they no longer need to a third party for compensation, typically cash. While *viatical settlements* are still used for terminally ill individuals, most states regulate policies sold to a third party for compensation under the "Life Settlements" term.

In life settlements, the seller (the policy owner) could have a life expectancy of more than one year. They can sell their policies because they no longer need the coverage or the premium costs have become too high to justify continuing the policy.

The *business of life settlement* refers to any activity related to soliciting and selling life settlement contracts to third parties with no insurable interest in the insured.

The term *owner* refers to the policy owner who can seek to enter into a life settlement contract. The term does not include an insurer, a financing entity, a qualified institutional buyer, a special purpose entity, or a related provider trust.

The *insured* is the person covered under the policy that is considered for sale in a life settlement contract.

A *qualified institutional buyer* is a person that owns and invests at least $100 million in securities and is allowed by the SEC to trade in unregistered securities. A life settlement provider can sell or transfer ownership of a settled policy to a qualified institutional buyer or other investment entity approved by the Commissioner.

Life expectancy is an essential concept in life settlement contracts. It refers to a calculation based on the average number of months the insured is projected to live because of medical history and mortality factors (an arithmetic mean).

The *life settlement contract* establishes the terms under which the life settlement provider will compensate the policy owner in return for the absolute assignment, transfer, sale, or release of any portion of any of the following:

- Policy ownership;
- The death benefit;
- Any beneficial interest; or
- Interest in a trust or any other entity that owns the policy.

A life settlement contract also includes a premium finance loan that is made on or before the policy's issue date if one or more of the following conditions apply:

- The loan proceeds are not used exclusively to pay premiums for the policy;
- The owner receives a guarantee of the policy's future life settlement value; and
- The owner agrees to sell the policy in case of default.

The following *would not comprise* a life settlement contract:

- A policy loan issued by a life insurance provider;
- A loan made by a lender or a bank;
- A collateral assignment of a life insurance policy by the policy owner;
- An agreement between closely related parties (by law or by blood);
- A bona fide business succession agreement;
- Employer-owned life insurance for key employees;
- A contract or agreement between a service recipient and a service provider;
- Any other form identified by the Commissioner.

The *financing entity* includes any accredited investor who provides funds for purchasing one or more life settlement contracts and has an agreement in writing to do so.

A *financing transaction* occurs when a licensed settlement provider secures funds from the financing entity.

Before an individual can act as a life settlement broker in California, they must be appropriately licensed. The following qualifications are required for a licensee:

- Complete the required pre-licensing education (15-hour training course);
- Pass the licensing examination;
- Submit an application on the approved form to the Commissioner;
- Pay any required fees; and
- Be competent, determined, and trustworthy.

If an individual has been licensed as a *life agent for at least one year*, they can act as a life settlement broker. However, they must inform the California Department of Insurance (CDI) within ten days of transacting life settlements. Instead of a broker's license, life agents will be required to pay the notification fee and renew that notification biennially at the time of their life license renewal.

Licensed *viatical settlement brokers* or providers will be deemed to have met the licensing requirements for life settlement brokers or providers.

Solicitors

An insurance *solicitor* is a *natural person* employed to assist a property and casualty broker-agent acting as an insurance broker or insurance agent in transacting insurance *other than life, health, or disability* (Cal. Ins. Code Section 1624). In California, an insurance solicitor is not eligible to act simultaneously as an insurance broker or agent. An individual authorized to act as an insurance broker or agent is not eligible to work simultaneously as an insurance solicitor.

Solicitors can make prospecting telephone calls, set appointments, offer quotes, or even take applications for insurance other than life insurance. A solicitor can be employed by more than one broker-agent at a time. A notice of appointment can be filed by a second or subsequent property and casualty broker-agent to appoint a solicitor. To perform the duties of an insurance solicitor, the Insurance Code requires that an individual hold an insurance solicitor's license.

A "life solicitor" license does not exist (Cal. Ins. Code Section 1704(d)).

Errors and Omissions

An insurance broker or agent might seek professional liability insurance to protect against financial losses that could happen because of the agent's negligent acts or actions. This coverage is known as *errors and omissions (E&O)* liability insurance.

Types of Coverage – E&O insurance is written for professionals (such as insurance agents) to provide protection resulting from actions charging that the professional failed to render reasonable services or duties. Some professional liability insurance coverage is written with a limit of liability on an occurrence basis. The insurer must obtain the insured's consent for any out-of-court settlement. The modern trend is to provide coverage on a claims-made basis and to remove previous requirements for the insured's consent for out-of-court settlements.

Errors and omissions liability contracts are renewable annually. They are typically written with "per claim" deductibles of at least $500 or $1,000. They have either a "limit for all claims during the policy period" or a "limit per claim" provision that specifies the contract's maximum benefit.

Types of Losses – The following examples of acts or omissions may lead to professional liability claims:

- An agent unintentionally records an answer incorrectly on an insurance application, concealing the client's actual response to a question concerning qualifying information. Upon investigating a claim, the insurance provider discovers the correct information, legally rejects the claim, and voids the contract based on the incorrect answers in the application, refunding the premiums paid. The E&O policy pays for the actual claim losses of the agent's client.

- The agent fails to disclose material information about a contract of insurance, such as coinsurance, deductibles, copayments, premium increases, surrender charges, or principal exclusions. The E&O policy could cover actual damages incurred by the agent's client.
- The agent tells a client, "I suppose I made a mistake" in calculating the original premium quotation when, in fact, the increased premium was because of the client's substandard rating. Suppose an insured later discovers the misrepresentation and elects to cancel the contract. In that situation, an E&O policy could pay the difference between the actual premiums paid and what the client was initially quoted as the periodic premium from the date the client discovered the error.
- The agent leads a client to believe that the sales illustration for a contract with non-guaranteed interest, or that projected investment results in a variable contract, are guaranteed elements of the contract. An E&O policy could pay for actual client losses.
- The agent collects a check from a client, representing an unscheduled deposit to the cash account in a variable or flexible premium policy, and fails to send it to the insurance provider promptly. An E&O policy could restore actual investment or interest losses.

Losses Not Covered – Errors and Omissions insurance does not protect against liabilities caused by a person's criminal acts. Such acts include unfair trade practices, fiduciary crimes, or material misrepresentations that cause damages or financial loss to a client.

It is worth noting that the E&O policy will not pay the claim if any of the previously named liability claims arise out of a criminal conviction or result in a criminal conviction. The broker or agent will remain personally liable for the client's damages.

Need for Coverage – E&O insurance is necessary because of the risk of injuring an individual due to the advice or services rendered (an error) or not rendered (an omission) to that individual.

At any time during the sales process, there can be a misrepresentation or misunderstanding that could lead to legal action being taken by the insured. Producers should document all requests for information, interviews, phone conversations, etc. The sales interview and the policy delivery are commonly the time for E&O situations.

Prohibited Acts Regarding Non-Admitted Insurers

A non-admitted insurer has not satisfied the requirements, either by failure or choice, to legally have its representatives physically present to transact insurance business in California. Such an insurer can be represented within California by specially licensed individuals, known as surplus lines brokers. These non-admitted insurers must obtain a valid Certificate of Authority from the California Department of Insurance before conducting business in the state.

Surplus lines brokers are of value to California residents because they help the residents purchase types of property and casualty insurance that are not available from admitted insurers.

The following acts are *misdemeanors* except when committed by a surplus lines broker:

- Acting as an agent on behalf of a non-admitted insurer in an insurance transaction;
- Advertising for a non-admitted insurer;
- Aiding a non-admitted insurer to transact insurance.

Along with any penalty for committing a misdemeanor, individuals violating any provision will be fined $500 and $100 for each month the individual continues the violation.

New legislation was recently enacted to streamline the surplus lines broker licensing laws, and the following changes were included. All individuals are required to hold an individual surplus lines broker license. Applicants for such a license must already be licensed to transact property and casualty insurance.

Also, a surplus lines broker's application and renewal fee allow for a 2-year license term.

It is essential to note there is a fee for a licensed surplus lines broker organization to endorse a licensed individual lines broker. The California Department of Insurance must be advised when terminating such a broker.

Surplus lines brokers transacting insurance for a licensed surplus lines broker organization will not have to file a bond. However, all other surplus lines brokers must file a $50,000 surplus lines broker bond.

Prohibitions of Free Insurance

The state has adopted the philosophy that insurance is a product of sufficient importance. It should be paid for by the insured for its intrinsic value to preserve the integrity of the insurance industry in California. To this end, it is *illegal* for any insurance licensee to offer *free insurance* as an incentive to transact some other type of business.

Suppose any insurance provider, broker, agent or solicitor willfully violates this provision. In that situation, the Insurance Commissioner can revoke or suspend that individual's certificate, license, or other authority to conduct business for a period not exceeding one year.

The following *exceptions* to the free insurance prohibition include:

- Insurance provided in association with newspaper subscriptions;
- The purchase of credit union shares;
- Insurance to guarantee the performance of a product and reimburse a customer for losses caused by such a product's failure;
- Title, life, or disability insurance which will pay off a debt in case a debtor dies or becomes disabled;
- Services provided by an attorney; and
- The services of a motor club, like AAA, regarding emergency roadside service, towing, bail bond service, DMV transactions, or other services that are not considered transacting insurance.

Miscellaneous Code Requirements and Specifications

Agency Name, Use of Name – California state law cannot limit a person's right to use their actual name to transact insurance business. Other than that, the insurance regulators are responsible for ensuring that California residents are not misled by the name or names attached to a licensed entity.

Every licensee, individual, and corporate entity must reveal to the Insurance Commissioner the actual name of the legal person and all Doing Business As (DBA) names intended for use. To prevent confusing the insurance consumer, the Commissioner can deny the use of a name for any of the following reasons:

- The name would interfere with another business or is too similar to the name of another;
- The name would mislead the consumer;
- The name gives the impression that the licensee is authorized to conduct a type of business that it cannot legally conduct;
- The terms "Chartered Life Underwriter" and "Chartered Property and Casualty Underwriter" are frequently used by those who earned those designations. It is not acceptable to use the term "underwriter" to give the impression that the licensee is authorized to act in such a capacity. The term "underwriter" can be used in the name of an organization of insurance agents who are individually licensed; or

- The licensee is already using two approved names. The exception is a licensee who acquires ownership of another licensee, where the use of two names for each entity is permitted.

There is room for negotiation with the Commissioner when there are extenuating circumstances concerning "fictitious" names like a DBA.

Suppose a broker or agent has a contract to provide service for a corporation that holds an insurance license in its own name, is a member of an incorporated agency, or is a stockholder in a licensed corporation. In that circumstance, the broker or agent can use the name of such organization in printed materials provided that the broker or agent identifies the relationship.

The following are acceptable relationship identifiers:

- "Representing _____;"
- "A stockholder of _____;"
- "Placing business through _____;" and
- "Using services of _____."

Licensed agents or brokers who advertise online must identify the following information, even if they are not responsible for maintaining their Internet presence:

- The licensee's name approved by the Commissioner;
- The state of the licensee's principal place of business; and
- The licensee's license number.

Anyone who conducts the following actions online is transacting insurance in this state:

- Provides insurance premium quotes to California residents;
- Accepts applications from California residents; or
- Communicates with California residents regarding the terms of an insurance agreement.

Change of Address – On their initial license application, every licensee has to provide their business, residence, and mailing addresses. The licensee's responsibility is to immediately notify the Commissioner of any changes in the principal business, mailing, residence, or e-mail addresses through an electronic service approved by the Commissioner (Cal. Ins. Code 1729).

Reporting Administrative Actions and Criminal Convictions – Every licensee and applicant for licenses must report any *background changes, administrative actions, or criminal convictions* to the California Department of Insurance Producer Licensing Bureau *within 30 days* of the matter's final disposition. Background information that needs to be reported includes the following:

- Filing of felony criminal charges against the licensee in federal or state court;
- Misdemeanor or felony convictions;
- Administrative actions regarding an occupational license;
- Personal or organizational bankruptcy filings; or breach
- Any financial misappropriation or.

Licensees and applicants must submit supporting documents, like certified court documents, a statement regarding the background change, administrative documents, or other related documents.

To report this information to the Department, licensees can use the background change disclosure form available at the California state insurance website, insurance.ca.gov.

Filing License Renewal Application – Insurance licenses in this state must be renewed every *two years*. Suppose a licensee delays completing the renewal requirements and finds themselves near the license expiration date. In that case, the licensee can continue transacting insurance for *60 days* past that expiration date, provided they complete all requirements and remit the license renewal fee no later than the expiration date (Cal. Ins. Code Section 1720).

Printing License Number on Documents – To facilitate a potential client's investigation of an agent, each agent must place their license number on all printed materials provided to the public in California, including proposals, business cards, and all print advertisements. (Cal. Ins. Code Section 1725.5).

The license number must be printed as large as the smallest telephone number or address on the same document. This requirement ensures the number is not minimized and would not be missed by a prospective insurance consumer. A single license number will be sufficient for licensees with more than one license. Solicitors are required to use the license number of their employer.

A first offense for being caught using illegal documents will be punished by a $200 fine, a second by a $500 fine, and a third by a $1,000 fine. A separate penalty, however, cannot be imposed for each piece of illegal material used. The Commissioner can consider extenuating circumstances and relieve the licensee of the penalty.

The one exception to the license number requirement is motor club (AAA, etc.) advertisements. These materials include insurance in a general list of services offered without providing details regarding the insurance products.

Record Maintenance

One of the challenges facing new brokers and agents is accepting the responsibility to obtain and maintain legible, accurate records. These records must be available within 30 days after a request to the insurance provider from the Department of Insurance. Each admitted insurance provider must maintain specific records regarding its life activities, life and disability, and disability agents for *five years*. Life, life and disability, and disability insurance agents must also maintain all applicable records at their primary place of business for a minimum of five years. The records need to be maintained in an orderly manner and be available for the Commissioner's review at all times (Cal. Ins. Code Sections 10508 through 10508.5).

The records can be in the form of copies, originals, or electronic data-processing records and must include the following:

- Policy number;
- Name of the insurance provider;
- Name of the insured;
- The date insurance becomes effective and any date it ceases to be in force;
- Renewals;
- All information regarding binders;
- Coverage changes;
- A copy of the application or other request for insurance;
- Proposals, including comparisons with existing coverage;
- All correspondence or other written records that describe the transaction, except printed materials in general usage;

- All correspondence regarding cessation of coverage; and
- Legally required disclosure statements or outlines of coverage.

Brokers and agents must keep the following records regarding policies, premium payments, and commissions:

- The original policy application;
- Amount of premiums received by the insurance provider;
- Production records that show policies sold by each agent;
- Itemization of the premiums received;
- All written communications sent by the insurance provider or its agents to a prospect, applicant, or insured;
- A copy of the disclosure statements or outlines of coverage.

Life Insurance Policy Illustrations

Insurance laws ensure that illustrations do not mislead life insurance consumers. They also seek to make illustrations more understandable by establishing standards and formats to be followed whenever illustrations are utilized. These laws must also specify the required disclosures used with illustrations (Cal. Ins. Code Sections 10509.950 through 10509.965).

Whenever possible, insurance providers should eliminate the use of caveats and footnotes and explain terms used in the illustration in language that is understandable by the average person.

Each insurance provider must notify the Commissioner when filing whether a policy will be marketed with or without an illustration.

Suppose the insurance provider recognizes a particular policy form to be marketed *without an illustration*. In that case, any use of an illustration for a policy before the first policy anniversary is prohibited. When a policy form is to be marketed *with an illustration*, the insurance provider must prepare and deliver a basic illustration.

An illustration used in the sale of a life insurance policy has to be prominently labeled "life insurance illustration" and include (but not be limited to) the following:

- Name of the insurance provider;
- Name and business address of the agent or insurance provider's authorized representative, if any;
- Name, age, and sex of the proposed insured, except where a composite illustration is allowed;
- Rating classification or underwriting upon which the illustration is based;
- The form number, the generic name of the policy, and the company product name, if different;
- Initial death benefit; and
- If applicable, the dividend option election or the application of nonguaranteed elements.

Application and License Specifications

Producer Application Investigation – The Commissioner is obligated to the consumers of California to ensure that each insurance licensee is qualified regarding their character and knowledge. The Commissioner is authorized to require the provision of any documents or information necessary to make such a determination. After the investigation is complete, the applicant can be authorized to conduct business.

Alterations on a Disability Application – No alteration of any written application for a disability policy can be made by any individual other than the applicant without the applicant's written consent. However, the insurance provider can make insertions for administrative purposes only if they do not pertain to the applicant.

Making any other alteration without the applicant's consent is considered a *misdemeanor*. It is essential to note that if the producer alters the application, the insurance provider will be the liable party.

Denial of Applications – There are many possible causes listed in the Insurance Code for denying an insurance license. Remember that these causes apply to legal "persons," which include individuals and business entities such as corporations and agencies. The applicant can be denied licensure if the applicant is unqualified or if licensing the applicant would be against the public's best interest.

An applicant's license *can be denied* if the applicant:

- Has no intention of selling the type of insurance allowed by the license;
- Lacks integrity;
- Does not have a respectable business reputation;
- Was denied or lost another state license within the previous five years for a reason which would also result in an insurance license being denied;
- Wants the license to avoid insurance law consequences;
- Previously acted dishonestly in business;
- Has lied on their application;
- Lied about an insurance policy;
- Exposed the public to loss as a result of incompetence or lack of trustworthiness;
- Has either not done something required by or has done something forbidden by the Insurance Code;
- Has been convicted of (not charged with) any misdemeanor violation or a felony of insurance law;
- Has helped someone else commit a crime that would make that other individual lose or be denied a license;
- Has allowed an employee to violate the Insurance Code;
- Has acted as a licensed individual before the issuance of a license; or
- Has submitted a fraudulent educational certificate.

The applicant can be *denied a license* without the right to a hearing if they have a history of any of the following:

- Misdemeanor violations of insurance law;
- Felony convictions;
- Denial of an insurance license within the past five years; or
- Insurance license revocation or suspension within the past five years.

Anyone *caught cheating* on the licensing exam will be barred from taking any licensing examination and holding an active license for *five years*.

Regarding what could constitute a conviction, any applicant for licensure in California will be considered convicted of a misdemeanor or felony if they were found guilty or convicted after entering a "no contest" plea.

It is important to remember that *every conviction* has to be disclosed on the license application at *any time* in an applicant's past. This stipulation applies to convictions where the charges were later expunged or dismissed or where an individual was given probation or received a suspended sentence. If an applicant does not disclose all convictions, the application for a producer license will be denied.

Suspension or Revocation of a License – A permanent license can be revoked for the same reason a license could be denied. Hearings will not be permitted if any of the four previously discussed conditions exist.

Termination of a License, Dissolving Partnerships

A licensee can surrender their insurance license at any time, either by returning the license to the Commissioner or submitting a notice of resignation if not in possession of the license.

An insurance license automatically terminates upon the licensee's death. If the licensee is an organization, the license will terminate if its corporation, association, or partnership is dissolved. Also, a partnership will lose its license if it changes the individuals listed as partners. When a new partner joins, a partnership can continue its license if it files a notice with the Department within 30 days and the changes are approved.

Suppose any of the above organizations cease to exist. In that situation, they can continue conducting business under another name, provided the same individuals remain involved. The necessary paperwork must be filed within 30 days (Cal. Ins. Code Sections 1708 through 1712.5).

Appointment Regulations

An insurance producer or agent cannot legally act as an agent of an insurance provider unless they become an *appointed agent* of that insurance company. An insurance producer who does not act as an agent of an authorized insurance provider does not have to become appointed.

The insurance provider must submit a notice of appointment within *14 days* to the Commissioner to legitimize and validate the insurance contract and the agency relationship. The licensee will be legal to conduct business, and the insurance provider will become responsible for the acts of the licensee as of the date the insurance company signs the appointment.

An appointment will cease, and the licensee will become unable to conduct business for the insurance provider when any of the following conditions exist:

- The licensee loses their license; or
- The licensee resigns their appointment or is terminated.

Life Insurance – Upon signing and submitting an appointment for an original license, an insurance company is inherently confirming to the Department of Insurance that the applicant has a good reputation and is worthy of being issued the license. This application also ensures that the applicant has sufficient education or experience or will soon receive the education necessary to satisfy the license requirements (within 30 days). If the applicant is a business entity, this is true for the entity and each of its natural individuals.

When a licensed business entity adds a person to its license, the above declarations are presumed to be about that individual.

A life or accident and health or sickness agent can present a coverage proposal to a client for an insurance provider with whom the agent is not appointed. Suppose the proposal results in an application to the insurance company, and a policy is issued. In that scenario, it is assumed that the insurance provider is appointing the agent. *Within 14 days*, the insurer must file the notice of appointment with the Department. All payments from the client regarding such a policy must be made payable to the insurer. The following exceptions to this rule include:

- An unappointed agent cannot present a proposal or accept an application for an insurance provider that uses only "career" agents, agents that exclusively represent only a single insurer or group of insurers; and
- The insurance provider requires that it be the first insurer to whom its agents present policy applications.

Disability Insurance – A person licensed as a life-only agent, a property and casualty broker-agent, or an accident and health or sickness agent can transact disability insurance on behalf of any insurer authorized to transact disability insurance. The authority to transact disability insurance takes effect the day the insurance company signs the notice of appointment. This authority will apply to transactions after that date and to determine the insurance provider's liability for acts of appointed agents.

Inactive License – A licensee does not lose their license when they have no active appointments. The insurance license is the result of the licensee's relationship with the Department of Insurance, and a lack of appointments does not change that relationship. A licensee with no appointments has a license that is designated as *inactive*. Upon being appointed by any insurance provider, the license becomes *active* again.

Cancellation of a License by the Licensee – A licensee can surrender their license for cancellation at any time. If the license is in the licensee's possession, they can surrender the license by delivering it to the Commissioner. When the license is in the possession of the insurance provider or the licensee's employer, the licensee can still surrender the license by submitting a written notice of surrender to the Commissioner.

Acting as an Agent without Appointment – A licensed life or accident and health or sickness agent who is not specifically appointed for a particular insurance provider cannot solicit insurance to a prospective client with that insurance company or give an insurance application to that insurer if the insurer requires that all its agents represent only that insurance company.

Suppose an insurance provider does not explicitly require its agents to be appointed. In that situation, any licensed agent can present an insurance proposal to a potential client on behalf of an insurer for which the agent is not specifically appointed. The agent can also pass on an application for insurance to that insurer. When insurance policies are issued, the insurer is considered to have authorized the agent to act on its behalf. The insurer is responsible for its agents' actions relating to the application and policy as if the insurance company had appointed the agent. The insurer must forward a *notice of appointment* of the agent to the Commissioner within *14 days* after the agent submits the insurance application. An insurer is not obligated to accept an application for underwriting from a life insurance agent.

Some insurance providers employ *exclusive/captive/career* agents and will not allow other agents to sell their products. The Department of Insurance requires that licensed agents not contracted with such companies are not allowed to present insurance applications to those companies. However, suppose an insurer does not stipulate that they appoint all agents to sell their products. In that case, agents can represent that insurer to a client and receive an application for insurance with that insurer. All client payments must be made payable to the insurance provider, not to the agent. If the insurer does not accept the application, no agency appointment exists. By issuing a policy in response to an application, the insurance provider is considered to have appointed that agent. The insurer has to inform the Commissioner of that appointment within *two weeks* of receiving the application.

Fiduciary

The term *fiduciary* describes the inherent responsibility in handling another individual's financial affairs and the person with such a responsibility. Insurance licensees frequently act as a conduit, receiving and transferring funds from the client to the insurance company and, eventually, from the insurance company to the client. Any individual who appropriates or diverts fiduciary funds to their own use is guilty of theft and punishable for *theft* as the law provides (Cal. Ins. Code Sections 1733 through 1735).

If a licensed agent receives fiduciary funds, they must ensure the following:

- Pay and return premiums received to the insurance provider (minus any commissions due); and
- Maintain fiduciary funds in a trustee bank account separate from any other accounts. The amount must be at a minimum equal to the premium and return premiums received by the agent and unpaid to the individual entitled to those funds.

Continuing Education Requirements

Continuing education rules aim to protect the public by maintaining high standards of professional competence in the insurance industry and maintaining and improving licensed producers' insurance skills and knowledge. The State of California has implemented pre-licensing and continuing education requirements for initial applicants and license renewals that apply equally to the following: life-only agents, accident and health or sickness agents, property and casualty broker-agents (formerly fire and casualty broker-agents).

Any licensee must complete *24 hours* of continuing education (CE), including *three hours of ethics*, per each 2-year license renewal term for the particular license (Cal. Ins. Code Sections 1749.3(b) and 1749.33(a)). This regulation applies to the following licenses:

- Life-only agent;
- Accident and health or sickness agent;
- Life and accident and health or sickness agent
- Property and casualty broker-agent; and
- Personal lines broker-agent.

Licensees can complete these hours at any time before the license renewal date. The Commissioner must approve all continuing education programs and courses.

Suppose an agent holds two types of licenses (for example, a life agent and a property and casualty broker-agent license). In that case, the agent can satisfy the CE requirement by completing it for any license type.

It may not be practical to complete the minimum number of CE units during a license period. While it is not possible to renew a license without the required number of credits, any credits above the required number will be carried over into the next licensing period.

It is worth noting, however, that licensees can carry over only those hours completed during the second year of the licensing period. The number of hours a licensee can carry over cannot exceed the hours required to renew the license.

Licensees can complete continuing education in a variety of settings. Courses are available with a live instructor, known as a "contact" setting. They are also available via mail-order as a "self-study" course and by computer over the Internet, which is also a "self-study" method. Before purchasing a continuing education course, producers should ensure that the California Department of Insurance has approved it. A licensee can gain valuable knowledge by taking any CE course, but only approved courses will meet license renewal requirements.

Life-only Agent – Life-only agents, accident and health or sickness agents, or property and casualty broker-agents can only receive credit for CE courses approved for their respective licenses. Agents holding licenses in more than one line of authority must satisfy the continuing education requirements by completing the approved courses or programs of instruction for any of the license types held.

Licensees who have been in good standing for 30 continuous years in California and who are 70 years of age or older do not have to comply with the continuing education requirements.

Agents Selling Annuity Products – Every life agent who sells annuities to individual consumers must complete *eight hours* of training before soliciting sales of annuity contracts. Every two years after that, agents must complete *four hours* of training, which are part of the overall CE requirement. The training needs to be approved by the Commissioner. It must include topics related to California law, regulations, annuities, and requirements associated with annuities, unfair trade practices, and prohibited sales practices (Cal. Ins. Code Section 1749.8).

It is worth noting that this requirement does not impact the total number of required continuing education hours for the life-only agent.

Agents Writing California Partnership Coverage – Accident and health agents who intend to sell California Partnership for Long-Term Care (CPLTC) insurance must also satisfy the continuing education requirement for those courses. These agents must complete one designated long-term care training course and one designated 8-hour California Partnership for Long-Term Care classroom course. Once the initial training requirement has been satisfied, the agents must complete an 8-hour classroom CE course on the Partnership every 2-year licensing period.

Life-only agents can be authorized to solicit long-term care (LTC) riders to a life insurance policy after meeting the proper training requirements. It is worth noting that the total number of continuing education hours required for the accident and health or sickness agent is *not impacted* by the CE requirement for LTC or CPLTC.

Accelerated Death Benefits and Long-Term Care Benefits

Long-term care training is *required* when an agent transacts accelerated death benefit riders or provisions requiring *services* provided to chronically ill insureds. LTC training is *not required* when an agent transacts accelerated death benefit riders or provisions that do not require services.

The required training is eight hours in each of the first four 12-month periods starting from the date of original license issuance and eight hours of training before each license renewal after that.

Insurers must ensure that agents marketing, offering, or selling accelerated death benefits can explain the differences between the benefits provided under an accelerated death benefit and the benefits provided under long-term care insurance. These distinctions include:

- The differences between benefit eligibility criteria;
- The difference between the benefits provided to an insured through an accelerated death benefit and a long-term care insurance policy or rider;
- The benefits provided under the accelerated death benefit or long-term care insurance if benefits are never needed;
- Whether an elimination period applies to an accelerated death benefit or long-term care insurance and a description of the elimination period;
- The benefits provided under the accelerated death benefit or long-term care insurance if benefits are needed;
- Restrictions on benefit amounts;
- Tax treatment of benefits; and
- Income and death benefit considerations.

Administrators

Although administrators have to meet the same general qualifications and pay the same license fees as life agents, they are not licensed as agents. *Administrators* are individuals who perform life and health insurance-related services like settling claims on behalf of or collecting premiums from insurers and insureds. Also referred to as *third-party administrators*, these individuals have to satisfy all the basic requirements of a life agent and have a written agreement with the insurance provider stipulating their responsibilities and compensation arrangements (if any) with the insurance company.

Administrators are also required to hold a *certificate of registration* from the Commissioner of Insurance. Payments from insureds to administrators are considered received by the insurance provider. However, payments from insurers to administrators are not considered received by an insured until the administrator has delivered the payment.

The Insurance Code identifies individuals who can perform duties similar to administrators but are not considered administrators. They include the following:

- A union on behalf of its members;
- An employer acting on behalf of employees;
- A life-only agent exclusively selling life or disability insurance;
- An insurance provider in connection with its contracts of insurance;
- A trust, its trustees, or its employees in the performance of their duties;
- A creditor on behalf of its debtors and their debts;
- Employees, trusts, or trustees of IRC 501(c) organizations, or custodians or agents of custodial accounts defined by IRC 401(f);
- A bank, credit union, or financial institution;
- Credit card companies collecting premiums from cardholders but are not involved in adjusting or settling claims;
- Attorneys who settle or adjust claims but do not collect charges or premiums for life or disability insurance;
- Licensed adjusters in the course of their responsibilities;
- A nonprofit agricultural association (e.g., a "Farm Bureau" or a "Grange"); and
- Managed Health Care provider organizations (HMOs, PPOs, etc.) or their employees.

Ethics

A producer should be able to *identify and apply* the meaning of the following:

- Put the customer's interest first;
- Know the job and continue to increase competence levels;
- Identify and recommend products and services that meet the customer's needs;
- Truthfully and accurately represent products and services;
- Use simple language that insurance consumers can understand;
- Stay in contact with customers and conduct periodic coverage reviews;
- Protect the confidential relationship with a client;
- Keep informed of and follow all insurance laws and regulations;
- Provide exemplary service to clients; and
- Avoid making inaccurate or unfair remarks about the competition.

It is worth noting that the California Code of Regulations and the California Insurance Code (Cal. Ins. Code) identify many unethical or illegal practices. It is impossible, however, to write legislation for each possible unethical act that could occur.

A producer's role in the insurance industry is a great responsibility toward others. The Insurance Code articulates the ethical and legal aspects of the client-agent relationship in many ways. Fiduciary responsibilities are very high on the list, including the contact a producer has with the insureds' premiums or the recommendations and advice given to others that have implications for their money or financial security.

An insurance agent must practice and demonstrate the highest integrity, ethics, and morals. Failures or lapses in any of these areas can cause significant financial harm to others. Misrepresentation, concealment, twisting, commingling client money with general business funds and other practices that lack integrity are unethical and prohibited by the Insurance Code. Failing to answer or providing an intentionally wrong answer to questions that prospects or insureds ask is also an ethical problem. It can lead a client to make a decision that might not be in their best interest. Unethical conduct can lead to the loss or suspension of a license, monetary penalties, and even time in jail or prison.

Producers must make recommendations to clients based on the clients' best interests. For a producer to recommend products or services to an individual that they would not recommend for themselves in the same situations is an ethical dilemma. This dilemma is regularly described as a conflict of interest. The normal conduct of business, especially in the insurance industry, can give producers many opportunities for conflicts of interest.

Agents are usually paid on a commission basis. Commissions are typically calculated based on an annual premium submitted, even though the client may have paid just the initial monthly installment with their application. For an agent, the higher the premium collected, the higher the commission. When the higher premium and the higher commission result from an inappropriate recommendation for the client, that is an unethical act and a conflict of interest.

An agent's opportunity to represent multiple insurance providers can be in the client's best interest. It can also lead to conflicts of interest, especially if a decision to book business with a particular insurer is made based on which insurer offers the best "perk" to its agents. Incentives like trips or cruises, commission bonuses, computers, or other sales-based contests present opportunities to do what is right for the agent. They do not offer opportunities to do what is right for the client.

Ethics demands that the other individual and their family are of primary importance. A producer with the highest respect for others will succeed the most. Producers who neglect this respect for others might have success initially, but they rarely achieve long-term success. The responsibility for ethical behavior is squarely on the producer.

Special Ethical Concerns Regarding Seniors – Senior citizens are the least likely to report abuses or financial crimes against them. They may feel embarrassed at being taken advantage of and do not want to appear to be losing the ability to manage their daily lives or personal finances.

Unethical agents have been caught selling multiple duplicative policies to senior citizens. Such agents propose one insurance policy or annuity contract but deliver another (bait and switch). They also mislead senior consumers into believing that an annuity product is a long-term care contract (or vice-versa).

California's Medicare supplement and LTC insurance regulations address unethical practices. Such practices include:

- Misleading or inaccurate comparisons of existing and proposed replacement contracts; and
- Selling an insured a third LTC policy within 12 months or a second Medicare supplement policy.

California passed the Financial Elder Abuse statutes in 2002, which, in part, explicitly addresses insurance agent abuses of individuals age 65 or older (Cal. Ins. Code Sections 785 through 789.10).

In most cases, insurance institutions, producers, and insurance-support organizations are not allowed to use pretext interviews to acquire information about an insurance transaction.

In an attempt to gain information about another natural person, a *pretext interview* is conducted when any individual does one or more of the following:

- Pretends to represent someone they do not actually represent;
- Pretends to be someone they are not;
- Misrepresents the purpose of the interview; or
- Refuses to identify themselves upon request.

Pretext interviews are prohibited during any phase of the insurance transaction process, including information gathering during underwriting. Using a pretext interview could reveal privileged information that would not usually be available to the insurance provider or producer. It could result in an *adverse underwriting decision*. As an investigative technique, pretext interviews are allowed when investigating a claim, particularly when fraud is presumed.

The purpose of the interview must be to investigate a claim where there is a reasonable basis for suspecting fraud, criminal activity, material misrepresentation, or material nondisclosure.

Insurers

Insurance is available to consumers from both private insurers and the government. The primary difference between government and private insurance is that government programs are funded with taxpayer dollars and serve national and state social purposes. Premiums, on the other hand, fund private insurance policies.

Private insurers can be classified in a variety of ways:

- Ownership;
- Domicile (location);
- Authority to transact business;
- Marketing and distribution systems; or
- Financial strength (rating).

As you read about different classifications of insurance companies, remember that these categories are not mutually exclusive. The same company can be described based on who owns it, where it is located and allowed to transact insurance, and what type of agents it appoints.

Admitted vs. Non-Admitted

Before insurers can transact business in a state, they must be granted a license or *certificate of authority* from the Department of Insurance and meet the state's financial capital and surplus requirements. Insurance providers who meet the state's financial requirements and are approved to do business in the state are considered *authorized or admitted* into the state as legal insurance companies. Insurance providers not approved to do business in California are deemed *unauthorized or non-admitted*. Many states do not allow unauthorized insurance companies to do business in the state, except through excess and surplus lines brokers (Cal. Ins. Code Sections 24 and 25).

Regulation of Admitted and Non-Admitted Insurers – The Insurance Code provisions limit the insurance that can be placed with non-admitted insurers to the following:

- Insurance against perils of navigation, transportation, transit, or other shipowner property, or marine insurance needs;

- Reinsurance of the liability of an admitted insurer;
- Aircraft or spacecraft insurance; and
- Insurance on property or railroad operations in interstate commerce.

These insurance types can only be placed with a non-admitted insurer through a licensed surplus lines broker.

Placing insurance in violation of these regulations is a *misdemeanor*.

Penalty for Acting as an Insurer without a Certificate of Authority – Transacting insurance business in California without a certificate of authority is a *public offense punishable* by:

- Fine up $100,000; or
- Imprisonment according to the Penal Code; or
- Imprisonment for up to one year in county jail; or
- Both the fine and imprisonment.

In California, except when performed by a surplus lines broker, the following acts are *misdemeanors*:

- Acting as an agent for a non-admitted insurance company;
- Advertising in any form of a non-admitted insurance company;
- In any other manner aiding a non-admitted insurance company to transact insurance business.

Individuals violating any provision of this section will be fined $500 and $100 for each month they continue the violation.

These rules are not applicable to sanctioned advertising.

Domestic, Foreign, and Alien Insurers

Insurance companies are classified according to where they are incorporated. An insurance company must obtain a certificate of authority before transacting insurance within the state, regardless of the location of incorporation (domicile) (Cal. Ins. Code Sections 26, 27, and 1580).

A *domestic insurer* is an insurance company that is incorporated in this state. In most cases, the company's home office is in the state where it was formed (the company's domicile). For instance, a company chartered in Colorado would be considered a Colorado domestic company.

Insurance companies incorporated in another state, the District of Columbia, or a territorial possession are known as *foreign insurers*. Presently, the United States has five major U.S. territories, including Puerto Rico, the Northern Mariana Islands, Guam, American Samoa, and the U.S. Virgin Islands.

An *alien insurer* is an insurance company incorporated outside the United States.

Mutual, Stock, and Fraternal Insurers

The most common types of ownership include the following:

Stock companies are owned by the stockholders who supply the capital necessary to establish and operate the insurance company and share any profits or losses. Officers manage stock insurance companies and are elected by the stockholders. Stock companies generally issue *nonparticipating policies*, where policy owners do not share in losses or profits.

Policy owners of nonparticipating policies do not receive dividends; however, stockholders are paid taxable dividends.

Mutual companies are owned by the policy owners and issue *participating policies*. Policy owners are entitled to dividends, which are a return of excess premiums that are *not taxable*. Dividends are generated when the combined earnings and premiums create a surplus that exceeds the coverage costs. Dividends are not guaranteed.

A *fraternal benefit society* is an organization formed to offer insurance for members of a religious organization, affiliated lodge, or fraternal organization with a representative form of government. Fraternals only sell insurance to their members and are considered charitable institutions, *not insurers*. They are not subject to all the regulations that apply to the insurance providers offering coverage to the public at large.

Earned Surplus and Policy Dividends – An *earned surplus* refers to unassigned funds that must be reported on the insurance provider's annual statement. A stock insurance company's dividend is paid from its earned surplus. However, the dividends cannot be declared out of earned surplus derived merely from the net appreciation in the value of assets not yet realized. It can only be returned to the stockholders once earned and is not needed for liabilities, expenses, reserves, etc.

The underwriting income of mutual insurance companies comes from *policy dividends*. They are not considered income or profit; they are refunds. Dividends are paid to the company's policy owners. They are also not guaranteed because an insurer's expenses can never be fully anticipated. Certain dividend options allow the purchase of additional insurance.

Operating Divisions

Insurers operate with many different divisions and departments. Among them are four principal departments responsible for the primary functions: Sales or Marketing, Underwriting, Claims, and Actuarial. These departments each have a specific purpose within the structure of an insurance company, and each can have an impact, positive or negative, on the company's profitability.

Sales and Marketing – The *marketing department* is responsible for promoting, advertising, and distributing an insurance provider's products to the public. This department also trains the producers, sells the products and develops any materials related to the marketing process. Agents are field representatives of the marketing department, responsible for putting the company's products and services into clients' hands. The marketing department can also handle monitoring compliance with the various laws regarding the conduct of producers and the transacting of contracts. It is also responsible for observing consumer trends and then researching and developing or modifying products and services to meet the demands or needs of the marketplace.

Underwriting – The *underwriting department* is responsible for accepting insurance applications and evaluating them according to established guidelines. Applications are either declined or approved. Declined applications do not meet the insurer's guidelines, but not all approved applicants are equal. The insurance company is willing to insure many applicants' risks that are more significant than the average risks the company expects to insure. These risks are classified as *substandard*. Certain applicants will also have risks more favorable than average, and those will be classified as *preferred*.

The underwriting department's primary objective is to prevent an imbalance of risks or the selection of poor risks, including too many substandard risks compared to preferred and standard risks. The prevention of selecting these poor risks is known as *adverse selection*. When the underwriting department approves too many poor risks, the statistical predictions of the actuaries may not hold up. Under these circumstances, the insurer will not attain the level of profit expected and could potentially suffer a loss.

Claims – The *claims department* is responsible for accepting claim requests, evaluating them in light of the actual contract, paying those claims which are covered by the terms of the contract, and rejecting those which are not. The claims department can employ or contract with adjusters or other investigators to assist in evaluating claims or to seek evidence of fraudulent or false claims. When the claims department does not settle claims fairly or promptly or makes payments for claims that are not covered by the contract, the insurance company's profitability can be affected.

Actuarial – The *actuarial department* is where the science of statistics is put into practice. Insurance company actuaries study morbidity and mortality statistics, the nature of claims, and actual claims experience. They even weigh the potential for fraudulent claims and the financial impact of those claims, including investigating fraudulent claims and payments. The actuaries must also account for the everyday expenses of doing business. These expenses include the payment of claims and making a conservative estimate of earnings from invested reserves (premiums received by the insurer but not currently needed to pay the expenses). After the analysis and calculations have been made, the actuaries publish the rates that must be charged for each line of business the company insures to achieve profitability.

Insurer's Qualifications

Any individual capable of making a contract can be an insurance provider, subject to the Code restrictions. To become an admitted insurer (legally entitled to transact insurance business in this state), an insurer must meet many technical, financial, and legal qualifications. The Code regulation is intended to prevent unqualified individuals from offering insurance to the public (Cal. Ins. Code Section 150).

The term *person* is used in the law to refer to any entity which is lawfully capable of performing legal acts, like making contracts, on its own behalf. In California, a person can be either a natural person *at least age 18* who is legally competent or any of the following entities:

- Organization;
- Association;
- Partnership;
- Limited liability company;
- Corporation; or
- Business trust.

Any person can be an insurance provider by satisfying the following guidelines of the California Insurance Code:

- Using only licensed brokers and agents;
- Submitting all products, forms, premiums, and advertising for approval before use;
- Using acceptable Doing Business As (DBA) names; and
- Maintaining required financial reserves.

Primary Insurer in Reinsurance

Reinsurance is insurance obtained by a primary insurer to protect itself against the catastrophe of a comparatively large single loss or a large number of small losses caused by a single occurrence. The reinsurance contract is between two parties:

1. **Reinsurer** – In consideration of the premium paid, a reinsurer is the company that assumes a part of the risk over an amount retained by the primary insurer, known as the *net line*.
2. **Primary insurer** – The primary insurer covers losses on a first dollar basis (sometimes subject to a deductible) and issues the policy over which reinsurance is obtained. The primary insurer is also called the *ceding company* in the reinsurance contract.

The contract between the reinsurer and the primary insurer is called a treaty. There are two types of reinsurance treaties:

1. **Automatic treaty** – The reinsurer agrees in advance to accept a portion of the gross line of the primary insurer's risks that meet the reinsurer's underwriting rules.
2. **Facultative treaty** – Every risk is considered individually by both parties. A risk is presented to the reinsurer for acceptance or rejection. If the risk is accepted, the primary insurer can accept or reject the rates and terms of the offer.

Retrocession refers to when a reinsurance company reinsures risks with other reinsurers.

Insolvent Insurers

Insolvency (Cal. Ins. Code Section 985) refers to either of the following:

- Any impairment of the minimum paid-in capital required of an insurance provider by the Insurance Code provisions for the class, or classes, of insurance that it transacts anywhere;
- An incapacity to reinsure any risk over and above the state's retention limits; or
- An inability of the insurance provider to meet its financial obligations when they are due.

When the insurer can provide reinsurance of all outstanding risks and liabilities, it cannot escape insolvency unless it has additional assets equal to the aggregate paid-in capital required by the state.

Paid-in Capital – *Paid-in capital* or *capital paid-in* (Cal. Ins. Code Section 36) refers to the following:

- In the circumstance of a *foreign mutual insurer* not issuing or having outstanding capital stock, the value of its assets over and above the sum of its liabilities for losses reported, taxes, expenses, and all other indebtedness and reinsurance of outstanding risks as provided by law. However, foreign mutual insurers cannot be admitted unless their paid-in capital consists of available cash assets amounting to at least $200,000.
- In the circumstance of a *foreign joint stock and mutual insurer*, its paid-in capital is calculated, according to its desire, based on the standards for subdivision (a) or subdivision (c). If paid-in capital is calculated according to subdivision (a), then its admission is subject to the same qualifications.
- In the case of *all other insurance providers*, its paid-in capital is the lesser of:
  o The value of its assets over and above the sum of its liabilities for losses reported, taxes, expenses, and all other debt and reinsurance of outstanding risks; or
  o The total par value of issued shares of stock, including treasury shares. Shares of stock are not considered liabilities to calculate paid-in capital or capital paid-in.

Refusal to Issue Information – Suppose the Commissioner learns that irreparable loss and injury to the property and business of an individual has occurred or could occur unless the Commissioner acts. In that case, before applying to the court for any order, the Commissioner can take possession of the business, property, records, books, and accounts of the individual and their office. The Commissioner can continue to retain possession after receiving a court order.

Anyone against whom a seizure order has been issued and who refuses to deliver pertinent records, books, or assets will be guilty of a *misdemeanor*. This violation may be punishable by a maximum fine of $1,000, imprisonment for no longer than one year, or both.

Market Regulation – General

California Insurance Code

The *California Insurance Code (CIC)* is the main body of laws set up by the state legislature, which regulates the insurance industry in California. The present form of the Code was enacted in 1935 as a restatement and expansion of previously established law. It is a dynamic, fluid device, constantly being reviewed, added to, amended, and even having outdated sections repealed. The CIC remains consistent with current practices and issues in the marketplace.

How the Code May be Changed – Legislative action is required to change the Insurance Code in any way. A bill repealing or amending an existing section or adding something new is introduced into the Assembly or the Senate. Here, it undergoes a variety of committee hearings and revisions before the bill is presented to the entire body for a vote. If approved, it goes to the other house for the same process. If additional changes are made before the bill is approved, it must be returned to the first body for re-approval. Once approved by both houses, the bill goes to the Governor for approval or veto, or it can also become law without the Governor's action.

Definitions

Shall and May – Certain terms or concepts have particular relevance to insurance but do not have different legal interpretations in insurance law. For example, the words "shall" and "may" always have the same implications, whether they appear in the Insurance Code or any other law (Cal. Ins. Code Section 16).

Shall is a word that compels action; it usually indicates that a specific action or response is required. Where the Code states that a person "shall" or "shall not" do something, there is usually no room for misunderstanding. On the other hand, *may* is a word of options or permission; it leaves room to act or not to act and remains in compliance with the law. However, the Code opens the possibility that, in context, even the word "may" could be interpreted the same as the word "shall."

Person – Even the word "person" is expansive. A *person* does not simply refer to a living, breathing human being (a natural person). A person can also refer to organizations, associations, partnerships, limited liability companies, corporations, and even trusts (all non-natural persons). Whether natural or non-natural, all persons are distinguished by their ability to contract, sue, or be sued. Non-natural persons only have to designate a natural person to represent them or act as their agent.

California Code of Regulations

The *California Code of Regulations (CCR)*, also called the *California Administrative Code*, is the set of regulations issued by the Department of Insurance that identifies the standards for the Insurance Code, and how it is to be administered. The CCR includes the regulations that have been issued by the Insurance Commissioner for clarification and administration of the Code.

The Commissioner

Selection of the Commissioner – In California, the Commissioner of Insurance is an *elected official*. The Commissioner is elected to serve not more than *two consecutive 4-year terms*.

The Commissioner is expected to be an individual knowledgeable in the insurance industry but cannot be an active agent, director, officer, or employee of an insurance company. If a licensed person is elected Commissioner, they must surrender their license within ten days of taking office. At the end of their term, they can have their license reinstated for the balance of the license term without penalties or fees.

Responsibilities – The Commissioner of Insurance has no authority or power to write or change the law but has the authority to enforce the law. The Commissioner's responsibility is to issue regulations establishing how the Department of Insurance intends to interpret and enforce the law. The regulations proposed by the Commissioner have to undergo a public hearing to determine their fairness or applicability before they can go into effect (Cal. Ins. Code Sections 12900 and 12921).

The Commissioner must oversee the California Department of Insurance (CDI) and direct all of the CDI's affairs and staff.

The Commissioner can appoint individuals to act on their behalf. These representatives can negotiate settlements with insurers or agents who have violated the Code. However, it is the responsibility of the Commissioner to make the final approval of a sanction.

The Commissioner is responsible for responding to inquiries and investigating complaints. When warranted, the Commissioner can bring enforcement actions against insurance providers. The system for managing complaints needs to include the following:

- A toll-free number published in telephone books throughout the state of California, dedicated to handling inquiries and complaints;
- Public service announcements to update consumers on the toll-free telephone number and how to report a complaint or make an inquiry to the California Department of Insurance;
- A simple, standardized complaint form intended to assure that complaints are appropriately registered and tracked;
- Retention of records related to complaints for at least three years;
- Guidelines to disseminate complaint and enforcement information to the public. This information contains license status, the number and type of complaints filed within the previous calendar year, the violations found, and any enforcement actions. Also included is the ratio of complaints received to total policies in force, premium dollars paid in a particular line, or both.

The Commissioner is responsible for giving the insurance provider an explanation of any complaint against the company that the Commissioner received and considered to be justified. This information must be provided at least 30 days before the public release of a report summarizing the required information. The summary includes:

- The date it was filed;
- The complainant's name;
- A description of facts; and
- A statement of the CDI's reasoning for determining whether the complaint is valid.

The Commissioner must prepare a report made available by the Department to interested individuals upon written request that details complaint and enforcement information on individual insurance providers according to the CIC. This report has to be made available by telephone, mail, Internet, and email.

Every public record of the Department and the Commissioner must be available for inspection and copying.

The Commissioner receives inquiries and complaints, investigates complaints, prosecutes insurance companies according to guidelines determined by the California Insurance Code, and responds to complaints and questions regarding alleged misconduct. The Commissioner is required to notify the complainant of receipt within *ten working days*. Once a determination is made, the Commissioner will inform the complainant of the final order within 30 days of judgment.

The Commissioner can issue a *cease and desist order* against the following: any individual acting as a broker or agent without being licensed and any individual transacting insurance without a certificate of authority. The Commissioner can also issue a cease and desist order without holding a hearing before allocating the order. A fine of up to $5,000 can be issued for each day the individual violates the order. An individual to whom a cease and desist order is issued can request a hearing by filing a request with the Commissioner within seven days after receiving the order.

Gramm-Leach-Bliley Act (GLBA)

The *Gramm-Leach-Bliley Act (GLBA)* mandates that an insurance provider cannot divulge nonpublic information to a nonaffiliated third party except for the following reasons:

- The insurance provider discloses to the consumer in writing that information may be disclosed to a third party;
- The consumer is given a chance, before the information is initially disclosed, to require that the information not be divulged to the third party; or
- The consumer receives an explanation of how the consumer can exercise a nondisclosure option.

The Gramm-Leach-Bliley Act requires two disclosures to a customer (a consumer who has an ongoing financial relationship with a financial institution):

1. When the customer relationship is established (e.g., a policy is purchased); and
2. Before disclosing protected information.

The customer must be given an annual privacy disclosure and the right to opt out or decide not to have their private information shared with other parties.

California Financial Information Privacy Act

The California Financial Information Privacy Act was enacted on July 1, 2004. It allows consumers to control how their nonpublic personal information is shared or sold to third-party financial institutions. The act provides greater privacy protections than the federal Gramm-Leach-Bliley Act (GLBA).

The act restricts the financial profiling of consumers. It makes consumers aware of their rights through a written and easy-to-understand notice, allowing them to opt in or out of sharing nonpublic personal information.

Nonpublic personal information refers to personally identifiable information collected by a financial institution through the consumer, a transaction between the institution and consumer, or some other means.

Examples of *personally-identifiable information* include:

- Information about an application obtaining credit cards, loans, or other financial services or products;
- Payment history, debit or credit card purchase information, and account balance information;
- Information from past and current financial institutions used by a consumer;
- Financial information gathered through web servers or internet cookies; and
- Information contained on a consumer report.

Authorized privacy notices must include the following:

- A form, statement, or writing that remains separate from other documents;
- A title that reads "Important Privacy Choices for Consumers;"

- The date and the consumer's signature;
- A disclosure stating the consumer consents to the release of personally identifiable information to a nonaffiliated third party;
- A disclosure confirming that consent will remain in effect unless revoked or modified by the consumer;
- A process for the consumer to revoke consent; and
- A statement confirming that the financial institution will maintain the notice, and the consumer can receive a copy upon request.

A financial institution is not required to obtain a consumer's consent if nonpublic personal information is shared with its wholly owned financial institution subsidiaries.

Suppose a financial institution violates the California Financial Information Privacy Act. In that circumstance, the institution may be fined up to $2,500 per violation of one consumer's information being released or $500,000 for multiple consumers.

Insurance Information and Privacy Protection Act

Practices – Cal. Ins. Code Section 791 is concerned with the collection and distribution of, or the access to, a person's private or privileged information, which can be necessary to obtain in connection with an insurance application. The law is sensitive to a consumer's desire to keep certain information private. However, it also acknowledges that an insurance provider might approve an individual for insurance without that information. The insurer could lawfully decline coverage if it knew that information.

Section 791 of the CIC balances fairness for applicants and insurance providers when gathering and using information. The law is designed to apply to natural persons who are residents of the state and are seeking life or disability insurance. It also applies to any individual seeking property or casualty insurance for policies issued or delivered in California.

The information necessary for proper underwriting can be personal and highly sensitive. Because of this, there is great potential for harm to an individual if their personal information is disclosed to others who have no legitimate reason for receiving it. How and from whom that information is collected, obtained, kept, and when or how it will be disseminated to others must be disclosed to insurance applicants.

In some cases, insurance providers can decide to conduct an investigative consumer report with an application. An investigative consumer report goes beyond simply gathering information from the Medical Information Bureau (MIB) or the credit reporting bureaus. It can include interviews with applicants, employers, their relatives, neighbors, or any other individual with information about the person's general reputation, character, personal characteristics, and lifestyle. The Insurance Code allows individuals to request that they be interviewed personally. It also requires that the person be given a copy of the report upon request and provided with a mechanism to protest and request a correction of inaccurate information about them. The individual has a right to know to whom the information has been given and the source or sources.

If an adverse underwriting decision occurs, the individual must be given the reason for the decision. The reason can include being declined, rated, or considered less than a standard risk. It can also mean being issued coverage by an insurer other than the one to which the applicant initially intended to apply. Insurers must give this information to the individual in writing. An insurer can also advise these individuals that they may request the reason for the action to be furnished to them in writing.

Suppose the information is medically-related and supplied by a medical professional or medical care institution. In that situation, it must be disclosed (upon request) directly to the individual or a licensed medical professional to treat the person for the condition to which the information relates. When the information is related to an individual's mental health, it can only be disclosed with the consent of the medical professional who is responsible for the treatment related to that information.

Prohibitions – The Insurance Code also describes how information about an individual's previous adverse underwriting decisions cannot be used as the basis of a new underwriting decision. An exception is made if it is received directly from the agent or insurer who made the adverse decision. Being declined or rated for insurance in the past or having insurance provided by a residual insurer is insufficient for denying or rating an individual for new insurance. A residual insurer is one other than the original insurer to which the application for coverage was submitted.

Additionally, applications for insurance that include questions that are not intended to gather information about the applicant but are intended for marketing or other purposes need to be clearly identified. Marketing or research questions could include those designed to reveal an individual's shopping habits, for example. Still, they could disclose other *privileged information* that the agent or insurer has no reason to need or possess. These questions do not have to be answered, and a decision not to answer such questions may not be used as the basis for an adverse underwriting decision.

Penalties – Section 791 of the CIC details under what circumstances the Commissioner can examine insurance providers, agents, and others engaged in the information collecting processes. It also details how these individuals must maintain or distribute the information gathered. There are a variety of penalties that may be applied to the various violations that can be committed. Some of the penalties include:

- Suspension or loss of license; and
- Civil fines for violating cease and desist orders of up to $10,000 per violation; or
- Up to $50,000 if the violations are discovered to be committed with a frequency indicating they are a general business practice.

Agents or insurers can also be liable for civil damages and legal fees arising from the unlawful collection or distribution of private or privileged information about an individual that causes harm. Certain acts could also violate other criminal laws and subject an individual to prosecution, resulting in fines or imprisonment.

Cal-GLBA

The California Financial Information Privacy Act provides standards for financial institutions regarding sharing or selling nonpublic personal information about consumers. California legislation known as *Cal-GLBA* delivers greater privacy protection to consumers than the federal Gramm-Leach-Bliley Act. Cal-GLBA outlines consumer privacy choices and rights and allows California consumers to have greater control over disclosing nonpublic personal information.

As defined by the California Financial Code, *nonpublic personal information* refers to any financial information that is

- Provided to a financial institution by a consumer;
- Acquired as a result of a transaction with the consumer; or
- Acquired by a financial institution through any other means.

Conservation Proceedings

Insurers are exempted explicitly under federal bankruptcy laws, which means that any *liquidation* of an insolvent insurance company is strictly a matter for the state to pursue. To accomplish this, California has adopted the *Uniform Insurers Rehabilitation Act*. This Act describes the steps the Commissioner must take when attempting to rehabilitate a *delinquent* or *insolvent* insurer to sound financial condition or liquidate an insurer that cannot be rehabilitated. The Code also describes the superior court's mandatory action when the Commissioner presents a petition for either a conservation or liquidation order (Cal. Ins. Code Sections 1011, 1013, and 1016).

Each year, on or before March 1, every insurer conducting business in California must report its financial condition to the Commissioner. When an insurance provider's legal reserve funds are less than the minimum required by law, the insurer is *impaired* in its ability to pay claims and is technically *insolvent*. The Commissioner has authority under the Code to take control of the insurance company, and the superior court must grant the Commissioner's petition for conservation. There is no long, drawn-out legal battle (the insurance provider has no power to prevent the act of conservation).

The court order gives the Commissioner absolute control over the operations and assets of the insurer. The Commissioner's first responsibility is to try to rehabilitate the insurer, if at all possible. Initially, every new business transaction is terminated. Existing and new claims are paid, and ways to return the insurer to solvency are explored. When there is no possibility of rehabilitating the insurer, the Commissioner's final move will be to liquidate the insurer and sell assets to continue to pay claims. If all claims have been satisfied, the insurer will use any remaining assets to satisfy the claims of other creditors.

If the insurer cannot pay its claims, the two Guarantee Associations in California are prepared to pay a portion of the claims, depending on the type of policy. Suppose one or both of the Guarantee Associations must pay claims because of the inability of the insurer to pay. In that situation, they become creditors of the insurer and can seek repayment through the liquidation process.

In a conservation or liquidation effort, the Commissioner also has the power to sue directors, officers, or others who might bear responsibility for the company's condition. These individuals include managing general agents, actuaries, auditors, and accountants to add to the "estate" of the insurer to pay the claims of insureds or creditors. Even industry rating companies have been held responsible for their published inaccuracies.

Additionally, in a liquidation, other parties not generally associated with the claims-paying responsibility of the insurer can have their assets seized. Suppose the insolvent insurance provider was a substantial owner of another business or partnership. In that circumstance, those assets can satisfy the insurer's obligations, regardless of whether that business was involved in the insurance industry.

When the Commissioner is involved in liquidating an insurer, there is a legal requirement to publish the notice of liquidation for four consecutive weeks. In most cases, the Commissioner must also mail notices to known potential claimants against the insurer's estate. Once the notices have been published or mailed, claimants have no more than six months to file their claims. The Insurance Code establishes the priority of claims. Only when the claims of a class or group have been fully satisfied will the next claimant in order be entitled to pursue their claims.

Discontinuance and Replacement of Group Life Insurance

When individuals are covered under a group life or disability insurance policy, there are provisions in the Insurance Code to protect them in the event the coverage is discontinued. These provisions also protect the individuals if they are no longer eligible for coverage under the policy. The Code explains these provisions as discontinuance, an extension of benefits, and replacement coverage (Cal. Ins. Code Section 10128.1 through 10128.4).

The term *discontinuance* is described as the termination of an insurance plan between the insurance provider and the entire group of employees. It does not refer to the termination of benefits for terminated employees or those whose eligibility under the group plan was affected by reduced work hours or other qualifying factors.

Insurers established *extension of benefits* provisions to protect covered individuals, dependents, or employees who are totally disabled before discontinuing or terminating their group insurance while they remain disabled. The Insurance Code allows up to 12 months of continued coverage for health care and disability claims beyond the termination of the preceding policy, provided the person remains totally disabled.

When a new group policy replaces an existing one, the new policy *must* accept all the insureds covered under the previous policy. However, the insurance provider is not required to take over existing claims. In this case, an individual who is totally disabled at the time of replacement must have their continuing claim paid for by the former insurer if the new insurer chooses not to cover pre-existing claims. However, a replacing insurer can accept all covered individuals and their existing claims.

An insurer must not cover a continuing claim longer than 12 months after the replacement date. This period is the same time a former insurance provider would have been required to provide coverage under the discontinuance provision. Each new claim unrelated to the individual's total disability would have to be covered by the new policy. This concept is also referred to as *no loss, no gain*. The covered individual would not be entitled to receive more or fewer benefits than the preceding insurer would have been required to provide. They must be treated the same as any other covered employee concerning new claims.

Suppose replacement coverage does not become effective at the same time the former policy ends. In that scenario, every covered individual as of the discontinuance date must be covered by the new policy without exception. The new policy must take effect within 60 days of the date of discontinuance.

A replacement policy taking effect more than 60 days after discontinuing a previous policy must also allow the conversion to an individual policy at the end of the extension of the benefits period. This requirement also applies to any group policy that includes a life insurance benefit and allows conversion to an individual insurance plan if eligibility is lost. Replacement enables an individual to have a continuous period of total disability covered without paying further premiums for up to 12 months. It then lets the protected person, even if still totally disabled, convert the group coverage to individual coverage without proof of insurability.

Notice by Mail

There is always the possibility that a party to a policy could attempt to avoid responsibility under the policy. They may falsely claim they sent a notice or that the other party never sent the required notice. The law explains what is considered to be sufficient proof of mailing.

Suppose the notice had postage applied and was put in the hands of the U.S. Postal Service with the recipient's last known address on it. In that case, an affidavit by the sender stating such facts is proof of the mailing. Any notice provided by electronic transmission must be treated as if mailed or given for any provision of the Insurance Code. A valid electronic signature will be sufficient for any provision of law requiring a written signature (Cal. Ins. Code Sections 38 and 38.6).

The insurer must retain a copy of the confirmation and electronic signature with the policy information. The insurer must be able to retrieve them upon request by the Department of Insurance when the policy is effective and for five years after that.

A licensee must acquire an insured's consent to opt-in to receive records electronically. Additionally, a licensee must disclose to insureds that they may opt-out of electronic transmission at any time. Licensees must also disclose a description of the records the insured will receive, a process to change or correct an insured's email address, and the licensee's contact information.

Upon the insured's request, a licensee must provide at least one free printed copy of records annually.

When required to transmit a record by return receipt, a licensee may demonstrate actual delivery by:

- Having the recipient acknowledge the receipt;
- Have the record securely posted on the licensee's website; or
- Having the record transmitted to the named insured through a secure application.

A licensee must contact the insured to confirm their email address when a record is not delivered directly to the insured's email. Licensees can also resend the record by regular mail within five business days.

California Life and Health Insurance Guarantee Association

The *California Life and Health Insurance Guarantee Association (CLHIGA)* exists to pay the claims of insureds or beneficiaries when an insurance provider is *impaired* or *insolvent* (Cal. Ins. Code Sections 1067.02(a)(1) and 1067.02(b)(1)). The Association covers the following:

- Most life and health insurance contracts and annuities;
- Individuals who are state residents and, in certain situations, those who are nonresidents; and
- Structured settlement annuities.

At most, the Association is *liable* for the lesser of the following benefits:

- 80% of the contractual obligations of the insurance provider if it had not become insolvent;
- $100,000 in total net cash withdrawal and net cash surrender values for life insurance;
- $250,000 in net cash withdrawal and net cash surrender values for deferred annuity contracts; or
- $300,000 for all benefits, including cash values, concerning any one life.

In no event would the Association be required to pay more than an aggregate of $300,000 in benefits concerning any one life. Regarding a single owner of multiple nongroup life insurance policies, the Association is not liable for more than $5,000,000 in benefits, irrespective of the number of contracts and policies.

For health insurance claims, the CLHIGA must cover the lesser of the covered claims of an insured but not more than $200,000 in health insurance benefits, adjusted for inflation based on increases or decreases in the health care component of the Consumer Price Index (CPI) from January 1, 1991, to the actual date of insolvency. The following are not included in health insurance claims:

- Disability income, credit disability, or indemnity;
- Accidental death or dismemberment;
- Workers compensation; or
- Long-term care.

CLHIGA comprises all insurance providers who legally conduct business in the state. It evaluates members according to the lines of business it transacts and maintains two separate accounts:

1. Life insurance and annuity account, which includes two subaccounts (the life insurance account and the annuity account); and
2. Health insurance.

Member insurers pay a maximum of 1% of annual premiums in each line of business for the future payment of claims, as reported to the Commissioner in their annual financial reports. This amount is based on a formula established by the Association's board of directors.

Suppose there are insufficient funds in any account to cover the Association's obligations. In that situation, member insurers can be assessed an additional amount, in proportion to their total premiums, necessary to fund the claims against the Association. Also, insurers can recoup these additional assessments for health insurance by passing the cost on to current policy owners over a reasonable period as a premium surcharge.

The California Life and Health Insurance Guarantee Association *does not cover* the following:

- Any portion of a policy not guaranteed by the insurance provider or under which the policy owner bears the risk;
- Any policy of reinsurance, unless assumption certificates have been issued;
- Any portion of a policy to the extent that the interest rate on which it is based exceeds a rate of interest calculated by subtracting six percentage points from Moody's Corporate Bond Yield Average;
- Guaranteed interest contracts, guaranteed investment contracts, deposit administration contracts, funding agreements, and all other unallocated annuity contracts;
- An individual who is a payee, or beneficiary, of a contract owner resident of California, if the payee, or beneficiary, is provided coverage by another state's Association;
- Any employer or Association plan to provide benefits to its members to the extent that the program is uninsured or self-funded;
- Any portion of a policy to the extent that it provides experience rating credits or dividends or stipulates that any fees or allowances be paid to any individual;
- Any annuity issued through a charitable organization not primarily involved in the insurance business; or
- Any policy or contract issued at a time when the member insurer did not have a certificate of authority or was not licensed.

Unfair Trade Practices

After passing the McCarran-Ferguson Act in 1945, California adopted regulations concerning unfair practices, affirming the state's role in insurance regulation. This section of the CIC, together with its subparts, contains different practices that the Code has identified explicitly as unfair and the other regulations and penalties related to unfair practices. The Code is also clear regarding any other undefined act or practice that the Commissioner determines to be unfair to insurers or consumers. Even though they are not mentioned in particular, such acts or practices can still violate the Code. (Cal. Ins. Code Sections 790 through 790.15).

General Prohibitions – Many of the most prevalent practices which are problems include things like misrepresentations in sales illustrations or advertised policy terms, or in the financial condition of an insurance provider, including its reserves and policy titles which could mislead an individual into believing that the contract performs differently, or other misrepresentations which could lead a person to forfeit, surrender, or lapse a policy. Additionally, acts such as unfairly discriminating against classes of insureds, filing false financial documents, or simply making false statements that should be known as untrue by using reasonable care are identified as unfair practices.

Unfair claims settlement practices include the following:

- Misrepresenting facts or provisions of policy coverage;
- Failure to determine within a reasonable amount of time after the submission of proof of loss forms whether or not a claim is payable;
- Not making a fair settlement of a claim after the insurance company's liability has been made clear;
- Compelling insureds to sue the insurer to obtain a judgment to enforce a claim by offering substantially less than the insured receives following a trial, only to collect an amount the same or nearly the same as the insured hoped to receive;

- Advertising insurance that the insurer will not sell; and
- Providing untrue or deceptive information about an individual or entity engaged in insurance.

Also included in this subpart are other offenses, such as the following:

- An insurance provider attempting to appeal arbitration awards to get the insured to accept a compromise or settlement for less than the arbitration award;
- Requiring insureds to submit preliminary claim reports followed later by a request to submit essentially the same information to either deny or accept a claim;
- Advising an insured not to seek or retain an attorney;
- Delaying payment regarding hospital, medical, or surgical claims for individuals with HIV or AIDS for more than 60 days after filing a claim to attempt to invoke a pre-existing condition exclusion;
- Advertising membership in the state's Guarantee Association;
- Unfair discrimination;
- Filing false financial statements; and
- Intimidation, coercion, boycott.

Specific Unfair Trade Practices Defined

False Advertising – Advertising covers a wide range of communication, from publishing an ad in a magazine or newspaper to broadcasting a commercial on television or the Internet. Advertisements cannot include any deceptive, untrue, or misleading statements that apply to the business of insurance or anyone who conducts it. Violating this rule is called *false advertising*.

It is forbidden to advertise or circulate any materials that are deceptive, untrue, or misleading. Deceptive or false advertising specifically includes *misrepresenting* any of the following:

- Benefits, terms, conditions, or advantages of any insurance policy;
- The financial condition of any individual or the insurance carrier;
- Any dividends to be received from the policy or previously paid out; or
- The true intention of an assignment or loan against a policy.

Representing an insurance policy as a share of stock or utilizing names or titles that could misrepresent the true nature of a policy will be considered false advertising. Also, a person or an entity cannot use a name that deceptively suggests it is an insurance provider.

Misrepresentation – It is illegal to publish, issue, or circulate any illustration or sales material that is misleading, false, or deceptive as to the policy benefits or terms, the payment of dividends, etc. This illegal activity also refers to oral statements and is known as *misrepresentation*.

Rebating – *Rebating* is any inducement offered to the insured during the sale of insurance products not specified in the policy. Both the offer and the acceptance of a rebate are illegal. Rebates can include, but are not limited to, the following:

- Rebates of policy premiums;
- Special services or favors;
- Kickbacks for referrals;
- Advantages in dividends or other benefits; and
- Securities, stocks, bonds, and their profits or dividends.

Twisting – *Twisting* s a misrepresentation. It is also a fraudulent or incomplete comparison of insurance that persuades a policy owner, to their detriment, to lapse, cancel, switch policies, or take out a policy with another insurer. Twisting is prohibited.

Unfair Discrimination – *Discrimination* in premiums, rates, or policy benefits for individuals within the *same class* or with the same life expectancy is illegal. Insurers cannot discriminate based on a person's race, national origin, marital status, sexual orientation, gender identity, creed, or ancestry unless it is for business purposes or required by law.

Defamation – *Defamation* occurs when oral or written statements are intended to injure a person engaged in the insurance business. It also applies to statements that are maliciously critical of the financial condition of any individual or company.

Boycott, Coercion, and Intimidation – It is illegal to engage in any activity of *boycott, coercion, or intimidation* intended to create a monopoly or restrict fair trade. This activity also would include unfair behavior that influences clients, competing brokers, and agents.

Coercion is to require, as a condition of a loan, that the applicant purchase insurance from a specific insurance company.

Penalties – Whenever the Commissioner has reason to believe that an individual is engaging in or has engaged in any unfair trade practices, the Commissioner must issue a cease and desist order. The cease and desist order must show cause, in addition to the individual's liability, and it must accompany the notice of a hearing, which must be at least *30 days* from the date of the order. The Commissioner can issue a penalty if the charges are justified at the hearing.

The *civil penalties* that can be assessed for violations of unfair trade practices are $5,000 for each act in violation of the Code, whether intentional or not. However, suppose the act or practice is determined to be a willful violation or a general business practice. In that case, the penalty increases to a maximum of $10,000 for each violation. The Commissioner can also act against a licensee who engages in any unfair practice.

When the Commissioner believes an individual has violated a cease and desist order, after a hearing, the Commissioner can order that individual to pay a sum not to exceed $5,000. This amount may be recouped in a civil action. If the violation is willful, the amount of the penalty can be a sum not to exceed $55,000. These fines are in addition to civil penalties for violation of the Insurance Code ($5,000 per act) and intentional violation of the Insurance Code ($10,000 per act).

Unfairly Discriminatory Practices

Insurance has two types of discrimination: fair and unfair discrimination (Cal. Ins. Code Sections 10140 through10145). *Fair discrimination* occurs when an insurance provider's underwriting department finds information that indicates an increase in risk that can be verified through statistical (actuarial) proof. Suppose an insurer decides to limit coverage or other policy benefits, increase premiums, or refuse coverage for that type of client (discriminate). In that case, it is appropriate for them to do so since the law permits it.

Unfair discrimination is morally unacceptable and illegal. One step in enabling insurance providers to avoid unfair discrimination is to place applicants and insureds in classifications based on actuarially acceptable guidelines. Such classifications upon which risk and insurability can be based will inherently vary with the specific type of coverage. Generally, they can include the following:

- Gender;
- Age;

- Tobacco use;
- Height/weight ratio;
- Geographic location; or
- Profession and avocations (hobbies).

Insurers can use a combination of these, but only if statistics prove that the classification increases a claim's risk on the specific type of insurance being considered.

For example, it would be unacceptable for an insurer to charge life insurance clients a higher premium based on their ZIP code. Their geographic location does not increase their risk of death. However, it would be acceptable to charge these same clients a higher or lower premium for health insurance, provided the costs of care in their ZIP code are higher or lower than the average. For this reason, it is typical for insurers to apply a *rating factor* to raise or lower a health insurance premium based solely on the ZIP code.

Once a client's actuarial classifications have been determined, that client must be treated the same as every other client within the same classifications. The person cannot be provided with different policy benefits or charged a different premium than everyone else in those classifications.

The following are specific classifications that *cannot* exist:

- Race;
- Color;
- Religion;
- National origin;
- Ancestry;
- Sexual orientation; and
- Physical and mental impairments that do not increase risk or vision impairment, including blindness.

Classifying people according to these classifications would be unfair as these characteristics do not affect the client's risk. It is forbidden for insurance providers or their representatives to request, acquire, or share such information. It is acceptable to ask an applicant for their place of birth if that information is only used for identification purposes.

Regarding sexual orientation, it would be a blatant violation for an insurance provider to ask an applicant any question regarding the subject. While insurers won't ask a direct question, they can attempt to conclude sexual orientation by analyzing other factors in the applicant's life. Then, the insurer can adjust the benefits or the premium based on a presumption of an increased risk of AIDS. Insurance providers cannot use the following to attempt to make a judgment about sexual orientation:

- Gender;
- Marital status;
- Living arrangement;
- Jobs;
- Beneficiary;
- ZIP code or any other geographic classification; or
- Any combination of these.

Therefore, if an insurance provider is concerned about the risk of claims resulting from AIDS and wishes to test for HIV, it is necessary to test everyone under the same guidelines.

Suppose an insured with a condition expected to cause death within one year requests an experimental treatment and is refused by their insurance provider. In that case, the insurer has to provide the following:

- The specific medical and scientific reasons for the denial and specific references to related policy provisions upon which the denial is based;
- A description of the alternative treatments or medical procedures covered by the policy, if any; and
- A description of the appeal/review process within 30 days or five days if delaying treatment would be detrimental.

Insurance providers offering life or health insurance cannot affect the coverage or premium of anyone because the insurer suspects the individual may become a victim of *domestic violence*. Underwriters are, however, allowed to consider an actual medical condition that does exist, as long as they don't consider whether the condition was caused by domestic violence. Intentional acts of the insured can still result in the loss of benefits.

Section 6211 of the California Family Code defines *domestic violence* as abuse perpetrated against any of the following:

- A cohabitant or former cohabitant;
- A spouse or former spouse;
- An individual with whom the respondent is having or has had a dating or engagement relationship;
- An individual with whom the respondent has had a child, where it is presumed that the male parent is the child's father and the female parent is the mother under the Uniform Parentage Act;
- A child of a party or a child who is the subject of an action under the Uniform Parentage Act, where the male parent is the father of the child to be protected; or
- Any other individual related by blood or affinity within the second degree.

Medical policies must include coverage for diagnosing and treating severe mental illness for every insured and serious emotional disturbances in children. This coverage then excludes insurance providers from offering any specific-coverage policy, such as accident only, dental, etc.

Penalties – In addition to any other remedy permitted by law, the Commissioner has the administrative authority to assess penalties against life or disability insurance companies for violations of the Insurance Code section on discriminatory practices. The penalties for the insurance provider for *unfair discrimination* violations are as follows:

- 1st violation – $2,500;
- Subsequent violations – $5,000 each;
- Violations so frequent as to indicate they are a general business practice of that insurer – $15,000 - $100,000 per violation.

Any individual who *negligently discloses* the results of a genetic test for an unauthorized third party will be assessed a civil penalty of up to $1,000, plus court costs, payable to the test subject. Any willful violations will be subject to a civil penalty between $1,000 and $5,000, plus court costs.

When the subject suffers bodily, emotional, or economic harm, the violation becomes a misdemeanor punishable by a fine of up to $10,000. Each unauthorized disclosure is considered a separate violation. Suppose an individual decides to share that information with the public. In that case, the penalty and damages could be hundreds of thousands of dollars.

Fraud

Common Circumstances – Insurance fraud is a significant problem for insurers and insureds. Premiums for most forms of insurance have risen in recent years due to the increasing number of fraudulent claims being presented to insurance companies for payment. The most common forms of insurance fraud include:

- Fraudulent health care billings;
- Staged automobile accidents;
- False or inflated property loss claims;
- Phony workers compensation claims;
- Fraudulent denial of workers compensation benefits;
- Workers compensation premium fraud by employers;
- Fake life insurance claims; and
- Arson for profit.

In 2002, the California Department of Insurance estimated that up to 50% of all automobile insurance claims might be fraudulent. Many of them are being "staged" on paper instead of occurring. This automobile insurance fraud is estimated to cost California consumers as much as $500,000,000 annually. Due to the high cost of medical claims, California has the highest rates for workers compensation insurance, even though the actual compensation benefits are among the lowest in the country.

Efforts to Combat Fraud – Federal, state, and local law enforcement officials work together with insurers and industry support organizations to combat insurance fraud. The California Department of Insurance has created the *Fraud Division* to enforce the Penal Code's provisions and administer the fraud reporting provisions.

Among other agencies and systems to help combat fraud is the Arson Information Reporting System. It allows for cooperation between insurance providers, fire investigating agencies, law enforcement agencies, and district attorneys. This system permits all parties to deposit arson case information in a common database within the Department of Justice.

All insurance providers must report covered private passenger vehicles involved in theft to prevent auto insurance-related fraud. Insurers must include the vehicle identification number (VIN) and any other relevant information to the National Automobile Theft Bureau or a similar organization approved by the Commissioner. Before the payment of theft losses, insurance companies have to comply with verification procedures according to the regulations adopted by the Commissioner.

Insurers, brokers, and agents also have a legal responsibility to report suspected fraud. Suppose an insurer or licensed rating organization knows the identity of an individual or entity that has perpetrated fraud relating to a workers compensation insurance policy or claim. In that case, the insurer must notify the local district attorney's office and the Fraud Division of the Department of Insurance. It can inform any other authorized government agency of that suspected fraud and provide additional information.

The Commissioner can license an organization as an *Insurance Claims Analysis Bureau*, provided that it is a nonprofit corporation organized for fraud prevention with at least two years of relevant experience. An Insurance Claims Analysis Bureau must perform the following functions:

- Gather and compile information and data from members concerning the insurance claims;
- Disseminate claims-related information to members to suppress and prevent insurance fraud;
- Promote training and education related to suppression, investigation, and prosecution of insurance fraud; and

- Provide to the Commissioner (without fee or charge) all state data and information contained in the records of the Bureau to further prevent and prosecute insurance fraud.

Every insurance company admitted to conducting business in this state must allow for the continuous operation of a unit or division to investigate possible fraudulent claims for services or repairs against policies held by insureds.

Insurers, brokers, and agents have legal immunity from civil suits claiming libel or slander. These lawsuits could result from filing reports, giving statements, or furnishing any other information, provided the information is offered *in good faith and without malice*.

Fraudulent Claim Forms – If a claimant signs a fraudulent claim form, the claimant can be found guilty of *perjury*.

False and Fraudulent Claims Article – Chapter 12 of the Insurance Code is devoted exclusively to the Insurance Fraud Prevention Act. The Insurance Code explains the primary responsibilities that the Commissioner, law enforcement agencies, insurers, brokers, agents, and others have when aggressively confronting the problem of insurance fraud in this state.

State insurance claim forms must carry a notice informing claimants of their liability in the event of a fraudulent claim.

Every individual who *commits insurance fraud* can be punished as follows:

- A fine up to $150,000 or twice the dollar amount of the fraud, whichever is greater;
- Imprisonment in county jail for one year, or in state prison for up to five years; or
- Both imprisonment and fine.

The court will determine the restitution amount and where the restitution needs to be paid. An individual convicted can be charged for the costs of the investigation at the court's discretion.

An individual who commits insurance fraud and has a prior felony conviction will receive a *2-year enhancement* for each prior conviction in addition to the sentence provided.

Fair Claims Settlement Practice Regulations

Definitions

A *claimant* is any individual who maintains a right of recovery under a surety bond (10 Cal. Code Regs. Section 2695.2(c)). Claimants can also include an attorney, any individual authorized by law to represent the claimant, or any of the following individuals properly designated by the claimant:

- Insurance adjuster;
- Public adjuster; or
- Any member of the claimant's family.

A *notice of legal action* is a document confirming a legal action has been initiated against the insurer regarding a claim or notice of action against the insured (10 Cal. Code Regs. Section 2695.2(o)). A notice of action against the principal under a bond can also be initiated, including any arbitration proceeding.

A *proof of claim* is any documentation in the claimant's possession submitted to the insurer that provides evidence of the claim and supports the amount of the claimed loss (10 Cal. Code Regs. Section 2695.2(s)).

File and Record Documentation

The Commissioner reserves the right to examine every licensee's claim files, including all notes, documents, and work papers (including copies of all correspondence). The files should be detailed so the Commissioner can reconstruct all events and dates and determine the licensee's actions (10 Cal. Code Regs. Section 2695.3).

Insurance providers must do the following:

- Maintain claim records that are legible, accessible, and retrievable;
- Record the dates the licensee received, processed, and transmitted or mailed relevant documents in the file; and
- Maintain hard copy files. If the files are not hard copies, they have to be in a format that is legible, accessible, and capable of being duplicated into hard copies.

When the licensee cannot construct complete records, they must document the difficulty or inability to obtain data for the Commissioner because of catastrophic losses or other unusual circumstances.

In this case, the licensee needs to submit to the Commissioner a plan for file and record documentation to be utilized while the circumstances that keep the licensee from compiling a complete record persist.

Duties upon Receipt of Communications

Upon receiving any inquiry from the Department of Insurance regarding a claim, the licensee has to respond within *21 calendar days*. The response must address all issues the Department of Insurance raised in its inquiry.

Upon receiving any communication from a claimant (concerning a claim) that reasonably suggests that a response is expected, every licensee has to furnish the claimant with a complete response within *15 days*.

A designation of claimant needs to be in writing, signed and dated by the claimant, and must indicate that the designated individual is authorized to handle the claim. All designations must be given to the insurance provider and will be valid from the date of execution until the designation is revoked or the claim is settled. A designation can be revoked by a written communication given to the insurance provider, signed and dated by the claimant, indicating that the designation is to be revoked and the effective date of the revocation.

Upon receipt, every licensee must immediately communicate a notice of claim to the insurance company. The licensee's duty to convey the information will be met when the licensee complies with proper written instructions from the insurer.

Upon receiving a notice of claim, every insurance provider must do the following (unless the notice of claim is a notice of legal action) within *15 days*:

- Acknowledge receipt of the notice to the claimant unless payment is made within that period. If the acknowledgment is not in writing, a notation of acknowledgment has to be made in the insurance provider's claim file and dated. Failure of an insurance agent to promptly transmit a notice of claim to the insurance provider will be attributed to the insurer;
- Provide to the claimant instructions, reasonable assistance, and necessary forms. This information includes specifying that the claimant must provide proof of claim; and
- Begin any necessary investigation of the claim.

Standards for Prompt, Fair and Equitable Settlements

Insurance providers cannot discriminate in their claims settlement practices based on a claimant's age, gender, race, language, income, religion, sexual orientation, national origin, ancestry, physical disability, or the territory of the property or person insured (10 Cal. Code Regs. Sections 2695.7(a), (b), (c), (g), (h)).

Once the claim is received, insurers have to either accept or deny it within *40 calendar days*. The amounts accepted or denied must be documented unless the claim has been denied in its entirety. The time frame does not apply to claims arising from disability insurance and disability income insurance policies or to automobile repair bills arising from policies of automobile collision and comprehensive insurance.

If an insurance provider rejects a first-party claim, it must do so in writing and state the basis for the rejection. Insurers are protected from disclosing information that could alert a claimant that a claim is being investigated as a suspected fraudulent claim.

Written notification must include a statement confirming a claimant can have a claim reviewed by the California Department of Insurance. A claimant may request a review if they suspect the claim has been rejected or denied wrongfully. The notice will include the address and telephone number of the unit of the Department which reviews claims practices.

Suppose an insurer needs more time to determine if a claim should be accepted or denied. In that case, within the 40-day acceptance period, it must inform the claimant in writing of the need for more time, any additional information the insurer needs, and any continuing reasons for the insurer's inability to decide. Subsequently, the written notice has to be submitted every 30 calendar days until a determination is made or notice of legal action is served.

An insurer cannot try to settle a claim by making an unreasonably low settlement offer. Upon acceptance of the claim, insurers must provide payment within *30 days*.

Chapter Review

This chapter explained the concepts relevant to the insurance marketplace in the state of California. Let's review some of the key points:

PRODUCERS	
Authority and Powers of Producers	• *Law of agency* – agents or producers always represent the insurance provider • *Three agent authority types* – express, implied, and apparent
Transacting Insurance	• Solicitation of insurance • Negotiations before the execution of a contract • The actual execution of a contract • Any later transactions that arise from the operation of the contract
Types of Licenses	• Property and casualty broker-agent • Life-only agent (formerly life agent) • Accident and health or sickness agent (formerly life agent) • Life and accident and health or sickness agent • Personal lines agent • Surplus lines broker

PRODUCERS *(Continued)*	
Agents vs. Brokers	• Agents legally represent the insurer, not their clients • Brokers legally represent their clients, not insurers
Continuing Education Requirements	• Any licensee must complete 24 hours of continuing education, including three hours of ethics, every two years • Agents holding two types of licenses can satisfy the CE requirement by completing it for any license type • Any credits above the required number will be carried over into the next licensing period
INSURERS	
Admitted vs. Non-Admitted	• Insurers must be granted a license or certificate of authority from the Department and meet the state's financial capital and surplus requirement • *Authorized or admitted* – insurers who meet the state's financial requirements and are approved to do business in the state • *Unauthorized or non-admitted* – insurers not approved to do business in California
Domicile	• *Domestic* – the home office is chartered or incorporated in the same state where policies are being sold • *Foreign* – the home office is located in a different state than the one where policies are being sold • *Alien* – the home office is chartered in any country other than the United States; considered an alien insurer in all U.S. states and territories
Ownership	• *Stock* – owned and controlled by stockholders; participating and nonparticipating policies; dividends are a share of profits and are taxable • Mutual – owned and controlled by its policyholders; only participating policies; dividends are a return of premium and are not taxable • Fraternal Benefit Society – operates as a corporation, association, or society; is for the benefit of its members and beneficiaries; is a not for profit lodge system
MARKET REGULATION – GENERAL	
The Commissioner	• In California, the Commissioner of Insurance is an elected official who will serve not more than two consecutive 4-year terms • The Commissioner's responsibility is to issue regulations and cease and desist orders, respond to inquiries, and investigate complaints
Consumer Privacy Regulations	• Gramm-Leach Bliley Act (GLBA) • California Financial Information Privacy Act • Insurance Information and Privacy Protection Act • Cal-GLBA
CLHIGA	• The California Life and Health Insurance Guarantee Association (CLHIGA) pays the claims of insureds or beneficiaries when an insurer is impaired or insolvent
Unfair Trade Practices	• *Unfair trade practices* - false advertising, misrepresentation, rebating, twisting, unfair discrimination, defamation, boycott/coercion/intimidation, and fraud
Fair Claims Settlement	• Insurers cannot discriminate in their claims settlement practices • Upon receiving a claim, insurers must accept or deny it within 40 calendar days • An insurer cannot try to settle a claim by making a low settlement offer

CHAPTER 4:
Life Insurance – Basics

Now that you have learned some basic insurance terminology and understand the insurance marketplace in California, you will now focus on the specific concepts pertinent to life insurance. You will learn about personal and business uses of life insurance, risk management, and the idea of insurable interest. The fundamentals presented in this chapter are essential for your exam and your future career as an insurance professional.

- Uses of Life Insurance
- Process of Issuing a Life Insurance Policy
- Life Settlements

Uses of Life Insurance

In life insurance, an insured pays a premium to an insurer, and in return, the insurer assumes the risk of that person dying prematurely. The premium (a small certain loss) is exchanged for a large uncertain loss. The insurer is insuring many lives, so it is spreading the risk of premature death among a large group of lives.

Life insurance is not typically viewed as property like real estate and other personal property. It has value like other property in the following ways:

- It can be a valuable part of an individual's estate, providing financial security to the insured's survivors and providing immediate cash to pay debts;
- Like land or buildings, the cash value of a life insurance policy can be used as collateral to obtain a loan; and
- Policy owners can pay for life insurance in manageable installments called *premiums*.

Insureds who are the breadwinners of their families will have different income needs at various stages of their lives. The needs that are protected with insurance can be divided into three different income periods. Today, with the wide variety of policies and riders available, it is possible to structure an insurance program to satisfy all of these needs. As an insurance producer, you are responsible for assisting the insured in developing such a program. The three income periods that most insureds are exposed to are the following:

1. **Family Dependency Period** – Should the insured die prematurely, this is the period when the surviving spouse will have to support dependent children. The family's income needs will be the greatest during this period.
2. **Preretirement Period** – This is the period after the children are no longer dependent upon the surviving spouse for support but before the surviving spouse qualifies for Social Security survivor benefits (Blackout Period). The surviving spouse's income needs are reduced during this period; however, until the surviving spouse reaches age 60, Social Security benefits are unavailable.
3. **Retirement Period** – During this period, the employment income of the surviving spouse ends, and their Social Security benefits begin. Since the surviving spouse's standard of living does not lessen, they will need an income comparable to the Preretirement Period during this time.

Personal Finance Planning

The type of information that must be gathered falls under four categories:

1. Debt;
2. Income;
3. Mortgage; and
4. Expenses.

These costs would consider the final medical expenses of the insured, such as funeral expenses and day-to-day expenses of maintaining the family, including mortgage or rent, car payments, groceries, utilities, etc.

Other needs and objectives include insurance premiums, daycare, estate taxes, and similar expenses.

Debt Cancellation – Insurance can be used to create a fund to pay off any debts of the insured, such as a home mortgage or auto loans.

Emergency Reserve Funds – Insurance proceeds can be used to assist in paying for sudden expenses after the insured's death, such as travel expenses and lodging for family members traveling from a distance.

Education Funds – Insurance proceeds can be used to pay for children's education expenses so they can remain in school. Sometimes, a surviving spouse who has worked in the home caring for children will need training or education to re-enter the job market.

Retirement Fund – Insurance proceeds can be used as a source of retirement income.

Bequests – An insured can wish to leave funds to their church, school, or other organization at the time of their death.

Unless funded by insurance, the surviving spouse who was the caregiver of the children may have to train to enter the job market. If they work outside the home, daycare expenses must be considered.

Selling assets, or *liquidation*, is a method of raising capital. Retention is the retaining of assets. If the principal asset is the home, selling the house would mean the survivors pay rent. Using the retention of capital approach, enough insurance is obtained so that when added to other liquid assets, there are enough funds to pay income benefits without invading the principal.

Life Insurance Creates an Immediate Estate

An individual can create an estate through savings, earnings, and investments, which require discipline and time. Purchasing life insurance, however, *creates an immediate estate*. Estate creation is significant for young families who have not yet had time to accumulate assets. When an insured buys a life insurance policy, they will immediately have an estate of at least that amount when the first premium is paid. No other legal method exists by which a person can create an immediate estate at such a small cost.

Life insurance can be used to accumulate specific amounts of money for particular needs, guaranteeing that the funds will be available when needed. For instance, some life insurance policies, such as whole life, provide permanent protection and accumulate a cash value available to the policyholder during the policy term.

The cash accumulation feature allows some life insurance policies to provide *liquidity* to the policyholder. That means the policy's cash value can be borrowed anytime and used for immediate needs.

The proceeds from life insurance can be used to pay federal estate and inheritance taxes so that beneficiaries do not need to sell off their assets.

Determining the Amount of Life Insurance

Human Life Value Approach – The human life value approach provides the insured with an estimate of what the family would lose in the event of the insured's premature death. It calculates an individual's life value by looking at the insured's wages, the number of years to retirement, inflation, and the time value of money.

Example 4.1 – Let's assume that a 40-year-old insured earns $50,000 yearly and expects to earn the same amount until she retires at age 65. Out of her annual income, $40,000 is spent on family needs, and the remaining $10,000 goes to the insured's own expenses. The human life value of this insured to her family is $1,000,000 ($40,000 a year spent on family needs x 25 years to retirement). Based on this assumption, and taking interest and inflation into consideration, the insurer will determine the right amount of insurance to produce the same annual income for the family should the insured die.

Needs Approach – The needs approach is based on the predicted needs of a family after the insured's premature death. Some factors considered in the needs approach are income, the amount of debt (including a mortgage), investments, and other ongoing expenses.

Business Uses of Life Insurance

For the same reason individuals use life insurance, businesses use life insurance to create an immediate payment upon the insured's death.

Businesses commonly use life insurance as an employee benefit, protecting employees and their beneficiaries. Other forms of life insurance can even cover the company itself and serve business owners and their survivors. These include compensating executives, funding business continuation agreements, and protecting the business against financial loss caused by the disability or death of key employees.

Key Person – Businesses can suffer a devastating financial loss due to the premature death of a key employee, who is someone with skills, business contacts, or specialized knowledge. A business can reduce the risk of such a loss using *key person insurance*. Under this coverage, the insured is the key employee, and the employer is the:

- Applicant;
- Policy owner;
- Premium payer; and
- Beneficiary.

If a key employee dies, the business will use the money for the additional costs of operating the company and replacing the employee. The business cannot take a tax deduction for the premium expense. However, in the event of a key employee's death, the benefits paid to the business are typically received as tax-free income. The employee does not require any special contracts or agreements. They only need to provide their permission for this coverage.

Buy-Sell Insurance – A *buy-sell* agreement is a legal contract determining what will be done with a business if an owner becomes disabled or dies. This contract is also known as a business continuation agreement.

There are several types of buy-sell agreements that are used by partnerships and corporations:

- **Cross Purchase** – used in partnerships when each partner purchases a policy on the other;
- **Entity Purchase** – used when the partnership purchases the policies on the partners;
- **Stock Purchase** – used by privately owned corporations when each stockholder purchases a policy on each of the other stockholder's lives;
- **Stock Redemption** – used when the corporation buys one policy on every shareholder.

Example 4.2 – In this example of a cross-purchase buy-sell agreement, Partnership AB has two partners, A and B. The value of the business is $1,000,000. Each partner has an equal interest ($500,000 each). Partner A purchases a life policy on Partner B for $500,000, and Partner B purchases a life policy on Partner A for $500,000. If Partner A dies, Partner B gets 100% business ownership, and Partner A's heirs receive $500,000.

Business Overhead Expense – The *business overhead expense (BOE)* policy is insurance sold to small business owners to meet overhead expenses. Such expenses can include employee salaries, rent, utilities, leased equipment, installment purchases, etc., following a disability. Business overhead expense policies reimburse the business owner for the incurred overhead expenses while the business owner is disabled. This policy does not reimburse the business owner for their compensation, salary, or other forms of income lost due to a disability. There is generally an elimination period of 15 to 30 days, and benefit payments typically last for one or two years.

The benefits are usually limited to the maximum monthly amount stated in the policy or the covered expenses incurred. The premiums paid for BOE insurance are tax-deductible to the business as a business expense; however, the benefits received by the company are taxable.

Executive Bonuses – An *executive bonus* is an arrangement where the employer offers to give the employee a wage increase in the premium amount on a new life insurance policy taken out on the employee. The employee owns the policy and has all the control. Since the employer treated the premium payment as a bonus, that premium amount is *tax-deductible to the employer* and *income taxable to the employee*. The employer would not offer the benefit if the employee were unwilling to accept these conditions.

Business Continuation – A *business continuation* plan is an arrangement between business owners that allows for shares owned by any of them who becomes disabled or dies to be sold to and purchased by the other co-owners or the business.

Limit of Liability – The *limit of liability* is the face value or death benefit of an individual life insurance policy, subject to any applicable exclusions or riders, minus any outstanding policy loans and interest payments due to the insurance provider.

Process of Issuing a Life Insurance Policy

Solicitation and Sales Presentations

The process of issuing a life insurance policy starts with solicitation. Soliciting insurance means persuading an individual to purchase an insurance policy, which can be done orally or in writing. This process also includes offering information about available products, explaining the policy benefits, making recommendations about a specific type of policy, and trying to secure a contract between the applicant and the insurer.

Any sales presentations that insurance companies or agents use in communication with the public must be complete and accurate.

Each applicant for life insurance must be given a written disclosure statement that provides basic information about the coverage and cost of the insurance policy being solicited. This disclosure statement has to be given to the applicant no later than the time the insurance application is signed. Disclosure statements will help applicants to make more informed and educated decisions about their choice of insurance.

Illustrations – The term illustration refers to a depiction or presentation that includes a policy's nonguaranteed elements of individual or group life insurance during a future period. A life insurance illustration needs to do the following:

- Distinguish between projected and guaranteed amounts;
- Specify that an illustration is not a part of the contract; and
- Identify any values that are not guaranteed.

An agent can only use the illustrations of the insurance provider that have been approved and cannot change them in any way.

An illustration used during the sale of a life insurance policy is required to contain the following basic information:

- Name of the insurance company;
- Name and business address of the producer or the insurance provider's authorized representative, if any;
- Name, age, and sex of the proposed insured, except when a composite illustration is allowed under this regulation;
- Rating classification or underwriting used to create the illustration;
- Generic name of the policy, the product name (if different), and form number;
- Initial death benefit;
- Dividend option or application of non-guaranteed elements (if applicable)
- Illustration date; and
- A prominent label stating "Life Insurance Illustration."

When using an illustration during the sale of a life insurance policy, an insurer or its agents may not:

- Depict the policy as anything other than a life insurance policy;
- Describe non-guaranteed elements in a way that could be misleading;
- Use an illustration that portrays a policy's performance as being more favorable than it is;
- Provide an incomplete illustration;
- Claim that premium payments will not be required for each year of the policy unless that is the fact;
- Use the term "vanish" or "vanishing premium," or a similar term that suggests the policy becomes paid-up; or
- Use illustrations that are not self-supporting.

Suppose an illustration shows an interest rate used to determine the illustrated non-guaranteed elements. In that situation, it cannot be greater than the earned interest rate underlying the disciplined current scale.

Buyer's Guide – A *buyer's guide* provides prospective applicants with basic, general information about life insurance policies limited to language approved by the Department of Insurance. This document explains how a buyer should select the type and amount of insurance to purchase and how a buyer can save money by comparing the costs of similar policies. Before accepting the initial premium, insurance companies must provide a buyer's guide to all potential applicants. The policy includes a free-look period (unconditional refund provision) of at least ten days. In that instance, producers can deliver a buyer's guide with the policy.

Policy Summary – A *policy summary* is a written statement describing the elements and features of the issued policy. It includes the agent's name and address, the insurer's full name and administrative office or home office address, and the generic name of the basic policy and each rider. A policy summary will include a cash value, premiums, dividends, surrender value, and death benefit figures for specific policy years. When the policy is delivered, agents must also provide the policy summary.

Cost Indexes – The insurance industry developed specific methods and indexes that measure and compare the actual policy costs. This comparison helps consumers make informed decisions about buying life insurance and is typically included in policy illustrations.

The *Traditional Net Cost Index* compares the cash values available to buyers if they surrender the policy in 10 or 20 years. This index does not consider the time value of money or investment return on the insurance premium had it been invested elsewhere.

The *Interest-Adjusted Net Cost Index* compares the death benefits paid at death in 10 or 20 years if the insured died at that time. It considers the time value of money.

By regulation, the Commissioner can adopt a term life insurance monetary value index (similar to the Life Insurance Surrender Cost Index) to be disclosed in all advertisements and policies of term life insurance for individuals 55 or older. In developing a term life insurance monetary value index, the Commissioner must consider actual policy benefits and premiums and how they are affected over time. Any term life insurance monetary value index assumes that the insured would want to retain coverage for at least ten years.

Underwriting

Underwriting is the process of risk selection. The underwriter's duties include selecting only those risks that are considered insurable and meet the insurance provider's underwriting standards. The purpose of underwriting is to protect the insurance company against *adverse selection* (risks that are more likely to sustain a loss).

The main criteria an underwriter will use in evaluating the desirability of a particular candidate for life insurance includes the applicant's health (current and past), lifestyle, occupation, and hobbies or habits. The underwriter will use many different information sources to assess the insurability of the individual risk. The specific underwriting requirements will also vary by insurer.

Field Underwriting – The agent serves as the front line for an insurance provider and is referred to as a field underwriter because the agent is typically the one who has solicited the proposed insured. As a field underwriter, the agent has several essential responsibilities to fulfill during the process of underwriting and beyond, including:

- Preventing adverse selection;
- Properly soliciting prospective applicants;
- Completing the application;
- Obtaining required signatures;
- Collecting the initial premium and, if applicable, issuing the receipt; and
- Delivering the policy and collecting any premium that might be due.

Application – The *application* is the building block and primary source of information used by the insurance company during the risk selection process. Although applications are not uniform and can vary from one insurance provider to another, they all contain the same essential elements.

Part 1 – General Information of the application includes the general questions about the applicant, such as name, age, gender, birth date, address, marital status, occupation, and income. It will also inquire about existing policies and whether the proposed insurance will replace them. Part 1 identifies the policy type and the coverage amount and typically contains information regarding the beneficiary.

Part 2 – Medical Information of the application includes information regarding the proposed insured's medical history, present health condition, any medical visits in recent years, the medical status of living relatives, and the causes of death of deceased relatives. If the insurance amount is relatively small, the agent and the prospective insured will complete all the medical information making it a nonmedical application. The insurance provider generally requires a medical exam for more significant insurance amounts.

The agent's (or producer's) responsibility is to ensure that the application is completed correctly, completely, and to the best of the applicant's knowledge. The agent must probe beyond the stated questions in the application if they have a reason to believe the applicant is concealing or misrepresenting information. Agents must also be able to help applicants who do not understand specific questions. Any inaccurate, misleading, or illegible information might delay the issuance of the policy. If the producer suspects there could be some misrepresentation, they must notify the insurer. Some insurance companies require that the applicant complete the application within the agent's presence. In contrast, other insurers require that the agent fills out the application to help avoid unanswered questions and mistakes.

Attachment of Application to Policy – When an application is taken at the time of purchase, and a policy is issued, the application must be attached to the policy. The policy and the application constitute the entire contract between the parties, and no additional documents can be incorporated into the agreement unless endorsed and attached to the policy. Any statements made by the insured in the application are considered representations and not warranties.

Agent's Report – As a field underwriter, the agent is considered the most critical information source available to the insurance provider's underwriters. The agent's report provides an insurer with personal observations regarding the proposed insured. It is not included in the entire contract, although it is a crucial part of the application process.

Required Signatures – Both the producer and the prospective insured, which is typically the applicant, must sign the application. The proposed insured and the policy owner does not have to be the same person. It can also be a business purchasing insurance for an employee. In that case, the policy owner must also sign the application. An exception to the prospective insured signing the application would be in the circumstance of an adult, as a parent or guardian, applying for an insurance policy on a minor child.

Changes on the Application – Depending on the insurer, when a correction to the application is required, agents can update the information and have the applicant initial the change or complete an entirely new application. An agent should never erase or use white-out to delete any information on an insurance application.

Consequences of Incomplete Applications – Before a policy can be issued, the applicant must answer each question on the application. If the insurance provider receives an incomplete application, they must return it to the applicant for completion. When an insurer issues a policy with unanswered questions, the contract is issued as if the insurance provider surrendered or waived its right to have an answer to the question. In other words, the insurance provider cannot deny coverage based on any information that the unanswered question might have included.

Premiums with the Application – Most insurance agents will try to collect the initial premium and submit it along with the application to the insurance provider. In addition, receiving the initial premium payment at the time of the application increases the likelihood that the applicant will accept the policy once it is issued. Whenever the agent collects a premium, the agent is required to issue a premium receipt. The type of receipt issued to the insured will determine when coverage becomes effective.

Conditional vs. Binding Receipt – The most common type of receipt is a *conditional receipt*. Agents provide this receipt when the applicant turns in a prepaid application. The conditional receipt stipulates that coverage becomes effective on the application date or the date of the medical examination, whichever occurs last, provided that the applicant is insurable as a standard risk. The insurer issues the policy to the applicant per the application. This rule will not apply if the applicant declines a policy or if the policy is rated or issued with riders excluding specific coverages.

Example 4.3 – An agent or producer collects the initial premium from an applicant and provides the applicant with a conditional receipt. When the applicant dies the following day, the underwriting process will continue as though the applicant were still alive. If the insurance provider approves the coverage, the applicant's beneficiary will receive the policy's death benefit. On the other hand, if the insurance provider concludes that the applicant was not an acceptable risk and declines the coverage, the premium is refunded to the beneficiary. The insurance provider does not have to pay the death benefit.

The *approval conditional receipt* coverage begins when the insurance provider approves the pre-paid application before the policy is delivered. In other words, there is no coverage during the initial underwriting process. This type of receipt is rarely used.

The *unconditional (binding) receipt* is seldom used in life insurance. Binders are more commonly found in property insurance. Coverage begins immediately for a specific period when the agent issues a binding receipt, even if the applicant is later deemed uninsurable. Binding receipts typically specify that coverage is effective from the date of the application for only a certain period, like 60 days, or until the insurer either issues or declines coverage, whichever happens first.

It is important to note that written binders are considered valid insurance policies to prove that the insured has coverage. This consideration does not apply to life insurance because binders are prohibited in life and disability policies.

Temporary Insurance Agreement – The underwriting process can often require considerable time. To bridge the gap between the applicant's request for immediate coverage and the insurance provider's need for thorough underwriting, insurance companies offer their customers a *temporary (or interim) insuring agreement*. This agreement requires payment of the first premium when submitting the application. However, it does not guarantee that a policy will be issued.

There are three types of temporary insuring agreements:

- Conditional Receipt (most commonly used);
- 30-day Interim Term Receipt; and
- Acceptance Form of Receipt.

The *temporary term* is the period of protection offered by binding receipts. An insurer is liable for the maximum amount guaranteed under the binding receipt/temporary insurance agreement during this period.

Nonmedical Application and Required Medical Examinations – A *nonmedical application* is the medical portion of an application that accepts a completed health questionnaire signed by the applicant and the agent and does not require a medical examination.

Limitations on Pre-Selection and Post-Selection Activities

Pre-selection – The broker or agent can achieve a good pre-selection by accurate, complete, and thorough completion of the insurance application. The application will ask for all the legally allowed information that an insurance provider can collect to perform effective post-selection underwriting.

During the application process, the producer is in a position to terminate at any time if they find that the client poses an untenable risk to the insurer. Producers must also explain to the client why their risk might be higher than usual. Notifying clients of a possible premium rating can help them overcome "sticker shock" later.

For example, suppose an applicant is morbidly obese. In that case, they could still submit the application to the insurance provider. Still, the producer should warn the applicant that since their height/weight ratio is out of the standard range, they can expect to pay a significantly higher premium rate. The same applies to extreme sports enthusiasts, smokers, skin divers, and individuals of similar risk.

The producer is not allowed to gather information not asked for on the application but can seek details for those items that do appear. This information can include the extent of involvement in hazardous activities, dosages and frequency of use of medications, specifics regarding employment duties, etc.

It is also necessary to emphasize the producer's responsibility to not withhold from the principal any information that could be harmful regarding the client's risk.

Post-selection – Once the agent has chosen to complete and submit an insurance application, the in-house underwriters begin the post-selection process.

Using the application as a foundation, the underwriter starts an investigation of the client's complete risk profile. Federal and state law delineates the types and extent of information that can be obtained and considered, which we will see below. After considering the legally available information, the underwriter will classify the client as *standard*, *substandard*, or *uninsurable*.

If the client is sub-standard, they will be offered the opportunity to obtain coverage under a higher-than-standard premium. The client can decline to be insured under the stated conditions.

After the producer receives a signed authorization for disclosure of information, the underwriter can begin an investigation using the following sources of information:

- **MIB** – The Medical Information Bureau (MIB) is a centralized information database into which insurance companies provide information from applications and claims. Subscribing insurance providers can then search the MIB database for information regarding an applicant for insurance.
- **Department of Motor Vehicles** – Statistically, half of all accidental deaths in the United States occur due to traffic collisions. Therefore, insurance providers are very interested in the driving records of their applicants. A poor driving record can cause a rating or even a declination.
- **Physician/medical facility records** – The APS (attending physician statement) enables the insurance provider to receive the complete medical treatment history of the client.
- **Additional medical testing/Current physical** – The insurance provider can request that the applicant be examined by a physician and the results submitted for consideration. It is also common to require examination by a paramedical company and the use of urine, blood, or saliva samples to check for nicotine or other drug use and the presence of HIV. An insurer could also require an EKG (electrocardiogram).
- **Financial reports** – Using financial inspection reports and information from major credit reporting agencies, the insurance company can detect whether the client has a history of financial wrongdoing.
- **Personal interviews** – The underwriter can contact individuals with information about the applicant by telephone. These individuals can include relatives, neighbors, coworkers, or other acquaintances.
- **Hazardous activity questionnaire** – The insurer can also ask the applicant to fill out a separate hazardous activity questionnaire to determine the risk classification of the applicant. The questionnaire can include questions regarding scuba diving, hobby aviation, and auto, boat, or motorcycle racing.

Company Underwriting Information Sources and Regulations – The insurance provider must obtain the applicant's medical history and background information to correctly select and classify an insurance risk. Several sources of underwriting information are available to those who underwrite insurance policies.

Application – The individual applying for insurance must ask the insurance provider for approval before issuing a policy. The *application* is one of the insurer's primary sources of underwriting information.

Agent's Report – The *agent's report* lets the agent correspond with the underwriter and provide them with information regarding the applicant that might assist in the underwriting process.

Investigative Consumer Report (Inspection) – To supplement the information on the application, the underwriter may order an *inspection report* on the applicant from a credit agency or independent investigating firm, which covers moral and financial information. These are generic reports of the applicant's character, finances, employment, habits, and hobbies. Insurance companies that use inspection reports are subject to the rules and regulations included in the Fair Credit Reporting Act.

The *Fair Credit Reporting Act (FCRA)* created procedures that consumer-reporting agencies must follow. The FCRA ensures that records are accurate, confidential, relevant, and properly used. This law also protects consumers against obsolete or inaccurate financial or personal information.

Insurance providers determine risk acceptability by checking the individual risk against several factors directly related to the risk's potential for loss. Along with these factors, an underwriter will sometimes ask for additional information about a particular risk from an outside source. These reports usually fall into two categories: Consumer Reports and Investigative Consumer Reports. Someone with a legitimate business purpose can use both reports, including employment screening, underwriting, and credit transactions.

Consumer Reports include written and oral information about a consumer's character, credit, habits, or reputation collected by a reporting agency from credit reports, employment records, and other public sources.

Investigative Consumer Reports are comparable to Consumer Reports. They also provide information on the consumer's reputation, character, and habits. The main *difference* is that insurers obtain the data through an investigation and interviews with the consumer's friends, neighbors, and associates. In contrast to Consumer Reports, insurers cannot get an Investigative Report unless the consumer receives written notification about the report within three days of the date the consumer requested the report. Consumers must receive confirmation that they have a right to ask for additional information regarding the report. The reporting agency or insurance provider has five days to provide the consumer with the additional information.

The reporting agency and information users are subject to a civil action for failure to comply with the FCRA's provisions. Any individual who intentionally and deliberately obtains information on a consumer under pretenses from a consumer reporting agency may be fined or imprisoned for up to two years.

Any person who *unwittingly* violates the FCRA is liable in the amount equal to the loss to the consumer and any reasonable attorney fees incurred during the process.

Any individual who *knowingly* violates the FCRA enough to constitute an overall pattern or business practice will be subject to a penalty of up to $2,500.

Under the FCRA, if an insurance policy is modified or declined because of information in either an investigative or consumer report, the consumer must be notified and provided with the reporting agency's name and address. It is the consumer's right to know what information is in the report. Consumers have a right to know the identity of anyone who has obtained a report during the past year. When the consumer challenges any information in the report, the reporting agency must reinvestigate and amend the report if warranted. Also, when a consumer report is inaccurate and corrected, the agency must send the updated information to all parties who reported the erroneous information within the last two years.

Consumer reports cannot contain specific types of information if the bank or insurer requests a report in connection with a credit transaction of less than $150,000 or a life insurance policy. The *prohibited information* includes arrest records or convictions of crimes and bankruptcies more than ten years old. It also includes civil suits or other negative information over seven years old. The FCRA defines a negative report as providing information about a customer's delinquencies, late payments, insolvency, or defaults.

Medical Information and Consumer Reports – For policies with higher coverage amounts or if the application raised additional questions about the prospective insured's health, the underwriter might require the insured to undergo a medical examination. Depending on the reason for the medical examination, there are two options:

1. The insurance provider may only request a *paramedical report* that a registered nurse or a paramedic completes; and
2. The underwriter may require a medical practitioner who treated the applicant for a prior medical problem to provide an *Attending Physician's Statement (APS)*.

Medical Information Bureau (MIB) – The underwriter will typically request a *Medical Information Bureau (MIB)* report in addition to an attending physician's report. The MIB is a membership corporation owned by member insurers. It is a *nonprofit trade organization* that receives adverse medical information from insurers and maintains private medical impairment information on individuals. It is a systematic method for insurance companies to compare the information collected on a prospective insured with information already discovered by other insurance companies. The MIB can only help insurers know what areas of impairment they might need to investigate further. Insurance providers cannot refuse an applicant merely because of adverse information discovered through the MIB.

Medical Examinations and Lab Tests Including HIV – The insurance company may require paramedics or physicians to conduct medical examinations at the insurer's expense. Usually, such exams are not necessary for health insurance, subsequently emphasizing the importance of the agent or producer when recording medical information on the application. The medical exam requirement is relatively common in life insurance underwriting. If an insurance company requests a medical exam, the insurer is responsible for the exam costs.

It is common among insurance providers to require an HIV test when an applicant applies for a large amount of coverage or any increased and additional benefits. Insurers seek to protect the insured's privacy and ensure they correctly obtain and handle test results. States have also enacted the following laws and regulations for insurance providers requiring an applicant to submit to an HIV test:

- The insurance provider must disclose the use of testing to the applicant and obtain written consent from the applicant on the approved form.
- To ensure confidentiality, the insurance provider must establish written policies and procedures for the internal distribution of test results among its employees and producers.
- Test results cannot be provided to the MIB if the patient is identified.

The following are guidelines to help insurance providers avoid unfair underwriting for the risk of HIV/AIDS:

- If the tests were performed correctly, insurers could decline a potential insured if their medical sample returns "positive for HIV/AIDS" after two different tests. Insurers can also decline the applicant if they have already been diagnosed with AIDS/HIV by another medical professional.
- These tests must be paid for by the insurance company, not the insured.
- If an insurance provider tests for HIV, it must first obtain informed, written consent from the insured. This consent often involves a separate disclosure form signed by all insureds and agents. Producers should then give a copy of this duplicate form to the client. The information includes written details about the tests performed, their purposes and uses, and how the insurer will provide results to the insured. The form often asks for the name and address of a physician so that the client's doctor can get involved should a positive result come back. If the client has no physician, the insurance provider should urge the client to consult a physician or government health agency.
- Informed consent also includes supplying the client with information regarding AIDS/HIV counseling from third-party sources.

- The information that is gathered must be handled correctly and in compliance with confidentiality requirements by authorized personnel.
- If an insured correctly obtains coverage but later dies because of AIDS or AIDS-related conditions, coverage cannot be denied or limited.

From an ethical and nondiscrimination standpoint, no insurance provider or its agents can consider the individual's gender, occupation, marital status, sexual orientation, living arrangements, zip code, or other such related demographic characteristics in determining whether to take an application, provide coverage, or perform any medical testing. An insurance provider could not ask if the insured had been tested before unless it was for insurance purposes. None of this information should be either on the application or implied. This stipulation allows the underwriter to make an unbiased determination and avoid overt or apparent discrimination. The only acceptable standard that an insurance company can use to determine whether to test for HIV is the amount of insurance the applicant has applied for at specific age ranges.

Negligently disclosing confidential results or underwriting information to unauthorized third parties could result in a civil fine of up to $1,000 plus court costs. The fine can go up to $5,000 plus costs for willful violations. Suppose the violation causes bodily, psychological, or economic harm to the other party. In that circumstance, the penalty can include a *misdemeanor* charge, one year in jail, or a fine of up to $10,000.

Genetic characteristics refer to any scientifically or medically identifiable gene or chromosome that is known to be a cause of a disorder or disease. Such a gene or chromosome is associated with a statistically increased risk of developing a disorder or disease. Examples of genetic conditions include sickle cell, Tay-Sachs, and X-linked hemophilia.

Insurance providers cannot require a test of the presence of a genetic characteristic to determine insurability except in policies that are contingent upon testing for other medical conditions or diseases. The insurance provider must obtain the applicant's written consent to conduct a genetic characteristics test. The insurer must also notify the applicant of a test result directly or through a designated physician.

HIPAA – The *Health Insurance Portability and Accountability Act (HIPAA)* is a federal law that protects private health information. HIPAA regulations protect the privacy of certain personally identifiable health information. Payment information that can identify the person or demographic data related to a physical or mental health condition is *protected health information*. Under the Privacy Rule, patients have the right to view their medical records and the right to know who has accessed their records over the previous six years. The Privacy Rule, however, permits disclosures without individual authorization to public health authorities authorized by law to receive or collect the information to control or prevent injury, disease, or disability.

Use and Disclosure of Insurance Information – Insurance providers must first give the applicant or insured a written Disclosure Authorization Notice when they pursue and use information obtained from investigators. It will state the insurance provider's practice concerning collecting and using personal data. The disclosure authorization form needs to be in plain language; the head of the Department of Insurance must approve it.

Risk Classification – When classifying a risk, the insurance carrier's underwriting department will look at the applicant's current physical condition, prior medical history, occupation, habits, and morals. If the applicant is deemed acceptable, the underwriter must then determine the risk or *rating classification* to decide whether or not the applicant will pay a higher or lower premium. A potential insured may be rated as one of the three *standard*, *substandard*, or *preferred* classifications.

Standard – *Standard risks* are individuals who, according to an insurance company's underwriting standards, are entitled to insurance coverage without an extra rating or special restrictions. Standard risks are representative of the majority of people with similar lifestyles at their age. They are the average risk.

Preferred – *Preferred risks* are individuals who meet specific requirements that qualify them for lower premiums, unlike those who are a standard risk. These applicants are in peak physical condition and maintain healthy lifestyles and habits.

Substandard – *Substandard risks* or *high exposure* applicants are not acceptable at standard rates because of their occupation, current physical condition, personal or family history of illness, disease, or dangerous habits. These policies are "rated" because they could be issued with the *premium rated-up*, resulting in a higher premium payment.

Applicants who are not issued policies are considered *declined risks*, which are risks that the underwriting departments assess as uninsurable. Insurers can decline a risk for one of the following reasons:

- No insurable interest exists;
- The applicant is deemed medically unacceptable;
- It does not meet the definition of insurance because the potential for loss is so great; or
- Insurance is illegal or prohibited by public policy.

Premium Determination

Once the insurer concludes that an applicant is insurable, they must establish an appropriate policy premium. Insurers will use the premium to cover the expenses and costs to keep the policy in force. *Premiums are paid in advance.*

Three main factors are used in determining premiums: mortality (rate of death within a specific group), interest, and expense.

Mortality – *Mortality* is the ratio of the number of deaths in a certain population over a specific period versus the number of people living in that population. *Mortality tables* used by insurance providers indicate the number of individuals within a specified group who are expected to be alive at a subsequent age. Such individuals include males, females, smokers, and nonsmokers beginning at a certain age. In other words, these tables help the insurance providers predict the life expectancy and the probability of death for a given group.

Interest – Since premiums are paid before claims are incurred, insurers invest the premiums to earn *interest* on these funds (invested in stocks, bonds, mortgages, etc.). This interest is a significant factor in lowering premiums.

Expense – The *expense* factor, also referred to as the loading charge, also affects premium rates. Insurance providers have various operating expenses, so each premium has to carry a proportionate share of these operating costs. The insurance company's most significant expense is the commissions paid to its agents. Other ongoing expenses include rent, payroll, and taxes.

Premium Payment Mode – Regarding insurance premiums, mode refers to the policy owner's *frequency* of premium payments. An insurance policy's rates are based on the assumption that policy owners will pay the premium annually at the beginning of the policy year. Rates are also based on the assumption that the insurer will have the premium to invest an entire year before paying out on any claims. When the policy owner decides to pay the premium more frequently than annually, there will be an additional charge because the insurer will have additional expenses in billing the premium. However, the premium can be paid annually, semi-annually, quarterly, or monthly.

Suppose the insured dies during a period for which the premium has been paid. In that case, the insurance provider has to *refund any unearned premium*, and the policy proceeds.

Single premium – The policy owner makes one lump-sum payment to the insurance provider to create a policy. A single premium whole life policy generates immediate cash value because of the lump sum payment made to the insurer. Most insurance providers require a minimum premium of $5,000 or more for a single premium policy.

Limited pay – The policy is designed to have a level annual premium, so the policy owner will completely pay up coverage before age 100. Some of the more common types of limited-pay life include 20-pay life, where coverage is entirely paid for in 20 years, and life paid-up at 65 (LP-65), where the coverage is entirely paid for by the insured's age of 65. All other factors being equal, a higher annual premium is required when the premium-paying period is condensed to a shorter duration.

Modified pay – A lower premium is charged in the first few years of the policy, generally the first three to five years. Then, a higher-level premium is paid over the remainder of the insured's life. These policies were developed to make the purchase of whole life insurance more attractive for individuals just starting out and with limited financial resources.

Level – Most life insurance policies have a level premium, meaning the premium remains the same throughout the contract's duration.

Fixed vs. flexible – The same amount is paid periodically with a fixed premium. The policy owner can pay more or less than the planned premium rate with a flexible premium.

Guaranteed at Initial Level vs. Initial and Maximum Premiums – Premiums can either remain the same for the entire policy period, or increase and decrease at different times, depending on the policy type.

Term policies and most permanent policies have premiums *guaranteed at initial levels* (or level premiums for the policy's life). The insurance provider "overcharges" the insured in the policy's early years and applies that excess in the future to fund the increased mortality costs. Insurance providers use premium tables to calculate the cost of insurance based on the insured's age and other underwriting factors. These tables can also be used to compare the *initial premiums* and *maximum premiums* charged by two types of policies for a specific class of insureds.

Policy Issue and Delivery

Once underwriting has been completed and the policy is issued, the agent will deliver it to the policy owner. Although personal delivery of the policy is the best way to finalize the insurance transaction, mailing the policy directly to the policy owner is also acceptable. The policy is considered legally delivered when the insurance provider relinquishes control of the policy by sending it to the policy owner. However, it is advisable to obtain a signed *delivery receipt*.

Methods for Policy Delivery and Delivery Receipt – Life and disability insurance policies must be signed and dated to avoid conflict and remain valid. This requirement is fundamental to all contract law.

The California Insurance Code requires that all life and disability contracts be signed and dated by the policy owner on the day the owner or client receives the policy. Nothing added to the policy after this date will be considered part of the *entire contract* by any ruling judge unless agreed upon by both parties to the contract. These additions have to be signed by each party and attached to the original contract. Any statements made and incorporated into the policy are considered representations.

The following are acceptable methods of delivery:

- Personal delivery with a signed and dated written receipt of delivery;
- Registered or Certified Mail (requires a signature);
- First Class Mail with a signed and dated written receipt of delivery; or
- Any other reasonable means of delivery as determined by the Commissioner.

It is worth noting that without written and signed proof of delivery, the burden of proof of delivery falls on the insurance provider and its agent in any legal dispute. Without a signature and date, it is difficult to establish when the free-look period or right of rescission started. If a loss should occur during this time, it must be clear whether a claim should be paid and whether the policy owner accepted or rejected the policy. It is also a sound practice to get a signed and dated receipt/note when a client rejects a policy if they die shortly after that. Agents may require this documentation should the family expect an inaccurate death benefit.

The following are *advantages of personal delivery*:

- It is another chance to explain to the policy owner (insured) what they have purchased and why;
- It reinforces the personal relationship with the agent and the insurance provider that agent represents. The policyholder is more likely to give referrals to agents they trust and with whom they have a personal relationship;
- It gives the agent the chance to assess future needs for additional insurance or provide other needed products; and
- When the paperwork or information gathered during underwriting was incomplete or contradictory, the insurer could require the agent to revisit the client when delivering a policy. The agent may have to collect a signed confirmation that a condition does or does not exist to cover the client adequately.

Explaining the Policy – Personal delivery of the policy gives the agent a chance to ensure that the insured understands all aspects of the contract. Reviewing the contract with the client involves pointing out riders or provisions that may be different than anticipated and explaining their effect on the contract. Additionally, the agent should explain the rating procedure to the insured, especially if the policy is rated differently than when the client initially applied for it. The agent should also explain any other provisions and choices that may become active to the policy owner.

Information on Policy Title Page – The *policy title (specification) page* is the first page of a life insurance policy. This page includes a summary of the benefits and coverages the policy will provide. In addition, the following information is included on the title page:

- The type of policy, the amount of coverage, and the premium amount and mode to be paid;
- The insured's name, their gender and age, and the name of the policy owner;
- The date the policy becomes effective and the date of termination;
- The premium payment period;
- If the policy is a term policy, the "renewability" of the policy; and
- Any optional riders or provisions attached to the policy and the amount of premium to be paid for each.

Effective Date of Coverage – If the initial premium is not submitted with the application, the agent must collect the premium at the time of policy delivery. In this situation, the policy does not become effective until the premium is collected. The agent may also be required to obtain a *statement of good health* from the insured. This individual must sign the statement and verify that the insured has not sustained an injury or illness since the application date.

If the agent collected the entire premium with the application and the policy was issued as requested, the policy's coverage usually coincides with the application date if no medical exam is required. If a medical exam is required, the coverage date coincides with the exam's date.

No "Standard" Life Policy – Unlike property and casualty policies that use standard policy forms, there are no *"standard"* life insurance policies.

Life Settlements

The term *life settlement* pertains to any financial transaction where a life insurance policy owner sells their policy to a third party for compensation, usually cash. A life settlement requires an absolute (permanent) assignment of all rights to the policy from the original policy owner to the new policy owner.

Policy owners can sell their policies because the premium costs have grown too high to continue the policy. They can also sell their policies if coverage is no longer needed. However, in many situations, life settlement transactions are offered to senior citizens who may have a life-threatening illness and a short life expectancy. In these cases, the policy owner can sell the policy to a life settlement provider for an amount more significant than what they would receive if they surrendered the policy for a cash value.

Example 4.4 – An insured, age 70, owns a $1,000,000 life insurance policy. He recently sold his small business for $5,000,000 and decided he no longer needed the life insurance coverage. The cash value is $390,000, which the insurance provider would give the policy owner if he cashed in the policy. After reviewing his medical records, a life settlement provider may offer him $575,000 for the policy. Once the policy owner transfers ownership and has received the funds, the life settlement company will assume the premium payments until the insured dies. At that time, the life settlement company will receive the $1,000,000 policy proceeds.

Disclosures

The following information needs to be included in the disclosure to help the policy owner understand the benefits and consequences of a life settlement transaction, at a minimum:

- An explanation of possible alternatives, including accelerated benefits offered by the insurance provider;
- That some or all of the proceeds of a life settlement contract can be taxable;
- The proceeds of a life settlement contract can be subject to the claims of creditors;
- Receipt of the proceeds can adversely affect the recipient's eligibility for public assistance;
- That the proceeds will be given to the policy owner within three business days after the life settlement provider has received acknowledgment that ownership of the policy has been transferred and the beneficiary has been designated according to the life settlement contract's terms;
- That entering into a life settlement contract can cause other benefits under the policy, such as waiver of premium or conversion, to be forfeited by the policy owner;
- The total amount paid by the life settlement provider and the net amount to be paid to the policy owner;
- The date by which the funds will be available to the policy owner;
- That the life settlement provider is required to provide to the owner a consumer information booklet;
- That the insured can be contacted by either the life settlement provider or the broker to determine the insured's health status or to verify the address (the life settlement provider or broker must also disclose that the contact will be limited to once every three months if the insured's life expectancy is greater than one year, and no more than once a month if the insured is anticipated to live one year or less); and
- The name, business address, email address, and phone number of the life settlement provider.

A life settlement licensee or provider must disclose that the policy owner can rescind a life settlement contract within *30 days* after all parties execute the agreement and the policy owner receives all disclosures. Policy owners also have a right to rescind a life settlement contract within *15 days* of receiving the life settlement proceeds from the policy owner, whichever is sooner. Rescission is effective only if a notice of rescission is given and the policy owner repays all proceeds and any premiums, loans, and loan interest within the rescission period. Suppose the insured dies during the rescission period. In that scenario, the contract will be considered rescinded subject to repayment by the policy owner or their estate of all proceeds and any premiums, loans, and loan interest to the provider.

Fraudulent Life Settlements

Stranger-originated life insurance (STOLI) is an arrangement in which an individual with no relationship to the insured (a "stranger") purchases a life policy on the insured's life. The intention is to profit financially when the insured dies and sell the policy to an investor. In other words, STOLI can be used to finance and purchase insurance to sell for life settlements.

STOLI *violates the principle of insurable interest*, which is in place to ensure that an individual obtaining a life insurance policy is interested in the insured's longevity rather than the insured's death. For this reason, insurance providers take an aggressive legal stance against policies they suspect are involved in STOLI transactions (Cal. Ins. Code Section 10110).

Lawful life settlement contracts are not considered stranger-originated life insurance. Life settlement transactions result from existing life insurance policies. STOLI is used to initiate the purchase of a policy that would benefit an individual with no insurable interest in the insured's life.

Under California law, anyone purchasing life insurance on another person *must have an insurance interest* in that individual. If there is no insurable interest, the insurance provider has a basis for declaring the policy void. State law also prohibits issuing an insurance policy as a wager on a person's life. *STOLI arrangements violate these rules and are illegal in California.*

Chapter Review

This chapter broke down some of the basic principles and processes of life insurance underwriting. Let's review them:

USES OF LIFE INSURANCE	
Personal Uses	• Personal finance planning • Create an immediate estate
Determining Life Insurance Amounts	• *Human life approach* – estimates what a family would lose if the insured dies • *Needs approach* – predicts the needs of a family after an insured's death
Business Uses	• *Key person insurance* – the insured is the key employee; the employer is the applicant, policy owner, premium payer, and beneficiary • *Bull-sell insurance* – determines what will happen to a business if an owner becomes disabled or dies • *Business overhead expense* – helps owners meet overhead expenses • *Executive bonuses* – tax-deductible to the employer and taxable to the employee • *Business continuation* – allows co-owners to buy each other's ownership shares

PROCESS OF ISSUING A LIFE INSURANCE POLICY	
Underwriting	• Field Underwriting (by agent): - *Application* – must be completed correctly and signed - *Agent's report* – the agent's observations about the applicant that can assist in the underwriting process - Premiums are collected with the application, and conditional receipts are issued • Company Underwriting: - Multiple sources of information that include the application, consumer reports, and the MIB - *Risk classification* – three types of risk include standard, substandard, and preferred
Premium Determination	• Three critical factors for life insurance include mortality, interest, and expense • *Mode* – the more frequently a premium is paid by a policy owner, the higher the premium
Policy Issue and Delivery	• *Effective date of coverage* – if the premium is not paid with the application, the agent must obtain the premium and a statement of continued good health at the time of policy delivery
Sources of Insurability Information	• *Attending Physician Report* – provides the most accurate information on the applicant's medical history • *MIB report* – helps insurance companies share adverse medical information on insureds • *Credit Reports* – contain factors related to a risk's potential for loss, including consumer reports (information regarding a consumer's credit, character, reputation, or habits collected from employment records, credit reports, and other public sources) and investigative consumer reports (information obtained through an investigation and interviews with associates, friends, and neighbors of the consumer) • *Medical Exam Report* – conducted by paramedics or physicians
LIFE SETTLEMENTS	
Life Settlements	• Policy owners sell their life policies they no longer need to a third party • The insured does not have to be terminally ill • Requires an absolute assignment of all right to the policy from the original policy owner to the new policy owner
Fraudulent Life Settlements	• *Stranger-originated life insurance (STOLI)* – an individual with no relationship to the insured (a "stranger") purchases a life policy on the insured's life • STOLI violates the principle of insurable interest and are illegal in California

CHAPTER 5:
Types of Life Policies

Now that you understand general life insurance concepts, you are ready to learn about the different life insurance policies. By the end of this chapter, you will know the major types of life insurance policies, their functions and characteristics, and who is best served by each policy type. Determining the suitability of specific policies for different life situations can make it easier for you to distinguish between the various policies discussed in this chapter.

- Term Life Insurance
- Whole Life Insurance
- Special Coverages
- Flexible Premium Policies
- Variable Products
- Group Life Insurance
- Credit Life

Consumers have access to many types of life insurance products that are available. Although all life insurance products offer death protection, life insurance also includes unique features and benefits to serve the varying needs of insureds.

Every life insurance policy provides temporary and permanent protection regarding the length of coverage.

Term Life Insurance

Term insurance offers temporary protection because it only provides coverage for a specific time. It is also known as pure life insurance. Compared to any other form of protection, term insurance policies provide the most significant coverage for the lowest premium. There is a maximum age above which insurance providers will not renew or offer insurance coverage.

Term insurance provides insureds with *pure death protection*:

- If the insured dies during the policy term, the policy pays the death benefit to the beneficiary;
- If the policy is canceled or expires before the insured's death, there is no payment at the term's end; and
- There is no cash value or other living benefits.

Based on *how the face amount (death benefit) changes* during the policy term, there are three types of term coverage available:

- Level Term,
- Increasing Term, and
- Decreasing Term.

Irrespective of the type of term insurance purchased, the premium is level throughout the policy term. Only the death benefit amount may fluctuate depending on the term insurance. Upon converting, selling, or renewing the term policy, the insurer calculates the premium at the insured's age when the transaction occurs, also called attained age.

Level Term

The most common type of temporary protection that policy owners may purchase is *level term insurance*. The word "level" refers to the death benefit (or face amount) that does not change throughout the policy's life.

Level Premium Term – *Level premium term* provides a level premium and a level death benefit during the policy term. If the insured dies within the next ten years, a $100,000 10-year level term policy will provide a $100,000 death benefit. The premium remains level during the entire 10-year period. If the policy renews at the end of the ten years, the insurer will base the premium on the insured's attained age.

Annually Renewable Term

The purest form of term insurance is *annually renewable term (ART)* insurance. The death benefit remains level, and the policy may be guaranteed renewable each year without proof of insurability. However, as the probability of death increases, the premium increases annually according to the attained age.

Indeterminate Level Premium – An indeterminate premium term policy includes a provision that provides a current premium scale (nonguaranteed) and a maximum premium scale (guaranteed), beyond which premiums cannot be raised.

Decreasing Term

Decreasing term policies feature a level premium and a death benefit that decreases yearly over the policy's lifespan. Decreasing term is most appropriate when the amount of needed protection is time-sensitive or decreases over time. Credit life insurance with decreasing term coverage is commonly purchased to insure a *mortgage payment or other debts* if the insured dies prematurely. The amount of coverage consequently decreases as the outstanding loan balance decreases each year. A decreasing term policy is typically convertible. It is usually not renewable since the death benefit is $0 at the end of the policy term.

Increasing Term

Increasing term has level premiums and a death benefit that increases yearly over the length of the policy term. The amount of the death benefit increase is typically expressed as a specific amount or a percentage of the original amount. Insurers use increasing term to fund specific riders that provide a gradual increase in total coverage or a *refund of premiums*, such as the cost of living or return of premium riders.

This type of policy would be ideal for dealing with inflation and the rising cost of living. It is also frequently added to another policy as a rider, such as with the return of premium policies.

Return of Premium – *Return of premium (ROP)* life insurance is an increasing term insurance policy that pays the beneficiary an additional death benefit which equals the amount of the premiums paid. Insurers will return the paid premiums if the death happens within a specified period or if the insured outlives the policy term.

ROP policies are structured to consider the low-risk factor of a term policy but at a significant increase in the premium cost, sometimes as much as 25-50% more. Traditional term policies offer a simple, low-cost death benefit for a specified term. They have no cash value or investment component. The policy expires when the term ends, and the insured is no longer covered. An ROP policy offers the pure protection of a term policy. However, when the insured remains healthy and is still alive once the term expires, the insurance provider guarantees a return of the premium. Notwithstanding, the returned premiums are not taxable since the amount returned equals the amount paid.

Example 5.1 – A healthy, 35-year-old man pays $360 annually for a $250,000, 30-year term policy. At the end of the 30 years, he has spent $10,800 in premiums which the insurer will return if he outlives the policy term. The insurer has determined that $250 per year, or $7,500 over 30 years, will cover the actual cost of protection. The excess funds, which the insurance company invests, provide the cash for the returned premiums.

Special Features: Renewable and Convertible

Most term insurance contracts are renewable, convertible, or both renewable and convertible (R&C). The *renewable* provision lets a policy owner renew their coverage without evidence of insurability. Insurers will base the new premium for the term policy on the insured's current age. For instance, a 10-year renewable term policy can be renewed at the end of the ten years for a subsequent 10-year period without evidence of insurability. However, the insured will have to pay the premium based on their attained age. When an individual buys a 10-year term policy at age 30, they will pay a premium based on age 40 upon renewal.

The *convertible* provision allows policy owners to convert the policy to permanent insurance without evidence of insurability. Insurance providers will base the premium on the insured's attained age at conversion.

Whole Life Insurance

Whole life insurance includes a cash value (or savings element) and provides lifetime protection. Whole life policies are endowed when the insured reaches the age of 100. In other words, the cash value created by the accumulating premiums equals the face amount of the policy at the age of 100. Insurance carriers calculate the policy premium, assuming that the policyholder will continue paying the premium until that age. Premium payments for whole life policies are generally higher than premiums for term insurance.

The key characteristics of whole life insurance include:

- **Level premium** – Insurers base the premium for a whole life policy on the age at policy issue; therefore, it remains the same throughout the policy period.
- **Death benefit** – The death benefit is guaranteed and remains level for the policy's life.
- **Cash value** – The cash value created by the accumulation of premiums will equal the face amount of the policy when the policy matures (the insured reaches age 100). At policy maturity, insurers pay cash values to the policyholder. Remember, the insured and the policyholder do not have to be the same person. The policy's cash values are credited regularly and have a guaranteed interest rate.
- **Living benefits** – Policyholders can borrow against the cash value when the policy is effective. The policy owner can receive the cash value when they surrender the policy. The cash value, also known as the nonforfeiture value, does not typically accumulate until the third policy year, and it grows tax-deferred.

Three primary forms of whole life insurance include straight life, limited-pay whole life, and single premium whole life. However, other forms and combination plans may also be available.

Straight Life (Continuous Premium)

Straight life, also known as ordinary life or continuous premium whole life, is the most basic whole life policy. The policyholder pays the premium from when the insurer issues the policy until the insured's death or age 100, whichever occurs first. Straight life will have the lowest annual premium of all whole life policies.

Limited Payment

The coverage premiums of limited-pay whole life will be entirely paid up well before age 100, unlike straight life. A typical version of limited-pay life is 20-pay life, where policy owners pay for coverage over 20 years. LP-65 (life paid-up at 65) is another version of limited-pay life. In LP-65 policies, policy owners pay for coverage by age 65. All other factors being equal, this type of policy has a shorter premium paying period than straight life insurance. Therefore, the annual premium will be higher. Cash value builds up faster for these limited-pay policies.

Limited-pay policies are well suited for insureds who do not want to pay premiums beyond a specific time. For instance, an individual might need some protection after retirement but does not want to pay premiums. A limited-pay (paid-up at 65) policy purchased during the individual's working years will accomplish that objective.

Single Premium

Single premium whole life (SPWL) provides a level death benefit until the insured reaches age 100 for a one-time, lump-sum payment. The policy is fully paid after one premium payment and generates immediate cash.

	TERM LIFE	WHOLE LIFE
Type of protection	Temporary	Permanent until age 100
Premium	Level	Level
Death benefit	• Level • Increasing • Decreasing	Level
Living benefits	Not available	• Cash values • Policy loans • Nonforfeiture values

Interest-Sensitive Whole Life

Interest-sensitive whole life, also known as current assumption life, is a whole life insurance policy that delivers a guaranteed death benefit to age 100. The insurance provider sets the initial premium based on current risk, interest, and expenses assumptions. If the actual values change, the insurance provider will lower or raise the premium at designated intervals. Also, interest-sensitive whole life policies credit the cash value with the current interest rate. This rate is typically comparable to money market rates and can be higher than the guaranteed levels. The policy also provides a minimum guaranteed interest rate.

Interest-sensitive whole life provides the same benefits as other traditional whole life policies. It has the added benefit of current interest rates, which may allow for either a shorter premium paying period or greater cash value accumulation.

Modified and Graded Premium Whole Life

Modified life is a whole life policy that charges a lower premium in the first few policy years, typically the first three to five years. Then, policy owners pay a higher premium for the rest of the insured's life. The subsequent premium is usually higher than a straight life premium for the same age and amount of coverage. These policies were created to make the purchase of whole life insurance more attractive for those who are just starting out and have limited financial resources but will be able to pay for the higher premiums as their income grows.

Graded-premium whole life is similar to modified life in that premiums start out relatively low and then level off at a future point. A graded premium whole life policy usually starts with a premium that is approximately 50% or lower than the premium of a straight life policy. The premium gradually increases each year for five or ten years and then remains level.

Modified life and graded-premium life policies are helpful as a compromise between straight life and convertible term insurance. The premium is less than straight life in the early years while some cash value accumulates. The actual premiums paid over the contract's life for a modified or graded premium policy are the same as paying for a straight life policy to age 100.

Indeterminate Premium – *Indeterminate premium* whole life policies have a premium rate that can vary yearly. These policies specify two premium rates: a *guaranteed* level premium stated in the contract (maximum premium) and a *nonguaranteed* lower premium rate that the policy owner pays for a set period. After the initial period (typically 2-3 years), the insurer establishes a new rate that it could raise, keep the same, or lower based on the company's expected mortality, expenses, and investments. The premium can never be higher than the guaranteed maximum.

Special Coverages

Family Protection, Family Policy, and Family Rider

A *family maintenance* policy is life insurance based on a family income policy. It combines *whole life* with *level term* insurance to provide income to a beneficiary over a specified period (e.g., 15 or 20 years) if the insured passes away during that period. When the insured dies within the period, the level term insurance is adequate to pay the monthly income portion of the contract. Also, the policy contains permanent life insurance protection to be paid upon the insured's death. The term portion expires without value if the insured survives the specified period. The contract is left with only permanent life protection.

A *family* policy, also called family protection, combines *whole life* with *term insurance* to insure family members in a single policy, providing coverage for every family member. The family policy usually provides whole life insurance on the family's breadwinner and convertible term insurance for the other family members. The spouse has the opportunity to convert their term coverage to permanent coverage up until age 65. Children are automatically insured after birth for a specified period, typically *30 or 31 days*. To continue coverage for the newborn after the initial period, the parents must notify the insurance provider of the birth within that period. The children can convert their term coverage to permanent coverage when they reach the age of 21, or the maximum age for coverage as a dependent that is specified in the policy, without evidence of insurability.

The *family income* policy combines *decreasing term insurance* and *whole life insurance* for the family's breadwinner. The policy provides an income period that begins from the policy's effective date and commonly runs for twenty years. Still, it is also issued for ten years or even until age 65. This income period is underwritten with decreasing term insurance. When the insured dies during the income period, the term coverage will provide the surviving family with a monthly income for the remainder of the income period. At the end of the income period, the face amount of the whole life policy is paid to the beneficiary. Should the insured pass away after the income period, the insurer will only pay the whole life portion to the beneficiary. This policy provides a family with a monthly income upon the insured's death while maintaining permanent coverage until the end of the income payments.

For example, suppose a person buys a 20-year family income policy and dies five years after the policy is issued. In that situation, the decreasing term portion of the plan would provide their surviving family members with a monthly income for 15 years. At the end of the 15 years, the whole life death benefit would be paid to the family.

The *family term rider* integrates the spouse term rider and the children's term rider into a single rider. When added to a whole life policy, the family term rider delivers level term life insurance benefits covering the spouse and all of the children in the family.

Joint Life and Survivorship Life

Joint life is a stand-alone policy designed to insure two or more lives. Joint life policies can be in the form of permanent insurance or term insurance. The premium payment for a joint life policy would be less than the same type and amount of coverage on the same insureds. It is also known as joint whole life, which performs similarly to an individual whole life policy with two noteworthy exceptions:

- Insurers base the premium payment on a *joint average age* of the insureds.
- Insurers only pay the death benefit upon the *first death*.

A premium based on a joint age is less than the sum of two premiums based on individual age. Therefore, it is common to find joint life policies purchased by husbands and wives. This situation is particularly the case if the need for insurance does not extend beyond the first death. Policy owners use joint life policies when there is a need for two or more individuals to be protected. However, the need for insurance is no longer present after the first insured dies.

For example, a married couple buying a house may purchase a joint life policy for mortgage protection if both spouses work and earn the same income. If one spouse dies, the policy covers the mortgage payments for the surviving spouse.

Business owners also use joint life to meet various business life insurance needs by insuring the lives of business partners through the funding of a buy-sell agreement. A buy-sell is a business continuation agreement that describes what will happen with the business if an owner becomes disabled or dies.

Survivorship life, also known as a "last survivor" or a "second-to-die" policy, is similar to joint life. It insures two or more lives for a *premium based on a joint age*. The primary difference is that survivorship life *pays on the last death* rather than upon the first death. Since the insurer does not pay the death benefit until the last death, the joint life expectancy, in a sense, is extended. This "extension" results in a lower premium payment for joint life, which pays upon the first death. Policy owners often use this insurance policy to *offset the estate tax liability* upon the death of the last insured.

Juvenile Policies

Jumping Juvenile – As the name implies, juvenile life insurance is any life insurance written on the life of a minor. A standard-issue juvenile policy is the *jumping juvenile* policy because the face amount increases at a predetermined age, often *21*. Under this policy type, the face amount "jumps" while the premium remains level.

Payor Benefit Rider – The *payor benefit* rider is mainly associated with juvenile policies or any life insurance policy written on the life of a minor. Otherwise, it functions as a waiver of premium rider. When the payor, typically a guardian or parent, becomes disabled for at least six months or dies, the insurance provider will waive the premiums until the minor reaches a certain age, such as 21. This rider is also appropriate when the policy owner and the insured are two different individuals.

Mortgage Redemption

A *mortgage redemption* provision covers borrowers for an amount that is equal to their mortgages. If the borrower/insured dies, the insurance provider assumes responsibility for paying the outstanding loan balance to the insured's creditor.

Return of Premium

The *return of premium* rider uses increasing term insurance. When a policy owner adds this rider to a whole life policy, it specifies that the original face amount is payable when death occurs before a given age. Nevertheless, the insurer owes the beneficiary an amount equal to all previously paid premiums. The return of premium rider typically expires at a specified time, such as age 60.

Policies Linked to Indexes

The central feature of *indexed whole life*, or equity index whole life, is a guaranteed minimum interest rate. The cash value is dependent upon the performance of the equity index, like the S&P 500. The policy's face amount increases yearly to keep pace with inflation as the Consumer Price Index increases. Also, evidence of insurability is not required. Indexed whole life policies are classified depending on whether the insurance provider or the policy owner assumes the inflation risk. If the insurance provider assumes the risk, the premium remains level. If the policyholder bears the risk, the policy premiums increase with the increases in the face amount.

Flexible Premium Policies

There are several other types of whole life insurance policies. While they all have the same fundamental characteristics, whole life policies offer unique features based on how the policy owner invests or pays the premium.

Adjustable Life

Insurance companies established *adjustable life* to provide the insured with term and permanent coverage. Adjustable life policies can take the form of either term insurance or permanent insurance. The insured generally determines the required coverage and an affordable premium amount. The insurance provider will select the appropriate type of insurance to meet the insured's needs. As the needs of the insured change, the policy owner can adjust their policy. Usually, the policy owner has the following options:

- Increase or reduce the premium or the premium-paying period;
- Increase or decrease the policy face amount; or
- Change the protection period.

The policy owner also chooses to convert from term life to whole life or vice versa. However, changing to a lower premium type of policy or increases in the death benefit will usually require proof of insurability. In the case of converting from a whole life policy to a term policy, the insurance carrier may adjust the death benefit. Under the permanent form, the policy owner can pay additional premiums above and beyond what is required to accumulate more cash value or shorten the premium paying period.

Adjustable life policies include most of the standard features of other whole life policies. The *cash value* of adjustable life policies only develops when the paid premiums are greater than the cost of the policy.

Universal Life

Universal life insurance is also referred to by the generic name of flexible premium adjustable life. This reference indicates that the policy owner has the flexibility to increase the amount of premium paid into the policy and then decrease it later again. Policy owners can even skip paying a premium. The policy will not lapse, provided that there is sufficient cash value to cover the monthly deductions for the cost of insurance. However, the policy will expire if the cash value is insufficient to cover the premium costs.

Since the premium can be adjusted, the insurance providers may give the policy owner a choice to pay either of the two types of premiums:

- The *minimum premium* amount keeps the policy in force for the current year. Paying the minimum premium makes the policy perform like an annually renewable term product.
- The *target premium* is a suggested amount that policy owners should pay on a policy to keep the policy in force for the duration of its lifetime and to cover the cost of insurance protection.

Universal life policies have two components: a *cash account* and an *insurance component*. *Annually renewable term insurance* is always the insurance component of a universal life policy.

Universal life policies allow the *partial surrender*, or *partial withdrawal*, of the policy cash value. However, there may be a charge for each withdrawal. There are typically limits on how much and how often policyholders can make a withdrawal. The interest earned on the withdrawn cash value may be subject to taxation during the withdrawal, depending upon the plan. The amount of any partial surrender will lower the death benefit. Additionally, a partial surrender from a universal life policy is not the same as a policy loan.

Death Benefit Options – Universal life insurance offers the policy owner one of two death benefit options. *Option A* provides a level death benefit, and *Option B* provides an increasing death benefit.

Under *Option A (Level Death Benefit)*, the death benefit remains level. At the same time, the cash value steadily increases, consequently lowering the pure insurance with the insurance provider in the later years. Pure insurance decreases as time passes, reducing the expenses, and allowing for a larger cash value in the older years. The increase in the death benefit at a later point is because the policy will comply with the "statutory definition of life insurance." The IRS established this definition, which applies to all life insurance products issued after December 31, 1984. According to this definition, a life insurance policy must maintain a specified "corridor" or gap between the death benefit and the cash value. The percentages that apply to the corridor appear in a table published by the IRS and vary based on the insured's age and the coverage amount. If this corridor is not maintained, the policy is no longer considered life insurance for tax purposes. Consequently, it loses most of the tax advantages associated with life insurance.

Under *Option B (Increasing Death Benefit)*, the death benefit gradually increases each year by the amount that the cash value increases. At any point in time, the face amount of the policy plus the current amount of cash value will always equal the total death benefit. The pure insurance with the insurer remains level for life, and the expenses of this option are higher than Option A. In this case, the cash value will be smaller in the older years.

Indexed Universal Life – *Indexed universal life* is a universal life policy with an equity index as its investment feature. It has many characteristics of variable universal life, including an adjustable death benefit, flexible premiums, and the policy owner deciding where the cash value will be invested. The investment feature is the primary difference between indexed universal life and variable universal life, where the policy's cash value depends on the performance of one or more investment funds. Under the equity index universal policy, the policy's cash value depends on the equity index performance. Death benefits and cash values are not guaranteed. The sale of equity-indexed universal life products does not require a securities license. However, the sale of variable universal life does require a life and securities license.

Guaranteed Universal Life – Unlike universal life, which accumulates interest depending on market indexes, *guaranteed universal life* eliminates the reliance on market risk. It also provides more affordable coverage. These policies do not accumulate cash value, which allows for lower monthly premiums compared to universal life insurance. Since there is no cash value component, the death benefit remains level throughout the policy's life. It has a no-lapse guarantee, meaning that coverage will remain in force as long as the policy owner pays the premium.

Guaranteed universal life is comparable to term life insurance because it provides coverage for a specific period. However, rather than the policy lasting for a particular number of years, insurers can establish guaranteed universal life for the rest of the insured's life. These policies can also be set to a specific age (typically 90, 95, or 100).

Survivorship Universal Life – Survivorship universal life (SUL), also known as second-to-die life insurance, is permanent life insurance that covers two people. SUL pays benefits after both insureds have passed away. Since SUL provides coverage for two people, it is usually more affordable than two individual permanent policies. SUL policies are suitable for insureds who intend to leave the policy proceeds to the beneficiaries, make charitable donations, or fund a buy-sell agreement on a business.

Under survivorship universal life policies, insurers can raise or lower premiums as required during the policy period.

The SUL policy's cash value grows tax deferred. Death benefits paid to a beneficiary are generally received income tax-free.

Variable Products

Variable Life

Variable life insurance, sometimes called variable whole life insurance, is a level, fixed premium, investment-based product. Similar to traditional forms of life insurance, these policies have a guaranteed minimum death benefit and fixed premiums. However, the cash value of the policy is not guaranteed. It fluctuates with the portfolio's performance in which the insurance provider has invested the premiums. In variable contracts, the policy owner bears the investment risk.

Because the insurer is not incurring the contract's investment risk, the contract's underlying assets cannot be kept in the insurer's general account. Insurers must hold these assets in a separate account, investing in stocks, bonds, and other securities. Any domestic insurance provider issuing variable contracts has to establish one or more separate accounts. Each account must maintain assets with a value that is at least equal to the amount held in reserves and other contract liabilities. Insurers must not commingle holdings in a separate account with assets in the general account.

Variable Universal Life

Variable universal life insurance combines universal life with variable life. Similar to universal life, it provides the policyholder with an adjustable death benefit and flexible premiums. Like variable life, the policyholder, rather than the insurance carrier, will decide where the cash value (net premiums) will be invested. Also, like variable life, the death benefit is not fixed, and the cash values are never guaranteed. The death benefit and cash value might increase or decrease over the policy's life depending on the investment performance of the underlying sub-account. The death benefit, however, usually cannot be reduced below the initial face amount of the policy. A producer must also hold a license for *securities* and *life insurance* to sell variable universal life.

Regulation of Variable Products (SEC, FINRA, and California)

Both state and federal governments *regulate* Variable life insurance products. Due to the investment risk, the federal government has established that variable contracts are securities. Consequently, the Securities and Exchange Commission (SEC) and the Financial Industry Regulatory Authority (FINRA) are responsible for regulating variable contracts. A state's Insurance Department also regulates variable life insurance as an insurance product.

Agents selling variable life insurance products must:

- Be registered with FINRA;
- Have a securities license; and
- Be licensed in a state to sell life insurance.

POLICIES COMPARED	
Adjustable Life	*Key Features* – Can be Term or Whole Life; can convert from one to the other *Premium* – Can be increased or decreased by policy owners *Face Amount* – Flexible; set by the policy owner with proof of insurability *Cash Value* – Fixed rate of return; general account *Policy Loans* – Can borrow cash value
Universal Life	*Key Features* – Permanent insurance with renewable term protection *Premium* – Flexible; minimum or target *Face Amount* – Flexible; set by the policy owner with proof of insurability *Cash Value* – Guaranteed at a minimum level; general account *Policy Loans* – Can borrow cash value
Variable Life	*Key Features* – Permanent insurance *Premium* – Fixed (if Whole Life); flexible (if Universal Life) *Face Amount* – Can increase or decrease to a stated minimum *Cash Value* – Not guaranteed; separate account *Policy Loans:* Can borrow cash value

Group Life Insurance

Individual life insurance is written on a single life. The rate and coverage are based upon the underwriting of that person.

Group life insurance is written as a master policy issued to the sponsoring organization, covering the lives of more than one member of that group. Individuals covered by group life insurance do not receive a policy; they receive a certificate of insurance from the master policy. The certificate holders' coverage amount must be determined according to non-discriminatory rules. The coverage and rate are based upon group underwriting, with all individuals covered for the same amount and rate. The cost of coverage paid by the employer that exceeds $50,000 is taxed on the employee.

Other characteristics of group policies include:

- The group must exist for a reason other than purchasing insurance; and
- Individual members covered under the group master policy must have the right to convert their coverage to an individual policy without proof of insurability should they leave the group.

Credit Life

Credit insurance is a particular type of coverage written to insure a debtor's life and pay off a loan balance if the debtor dies. *Credit life* is typically written as decreasing term insurance and can be written as an individual policy or a group plan. When coverage is written as a group policy, the creditor owns the master policy, and every debtor receives a certificate of insurance.

The creditor is the policy owner and beneficiary. At the same time, the premiums are usually paid by the borrower (or the debtor). Credit life insurance cannot pay out more than the debt balance, so there is no financial incentive for the insured's death. The creditors can require the debtor to have life insurance; however, they cannot require that the debtor purchases insurance from a specific insurance company.

Chapter Review

This chapter discussed the different types of life insurance policies. Let's review them:

TERM LIFE	
General Characteristics	• Pure protection • Lasts for specific term • No cash value • Maximum age above which coverage will not be offered or at which coverage cannot be renewed
Level Premium Term	• Level death benefit and level premium
Annually Renewable Term	• Renews each year without proof of insurability • Premiums increase due to attained age
Decreasing Term	• Coverage gradually decreases at predetermined times • Best used when the need for protection decreases from year to year
Features of Term Policies	• *Renewable* – can renew the policy without evidence of insurability • *Convertible* – the right to convert a term policy to a permanent policy without evidence of insurability
WHOLE LIFE	
General Characteristics	• Permanent protection • Guaranteed elements (premium, face amount, and cash value) until death or age 100 • Level premium • Cash value and other living benefits
Ordinary Whole Life (Continuous Premium)	• Level death benefit • The insured pays the premiums for life or until age 100
Limited Payment	• Premiums are paid until a certain time; coverage is in effect to age 100
Single Premium	• Premiums are paid in one single lump sum; coverage continues to age 100
OTHER TYPES OF POLICIES	
Flexible Premium	• A type of whole life insurance with a flexible premium
Universal Life	• An insurance component that comes in the form of annually renewable term • Two options for the death benefit: Option A (level), and Option B (increasing) • Can make a partial surrender/cash withdrawal
Variable Life	• Fixed premium, minimum death benefit • Cash value and the actual amount of the death benefit are not guaranteed • Assets held in separate accounts • Agents must be dually licensed in both insurance and securities

CHAPTER 6:
Individual Life Insurance Contract – Provisions and Options

Now, you have a solid working knowledge of the different life insurance policies and their suitability for other insured individuals. You will now learn about available provisions, options, and exclusions that can cause two policies of the same type to differ significantly.

- Common Life Policy Provisions
- Beneficiaries
- Policy Loans
- Nonforfeiture Options
- Dividend Options
- Settlement Options

Common Life Policy Provisions

Provisions define an insurance contract's characteristics and are relatively universal from one policy to the next. *Riders* are added to a policy to amend provisions that already exist. *Options* offer insurance providers and insureds ways to invest or distribute a sum of money available in a life policy. You need to understand the different provisions, riders, and options for future life insurance transactions.

The standard policy provisions adopted by the National Association of Insurance Commissioners (NAIC) create uniformity among life insurance policies. There is no "standard" policy form in life insurance.

Entire Contract

The *entire contract* provision states that *the policy, application copy, and any amendments or riders* make up the entire contract. Any statements made before the contract cannot be used to modify the agreement. Neither the insurance provider nor the insured can change policy provisions once the policy is effective unless both parties agree and the change is attached to the contract.

Insuring Clause

The insuring clause, also known as the insuring agreement, sets forth the basic contract between the insurance company and the insured. It states the insurance company's promise to pay the death benefit upon the insured's death. Policy owners can typically find the insuring clause on the face page of the policy. It also defines the parties to the contract, the premium payments to be made, the death benefit amount, and how long coverage will remain in force.

Consideration

Both parties to a contract or agreement must provide some *consideration*, or value, for the contract to be valid. The consideration provision stipulates that the policy owner's consideration or value is the premium and the statements made in the application. The consideration offered by the insurance company is the promise to pay per the terms of the contract. A consideration clause does not always appear as a separate provision. It is often in the entire contract provision. A separate provision regarding the payment of policy premiums is also usually found in the policy.

Ownership

The parties to the insurance contract are the insurance provider, the policy owner, the insured, and the beneficiary. The policy owner and the insured can be the same individual or different people. Regardless, only the policy owner has ownership rights under the policy, not the insured or the beneficiary. The ownership rights are naming and changing the beneficiary, selecting a payment option for receiving benefits, assigning the policy, and receiving the policy's living benefits.

The policy owner is responsible for paying the policy premiums. They are also the individual who must have an insurable interest in the insured when applying for insurance. When the policy owner and the insured are different individuals, the insurance arrangement is known as third-party ownership.

Assignment or Transfer of Policy – Life insurance policy owners can transfer complete or partial ownership of the policy to another individual without the insurer's consent. However, the owner must notify the insurer in writing of the assignment. Transfer of the life insurance policy *does not change the amount of coverage or the insured*; it only changes who has the policy ownership rights.

The assignment provision stipulates the policy owner's right to assign the policy or transfer ownership rights. The policy owner must notify the insurance provider in writing of the assignment. The following two types of policy assignment include:

- *Absolute Assignment* involves transferring *all ownership rights* to another person or entity. It is a permanent transfer, and the new policy owner does not need an insurable interest in the insured.
- *Collateral Assignment* involves a transfer of *partial rights* to another individual to secure a loan or some other transaction. A collateral assignment is a temporary and partial assignment of some policy rights. Once the policy owner repays the loan or debt, they regain these rights.

Selecting or Changing Premium Modes – A policy owner can change the premium payment frequency on any policy anniversary. The payment cannot be less than the minimum amount specified by the insurer.

Most insurance providers offer several ways in which policy owners can pay the premium, such as the following:

- Annually;
- Semiannually;
- Quarterly;
- Monthly; or
- An automated bank drafting method.

For premium modes other than annual, the insurance company can include a surcharge (loading) to cover the cost of the additional billings and the loss of investment income from not having the entire yearly premium to invest for the whole policy year.

Suppose, after a policy has been issued with an annual premium, the policy owner requests to change the premium payment to a more frequent mode (e.g., monthly or quarterly). In that circumstance, the insurance provider can require that the insured prove continued insurability.

Selecting or Changing Beneficiaries – The policy owner usually has the right to change beneficiaries by designating a revocable beneficiary. However, if a policy owner names an *irrevocable* beneficiary, the beneficiary's consent is required to change beneficiaries. Also, if an irrevocable beneficiary is designated, the policy owner would not be able to take out a policy loan without the irrevocable beneficiary's consent.

Selecting or Changing Settlement Options – Insureds and beneficiaries can choose how they can receive proceeds from life insurance policies. These choices are known as settlement options. The type of settlement option chosen usually depends on whether the beneficiary prefers a single, lump-sum payment or payments over time. Insureds and beneficiaries can select and change their settlement options. Insurance providers must pay benefits according to the option chosen within 30 days of the insured's death. When insurance providers do not pay within 30 days, beneficiaries have the right to have interest on the benefit amount paid to them.

Conversion Privilege – The conversion privilege in an individual life insurance policy allows the policy owner to choose to have a new policy issued before the expiration of an existing policy. A conversion right is often exercised when the policy owner converts the term policy to a cash-value permanent policy.

The conversion privilege can be exercised for coverage on dependents. When a dependent covered under an individual life insurance policy reaches the limiting age for coverage, the insurer must provide the privilege to convert coverage to an individual policy without evidence of insurability. Most states require that the insurance provider give a written explanation of the rights of the dependent before reaching such age.

Cash Values and Dividends – The policy owner can surrender the policy for its current cash value when coverage is no longer affordable or needed. Once this option is chosen, the insured is no longer covered.

An insurer's surplus is called *dividends*. Mutual companies issue the most participating policies. The owners of mutual companies are their insureds. As owners, the insureds have the right to share in any surplus the company earns every year. California law requires an insurer's dividends to be credited to participating policies on the anniversary date of the policies if all premiums are current. Extended term or reduced paid-up policies are excluded. Usually, insureds will not receive dividends on policies that have been in effect for less than five years because the early costs of the policy are being paid at this time.

Surrender Charges – A *surrender charge* is a fee charged to the insured when a policy or annuity is surrendered for its cash value.

Free Look (Right to Return and Right to Examine)

This provision allows the policyholder a specified number of days (at least ten) from receipt to review the policy and return it for a full refund of the premium if dissatisfied for any reason. The *free-look period begins when the policyholder receives the policy*, not when the insurance company issues the policy. Specific policies might require a longer free-look period, or state statute may set the period.

Payment of Premium

The policy states when the premiums are due, how often they are to be paid (annually, semiannually, quarterly, monthly, etc.), and to whom. Suppose the insured dies during the period for which the premium has been paid. In that case, the insurance provider has to refund any unearned premium, and the policy proceeds. The payment of premium provision also states that policy owners must pay premiums in advance.

Most life insurance policies have a level premium, meaning the premium remains the same throughout the contract's duration. Flexible premium policies let the policy owner increase or decrease the premium during the policy period.

Grace Period

A *grace period* refers to the time after the premium due date that the policyholder has to pay the premium before the policy lapses (usually 30 or 31 days). The grace period protects the policy owner against an unintentional policy lapse. If a policyholder dies during this period, the death benefit is payable; however, insurers will deduct any unpaid premiums from the death benefit.

In California, each individual life insurance policy has to include a provision for a grace period of at least *60 days* from the premium due date. The 60-day grace period cannot run concurrently with the period of paid coverage.

Reinstatement

A *reinstatement provision* allows policy owners to reinstate a lapsed policy. The maximum time limit for reinstatement is typically *three years* after the policy has lapsed. If the policy owner reinstates their policy, they must provide evidence of insurability. The policyholder must pay all back premiums with interest and could be required to repay any outstanding loans and interest. The advantage of reinstating a lapsed policy instead of purchasing a new one is that the insurer restores the policy to its original state. The policy retains the values calculated at the insured's issue age.

It is worth noting that a policy owner cannot reinstate a surrendered policy.

Incontestability

The *incontestability clause* prevents insurance companies from denying a claim due to statements in the application after the policy has been effective for *two years*. This provision is especially relevant when there is a concealment of a material fact or a material misstatement of facts. Insurers can contest a claim during the first two years of the policy if they feel the applicant was misleading or provided inaccurate information on the application. The incontestability period is not applicable in the event of nonpayment of premiums. It also does not typically apply to statements concerning sex, age, or identity.

Misstatement of Age and Sex

An insured's age and gender are essential to the premium the insurer will charge for a life insurance policy. Consequently, a policy provision allows the insurance provider to adjust the policy when a misstatement of age or gender occurs. When the applicant misstated their age or gender, in the case of a claim, insurers can adjust the benefits to an amount that the premium at the correct gender or age would have obtained. The insurer should base a proceeds calculation on their rate when the policy was issued.

Exclusions

Exclusions are the kinds of risks the policy will not cover. Specific exclusions are standard in all policies, and policy owners can attach other exclusions as riders. The most common exclusions in life insurance policies are aviation, hazardous occupations or hobbies, and war or military service.

Aviation – Most life insurance policies will insure a policy owner as a pilot on a regularly scheduled airline or a fare-paying passenger. However, they will exclude coverage for noncommercial pilots or require an additional premium.

Hazardous Occupations or Hobbies – Suppose the insured is employed in a hazardous occupation or participates in dangerous hobbies like auto racing or skydiving. In that scenario, insurers will exclude death from a hazardous occupation or hobby from coverage. The underwriter can also charge a higher premium for insuring these risks.

Military Service or War – Insurers do not exclude military service in most life insurance policies issued today. However, insurance providers can use two different exclusions to limit the death benefit if the insured dies because of war or serving in the military. The *status clause* of the policy excludes all causes of death while the insured is on active duty in the military. The *results clause* only eliminates the death benefit if the insured dies due to an act of declared or undeclared war.

Suicide – In life insurance policies, the *suicide provision* protects the insurance carriers from individuals who obtain life insurance intending to commit suicide. Insurance policies typically specify when the insurer will not pay death proceeds if the insured commits suicide. If the insured commits suicide within two years after the policy effective date (issue date), the insurance company's liability is limited to a premium refund. When the insured commits suicide after two years, the policy will pay the death benefit to the designated beneficiary as if the insured had died of natural causes.

Beneficiaries

Designation Options

The *beneficiary* is the individual or interest to which the insurer will pay policy proceeds upon the insured's death. The beneficiary can be a person, class of individuals (sometimes used with children of the insured), the insured's estate, or an institution or other entity such as a corporation, charity, foundation, or trustee of a trust. Trusts are commonly used with beneficiary designations for estate tax purposes or to manage life insurance proceeds for a minor. However, naming a trust as a beneficiary does not avoid estate taxes.

The beneficiary does not need to have an insurable interest in the insured. Additionally, the policy owner does not have to name a beneficiary for the policy to be valid.

Individuals – A life insurance policy owner can name any individual as a beneficiary for the policy proceeds. The owner can name more than one person, wherein the individual beneficiaries will split the benefit by the percentage stated in the policy.

Benefits designated to a minor will either be paid to the minor's guardian or paid to the trustee of the minor if the trust is the named beneficiary. The trustee and guardian can be the same individual. It is usually accepted not to be a sound practice to have life insurance benefits payable to a minor.

Classes – A beneficiary class uses a designation such as "my children." This designation can be vague if the insured has adopted children, has been married more than once, or has illegitimate children. An example of a less ambiguous class is "children of the union of Stan Smith and Francine Smith." Many insurance providers encourage the insured to name each child specifically and to state the percentage of benefits they are to receive.

When naming beneficiaries, it is wise to be specific by naming each person and by designating the amount to be given to them. Two class designations are available for use when an insured chooses to "group" the beneficiaries, which include Per Capita and Per Stirpes. Per Capita evenly distributes benefits among the living named beneficiaries. Per Stirpes distributes the benefits of a beneficiary who died before the insured to that beneficiary's heirs.

As an example, Brian purchased a $90,000 life insurance policy. He named his three children, Robert, Maria, and Michael, as beneficiaries for equal shares. Robert has two children of his own. Maria and Michael are both married but have no children. Unfortunately, Robert predeceases Brian.

If Brian chose the *Per Capita* designation, which means "by the head," with Robert deceased, only two named beneficiaries remain. Maria and Michael will each receive $45,000 ($90,000 divided by 2). Robert's children would not receive any benefits since they were not named as beneficiaries.

If Brian chose the *Per Stirpes* designation, meaning "by the bloodline," Maria and Michael would receive $30,000 each. Robert's children would share his allotment equally at $15,000 each.

Estates – When none of the beneficiaries are alive, or if there are no named beneficiaries when the insured dies, the insured's *estate* will automatically receive the proceeds of a life insurance policy. If this occurs, the policy's death benefit could be factored into the insured's taxable estate.

Trusts – *Trusts* are frequently established for minors or to create a scholarship fund. When used correctly, trusts can be used for estate planning purposes. They can keep life insurance death proceeds out of the insured's taxable estate. They are, however, expensive to administer.

Succession

The beneficiary designation can offer three levels of priority or choice. When the first beneficiary dies before the insured, the second (or sometimes third) level in the succession of beneficiaries will be entitled to the death benefits. Each level in the succession of beneficiaries is only eligible for the death proceeds if the beneficiary(s) in the level(s) above them predeceases the insured.

The *primary beneficiary* has the first claim to the policy proceeds following the insured's death. Policy owners can name more than one primary beneficiary and how the proceeds are divided.

The *contingent beneficiary* is also known as a secondary or tertiary beneficiary. Contingent beneficiaries have the second claim if the primary beneficiary predeceases the insured. They do not receive anything if the primary beneficiary is still alive when the insured dies.

When none of the beneficiaries are alive, or if there are no named beneficiaries when the insured dies, the insured's *estate* will automatically receive the proceeds of a life insurance policy. If this occurs, the policy's death benefit could be factored into the insured's taxable estate.

Revocable and Irrevocable

Beneficiary designations can be either revocable or irrevocable. Without the knowledge or consent of the beneficiary, the policy owner can change a revocable designation at any time. Policy owners cannot change an irrevocable designation without the beneficiary's written agreement. An irrevocable beneficiary has a vested interest in the policy; therefore, the policy owner cannot exercise certain rights without the beneficiary's consent. In addition to being unable to change the beneficiary designation, the policy owner cannot borrow against the policy's cash value; this loan would reduce the policy's face value. Also, policy owners cannot assign the policy to another individual without the beneficiary's consent.

Common Disaster Clause

When the insured and the primary beneficiary die at approximately the same time from a common accident with no clear indication of who died first, a problem could arise in identifying which party is eligible for the death benefit. The *Uniform Simultaneous Death Law* addresses this problem in most states; it protects the policy owner's original intent and the contingent beneficiary. Suppose the insured and the primary beneficiary die in the same accident with insufficient evidence to demonstrate who died first. In that circumstance, the insurance company will distribute the policy benefits as if the primary beneficiary was the first to die.

When added to a policy, the Common Disaster Clause states that if the insured and the primary beneficiary die in a common disaster, the insurer will assume that the primary beneficiary died first. Insurance providers would make this assumption even if the beneficiary outlived the insured by one or more days. The insurer will pay the proceeds to the contingent beneficiary or the insured's estate if no contingent beneficiary is designated. Most insurance providers specify a certain period, typically 14 to 30 days, in which death must occur for this provision to apply. Following the insured's death, the insurer will assume that the beneficiary died first as long as the beneficiary dies within this specified time. The law intends to fulfill the wishes of the policy owner regarding the payment of proceeds to beneficiaries.

Spendthrift Clause and Rights of Beneficiaries and Creditors

In a life insurance policy, the *spendthrift clause* protects beneficiaries from the claims of their creditors. This clause applies to the benefits paid in fixed-amount or fixed-period installments. The beneficiary does not have the right to select a different settlement option and also cannot borrow or assign any of the proceeds. The spendthrift clause protects life insurance policy proceeds that have not yet been paid to a named beneficiary from the claims of the policy owner's or beneficiary's creditors.

Policy Loans

The *policy loan option* is only in policies with a cash value. The policyholder is eligible to borrow an amount equal to the available cash value. Insurers deduct any outstanding loans and accrued interest from the policy proceeds upon the insured's death. An outstanding policy loan prevents the policy from lapsing unless the loan amount and accrued interest exceed the available cash value. However, the insurance company must provide *30 days' written notice* to the policyholder that the policy will lapse. Insurers can defer a policy loan request for up to six months unless the reason for the loan is to pay the policy premium. Policy loans are not subject to federal income taxation.

Cash Loans

When a policy has cash value, it also has loan value. The amount available to the policyholder for a loan equals the cash value minus any outstanding and unpaid policy loans, including interest. Suppose there are outstanding loans at the time of the insured's death. In that case, the loan amount will be treated like a debt to the policy, and the amount of the debt will decrease the death benefit.

Automatic Premium Loans

The automatic premium loan provision is typically added to contracts with a cash value at no additional charge but is not required. This type of loan *avoids the unintentional lapse of a policy* because of the nonpayment of premiums. The insurance provider automatically generates a loan against the policy's cash value for the amount of premium due when the policy owner has not paid the premium by the end of the grace period. Once the cash value is depleted, the policy will terminate. The insurance provider will charge interest on the loan. When the insured does not repay the loan and interest and dies suddenly, the insurer will deduct this amount from the death benefit. While the insurer can defer requests for other loans for up to *six months*, loan requests for payment of due premiums must be honored immediately. Generally, the policyholder must opt for this provision in writing to make it effective.

Nonforfeiture Options

Because a permanent life insurance policy has a cash value, insurers write certain guarantees into the policy that *the policy owner cannot forfeit*. These guarantees, called nonforfeiture values, are required by state law to be contained in the policy. Every policy has a table showing the nonforfeiture values for a minimum of 20 years. The policy owner selects one of the following nonforfeiture options: cash surrender value, reduced paid-up insurance, or extended-term.

Reduced Paid-up Insurance

Under this option, the insurance provider uses the policy's cash value as a single premium to purchase a paid-up permanent policy with a *reduced face amount* from the previous policy. The new reduced policy will remain in force until death or maturity and builds its cash value.

Extended Term

Under the *extended term* option, the insurance provider uses the policy's cash value to convert to term insurance for the *exact face amount* as the previous permanent policy. The length of the new coverage term lasts for as long a period as the amount of cash value will purchase. When the policy owner has not chosen one of these nonforfeiture options, if the insurer terminates the original policy, it will *automatically* apply the extended term option.

Cash Surrender Value

The policy owner can surrender the policy for the current cash value when coverage is no longer affordable or needed. Upon receiving the cash surrender value, the excess is taxed as ordinary income if the cash value exceeds the premiums paid. Once the policy owner chooses this option, the insured is no longer covered. Policies surrendered for their cash value cannot be reinstated. When the policy owner surrenders a life policy or annuity for its cash value, the insurer charges a fee known as a surrender charge.

Example 6.1 – Review the table on the following page. Suppose the insured decides to exercise the reduced paid-up option at the end of year 15. The cash value of $8,100 can be used as a single premium to obtain paid-up insurance of the same type as the original policy. The insured does not have to pay an additional premium while still retaining some life insurance, which in this case, is $21,750.

The extended term option specifies the option to use the policy's cash value to purchase a term insurance policy in a single premium equal to the original policy's face value, which in this example, is term insurance with a $50,000 face amount. The insurer determines that $8,100 of cash value is the equivalent of 18 years and eight days of $50,000 worth of protection for this insured.

Table of Guaranteed Values – $50,000 Whole Life Nonforfeiture Table (20 years)				
End of Policy Year	Cash or Loan Value	Reduced Paid-up	Extended-Term	
			Years	Days
1	$0	$0	0	60
2	$50	$250	0	122
3	$400	$1,600	2	147
4	$950	$3,600	5	27
5	$1,550	$5.650	7	183
6	$2,150	$7,600	9	185
7	$2,750	$9,400	11	52
8	$3,350	$11,100	12	186
9	$4,000	$12,850	13	315
10	$4,650	$14,500	15	6
11	$5,300	$16,050	15	333
12	$6,000	$17,600	16	249
13	$6,700	$19,100	17	95
14	$7,400	$20,450	17	255
15	**$8,100**	**$21,750**	**18**	**8**
16	$8,650	$23,050	18	116
17	$9,850	$24,440	18	208
18	$10,400	$25,550	18	227
19	$11,200	$26,750	18	231
20	$12,000	$27,850	18	20

Dividend Options

Dividends are paid only on participating policies. When the policy owner buys a policy from a participating insurance provider, they pay a higher premium. The higher premium is a safety measure if the insurance provider's losses are higher than expected. The insurance provider will return a dividend to the policy owner if the interest earned by the company exceeds the assumptions or if the actual mortality experience improves. Dividends are a return of surplus premiums and are *not taxable* to the policy owner. Insurance providers *cannot guarantee* dividends.

California law requires an insurance company's dividends to be paid as early as the 1st policy anniversary. Dividend payments must occur no later than the end of the 3rd policy year. From then on, dividends are typically paid yearly. Policy owners have the option of receiving their dividends in one of several different ways.

Cash Payments

The insurance provider usually sends the policy owner a check for the dividend amount as it is declared each year.

Reduction of Premiums

The insurance provider uses the dividend to reduce the following year's premium. For instance, if the policy owner typically pays an annual premium of $1,000 and the insurance provider declares a $100 dividend, the policyholder would only pay a $900 premium that year.

Accumulation at Interest

The insurer keeps the dividend in an account that accrues interest. The policy owner is allowed to withdraw the dividends at any time. The interest amount is specified in the policy and compounds annually. Although the dividends are not taxable, *the interest on the dividends is taxable* to the policy owner when credited to the policy, regardless of whether or not the policy owner receives the interest.

Paid-up Additions

Policy owners can use the dividends to buy a single premium policy in addition to the face amount of the permanent policy. No new separate policies are issued. However, each small single premium payment *increases the original policy's death benefit* by the amount the dividend will purchase. In addition, each of these paid-up policies will build cash value and pay dividends. The additional coverage that policy owners can buy with the dividend will depend on the insured's attained age when the dividend is declared.

One-year Term Option

The insurer uses the dividend to buy additional insurance in the form of *one-year term insurance* that increases the overall policy death benefit. The policy owner can use the dividend as a single premium on as much one-year term insurance as it will purchase. They can also buy term insurance equal to the policy's cash value for as long as it will remain in force. When the insured dies during the one-year term, the beneficiary receives both the death proceeds of the original policy and the death benefit of the one-year term insurance.

Settlement Options

Settlement options are the methods insurance companies use to pay a beneficiary the death proceeds upon the insured's death or to pay the endowment benefit if the insured lives to the endowment date. The policy owner can choose a settlement option when completing the policy application and may change that selection during the insured's life. Once the policy owner selects the settlement option, the beneficiary cannot change it. When the policy owner does not choose a settlement option, the beneficiary will be allowed to select one at the time of the insured's death.

Cash Payment (Lump Sum)

Upon the insured's death or at endowment, the contract pays the proceeds in a cash payment, called a *lump sum*, unless the recipient chooses a different mode of settlement. As a general rule, payments of the principal face amount following the insured's death are not taxable as income.

Life Income

The *life-income option*, also referred to as straight life, provides the recipient with an income that the policyholder cannot outlive. Insurers guarantee installment payments for as long as the recipient lives, regardless of the date of death. They base each paid installment on the principal amount and the *recipient's* life expectancy. If the beneficiary lives for a long time, payments can exceed the total principal. However, when the beneficiary dies after they start receiving installments, the policy owner forfeits the balance of the principal to the insurance provider. There is a chance that the beneficiary might not live long enough to receive all the life insurance proceeds. Consequently, insurance companies make options available that provide at least a partial guarantee that they will pay out some or all of the benefits. With each of the guarantees, an insurer reduces the installment's size.

Joint and Survivor – The *life income joint and survivor* option will provide guaranteed income payments for two or more recipients as long as they live. Most contracts specify that the surviving recipient will receive a reduced payment after the first recipient's death.

Typically, insurers write the reduced option as "joint and 1/2 survivor" or "joint and 2/3 survivor." The surviving beneficiary will receive either 1/2 or 2/3 of the death benefit when both beneficiaries are alive. Policy owners who want to protect two beneficiaries, like elderly parents, usually choose this option. Unless a period certain option is also selected, there is no guarantee that the insurer will pay out full life insurance benefits if all beneficiaries die soon after the installment payments begin. This option guarantees, however, a lifetime income for all beneficiaries.

Life Refund – The *life refund income* option comes in either a *cash refund* form or an *installment refund* form. Both options guarantee that the total annuity will be paid to the beneficiary or the annuitant. The difference between the two options is that under the cash refund option, if the annuitant dies before the annuity is depleted, the insurer will pay a lump-sum settlement of the remainder to the beneficiary. Under the installment refund option, the beneficiary will receive the remaining funds in the form of continued annuity payments.

Life with Period Certain – Under the *life income with period certain option*, the recipient has a lifetime income and a guaranteed installment period. Insurers guarantee these payments for the recipient's lifetime, but a specified period is also guaranteed. For example, a life income with a ten-year certain option will provide the recipient with an income for as long as they live. When the recipient dies shortly after beginning to receive payments, insurers will continue the installments to a beneficiary for the remainder of the ten years. As previously stated, the installments for the life income with period certain option will be smaller than the life income only option.

Interest-Only

Under the *interest-only option*, the insurer retains the policy proceeds. It pays interest on the proceeds to the recipient (beneficiary) monthly, quarterly, semiannually, or annually. The insurance provider typically guarantees a particular interest rate and pays interest over and above the guaranteed rate. An interest-only option is temporary because the insurance company retains the proceeds until they are paid out in a lump sum or under another settlement option. When the beneficiary can choose a settlement option, the interest option is sometimes used as a temporary option if the beneficiary requires some time to decide which settlement option to select. For example, the policy owner can specify that interest-only will be paid annually to the surviving spouse. The policy owner's children receive the principal at the surviving spouse's death or when they reach a particular age.

Fixed-Period Installments

With the *fixed-period installments option*, also referred to as *period certain*, a policy owner chooses a specified period of years. The insurer pays equal installments to the recipient. These payments will continue for the specified period even if the recipient dies before the end of that period. If the recipient dies, the payments will continue to a beneficiary. The insurer will determine the size of each installment payment based on the principal amount, guaranteed interest, and the length of the period selected. The longer the period chosen, the smaller each installment payment will be. This option does not ensure income for the beneficiary's lifetime; however, it guarantees the entire principal gets distributed.

Fixed-Amount Installments

Under the *fixed-amount installments option*, a specified, fixed dollar amount is paid in installments until the proceeds (principal and interest) are exhausted. When the beneficiary dies before the proceeds are distributed, a contingent beneficiary will continue receiving the installments until all proceeds are exhausted. With this option, the size of each installment payment will determine how long the beneficiary will receive benefits. The larger the installment payment, the shorter the income period will be. Like the fixed-period option, this option does not guarantee the beneficiary will receive payments for their lifetime. However, it does ensure that the insurance provider pays all proceeds.

OPTION TYPE	AVAILABLE OPTIONS
Nonforfeiture Options	• Reduced Paid-up • Extended Term (automatic) • Cash
Dividend Options	• Cash • Reduction of Premium • Accumulation at Interest • Paid-up Additions (automatic) • Paid-up Insurance • One-year Term
Riders Affecting Death Benefits	• Cash (automatic) • Life Income • Interest-Only • Fixed Period • Fixed Amount

Chapter Review

This chapter taught about life insurance policy provisions and options. Remember that provisions stipulate the rights and obligations under the contract, and options specify ways to distribute a policy's proceeds. Let's review the major points of the chapter:

POLICY PROVISIONS	
Standard Provisions	• *Consideration* – the parties to a contract exchange something of value • *Entire contract* – policy (with amendments and riders) and copy of the application • *Grace period* – the period after the premium is due during which the policy will not lapse • *Incontestability* – the insurance provider cannot contest misstatements on the application after a specified period • *Insuring clause* – the basic agreement between the insurance company and the policy owner • *Misstatement of age or gender* – the death benefit is adjusted according to the correct age and gender at policy issue • *Payment of premiums* – the policy owner pays premiums in advance • *Reinstatement* – policy owners can restore a policy within a specified period with proof of insurability

Beneficiaries	• *Designations* – can be a person (including minors), class of individuals, estates
	• *Succession* – the levels of priority or choice; each level in the succession is eligible only if the beneficiary in the level above has died:
	  - *Primary* – has first claim to the policy benefits
	  - *Contingent* (secondary, tertiary) – next claim after the primary
	• *Policy owner's right to change a beneficiary:*
	  - *Revocable* – the policy owner can change beneficiaries at any time
	  - *Irrevocable* – the policy owner can only change beneficiaries with the consent of the beneficiary
	• *Common disaster clause* – protects the rights of contingent beneficiaries; if the primary beneficiary and the insured died at approximately the same time, it is assumed that the primary beneficiary was the first to die

Other Provisions	• *Assignment* – absolute or collateral • *Exclusions* – noncommercial aviation, hazardous occupation, war or military service, suicide within a specified time period • *Free look* – applicants can return the policy for a refund of the premium within a specified period • *Ownership* – the policy owner has ownership rights
Policy Loans, Withdrawals and Partial Surrenders	• *Cash loans* – a policy's cash value with unpaid loans and interest deducted • *Automatic premium loans* – prevent an unintentional lapse in the policy due to nonpayment of premium
POLICY OPTIONS	
Dividend	• *Cash* – insurance companies send a check to the insured • *Reduction of premium* – dividends are applied to reduce the following year's premium payment • *Accumulation at interest* – insurance companies keep the dividend in an account where interest accumulates • *Paid-up addition* – dividends are used to increase the policy face amount • *Paid-up insurance* – dividends are used to pay up a policy early • *One-year term* – dividends are used to purchase additional insurance

POLICY OPTIONS *(Continued)*	
Nonforfeiture	• *Reduced paid-up insurance* – uses a policy's cash value as a single premium to purchase a permanent policy with a reduced face amount • *Extended term* – automatic option; uses a policy's cash value to convert to term insurance • *Cash surrender value* – no more insurance after that
Settlement	• *Cash* – a lump-sum payment that is usually not taxable • *Life income* – provides an income the beneficiary cannot outlive; if the beneficiary dies too soon, there is no guarantee that the entire principal will be paid out; available as either single life or as joint and survivor • *Interest-only* – the insurance provider retains the principal and only pays out interest • *Fixed period* – payments are received for a specified time period until all the proceeds are paid out • *Fixed amount* – payments are received in specified amounts until all the proceeds are paid out

CHAPTER 7:
Life Policy Riders

This chapter looks at different riders available in life insurance policies issued in this state. You will learn about riders that offer benefits in case of the insured's disability, such as waiver of premium, disability income, living needs, and accidental death and dismemberment. You will also learn about riders that offer protection from inflation or additional coverage based on the insured's needs. Finally, you will review riders available in variable annuities.

- Waiver of Premium and Waiver of Monthly Deduction
- Disability Income
- Accidental Death and Dismemberment
- Cost of Living
- Living Need
- No-Lapse Guaranteed Rider
- Guaranteed Insurability
- Long-Term Care
- Annuity Riders (Guaranteed Minimum Income and Withdrawal)

Waiver of Premium and Waiver of Monthly Deductions

The *waiver of premium* rider waives the policy premium if the insured becomes disabled. Coverage will remain in force until the insured can return to work. If the insured cannot return to work, the premiums will continue to be waived by the insurer. Most insurance providers impose a 6-month waiting period from the moment of disability until they waive the first premium. When the insured is still disabled after this waiting period, the insurance provider will refund the premium paid by the policy owner from the start of the disability. This rider typically expires when the policy owner reaches the age of 65.

The *waiver of monthly deductions* rider, also known as the waiver of cost of insurance rider, will pay all monthly deductions while the insured is disabled, following a 6-month waiting period. This rider only pays monthly deductions, not the total premium amount necessary to accumulate cash value. The period this rider will pay monthly deductions varies based on the age at which the insured becomes disabled. Insurers typically include this rider in Universal Life and Variable Universal Life policies.

Disability Income

With this rider, in the event of disability, the insurance provider will waive the policy premiums and pay a monthly income to the insured. The amount paid is usually based on a percentage of the policy's face amount to which it is attached.

Accidental Death and Dismemberment

The *accidental death* rider pays some multiple of the face amount if death is caused by an accident as defined by the policy. Generally, death must occur within 90 days of such an accident. The benefit is typically two times (*double indemnity*) the face amount. At the same time, some policies will pay triple the face amount (*triple indemnity*) for accidental death.

Each policy stipulates what will be considered accidental death. Accidental death does not include death caused by any disability or health problem. In addition, deaths resulting from war, self-inflicted injuries, or hazardous hobbies or avocations are generally not covered. They would be insured under the base policy unless expressly excluded.

This rider often expires when the insured reaches the age of 65. No additional cash value can accumulate because of this rider. The accidental death benefits apply only to the face amount of the base policy and not to any extra benefits that policy owners can purchase from the policy's dividends.

The *accidental death and dismemberment rider (AD&D)* pays the face amount for accidental death. It pays a percentage of that amount, called a capital sum, for accidental dismemberment. The rider's dismemberment portion will typically determine the benefit amount according to the injury's severity. Insurance providers will generally pay the total amount of the principal in the event of the loss of two hands, two arms, two legs, or the loss of vision in both eyes. A capital sum is generally limited to half of the face amount. It is payable for losing one hand, arm, leg, or eye. The dismemberment can be defined differently by insurers, from the loss of use to the actual severance of the limb.

Cost of Living

The *cost of living* rider contends with the inflation factor by automatically increasing the amount of insurance without requiring evidence of insurability from the insured. The face value of the policy can be increased by a cost of living factor tied to an inflation index like the Consumer Price Index (CPI).

Living Needs

The *Accelerated Benefits* or *Living Needs Rider* allows for the payment of a part of the policy's death benefit if the insured is diagnosed with a terminal condition that will result in death within two years. This rider's purpose is to provide the insured with the necessary funds to pay for all essential medical and nursing home expenses incurred by the terminal illness. Many insurers do not charge an additional premium for this rider since it is simply an advance payment of the death benefit. The beneficiary receives the remainder of the policy's proceeds at the insured's death.

In California, the accelerated death benefit is fixed at the time the insurance provider approves the request for the accelerated death benefit. The insured can take the accelerated death benefits *in a lump sum* upon a qualifying event or receive the benefit *in periodic payments* for a specified period of time only.

No-Lapse Guarantee

As the name implies, the *no-lapse guarantee* rider prevents a policy from lapsing even if the cash surrender value is inadequate to pay the policy's monthly charges. It is generally available in *universal life* policies. While it limits the policy owner's flexibility in premium payments, it removes the risk of the policy lapsing.

Guaranteed Insurability

The *guaranteed insurability* rider lets the policy owner purchase additional coverage at specified dates in the future. These purchases are typically allowed every three years between the age of 25 to 40. They are also allowed following events like marriage or the birth of a child, for an additional premium, without evidence of insurability. When this option is exercised, the insured purchases the extra coverage at their attained age. This rider usually expires when the insured reaches the age of 40.

The guaranteed insurability rider is not adjusted or overcome by the existence of other riders.

Example 7.1 – Bobby's life insurance policy includes the waiver of premium and guaranteed insurability riders. Three years after the policy was issued, Bobby was totally and permanently disabled. His insurer waived the life insurance premium payments. However, at the specified times or events stipulated in the policy, Bobby can purchase additional insurance with the premiums on those increases also waived.

Long-Term Care

Coverage for Long-Term Care (LTC), often a separate standalone policy, can also be marketed as a rider to a life insurance policy. These riders allow for the payment of part of the death benefit, also called accelerated benefits, to cover the insured's health care expenses incurred in a nursing or convalescent home. Like the living needs rider, payment of LTC benefits will reduce the amount payable to the beneficiary upon the insured's death.

Benefits from an LTC policy or rider are often activated by an impairment of activities of daily living (ADLs) regardless of the cause. ADLs include eating, bathing, dressing, transferring positions (also called mobility), toileting, and continence. Once the insured passes the elimination period, benefits are paid from the policy.

State Requirements for Insurers and Agents

The law requires that every insurer of long-term care in California establishes marketing procedures to avoid an unfair comparison of policies by the agents. It also prevents the sale of excessive insurance. The insurance companies must also submit a list of all agents authorized to transact long-term care insurance to the Commissioner. These lists have to be updated at least semiannually.

The insurance provider must ensure that its licensees have completed the initial training requirements before being authorized to transact individual long-term care insurance. The required training must cover the topic related to long-term care insurance and services, including, but not limited to, available long-term care services and facilities, state regulations and requirements, changes or improvements in long-term care insurance, and alternatives to purchasing private long-term care insurance.

Each agent authorized to solicit long-term care insurance must satisfy the training and continuing education requirements. The training requirements are as follows:

- Eight hours of LTC training annually for the first four years after the original license is issued; and
- Eight hours of training during each licensing period after that.

The required LTC training is *included* in the hours that are required for overall continuing education, not added to them. Long-term care training is *not required* when an agent is transacting accelerated death benefit provisions or riders that do not require services.

Annuity Riders – Guaranteed Minimum Income and Withdrawal

Annuity riders are features that let annuity investors obtain additional benefits not provided with the original annuity product. Several common riders available for variable annuities include the following:

- **Guaranteed Lifetime Withdrawal Benefit** – Lets the annuity owner withdraw from the annuity over their lifetime, which will at least equal the amount paid for the annuity. This rider protects annuity owners against losing their investments if the value of the annuity drops.
- **Guaranteed Minimum Income Benefit** – Lets investors receive at least a set income annually, regardless of how the underlying investments perform. This rider provides the same income guarantee to the annuity owner as a fixed annuity.

Chapter Review

This chapter taught about life insurance riders. Remember that riders modify provisions. Let's review the major points of the chapter:

LIFE POLICY RIDERS	
Disability	• *Waiver of premium* – waives the premium if the insured becomes totally disabled; 6-month waiting period before benefits start • *Waiver of monthly deductions* – waives the insurance cost in the event of the insured's disability • *Payor benefit* – performs like a waiver of premium rider; used for juvenile policies • *Disability income* – in the event of disability, the insurance provider will waive the policy premiums and pay monthly income to the insured
Additional Riders	• *Accidental death* – pays some multiple of the face amount if death is caused by an accident as defined by the policy • *Accidental death and dismemberment (AD&D)* – pays the face amount for accidental death; it pays a percentage of that amount (capital sum) • *Cost of living* – contends without the inflation factor by automatically increasing the amount of insurance with evidence of insurability • *No-lapse guaranteed* – prevents a policy from lapsing even if the cash surrender value is inadequate to pay the policy's monthly charges
Accelerated Benefits/Living Needs	• Early payment if the insured is diagnosed with a specified catastrophic illness • The insured receives a portion of the death proceeds • Death benefits are reduced by the amount paid plus the insurance provider's lost earnings
Riders that Affect the Death Benefit	• *Guaranteed insurability* – allows for the purchase of additional insurance at specified times at the attained age, without evidence of insurability • *Long-term care* – allows for the payment of part of the death benefit (accelerated benefits) to cover the insured's health care expenses incurred in a nursing or convalescent home

Long-Term Care	• Each agent authorized to solicit long-term care insurance must satisfy the training and continuing education requirement
	   o Eight hours of LTC training annually for the first four years after the original license is issued
	   o Eight hours of training during each licensing period after that
	• Training is not required when an agent is transacting accelerated death benefit provisions or riders that do not require services.

Annuity Riders	• *Guaranteed lifetime withdrawal benefit* – lets the annuity owner withdraw from the annuity over their lifetime • *Guaranteed minimum income benefit* – lets investors receive at least a set income annually, regardless of how the underlying investments perform

CHAPTER 8:
Annuities

This chapter includes a discussion about annuities. It is important for you to understand what annuities are and how they differ from life insurance. By the end of this chapter, you will be able to describe the different roles of the owner, annuitant, and beneficiary, discuss different classifications of annuities like immediate vs. deferred and fixed vs. variable, and identify proper uses of different types of annuities.

- Annuity Principles and Concepts
- Types of Annuities
- Uses of Annuities
- Senior Consumers

Annuity Principles and Concepts

Annuities are contracts that deliver income for a specified number of years or life. An annuity protects an individual against outliving their money. An annuity is not a life insurance product but rather a vehicle for accumulating money and *liquidating an estate*. Life insurance companies will often market annuities, and licensed life insurance agents are authorized to sell certain types of annuities.

Upon the annuitant's death, annuities do not pay a face amount. They do just the opposite. In most cases, the annuity payments stop upon the annuitant's death. Although annuities use mortality tables, these tables reflect a longer life expectancy than the mortality tables used for life insurance. Mortality tables indicate the number of individuals within a specified group, including males, females, smokers, and nonsmokers, starting at a certain age, who expect to be alive at a succeeding age.

The Parties

Owner – The individual who purchases the annuity contract is not necessarily the person who receives the benefits. *The annuity owner has all rights*, such as surrendering the annuity and naming the beneficiary. The annuity owner can be a corporation, trust, or legal entity.

Annuitant – The annuitant is the individual who receives payments or benefits from the annuity. Insurance providers use the annuitant's life expectancy when writing the annuity. The contract owner and the annuitant do not need to be the same person but are most of the time. A corporation, trust, or other legal entity can own an annuity, but *the annuitant must be a natural person*.

Beneficiary – The beneficiary is the individual who receives the annuity's assets (either the cash value or the amount paid into the annuity, whichever is greater) when the annuitant dies during the accumulation period. Beneficiaries also receive the balance of annuity benefits.

Accumulation Period vs. Annuitization Period

The *accumulation period* is also called the *pay-in period*. This period is when the annuity owner makes premium payments into an annuity. It is also when the premium payments earn interest on a tax-deferred basis.

The *annuity period* is also called the *annuitization period, liquidation period*, or *pay-out period*. It is when the total amount accumulated during the accumulation period converts into a stream of annuity income payments to the annuitant. The annuity period can last for the annuitant's lifetime or a specific time. The *annuitization date* starts when the annuity benefit payouts begin (trigger for benefits).

The amount of annuity income depends upon the following:

- The amount of cash value accumulated or premium paid;
- The frequency of premium payments;
- The interest rate; and
- The gender and age of the annuitant.

An annuitant with a longer life expectancy will receive smaller income installments. For instance, all other factors are equal. A 65-year-old male will have higher annuity income payments than a 45-year-old male because he is younger than a 65-year-old female due to the statistical fact that women have a longer life expectancy.

When an annuitant dies during the accumulation period, the insurance provider must return either the *cash value* or the *total paid premiums* to the beneficiary, whichever is greater. The insurer will pay the benefit to the annuitant's estate if a beneficiary is not designated.

Types of Annuities

Insurers classify annuities according to how they invest premiums, how annuity owners make premium payments, and when (and how) annuitants receive benefit payouts.

Premium Payment Options

Insurers classify annuities based on how they can be funded (paid for). Two options are a *single payment* (lump sum) or *periodic payments*. With periodic payments, the annuity owner pays premiums in installments over time. Periodic payment annuities can be either *level premium*, in which the annuitant/owner pays a fixed installment, or *flexible premium*. With a flexible premium, the frequency and amount of each installment will vary.

Immediate vs. Deferred Annuities

Insurers classify annuities according to when the annuity's income payments start. An *immediate annuity* is purchased with one lump-sum payment and provides a stream of income payments that begin *within one year* from the purchase date. Usually, an immediate annuity will make the first payment as early as one month from the date of purchase. This type of annuity is also known as a Single Premium Immediate Annuity (SPIA).

Income payments begin sometime *after one year* from the purchase date in a *deferred annuity*. Annuity owners fund deferred annuities through periodic payments such as Flexible Premium Deferred Annuities (FPDAs) or a single lump-sum payment, like Single Premium Deferred Annuities (SPDAs). Periodic payments can vary from year to year. More flexibility for premium payments is allowed when an annuity's deferral is longer.

Nonforfeiture – The nonforfeiture law specifies that a deferred annuity must have a guaranteed surrender value available if the annuity owner decides to surrender it before annuitization (e.g., 100% of the premium paid, less any prior withdrawals and surrender charges). However, a 10% penalty will be applied for early withdrawals before age 59 ½.

Surrender Charges – The purpose of the surrender charge is to help compensate the insurer for a loss of the investment value because of an early surrender of a deferred annuity.

A surrender charge is levied against the cash value and is usually a percentage that decreases over time. A common surrender charge could be 7% the first year, 6% the second year, and 5%, 4%, 3%, 2%, 1%, and 0% thereafter. Consequently, if the annuity is surrendered in the 8th year or later, there would be no further surrender charge. At the surrender, the owner receives the premium plus interest (the value of the annuity) minus the surrender charge.

Example 8.1 – Assume that the annuity owner paid $700 in premium, which accumulated $35 of interest, and a surrender charge is $70. If the annuity is surrendered early, what will the annuity value be at surrender? The answer is $665, which is calculated below.

($700 Premium + $35 Interest) - $70 Surrender Charge = $665 Value of the Annuity

Annuity Investment Options

Based on how insurers invest the premium payments, annuities can be fixed or variable.

Fixed Annuities – A *fixed annuity* offers the following features:

- A guaranteed minimum interest rate to be credited to the purchase payment(s);
- Annuity (income) payments that do not vary from one payment to the next;
- The insurer guarantees the length of the period of payments and the specified dollar amount for each payment as determined by the settlement option chosen by the annuitant.

With a fixed annuity, the annuitant knows the exact amount of every payment they receive from the annuity during the annuitization period. Fixed annuities have a *level benefit payment amount*. A disadvantage to fixed annuities is that inflation could erode their purchasing power over time.

General Account Assets – Fixed annuity premiums are deposited into the life insurance provider's *general account*. The general account consists of conservative investments like bonds. These investments are secure enough to allow the insurer to guarantee a specified rate of interest, as well as assure the future income payments that the annuity will provide.

Interest Rate Guarantees (Minimum vs. Current) – The insurance company bears the investment risk in fixed annuities. Future interest rates paid by an insurance provider are based upon the performance of the insurer's general account. However, the rate may not drop below a policy's *guaranteed minimum*, usually 3%. Should interest rates fall below this guaranteed rate, the insurance provider is obligated to pay the guaranteed rate amount.

During the accumulation phase, the insurer will invest the principal, or accumulation, and give the annuitant a guaranteed interest rate. This rate is based on a minimum rate stipulated in the annuity, or the current interest rate, whichever is higher. The minimum rate is the lowest rate the principal can earn according to the contract.

Equity-Indexed Annuities – *Indexed (or equity-indexed) annuities* are fixed annuities that invest on a fairly aggressive basis to aim for achieving higher returns. They have a guaranteed minimum interest rate, like a fixed annuity. The current interest rate that is credited corresponds to a familiar index such as the Standard and Poor's (S&P) 500.

Usually, the insurance providers reserve the initial returns for investment purposes but pay the excess to the annuitant. For instance, the company might keep the first 4% earned and credit any accumulation above 4% to the annuitant's account. Therefore, if the interest earned is 11%, the company keeps 4% and credits the client's account with 7%.

Equity-indexed annuities are less risky than a mutual fund or variable annuity. However, they expect to earn a higher interest rate than a fixed annuity.

Variable Annuities – A *variable annuity* operates as a hedge against inflation. It is variable from the standpoint that the annuitant could receive different return rates on the funds paid into the annuity. The three main characteristics of variable annuities are listed below:

- **Underlying Investment** – Insurance providers invest the annuitant's payments into their variable annuity in the insurer's separate account, not their general account. The separate account is not part of the insurer's investment portfolio. It is not subject to the restrictions on the insurer's general account.
- **Interest Rate** – The issuing insurance company does not guarantee a minimum interest rate.

- **License Requirements** – A variable annuity is considered a *security*. State regulators and the Securities Exchange Commission (SEC) regulate variable annuities. An agent selling variable annuities must have a securities license and a life insurance license. Companies or agents that sell variable annuities must also register with FINRA.

Like buying shares in a Mutual Fund, variable premiums purchase *accumulation units* in the fund. Accumulation units represent an ownership interest in the insurer's separate account. During the annuity period, the accumulation units convert to *annuity units*. The number of annuity units received remains level. However, the unit values will fluctuate until the insurer pays the annuitant.

The following table compares the features of fixed and variables annuities:

FEATURES	FIXED ANNUITY	VARIABLE ANNUITY
Interest Rate	Guaranteed by insurer	No guarantee
Underlying Investment	General account (safe, conservative)	Separate account (equities)
License Needed	Life insurance	Life insurance PLUS securities
Expenses	Guaranteed	Guaranteed
Income Payment	Guaranteed	No guarantee

Market Value Adjusted Annuities – A *market value* or *market value adjusted* annuity (MVA), also called a *modified guaranteed* annuity (MGA). A single-premium deferred annuity lets the owner secure a guaranteed interest rate over a specified maturity period, typically between three to ten years. In an MVA, penalties for an early surrender depend upon current interest rates at the time of surrender.

For example, assume that a client purchased a 10-year 6% fixed annuity tied to the Bond Fund Index Interest Rate (Moody's). If the client withdraws their money in 5 years and the current interest rate at that point is 6%, there is no adjustment. If the current interest rate at the time of surrender is 8%, a penalty will be assessed. If the interest rate at surrender is 4%, the insurer can pay a bonus. The market value adjustment is typically a percentage of the difference between the contracted interest rate in the annuity and the current rate at surrender. The insurer requires the annuitant to share the market risk of changing interest rates if the annuity is surrendered prematurely.

Annuity Benefit Payment Options

Annuity payment options stipulate how annuity funds are paid out. They are very similar to settlement options used in life insurance that determine how the policy proceeds are allocated to the beneficiaries.

Life Contingency Options – The life annuity will pay a specific amount for the rest of the annuitant's life. *Pure life*, also called *life-only* or *straight life*, ends payment at the annuitant's death, no matter how soon in the annuitization period. This option *offers the highest monthly benefits* for annuitants. With this option, while the annuity payments are guaranteed for the annuitant's lifetime, there is no guarantee all the proceeds will be fully paid.

Under the *life with guaranteed minimum* payment option, if the annuitant dies before the principal amount has been paid out, the balance of the principal amount will be refunded to the beneficiary. This option is also called *refund life*. It ensures that the insurance provider will pay out the entire principal amount. There are two types of refund life annuities:

- **Cash refund** – When an annuitant dies, the beneficiary will receive a lump-sum refund of the principal minus benefit payments already made to the annuitant. This option does not guarantee interest.
- **Installment refund** – When an annuitant dies, the beneficiary receives guaranteed installments until the entire principal amount has been paid.

Another life contingency payout option is *life with period certain*. Under this option, the annuity payments are guaranteed for the *annuitant's lifetime* and a specified period for the beneficiary. For example, a life income with a 20-year period certain option would provide the annuitant with an income while they are living (for the entire life). Suppose the annuitant dies soon after payments begin. In that case, the insurer will make the payments to a beneficiary for the remainder of the period (20 years).

Single Life vs. Multiple Life – *Single* life annuities only cover *one life*, and annuity payments are made regarding one life only. Contributions are made with either a single premium or on a periodic premium basis, with subsequent values accumulating until the contract is annuitized.

Multiple life annuities cover *two or more lives*. Joint life and joint and survivor are the most common multiple life annuities.

Joint Life – *Joint life* is a payout arrangement where two or more annuitants receive payments until the first death among the annuitants, and then payments end.

Joint and Survivor – The *joint and survivor* payment option is a modification of the life income option. It guarantees an income for two recipients that neither can outlive. Although the surviving recipient(s) can receive payments in the same amount as the first recipient to die, most contracts specify that the surviving recipients will receive a reduced payment. Generally, this option is written as "joint and 1/2 survivor" or "joint and 2/3 survivor," in which the surviving beneficiary receives 1/2 or 2/3 of the amount received when both beneficiaries were living. A couple in retirement commonly chooses this option. As with the life income option, there is no guarantee that all the proceeds will be paid out if both beneficiaries die soon after the installment payments begin.

Annuities Certain – Unlike life contingency benefit options, *annuities certain* are short-term annuities. They limit the annuity amounts paid to a certain fixed period or until a certain fixed amount is liquidated.

Fixed Period – With *fixed period* installments, the annuitant picks the period for the benefits, and the insurance provider determines how much each payment will be, based on the value of the account and future earnings projections. This option only pays for a specified amount of time, whether or not the annuitant is alive.

Fixed Amount – Under *fixed amount* installments, the annuitant chooses how much each payment will be. The insurance provider determines how long the benefits will be paid by analyzing the account's value and future earnings. This option pays a specific amount until funds are depleted, whether or not the annuitant is living.

Uses of Annuities

Personal Uses

Lump-sum Settlements – Annuities can be an ideal financial vehicle for anyone who comes into a large lump sum of money, such as inheritance, award of damages from a lawsuit, lottery, proceeds from a sale of a business, or a lump-sum distribution from a qualified pension plan. In this case, an individual can purchase a single premium immediate annuity, which will convert the lump sum into a series of periodic payments, providing income for the annuitant.

Retirement Income – Annuities are a popular means to provide retirement income. They are often utilized to fund *qualified retirement plans*, which means they meet the IRS guidelines to receive favorable tax treatment.

Qualified vs. Nonqualified – A *qualified* retirement plan adheres to federal tax laws requirements. It is approved by the Internal Revenue Service (IRS), which recognizes the employer's contributions to the plan as tax-deductible expenses. When a plan is qualified, it is given favorable tax treatment. Employer contributions are tax-deductible expenses when made. The employee is not taxed on the employer's contribution until the benefits are received. Also, the increase during the accumulation period is not subject to taxation until benefits are received. Another requirement for qualified plans is that they cannot discriminate in contributions, coverage, or benefits in favor of highly compensated shareholders, company officers, or employees.

A *nonqualified* retirement plan is one in which the contributions are not exempt from taxation. However, an increase in the funds during the accumulation period is not taxed until it is received.

Guaranteed Minimum Withdrawal Benefit – Retirement annuities can offer a *Guaranteed Minimum Withdrawal Benefit (GMWB)* option to the annuitant. With this option, the annuitant can withdraw a maximum percentage of their investment annually until the initial investment has been recovered. This option shields the annuitant against investment losses.

Qualified retirement annuities, like individual retirement accounts (IRAs), can be for an individual. They can also be for a group, like a tax-sheltered annuity (TSA) or profit-sharing pension plans.

Individual Retirement Annuity – Anyone with earned income can have an *IRA (Individual Retirement Annuity or Account)*. Individuals can contribute up to a specified dollar limit each year, or 100% of their salary, if it is less than the maximum allowable amount. A married couple could contribute a specified amount double the individual amount, even if only one spouse had earned income. Still, each must maintain a separate account not to exceed the individual limit. For traditional IRAs, the excess contribution penalty is 6% until withdrawn.

Earned income means wages, salary, and commissions but does not include income from trust funds, investments, unemployment benefits, etc.

Typically, a person's contributions to a traditional IRA are tax-deductible for the year of the contribution. Any eligible individual who does not participate in a qualified retirement plan can take a full deduction from taxable income up to the maximum limit. When they participate in another qualified retirement plan, there are income limitation tests to determine how much of one's IRA contribution is tax-deductible. Individuals not covered by an employer-sponsored plan can deduct the total amount of their IRA contributions regardless of their income level.

Irrespective of the IRA contribution's deductible status, IRA assets grow tax-deferred.

Tax-sheltered Annuity – 403(b) – A 403(b) plan or a tax-sheltered annuity (TSA) is a qualified plan available to employees of specific *nonprofit organizations* under Section 501(c)(3) of the Internal Revenue Code. It is also available to those who are employed by public school systems.

Contributions can be made by the employer or the employee through a salary reduction and are excluded from the employee's current income. As with any other qualified plan, 403(b) limits employee contributions to a maximum amount that changes annually, adjusted for inflation. The same catch-up provisions also apply.

Education Funds – In addition to providing income for estate liquidation and retirement, annuities can be used to accumulate funds for college education. An annuity can provide savings on a tax-deferred basis for the annuitant's education expenses.

Long-Term Care Needs – Under the Pension Protection Act of 2006, annuitants can transfer money from an annuity to cover long-term care insurance premiums tax-free. In the past, distributions from nonqualified annuities were taxed. However, now, distributions can be used to cover long-term care premiums and, in many cases, eliminate the taxes on the annuity gains. Consequently, many insurance providers now offer a hybrid annuity with a long-term care feature. These policies provide for long-term care, income, or both.

Business Uses

Annuities can be used in business as investment vehicles. Businesses commonly use them to fund employee retirement plans set up by the employer or jointly with a union or other employers. Employers can set up the plan for employees of a particular business, or it can be a multi-employer plan, serving the employees from several related or unrelated firms. These plans will supplement Social Security retirement benefits upon the employee's retirement. The employer benefits from the existence of the plan through higher employee retention.

Suitability

An annuity's primary use is to provide retirement income; however, an annuity can be used for any cash accumulation or liquidating an estate. Because of the various uses of annuities, producers should continually evaluate how well a recommended product will meet the applicant's needs and resources to determine a product's *suitability* (Cal. Ins. Code Sections 10509.913(i)(1- 14)).

An agent must ensure that annuity transactions meet the consumers' needs and financial objectives. To ensure suitability, producers must make a reasonable effort to obtain relevant information from the consumer and assess the following factors:

- Age;
- Marital status;
- Occupation and occupational status;
- Insurance needs and objectives;
- Number and types of dependents;
- Annual income and sources of income;
- Whether or not the consumer has long-term care (LTC) insurance;
- Existing assets and insurance products, including investment and life insurance holdings;
- Costs to the consumer and the consumer's ability to pay for the proposed transaction;
- Source of funds to pay premiums;
- Investment savings;
- Liquid net worth;
- Financial and investment experience;
- Tax status and need for tax advantages;
- Need for the preservation of principal;
- Intended use of the annuity; and
- Product/financial time horizon.

Insurance providers must establish standards and procedures and a system to supervise consumer recommendations resulting in transactions involving annuity products. In the case of a replacement or exchange of an annuity, the exchange or replacement must be suitable. The consumer must be informed of the annuity's various features, such as the potential surrender period and surrender charges, mortality and expense fees, tax penalties, charges for riders, and market risks.

Suability requirements do not apply to the following transactions:

- Direct response solicitations where there are no recommendations based on information collected from the consumer;
- Employee pensions or welfare benefit plans covered by the Employee Retirement Income Security Act (ERISA);
- Profit-sharing plans (401(k)) or tax-sheltered annuities (403(b));
- Government or church plans;
- Employer-sponsored nonqualified deferred compensation plans;
- Settlements of liabilities associated with personal injury litigation or any dispute or claim resolution process; and
- Prepaid funeral contracts.

Senior Consumers

All insurers, brokers, and agents soliciting insurance to insureds aged 65 or older owe those individuals *honesty, good faith, and fair dealing* (Cal. Ins. Code Sections 785 through 789.10).

Any advertisement that generates leads based on a response directed towards individuals aged 65 years or older must prominently disclose that a producer or agent can contact the applicant.

Insurers or agents cannot use real or fictitious names that are misleading or deceptive concerning the character, status, or representative capacity of the insurer or agent or the true purpose of the advertisement. The use of misleading advertising materials or terminology is also prohibited.

Suppose a life agent offers to sell any annuity product to a senior consumer. In that case, the agent must advise the senior in writing that the liquidation or sale of any stock, bond, certificate of deposit, individual retirement account, annuity, mutual fund, or another asset to fund the purchase of this product can have tax consequences, early withdrawal penalties, or other costs or penalties. The agent must also inform the senior that they might want to consult independent financial or legal advice before the transaction.

Individuals who violate these regulations are subject to the following administrative penalties:

- $1,000 for the first violation;
- $5,000 - $50,000 for the second or subsequent violations.

When the Commissioner concludes that the licensee's actions could cause significant harm to seniors, the Commissioner can suspend the agent's license. Insurance providers who violate these rules are liable for an administrative penalty of $10,000 for the first violation and $30,000 - $300,000 for each subsequent offense.

Disclosures

All individual annuities issued to seniors in California must have printed a notice on the cover page stating that the owner can return the annuity to the insurer or agent if dissatisfied. The period for the return has to be clearly stated and must be at least *30 days*.

During the 30 days, the premium for a variable annuity can be invested only in money-market funds and fixed-income investments unless the owner specifically directs that the premium is to be invested in the mutual funds within the annuity.

Suppose the annuitant waives the right to the fixed-income requirement by specifying that the funds be invested immediately and then cancels the annuity anyway. In that situation, the annuitant receives the account value on the date the annuity is returned to the insurer. This amount is not the total value initially guaranteed by the free look. The insurance provider must refund the account value within 30 days from the date the insurance company is notified that the owner has canceled the policy.

Chapter Review

This chapter discussed the various annuity types and various personal and business uses of annuities. Let's review the major points of the chapter:

ANNUITIES	

Types of Annuities	• *Fixed annuities:*
	  - Guaranteed
	  - Fixed payments
	  - Premiums are held in a general account
	• *Variable annuities*
	  - Payment is not guaranteed
	  - Premiums are held in a separate account
	  - Invested in stocks and bonds
	• *Indexed annuities:*
	  - Interest rates are tied to an index
	  - Earn a higher rate than fixed annuities
	  - Are not as risky as mutual funds or variable annuities

Phases	• *Accumulation (pay-in)* – payments made into the annuity • *Annuitization (pay-out)* – payments made to the annuitant from the annuity
Parties	• *Annuitant* – insured (must be a person); policy issued on the annuitant's life • *Beneficiary* – will receive any amount contributed to the annuity (plus any gain) if the annuitant dies during the accumulation period • *Owner* – has all rights to the policy (usually annuitant); can be a corporation or trust
Premium Payments	• *Single premium* – a single lump-sum payment; the principal is immediately created in both immediate and deferred annuities • *Periodic (Flexible) premium* – multiple payments; the principal is created over time (used for deferred annuities only)

Income Payments	• *Immediate:*
	  - Purchased with a single premium
	  - Income payments begin within 12 months from the purchase date
	• *Deferred:*
	  - Purchased with either a lump sum or periodic premium payments
	  - Benefits start sometime after one year from the date of purchase
	  - It is often used to accumulate funds for retirement

Interest Rate	• *Guaranteed:*
	  - The insurer must pay this minimum percentage, usually around 3%
	• *Current:*
	  - Exceeds the guaranteed rate
	  - Paid to the annuitant when an insurer's investment is better than expected

Payment Options	• *Life Only:*
	  - An insured cannot outlive their income
	  - Any funds not paid out are retained by the insurer at the insured's death
	  - Pays the highest monthly amount
	• *Refund Life Annuity:*
	  - Guaranteed lifetime income
	  - If an annuitant dies, the balance is "refunded" to the beneficiary
	  - The installment option pays the beneficiary until the purchase amount is paid out
	• - The cash refund pays the balance of an original annuity's purchase amount minus payments made to the annuitant
	• *Life with Period Certain:*
	  - Specific monthly payments for life and a specific period
	  - If an annuitant dies before the payment period is up, the payment goes to the beneficiary
	• *Joint Life:*
	  - Two or more annuitants receive payments until the first death, then payments end
	• *Joint and Survivor:*
	  - Income for two or more individuals that cannot be outlived
	  - Often used with period certain
	  - When one annuitant dies, the other receives either 1/2 or 2/3 of the original payment amount
	• *Lump-sum:*
	  - Paid at annuitization; all accumulated interest is taxable
	  - An additional 10% penalty is imposed before annuitants reach age 59 1/2.
	• *Annuities Certain:*
	  - Payments are guaranteed for a fixed period or until a certain fixed amount

CHAPTER 9:
Life Insurance and Annuities – Policy Replacement and Cancellation

This chapter will describe regulations regarding policy replacement and cancellation in California. You will learn about the insured's right to cancel and specific time requirements for those aged 60 or over. You will also learn about several required disclosures for policy replacement and immediate investments.

- Insured's Right to Cancel
- Policy Replacement

Insured's Right to Cancel

All individual life insurance policies or annuities initially issued in this state must have printed a notice on the cover page or the front of the policy stating that the policy owner can return the policy within a certain period. The policy owner has the chance to review the policy on their own and, if dissatisfied, *return it for a full refund of all paid premiums* with no questions asked.

Rescinding the policy means it effectively never existed. The owner exercises this right by returning the policy to the original producer or mailing it back to the insurance provider. This right must be clearly stated in the policy's text outlined on the title page. This timeframe begins when the policy is received and signed for by the owner. It does not start when the application is signed, or the policy is underwritten. This clarification is why a signed and dated "Acknowledgment of Delivery Receipt," as well as prompt delivery, is so important. It must be established precisely when this period starts and ends. A client can cancel a policy after this period but will not be entitled to a full refund.

Once the insurance provider receives the notification of rescission, the insurer has 30 days to issue the refund of premiums. When the policy is a variable life or annuity policy, the refund due is the value of the account and any policy fees.

Age 60 or Over

Suppose the annuitant on an annuity contract or the insured on an individual life policy is *60 or older*. In that case, the insured has the right to cancel the policy for a full refund within *30 days*. Each annuity contract or individual life policy (other than modified guaranteed contracts and variable contracts) delivered to a senior consumer must include a notice if the policy contains surrender charges or penalties. This notice must be printed on the cover page or policy jacket or a sticker attached to the cover page or policy jacket (Cal. Ins. Code Section 10127.10).

Less than 60 Years of Age

The *free look* or *right-to-return period* allowed for a new individual life policy must last at least ten days. By law, insurance companies can give up to 30 days but not less than ten. This period does not apply to credit life policies or term conversions.

If the policy is a replacement, a minimum *30-day* period is mandatory because this requires even more time for evaluation (Cal. Ins. Code Section 10127.9).

Investment Requirements During the Free-Look Period

During the 30-day free look (cancellation) period, the premium for a variable annuity can only be invested in money-market funds and fixed-income investments. However, it cannot be invested if the investor requests explicitly that the premium be invested in the mutual funds that underlie the variable annuity contract.

Provisions for Face Value Less than $10,000

All individual life insurance policies with a face value of less than $10,000 must include a notice stating that the policy owner can return the policy for cancellation by mailing it or delivering it to the insurance company or to the agent through whom it was purchased. The insurance provider can establish how long the policy owner will have to return the policy. This amount of time has to be between 10 and 30 days.

If the policy owner returns the policy, the agreement will be void from its beginning. The parties will be in the same position as if the policy had never been issued in the first place. All premiums and any policy fees that have previously been paid must be refunded to the policy owner.

Notice of the Right to Cancel a Policy

Every individual life insurance policy must include a notice stating that the owner can return the policy by delivering it to the insurer or agent through whom it was purchased. The period established by the insurance company for the return of the policy must be between 10 and 30 days. The insured can return the policy to the insurer at any time during the period specified in the notice. In the case of individual life insurance policies (other than modified guaranteed contracts and variable contracts), the policy owner will void the policy from the beginning by delivering the policy during the cancellation period. The parties will be in the same position as if no policy had ever been issued.

All premiums and policy fees paid for the policy must be refunded by the insurer to the owner within 30 days from the date the insurer receives notification that the insured has canceled the policy.

In the case of modified guaranteed contracts, variable life insurance contracts, and variable annuity contracts, returning the contract during the cancellation period entitles the owner to a refund of the account value plus any fee paid for the policy. The insurance provider must refund the account value and policy fee to the owner within 30 days from the date the insurer receives notification that the insured has canceled the policy.

Policy Replacement

Replacement is any transaction where a new annuity or life insurance policy is purchased. Consequently, the existing annuity or life insurance has been or will be any of the following:

- Surrendered, lapsed, forfeited, or terminated;
- Reissued with any decrease in cash value;
- Continued as extended term insurance, converted to reduced paid-up insurance, or reduced in value through nonforfeiture benefits or other policy values;
- Amended to affect either a reduction in benefits or in the term for which coverage would otherwise remain effective or for which benefits would be paid; or
- Used in a financed purchase.

A *replacing insurer* is the insurance company that issues the new policy, while an *existing insurer* is the insurance company whose policy is being replaced. The *responsibilities of the replacing producer* are to:

- Provide to the applicant a *Notice Regarding Replacement* that is signed by both the applicant and the producer. A copy has to be left with the applicant.
- Obtain a list of every existing life insurance policy or annuity to be replaced, including policy numbers and the names of the companies being replaced.
- Leave the applicant with the original or a copy of written or printed communications used for presenting to the applicant.
- Submit a copy of the replacement notice with the application to the replacing insurance company.

Every agent who initiates the application must submit the following to the insurance provider with or as part of each application:

- A statement signed by the applicant confirming whether replacing the existing annuity or life insurance is involved in the transaction; and
- A signed statement regarding whether the agent knows replacement is or could be involved in the transaction.

The *duties of the replacing insurance company* are to:

- Require from the agent a list of the applicant's annuity or life insurance contracts to be replaced and a copy of the replacement notice given to the applicant; and
- Send each existing insurer a written communication advising of the proposed replacement within a specified period of the date that the application is received in the replacing insurer's home or regional office. Insurers must include a policy summary or ledger statement containing policy data on the proposed annuity or life insurance.

Conservation refers to any attempt by the existing insurance company or its producers or by a broker to discourage a current policy owner from replacing existing annuities or life insurance. It does not include regular administrative procedures such as reminders for late payment, offers for late payment, or offers for reinstatement.

State Requirements

The burden of adhering to the replacement rules falls on the insurance company to ensure that its agents follow these guidelines correctly. These guidelines include making sure the applications and disclosures ask proper replacement questions and returning any applications that are not correctly completed to the agent.

The replacing insurer must provide a notice to the applicant of the right to an unconditional refund of all premiums within *30 days* starting from the date of policy delivery (free-look period).

The replacing and existing insurance providers must retain evidence of all signed applications, disclosures, and other materials used in replacement or conservation for no less than *three years*.

When no producer is involved in the replacement (e.g., direct response or internet marketing), the replacing insurer must present to the client a disclosure as soon as a replacement is suspected. The replacing insurer must also present the disclosure when the policy is delivered, typically via mail.

To maintain this standard, the insurance provider should still ask on the application what life insurance the applicant currently has and whether a replacement is involved. Not using producers does not excuse insurers from their replacement responsibility.

Exclusions

The replacement regulation *does not apply* to:

- Group life and group annuities;
- Credit life;
- Converting or changing the current policy with the same insurance provider; or
- New policy transactions where the replacing insurer and the existing insurer are the same.

Penalties

The replacement regulation for annuities and life insurance policies aims to ensure that policy owners receive the information they need to make informed and educated decisions. It also seeks to minimize the likelihood of misrepresentations and incomplete disclosures.

Any individual or entity that violates the Insurance Code's replacement provisions is liable for the following administrative penalties:

Agents

- A minimum of $1,000 for the first violation;
- No less than $5,000 and no more than $50,000 per violation for a second or subsequent violation.

Insurer

- $10,000 for the first violation;
- No less than $30,000 and no more than $300,000 per violation for a second or subsequent violation.

The Commissioner can revoke or suspend the license of any individual or entity that violates the Code.

Chapter Review

This chapter discussed the replacement and cancellation of life insurance and annuities. Let's review the major points of the chapter:

INSURED'S RIGHT TO CANCEL	
Policy Cancellation	• *Age 60 or over* – the insured has the right to cancel the policy for a full refund within 30 days • *Less than age 60* – the free look or right-to-return period allowed for a new individual life policy must last at least ten days • *Investment requirements during the free-look period* – during the 30-day free look (cancellation) period, the premium for a variable annuity can only be invested in money-market funds and fixed-income investments • *Provisions for face value less than $10,000* – policy owners can return the policy for cancellation, typically between 10 and 30 days • *Right to cancel a policy:* - The period established by the insurance company for the return of the policy must be between 10 and 30 days - Premiums and policy fees paid for the policy must be refunded by the insurer to the owner within 30 days
POLICY REPLACEMENT	
Duties of the Replacing Insurer	• *Replacing insurer* – the insurance company issuing the new policy • Provide to the applicant a Notice Regarding Replacement • Obtain a list of every existing life insurance policy or annuity to be replaced • Send each existing insurer a written communication advising of the proposed replacement within a specified period
State Requirements	• The replacing insurer must provide inform the applicant of the right to a refund of all premiums within 30 days from policy delivery (free-look period)
Exclusions	• Group life and group annuities, credit life • Converting or changing the current policy with the existing insurer

CHAPTER 10:
Group Life Insurance, Retirement Plans, and Social Security Disability

This chapter helps broaden your knowledge of life insurance. You will learn about various topics, from group life insurance and plans specifically for businesses to retirement plans and social security benefits.

- Third-Party Ownership
- Group Life Insurance
- Qualified Retirement Plans
- Social Security Disability Program

Third-Party Ownership

Insurers write most insurance policies where the policy owner is also the insured. However, there are instances where someone other than the insured may own the contract. These types of contracts are known as *third-party ownership*. "Third-party owner" is a legal term used to identify any person or entity not listed as an insured under the policy but has a legally enforceable right. Most third-party ownership policies are written in business situations or for minors where the parent is the policy owner.

Group Life Insurance

Insurers write individual life insurance on a single life and base coverage on the underwriting of that individual's life. In contrast, the sponsoring organization obtains group life insurance which covers the lives of more than one individual member of that group. Insurers generally write group insurance for employee-employer groups, but other types of groups also qualify for coverage. They typically write this coverage as annually renewable term insurance. Two features that differentiate group insurance from individual insurance are:

- Evidence of insurability is generally not required unless an applicant is enrolling for coverage outside of the regular enrollment period; and
- The plan's participants (insureds) do not receive a policy because they do not control or own it.

Instead, all insured participants under the group plan receive a *certificate of insurance* as evidence that they have coverage. It also includes policy benefits, exclusions, and procedures for filing a claim. The actual policy, or master policy/contract, is issued to the sponsoring organization of the group, which is often an employer. The group sponsor is the policy owner and is the one that exercises control over the policy.

Group underwriting is different from individual insurance underwriting and is based on the group's makeup and characteristics. Some of the characteristics that are of concern to group underwriters include the following:

- **Purpose of the group** – The group must exist for a purpose other than obtaining group insurance.
- **Size of the group** – Insurers base a group's size on the law of large numbers of similar risks. The larger the number of people in the group, the more accurate the projections of future loss experience will be.
- **Turnover of the group** – For the underwriter, a group should have a steady turnover in which younger, lower-risk employees enter the group and older, higher-risk employees leave the group.
- **The group's financial strength** – Group insurance is costly to administer. The underwriter must consider whether or not the group's financial resources are sufficient to pay the policy premiums and whether or not the group will be capable of renewing the coverage.

A unique aspect of group underwriting is that insurers base the cost of coverage on the ratio of men to women and the group's average age. In addition, to decrease *adverse selection*, the insurance company will require a minimum number of participants in the group, depending on whether the employees or the employer pay the insurance premium.

Policies and Certificates of Insurance

Insurers issue only one policy for group life insurance plans (*master policy*). It is issued to the sponsor of the group, which is often an employer. Each participant in an individual plan receives a *certificate of insurance*, which outlines the contract provisions and benefits.

The certificate of insurance is required to include the following information:

- The policy number;
- The name, address, and other contact information for the insurance provider;
- The name of the insured (the employer or sponsor of the group);
- The amount of insurance provided and to whom the benefit is payable; and
- Any principal exclusions that are found in the contract.

An individual certificate is considered "individualized" if it contains the name of the covered employee or another means of identifying the covered employee's individual certificate.

Enrollment

The *application* or *enrollment* process for group insurance refers to any steps required of a named insured in applying for a certificate under a group life policy. These steps may include completing an enrollment form or taking a medical examination if required by the insurance provider.

Medical Examinations and Eligibility

In California, a group policy must cover at least *ten* eligible group members.

Underwriting for group life insurance is performed on a group basis instead of an individual basis. Every participant completes a short application that identifies the insured and their beneficiary. Usually, when the group is large enough, there are *no medical questions* since the plan will be issued based on the nature of the group and previous claims experiences.

Contributory vs. Noncontributory

The employer or other group sponsor can share premiums with the employees or pay all premiums. When an employer pays all premiums, the plan is called a *noncontributory plan*. Under a noncontributory plan, an insurance provider will require 100% of eligible employees to enroll in the plan. When the employees and the employer split group insurance premiums, the plan is called a *contributory plan*. Under a contributory plan, an insurance provider will require that 75% of eligible employees enroll in the plan.

Selection of Coverage

In some employee benefit plans, the employer contributes a set amount to the plan for each employee. The employee can then choose from a group of benefits for the one that best meets their needs. The benefits include life insurance, health insurance, retirement annuity, etc. There can also be a choice of providers from which to select coverage.

Recordkeeping

Insurance providers issuing group life policies in California are required to keep records of all transactions (original or copies) for five years after delivering a policy or contract. The records are required to include the following:

- The original policy application;
- Records exposing the premiums received by the insurance provider;
- Records exposing the amount of commissions paid and to whom;
- Any correspondence, written solicitations, or proposals sent by the insurance provider to a prospect, applicant, or insured, or received by the insurance provider;
- A copy of the disclosure statement or outline of coverage;
- Any other pertinent records.

Characteristics of Group Life Insurance

Eligible Groups and Insureds – Group life insurance plans can be sponsored by employers, labor unions, debtor groups, credit unions, associations, and other organizations formed for reasons other than purchasing insurance. Insurance providers can establish a minimum number of individuals insured under a group plan.

Single Employers – When a policy is issued to an employer, the employer or trustee will be the policyholder to insure employees for the benefit of individuals besides the employer. A policy on which insured employees pay no part of the premium has to insure all eligible employees, except those who reject such coverage in writing.

Labor Unions – A policy issued to a labor union or similar organization to insure its members for the benefit of individuals other than the union or organization are subject to the following requirements:

- The eligible members for insurance under the policy must be every union or organization member.
- The policy premiums must be paid from the union's funds, from funds contributed by the insured members expressly for their insurance, or from both.
- An insurance provider can exclude or limit the coverage on any individual whose evidence of insurability is not satisfactory to the insurance company.

Associations – An *association group* (alumni or professional) can purchase group insurance for its members. The group must have been active for at least two years, be organized for reasons other than buying insurance, have at least 100 members, have a constitution and by-laws, and hold at least annual meetings. Examples of these groups include, but are not limited to, college alumni associations, professional associations, trade associations, veteran associations, customers of large retail chains, and saving account depositors. Association group plans can be either contributory or noncontributory.

Credit Unions – A group life policy can be issued to a credit union or to a trustee, or trustees or agents designated by two or more credit unions to insure members of such credit unions for the benefit of individuals other than the policyholder, subject to the following requirements:

- The members eligible for insurance will be every member of the credit union(s) or all of any class or classes thereof;
- The premium for the policy will be paid by the policyholder from the credit union's funds and has to insure every eligible member; and
- An insurer can exclude or limit coverage on any member whose evidence of insurability is unsatisfactory to the insurer.

Debtor Groups – A policy issued to a creditor that is considered to be the policy owner is subject to the following requirements:

- The eligible debtors for insurance under the policy must all be the creditor's debtors;
- The premium for the policy has to be paid from either the creditor's funds, from charges collected from the insured debtors or both;
- An insurance provider can exclude any debtors whose individual insurability is not satisfactory to the insurance company; and
- The amount of insurance on any debtor's life may at no time exceed the greater of the scheduled or actual amount of unpaid debt to the creditor.

Dependents of Insured Employees – Under group insurance policies, insurance can be extended to insure dependents of the insured in amounts according to a plan that precludes individual selection. The amounts cannot exceed 100% of the insurance on the life of the insured employee. The insurance premiums on the dependents can be paid by the employee or employer or paid jointly by both.

The term *dependents* include the insured's spouse and all children from birth *until 26 years* of age. Dependents can also be children older than 26 who are incapable of self-sustaining employment because of a physical handicap or intellectual disability. These individuals primarily depend on the insured employee for maintenance and support. A disabled child must be insured within 31 days of reaching the limiting age. Proof of incapacity and dependency might be required once a year after the first two years of the child's attainment of the limiting age. The premiums for the insurance on the dependents can be paid by the employee, the employer, or both.

Domestic Partnership – An insurance company in California must provide the registered domestic partner of an employee, policyholder, or insured the same coverage that would be provided to a spouse. The insurance provider must notify employers and guaranteed associations of this coverage.

A group health policy can require the status of the domestic partnership to be verified by providing the insurance provider a copy of a valid Declaration of Domestic Partnership. The policy can also require that the employee inform the insurance provider upon the termination of the domestic partnership. However, this information is necessary only if the insurer also requests verification of marital status and notification of dissolution of marriage from an employee whose spouse is provided coverage.

Types of Policies – According to the California Insurance Code, any life insurance company can issue life, term, disability, and endowment insurance on a group plan with premium rates lower than the usual rates for such insurance. Insurance under a franchise agreement or on a wholesale basis can be written using rates more or less than the customary rates for such insurance.

Blanket Life Insurance – A *blanket life* policy would cover a group of people exposed to the same hazard. It differs from the traditional group insurance in that it does not name individual insureds and doesn't issue certificates of insurance. The coverage under a blanket policy is temporary, and only for the time, the group is exposed to the hazards stipulated in the policy. Typical examples of blanket insurance would include airlines insuring passengers during a flight or schools insuring teachers and students during school hours.

The California Insurance Code allows insurers to offer blanket insurance to the following entities:

- Magazines, newspapers, or other similar publications to insure the following individuals:
    - Those who collect payments or deliver publications for the magazine or newspaper;
    - Those who supervise the collections or deliveries;
    - Those who are wholesalers; or
    - Others in the distribution, sales, or marketing process of the publication;
- Educational, recreational, athletic, religious, charitable, or civic organizations;
- Employers who pay the benefits provided by a voluntary plan of unemployment compensation disability insurance;
- Employers who provide benefits to any group of employees, dependents, or guests, limited to specified hazards or operations of the policyholder; and
- An entertainment production company that benefits any group of participants, audience members, volunteers, or contestants.

Blanket life insurance can be issued for a term *not exceeding one year* with premium rates less than the customary rates for such insurance. Blanket policies are renewable.

When the insured pays the policy premiums, the insured can request from the insurance provider a copy of the policy in the form of a certificate.

A person can elect not to be covered by a blanket insurance plan by submitting a written request to the insurance provider. Suppose more than 10% of the individuals eligible for coverage choose not to participate. In that case, the insurance contract cannot be put into effect, or if it has been in effect, it cannot be renewed.

Conversion Privilege – The conversion privilege is another characteristic of group insurance. When an employer terminates an employee's membership in the insured group, the employee has the right to convert to an individual policy at a standard rate *without proving insurability*, based on the person's attained age. The group life policy can convert to any form of insurance issued by the insurance provider (usually whole life), except for term insurance. The death benefit or face amount will equal the face amount of the group term insurance, but the premium will be higher. The employee typically has *31 days after terminating from the group* to exercise the conversion option. The employee still has access to coverage under the original group policy during this time.

Other rules that apply to conversion involve the disability or death of the insured and termination of the master policy. When the insured dies during the conversion period, whether or not the insured completed the application for an individual policy, a death benefit has to be paid by the group policy. Every individual who has been on the plan for at least *five years* can convert to individual permanent insurance of the same coverage in the event of the termination of the master contract.

Suppose the employee is not given notice by the employer or the insurance provider of their right to convert within 15 days of termination of employment. In that circumstance, the Insurance Code mandates that they be given an additional 25 days following the notice to apply for a conversion policy.

In no event will an employee be given more than 60 days after the end of any conversion period to choose to convert and pay the first premium for individual coverage. There is no coverage following the initial 31-day conversion period until a new premium is paid.

A spouse or child covered by the group policy as a dependent has the same right to convert to an individual insurance plan without providing evidence of insurability. All of the provisions previously described will apply to a dependent's conversion.

Incontestability – In California, the *incontestability* clause states that the insurer cannot contest the statements on the application after a policy has been in force for two years. The insurer cannot rescind the contract based on any error or misrepresentation on the part of the policy owner or insured after the policy has been effective for two years.

Misstatement of Age – The policy must include a provision for the fair adjustment of the premium or the insurance amount payable in the event of a misstatement of an employee's age.

War, Military, or Aviation Risk – Insurance providers can reduce or exclude liability for losses resulting from war, military or naval service, and aviation.

Qualified Retirement Plans

Individual Qualified Plans

Traditional IRAs and Roth IRAs are the most common qualified individual retirement plans. Anyone with *earned income* can contribute to either plan.

A traditional *Individual Retirement Account (IRA)* lets individuals make tax-deductible contributions regardless of age. Previously, individuals could contribute to the account until age 70 ½; however, the SECURE Act of 2019 removed the prior age limit for all contributions. Plan participants can contribute up to a specified dollar limit each year or 100% of their salary if it is less than the maximum allowable amount. Individuals aged 50 or older are qualified to make additional (catch-up) contributions. A married couple can contribute double the amount for an individual, even if only one spouse has an earned income. Each spouse must maintain a separate account that does not exceed the individual limit.

In traditional IRAs, the owner can withdraw funds at any time. However, withdrawals before age 59 ½ are considered early withdrawals and are subject to a 10% additional tax. At 59 ½, the owner can withdraw assets without paying the 10% tax. However, the owner must start to receive distributions from the IRA at age 72 (the 2019 SECURE Act extended the required minimum distribution age from 70 ½ to 72). At age 72, the owner must receive at least a minimum annual amount, known as the *required minimum distribution (RMD)*.

Roth IRAs are a type of individual retirement account funded with after-tax contributions. A person can contribute 100% of their earned income up to an IRS-specified maximum, similar to traditional IRAs (the dollar amounts change yearly). Roth contributions can continue regardless of the age of the account owner. In contrast with a traditional IRA, distributions do not have to begin at age 72 (previously 70 ½). Roth IRAs grow tax-free if the account is open for at least five years.

Plans for Employers

In addition to individual plans, other types of qualified plans are available. They have been designed for use by both large and small employers.

An employer-sponsored *qualified retirement plan* is approved by the IRS, which provides benefits to both the employer and employee, such as deductible contributions and tax-deferred growth.

The following characteristics are found in qualified plans:

- Intended for the exclusive benefit of the employees and their beneficiaries;
- Are officially written and communicated to employees;
- Use a contribution or benefit formula that does not discriminate in favor of the prohibited group - stockholders, officers, or highly paid employees;
- Are not exclusively geared to the prohibited group;
- Are approved by the IRS;
- Are permanent; and
- Have a vesting requirement.

Self-employed Plans (HR-10 or Keogh Plans) – HR-10 or Keogh Plans allow *self-employed individuals* to receive coverage under an IRS-qualified retirement plan. These plans let self-employed individuals fund their retirement programs with pre-tax dollars as if they were under a corporate retirement or pension plan. To be covered under a Keogh retirement plan, the individual must be self-employed or be a partner working full-time or part-time who owns at least 10% of the business.

Contribution limits are either the lesser of 100% of their total earned income or an established dollar limit. The contribution is tax-deductible, and it accumulates tax deferred until withdrawn.

Upon the death of a participant, payouts can become available immediately. If a participant becomes disabled, they may collect benefits directly, or the funds can be left to accumulate. When a participant enters retirement, funds distribution must occur no earlier than 59 ½ and no later than 70 ½. If an individual withdraws funds before age 59 ½, there is a 10% penalty. Individuals can discontinue payments without incurring a penalty, and funds can be left to accumulate.

Under eligibility requirements, a person must be included in the Keogh Plan if they:

- Are at least 21 years old;
- Have worked for a self-employed individual for one year or more; and
- Have worked full-time at least 1,000 hours per year.

The employer must contribute the same percentage of funds into the employee's account as they contribute to their retirement account.

Simplified Employee Pensions (SEPs) – A Simplified Employee Pension (SEP) is a qualified plan suited for the self-employed or the small employer. An employee establishes and maintains an individual retirement account in a SEP to receive employer contributions. An employee's gross income does not include employer contributions. The primary difference between SEPs and IRAs is the larger amount participants can contribute each year to a SEP. This amount can be 25% of the employee's compensation or an annual dollar limit established by the IRS, whichever is less.

SIMPLE Plans – A SIMPLE (Savings Incentive Match Plan for Employees) plan is available to eligible small businesses. They must have *no more than 100 employees* who received at least $5,000 in compensation from the employer during the previous year. To set up a SIMPLE plan, the employer must not already have a qualified retirement plan. Employees who decide to participate can defer up to a specified amount each year. The employer will make a matching contribution, dollar for dollar, up to an amount equal to 3% of the employee's yearly compensation. *Taxation is deferred* on earnings and contributions until funds are withdrawn.

Profit-Sharing and 401(k) Plans – Profit-sharing plans are qualified retirement plans. A portion of the company's profit is shared with employees and contributed to the plan. Suppose the plan does not provide a definitive formula for calculating the profits to be shared. In that circumstance, employer contributions have to be *systematic and substantial*.

A 401(k) qualified retirement plan lets employees reduce their current salaries by remitting amounts into a retirement plan. The company can also match the employee's contribution, whether on a percentage or dollar-for-dollar basis. Under a 401(k) plan, participants can elect to either have the money contributed to the 401(k) or receive taxable cash compensation, referred to as cash or deferred arrangement plans (CODA). The employee's gross income does not include contributions up to a dollar ceiling amount into the plan. The ceiling amount is adjusted each year for inflation. The plan allows participants age 50 or older to make additional contributions up to a limit at the end of the calendar year.

401(k) plans allow an early withdrawal for specific hardship reasons such as disability or death. Sometimes, they allow loans up to 50% of the participant's vested accrued benefit or a specific dollar limit (established annually by the IRS).

403(b) Tax-Sheltered Annuities (TSAs) – A 403(b) plan or a tax-sheltered annuity (TSA) is a qualified plan available to employees of public school systems and employees of certain *nonprofit corporations under Section 501(c)(3)* of the Internal Revenue Code.

The employee or the employer makes contributions through a salary reduction. The employee's current income does not include their contributions. As with any other qualified retirement plan, 403(b) plans limit employee contributions to a maximum amount that changes annually, adjusted for inflation. The same catch-up provisions are also applicable.

	ELIGIBILITY	WHO CONTRIBUTES
HR-10 (Keogh)	Self-employed	Employer matches employee's contribution
SEP	Small employer or self-employed	Employer only
SIMPLE	Small employers (no more than 100 employees)	Employer matches employee's contribution
401(k)	Any employer	Employer matches employee's contribution
403(b) – TSA	Nonprofit organizations	Employer and employee

Social Security Disability Program

Social Security, also known as *Old Age Survivors Disability Insurance (OASDI)*, is a Federal program enacted in 1935. This program protects eligible workers and dependents against financial loss because of old age, disability, or death. With a few exceptions, Social Security covers almost every individual. In some aspects, Social Security plays a role in federal life and health insurance, which is essential to consider when determining an individual's life insurance needs.

Social Security uses the Quarter of Coverage (QC) system to determine whether or not a person qualifies for Social Security benefits. The number of credits or QCs earned by a worker determines the type and amount of benefits. Anyone operating their own business or working in jobs covered by Social Security can earn up to 4 credits for each year of work.

The term *fully insured* refers to anyone who has earned *40 quarters of coverage* and is entitled to Social Security retirement, Medicare, and survivor benefits. Forty quarters is the equivalent of working for ten years.

Individuals can attain a *currently insured* status (or partially insured) and qualify for certain benefits. They need to have earned six quarters (or credits) of coverage during the 13 quarters ending with the quarter wherein the insured either:

- Dies;
- Qualifies for disability insurance benefits; or
- Qualifies for old-age insurance benefits.

For younger workers, the number of quarters required to be eligible for the benefits differs by age, according to a table established by Social Security.

To be eligible for *disability benefits* under Social Security, the disabled person must have earned a certain amount of credits. Each year, an individual can earn a maximum of 4 work credits. Usually, a person needs 40 credits, 20 of which they acquired in the last ten years before the disability. In other circumstances, the amount of required credits varies by age, as shown in the following table:

- **Before age 24** – Individuals can qualify for benefits with only six credits earned three years before the disability occurred.
- **Ages 24 - 31** – Individuals can qualify for benefits if they have credit for having worked half the time between age 21 and the start of the disability. For example, if a person becomes disabled at age 27, they would need 12 credits (or three years' worth) out of the previous six years (between ages 21 and 27).
- **After age 31** – The required work credits vary even more. Still, a person must have earned at least 20 credits in the ten years before becoming disabled.

AGE	CREDITS NEEDED
31-42	20
44	22
46	24
48	26
50	28
52	30
54	32
56	34
58	36
60	38
62+	40

The table shown below identifies the kinds of benefits paid and the insured status required for the following types of benefits:

CONDITIONS FOR PAYMENT	PAID TO	TYPE OF PAYMENT
RETIREMENT BENEFIT:		
Fully insured at age 66* (or reduced benefits at age 62)	Retired individual and eligible dependents	Monthly benefit equal to the primary insurance amount (PIA)
DISABILITY BENEFIT:		
Fully insured status and total and permanent disability prior to the retirement age	Disabled worker and spouse and eligible dependents	Monthly disability benefit after a 5-month waiting period
SURVIVOR BENEFIT:		
Worker's death	Surviving spouse and dependent children	Lump-sum burial benefit if fully or currently insured; Monthly income payments if fully insured

* The current full retirement age is 66, and is gradually increasing to age 67. For anyone born 1960 or later, full retirement benefits are payable at age 67.

Survivor benefits are death benefits paid to the worker's surviving spouse and dependent children under specified circumstances. A lump-sum burial benefit is available for a spouse who lives with the worker at the time of death, or a spouse or child who qualifies for Social Security during the month of the worker's death. Monthly income payments can also be paid to the following in the event of a fully insured (covered) worker's death:

- Surviving spouse, limited benefits available at age 60, full benefits payable upon full retirement age (varies depending on birth year).
- Surviving or divorced spouse, if they care for disabled children or minor children under age 16, sometimes called a parent's benefit. Once the minor reaches age 16, the parent is not eligible for Social Security retirement benefits until age 60 or retirement (Blackout Period).

- Dependent parents, age 62 or older.
- Unmarried children under age 18 or 19, if they are full-time elementary or secondary (high school) students.

Social Security is funded by the taxes levied on a worker's earned income. This is a payroll tax paid for by all employers and employees, including individuals that are self-employed. This tax is levied on a certain percentage of the employee's income, known as the taxable wage base. The employer subtracts the taxes from the employee's paycheck and contributes an equal amount. Part of the tax is applied to OASDI under *FICA* (the Federal Insurance Contributions Act), and part of the tax funds Medicare. Self-employed employees pay an amount that is equivalent to both the employee and the employer contribution.

Chapter Review

This chapter discussed group life insurance, retirement plans, and social security disability. Let's review the key points of the chapter:

GROUP LIFE INSURANCE	
General Features	<ul><li>Employers are the policy owners; employees are the insureds</li><li>No evidence of insurability</li><li>*Conversion* – no evidence of insurability within a specified number of days (typically 30 or 31 days of termination)</li><li>*Noncontributory* – employer pays 100% of the premium; requires 100% employee participation</li><li>*Contributory* – employer and employees share the cost of thepremium; requires 75% participation</li></ul>
QUALIFIED PLANS	
General Features	<ul><li>Approved by the IRS</li><li>Tax benefits for employers and employees</li><li>Must be permanent and have a vesting requirement</li><li>Cannot discriminate in favor of the prohibited group</li></ul>
Individual Qualified Retirement Plans	*Traditional IRA:*<ul><li>Earned income</li><li>Pretax contributions</li><li>Contributions: - No limiting age (SECURE Act recently changed this law) - Dollar limit – up to a maximum allowed amount - Married couples – double the amount for singles</li><li>Withdrawals can begin at age 59 ½ but not later than age 72</li></ul>*Roth IRA:*<ul><li>Earned income</li><li>After-tax contributions</li><li>Contributions: - No limiting age - *Dollar limit* – up to a maximum allowed amount</li><li>Withdrawals do not have to begin at age 72</li></ul>

QUALIFIED PLANS *(Continued)*	
Employer-sponsored Qualified Plans	• Contributions up to an IRS-specified amounts • Both employer and employee can contribute *Types of plans:* • *HR-10 (Keogh)* – self-employed • *SEP* – small employer/self-employed; employer funds employee's IRA • *SIMPLE* – small employer (no more than 100 employees); set up as IRA or as 401(k) • *401(k)* – any employer; cash or deferred arrangements; profit sharing • *403(b)* – nonprofit organizations; a tax-sheltered annuity
SOCIAL SECURITY BENEFITS	
Types of Benefits	• Retirement • Disability • Survivor
Insured Status	• *Fully insured* (40 quarters of coverage) – qualify for Social Security retirement, Medicare, and survivor benefits • *Currently insured* (6 quarters of coverage) – qualify for some benefits

CHAPTER 11:
Taxation of Life Insurance and Annuities – Premiums and Proceeds

This chapter will help expand your knowledge of life insurance and annuities by explaining the subject of taxation. You will learn the basic principles of taxation for policy benefits, dividends, and loans and the options available for nontaxable exchanges.

- Taxation of Life Insurance
- Taxation of Annuities
- Business Life Insurance
- Modified Endowment Contract

Taxation of Life Insurance

Generally speaking, the following taxation rules apply to individual life insurance policies:

- *Premiums* are not tax-deductible;
- *Death benefit:*
    - Tax-free if a named beneficiary takes the death benefit as a lump-sum distribution;
    - The principal is tax-free; interest is taxable if the insurer pays the death benefit in installments other than a lump sum.

Amounts Available to Policy Owners

As previously discussed, permanent life insurance provides living benefits. There are several ways policyholders may receive those living benefits from the policy.

Dividends – Dividends are a return of unused premiums and are not considered income for tax purposes. When dividends are left with the insurance provider to accumulate interest, the interest on the dividend is taxed as ordinary income every year it earns. The policy owner does not need to be paid out the interest for this to be the case.

Cash Value Accumulations – A policyholder can borrow against their policy's cash value accumulations or receive the cash value upon policy surrender. Cash values grow tax-deferred, and upon endowment or surrender, any cash value over and above the premium payments is taxable as ordinary income. Upon the policy owner's death, the insurer pays the face amount, and there is no more cash value. Death benefits are usually delivered to the beneficiary and are tax-free.

Policy Loans – The policy owner can borrow against the policy's cash value. Money borrowed against the cash value is not taxable income; however, the insurer charges interest on outstanding policy loans. Policy loans, with interest, can be repaid to the insurance company in any of the following ways:

- By the policy owner while the policy is in force;
- At policy surrender or maturity, deducted from the cash value; or
- At the insured's death, deducted from the death benefit.

Surrenders – When a policy owner surrenders a policy for a cash value, some cash value is taxed as income if the cash surrender value exceeds the premiums paid into the policy. When the policy owner withdraws cash value from a universal life policy through a partial surrender, the death benefit and the cash value are reduced by the surrender amount.

Example 11.1 – Consider the following scenario:

- Face amount: $300,000
- Premiums paid: $70,000
- Total cash value: $100,000

If the policy owner surrendered $30,000 of cash value, the $30,000 would be tax-free. If the policy owner took out $100,000, the last $30,000 would be taxable since the $100,000 exceeds the premiums paid in by $30,000.

Accelerated Benefits – A terminally ill insured receives accelerated benefits tax-free under a life insurance policy. When a chronically ill insured (e.g., Alzheimer's disease, cancer, or other severe illness) accepts accelerated benefit payments, these benefits are tax-free up to a specific limit. The insured must include any amount received over this dollar limit in their gross income.

Amounts Received by Beneficiaries

General Rule and Exceptions – Life insurance proceeds paid to a named beneficiary are usually *free of federal income tax* if received as a lump sum payment. An exception to this rule will apply if the benefit payment results from a transfer for value, which occurs when the life insurance policy owner sells the policy to another party before the insured's death.

Settlement Options – With *settlement options*, the interest portion of the payments is taxable as income when the beneficiary receives both principal and interest payments.

Example 11.2 – Suppose $100,000 of life insurance proceeds were used in a settlement option paying $13,000 per year for ten years. In that case, $10,000 per year would be tax-free, and $3,000 per year would be taxable income.

PERMANENT LIFE FEATURES	TAX TREATMENT
Premiums	Not tax deductible
Cash value exceeding paid premiums	Taxable at surrender
Policy Loans	Not income taxable
Policy dividends	Not taxable
Dividend interest	Taxable in the year earned
Lump-sum death benefit	Not income taxable

Group Life and Employer-Sponsored Plans

The *premiums* that an employer pays for a policy on an employee, whereby the life insurance is for the employee's benefit, are *tax-deductible to the employer* as a business expense. When the group life policy coverage is $50,000 or less, the employee does not have to report the premium paid by the employer as income (not taxable to the employee).

When a business is the named beneficiary of a life insurance policy or has a beneficial interest in the policy, premiums that the company pays for such insurance are not tax-deductible. When a business pays the premiums for any of the following arrangements, the premiums will not be deductible:

- Key-person (key-employee) insurance;
- Stock-redemption or entity purchase agreement; and
- Split-dollar insurance.

The *cash value* of a life insurance policy owned by a business or an employer-provided policy accumulates on a tax-deferred basis and is subject to taxation like an individually owned policy.

Policy loans are not taxable to a business. Unlike an individual taxpayer, a corporation can deduct interest on a life insurance policy loan for loans that do not exceed $50,000.

Policy death benefits paid under a business-owned or an employer-provided life insurance policy are received free of federal income tax by the beneficiary in the same manner as an individually owned policy.

If the qualified plan meets the general requirements, the following tax advantages will apply:

- Employer contributions are not taxed as income to the employee and are tax-deductible to the employer;
- The plan's earnings accumulate tax-deferred; and
- Lump-sum distributions to employees are received tax-free.

Section 1035 Exchange

Under Section 1035 of the Internal Revenue Code, specific life insurance policies and annuities exchanges can occur as nontaxable exchanges. When a policy owner exchanges a cash value life policy for another cash value life policy, exchanges a cash value life policy for an annuity, or exchanges an annuity for another one, the policies or annuities have to be on *the same life*. There will be no income tax on these types of transactions.

The following are allowable exchanges:

- A life insurance policy for another life insurance policy, an annuity contract, or an endowment contract;
- An endowment contract for another endowment contract or an annuity contract; or
- An annuity contract for another annuity contract.

It is essential to note that a policy owner cannot exchange funds from an annuity into a cash value life policy. Nor would term life be used in a 1035 Exchange because it has no cash value. The exchange cannot be from a less tax-advantaged contract to a more tax-advantaged contract, but *"same to same"* is acceptable.

Taxation of Annuities

Individually-Owned

A portion of every annuity benefit payment is taxable, and a portion is not. The nontaxable portion is the anticipated return of the paid principal, known as the *cost base*. The taxable amount is the interest earned on the principal is known as the *tax base*.

Accumulation Phase – The accumulation phase is the period after an annuity has been purchased and before distribution payments begin.

Tax-deferred Accumulation – The cost base represents the premium dollars that have already been taxed and will not be taxed again when withdrawn from the contract. The accumulated interest in an annuity is the tax base, but the taxes are deferred during the accumulation period.

Withdrawal of Interest and Principal – When funds are withdrawn from an annuity during the accumulation phase, the amounts are taxed on a Last In, First Out basis (LIFO). Therefore, all withdrawals will be taxable until the owner reaches the cost basis. After all the interest is received and taxed, the annuity owner will receive the principal without additional tax consequences.

(Lump) One-Sum Cash Surrenders – Cash surrender of an annuity results in immediate taxation of the earned interest.

Premature Distributions and Penalty Tax – The IRS imposes a penalty for certain early distributions under annuity contracts. In addition to ordinary income tax that may be due, a 10% penalty is assessed on the annuity tax base for early withdrawals before age 59 ½.

Example 11.3 – Assume a 56-year-old insured makes an early withdrawal from her annuity. If the total withdrawal is $6,000, and the entire amount is taxable, the insured will receive a penalty equal to 10% of the withdrawal, or $600.

Annuity Phase and the Exclusion Ratio – The *exclusion ratio* calculates the annuity amounts excluded from taxes. The annuitant can recover the nontaxable cost basis. The cost basis is the amount paid into the annuity, or the principal amount, and is excluded from taxes. The rest of each annuity payment is earned interest and is taxable.

Taxation of Individual Retirement Annuities (IRAs) – When an annuity funds a traditional IRA, distributions are taxable if contributions were made with pretax dollars. If the distributions are not large enough, or if there are no distributions at the required age, the penalty is *50%* of the shortfall from the required annual amount.

The following taxation rules apply to *contributions* made to traditional IRA plans:

- The income of the individual will determine the tax-deductible contributions for the year;
- Contributions must be made in *"cash"* to be tax-deductible (the term cash refers to any form of money, such as cash, check, or money order);
- As long as the excess amounts remain in the IRA, excess contributions are taxed at 6% per year;
- The IRS will not tax any money accumulated in the account (tax-deferred earnings) until withdrawal.

A *distribution* from an IRA is subject to income taxation when the withdrawal occurs. In case of an early distribution before 59 ½, a 10% penalty will also apply. There are certain conditions under which the 10% early withdrawal penalty would not be applicable (penalty tax exceptions):

- The participant is age 59 ½;
- The participant is disabled;
- The withdrawal goes toward the down payment on a home (not to exceed $10,000, and typically for first-time homebuyers);
- Withdrawals to pay for expenses relating to post-secondary education; and
- Withdrawals are used for catastrophic medical expenditures or upon death.

The following taxation rules apply to Roth IRAs:

- Contributions are not tax-deductible; and
- The IRS will assess a 6% tax penalty on excess contributions.

TRADITIONAL IRA	ROTH IRA
Contribute 100% of income up to an IRS-specified limit	
Excess contribution penalty is 6%	
Grows tax deferred	Grows tax free (if account open for at least 5 years)
Contributions are *tax deductible* (Made with "pre-tax dollars")	Contributions are *not tax deductible* (Made with "after-tax dollars")
10% penalty for early nonqualified distributions prior to age 59 ½ (some exceptions apply)	Qualified distribution cannot occur until the account is open for 5 years and owner is 59 ½
Distributions are *taxable*	Distributions are *not taxable*
Payouts must begin by 72	No required minimum age for payouts

Rollovers and Transfers – Situations arise where an individual may choose to move the money from one qualified retirement plan to another. However, benefits withdrawn from any qualified retirement plan are taxable the year they are received if the individual does not move the money correctly. The two ways to accomplish this are through a *rollover* and a *transfer* from one account to another.

A *rollover* is a tax-free cash distribution from one retirement plan to another. Usually, participants must complete IRA rollovers within 60 days after withdrawing the money from the first plan. Whenever the distribution from the first plan is paid directly to the participant, the payor must withhold 20% of the distribution. Suppose the individual moves the distribution *from the first plan to the new IRA plan's trustee or administrator/custodian*. In that scenario, an individual can avoid the 20% withholding of funds. This transaction is known as a *direct rollover*.

A *transfer (or direct transfer)* is a tax-free transfer of funds from one retirement program to a traditional IRA. It can also transfer an interest in a traditional IRA *from one trustee directly to another*.

Distributions at Death – If the annuity contract holder dies before the annuitization date, the interest accumulated in the annuity becomes taxable. However, if the annuity beneficiary is a spouse, the tax can continue to be deferred. Any unpaid annuity benefits after the death of an annuitant are paid to the beneficiary and are taxable.

Values Included in Annuitant's Estate – If the annuitant dies during the accumulation period, the insurer must return all or a portion of the values accumulated in the annuity (cash value). This amount will be included in the deceased annuitant's estate. Suppose the annuity is paid up and the annuitant dies during the annuity period. In that case, the annuity benefits will be taxable and included in the deceased annuitant's estate.

Corporate-Owned

A corporate-owned annuity has different tax implications than an individual annuity:

- Annuity growth is *not* tax-deferred;
- Interest income is *taxed* annually unless the corporation owns a group annuity for its employees and every employee receives a certificate of participation.

TAX CONSIDERATIONS FOR LIFE INSURANCE AND ANNUITIES	
Premiums	Not deductible (personal expense)
Death Benefit	Not taxable income (except for interest)
Cash Value Increases	Not taxable (as long as the policy is in force)
Cash Value Gains	Taxed at surrender
Dividends	Not taxable (return of unused premium; however, interest is taxable)
Accumulations	Interest taxable
Policy Loans	Not income taxable
Surrenders	Surrender value - past premium = amount taxable
Partial Surrenders	First In, First Out (FIFO)*
Settlement Options – Death benefit is spread evenly over an income period (averaged). Interest payments in excess of the death benefit portion are taxable.	
Estate Tax – If the insured is the policy owner, it will be included for estate tax purposes. If the policy is given away (e.g., trust) and the insured dies within three years, the death benefit is included in the estate.	

* FIFO only applies to Life Insurance. Annuities follow a LIFO format.

Business Life Insurance

Split Dollar

A *split-dollar* plan is an arrangement where the employee and employer agree to purchase and fund life insurance for an employee. In the most common form, the employer pays the part of the premium that equals the annual increase in the policy's cash value, while the employee pays the balance. If the employee dies, the employer recovers the total of its payments from the policy proceeds, with the balance being paid to the employee's beneficiary.

Deferred Compensation

Deferred compensation funding refers to any savings, employer retirement, or other deferred compensation plans that is not a qualified retirement plan. Funding involves a contractual commitment between the employee and employer to pay compensation in future years. Typically, funding is made with cash deposits to a life insurance or annuity contract.

Deferred compensation funding is split into two major classes:

- *In-addition funding plans* pay an amount in addition to the employee's qualified retirement plan.
- *Elective plans* allow the employee to defer part of their salary or bonus as tax-deferred savings.

Both plans are usually made with selected employees to provide additional retirement benefits.

Modified Endowment Contracts (MECs)

Generally speaking, an endowment policy is an investment instrument. Endowment life insurance policies promise to pay the face amount if the insured survives until the end of a specified period and if the insured dies within the same period. Such periods include 20 years, 30 years, or until the insured reaches age 65. Endowments require premiums far exceeding the amount needed to fund the death benefit.

The Tax Reform Act of 1984 eliminated numerous traditional tax shelters. Consequently, single premium life insurance remained one of the few financial products to offer significant tax advantages. Many of these policies were purchased to set aside large sums of money for the tax-deferred growth and the tax-free cash flow that is available via policy loans and partial surrenders.

To restrict this activity and identify if an owner has overfunded their insurance policy, the IRS established the *7-pay test*. Any life insurance policy that fails a 7-pay test is a *Modified Endowment Contract (MEC)*. It loses the standard tax benefits associated with a life insurance contract. In a MEC, the cumulative premiums paid during the first seven years of the policy exceed the total amount of net level premiums necessary to pay the policy up using guaranteed mortality costs and interest.

When a policy fails the 7-pay test and becomes a MEC, it remains a MEC.

Every life insurance policy is subject to the 7-pay test. When a material change to a policy occurs (e.g., an increase in the death benefit), a new 7-pay test is required. The death benefit received by a beneficiary is tax-free, whether from a life insurance policy or a MEC.

As defined by Section 7702A of the IRS Code, a Modified Endowment Contract is a contract that meets the requirements of a life insurance contract. These contracts do not meet the 7-pay test and are received in exchange for MECs.

The following taxation rules apply to a MEC's cash value:

- Accumulations are tax-deferred;
- Distributions are taxable, including policy loans and withdrawals;
- The IRS will tax distributions on a LIFO basis (Last In, First Out) – also called the "interest-first" rule;
- Distributions before age 59 ½ are subject to a 10% penalty.

Chapter Review

This chapter discussed the taxation of the premiums and proceeds of life insurance and annuities. Let's review the major points:

TAXATION	
Life Insurance	• *Premiums* – not tax deductible • *Cash value* – taxable only if the amount exceeds premiums (taxed on gain) • *Policy loans* – not taxable, interest not tax deductible • *Dividends* – not taxable as return of premium; any interest is taxable • *Death benefit* – not taxable if lump-sum; any interest is taxable
Annuities	• Tax-deferred accumulation • *Withdrawal of interest and principal* – taxed on a Last In, First Out basis (LIFO) • *Cash surrenders* – immediate taxation of the earned interest
IRAs	• *Contributions* – pretax dollars, tax deductible, must be made in "cash" • *Earnings* – tax deferred • *Distributions* – taxable; 10% penalty for early withdrawals
Roth IRAs	• *Contributions* – after-tax dollars, not tax deductible • *Distributions* – not taxable

Business Life Insurance	• Employer contributions:
	  - Tax deductible to the employer; not taxed as income to the employee
	  - The earnings grow tax deferred
	• Lump-sum distributions to employees have favorable tax treatment

OTHER RELATED CONCEPTS	
Rollovers and Transfers	• Tax-free transactions • Distribution of money from one qualified retirement plan to another • Must be completed within 60 days • If from plan to the participant, 20% of distribution is withheld • If from plan to trustee, no withholdings (direct rollover)
Modified Endowment Contracts (MECs)	• Overfunded life insurance policy (7-pay test) • *Accumulation* – tax deferred • *Distributions* – taxed on a Last In, First Out basis (LIFO) • Distributions before age 59 ½ – 10% penalty

CHAPTER 12:
Accident and Health or Sickness Insurance – Basics

This chapter will present various classes of health insurance policies and concepts that generally apply to health insurance. You will begin by learning about the principal types of losses and benefits, common exclusions from coverage, and a producer's responsibilities and liabilities for errors. This chapter will take an in-depth look at health insurance underwriting. This type of underwriting is especially prone to unfair discrimination because of the presence of certain health conditions and the use of genetic information. Finally, you will learn about the concept of policy replacement and factors to consider in determining the best course of action for the policyholder.

- Basic Health and Disability Insurance Principles, Concepts, and Marketplace
- Underwriting
- Rate-Making Components
- Duties of Insureds and Insurers in the Event of Loss

Basic Health and Disability Insurance Principles, Concepts, and Marketplace

Health insurance is a generic term encompassing several related insurance contracts designed to protect against different risks.

Two distinct types of insurance are included under the generic term health insurance. One type provides coverage for costs related to health care, and the second is designed to provide payments for a loss of income. The terminology used to reference health insurance differs from state to state and insurer to insurer. The health insurance policy designed to provide periodic payments when an insured cannot work because of sickness or injury is known as disability income insurance.

Important Terms

Accident vs. Sickness – Under a health insurance policy, there are two major causes of loss (perils). Policies can cover both accident and sickness or accident only.

Accidental bodily injury is an unintended and unforeseen injury resulting from an accident rather than a sickness.

Sickness usually refers to an illness that first manifests itself while the policy is effective. Most health insurance claims result from sickness instead of accidental injury. An emergency medical condition is so severe in pain or symptoms that, if not quickly and adequately treated, it could cause serious bodily harm or death.

Accidental Means vs. Accidental Results – Like many disability policies, Accidental Death and Dismemberment (AD&D) policies also distinguish between injuries due to *accidental means* and *accidental results*.

With policies that base payment on accident means, the injury and its cause must be unintended and unexpected. For instance, a man loses an arm in a car accident. The accident and the loss are both unexpected.

With policies that base payment on accidental results, only the injury has to be unintended and unexpected. For example, a man is cliff-diving and breaks his back. The man intentionally jumped off the cliff, but not to break his back.

Coinsurance – Most major medical policies contain a *coinsurance provision* that allows for sharing expenses between the insured and the insurer. After the insured satisfies the policy deductible, the insurer usually pays most of the costs, typically 80%, with the insured paying the remaining 20%. Other coinsurance arrangements such as 90/10, 75/25, or 50/50 are also available. The larger the percentage covered by the insured, the lower the required premium. This provision enables the insurer to control costs and discourage policy overutilization.

Deductible – A *deductible* is a stated dollar amount the insured must pay first before the insurer pays the policy benefits. A deductible intends to have the insured absorb the more minor claims, while the coverage provided under the policy absorbs the more significant claims. Consequently, the larger the deductible, the lower the premium the policy owner must pay.

Most major medical policies have an *annual deductible* (also known as a calendar year deductible) that is paid once in any year, regardless of the number of claims. These policies may contain an *individual deductible*, where each insured is personally responsible for a specified deductible amount each year. They may also include a *family deductible*. The annual deductible is satisfied if two or more family members pay a deductible in a given year, regardless of the number of claims incurred by other family members. Some policies contain what is known as a *per-occurrence deductible* or *flat deduct*ible, which the insured must pay for each claim. This type of deductible could result in the policy owner paying more than one deductible in a given year.

The policy may also contain the *common accident* provision, which applies when more than one family member is involved in a single accident. In this case, only one deductible applies to all family members injured in the same accident.

Some supplemental major medical plans also contain an *integrated deductible*. The amount paid under basic medical expense coverage may satisfy the deductible amount. For example, if the supplemental coverage had a $1,000 integrated deductible, and the insured incurs $1,000 in basic medical expenses, the deductible will be satisfied. If the basic policy only covers $800 of the basic costs, the insured must satisfy the remaining $200 difference.

Some policies also include a *carry-over provision*. Suppose the insured did not incur enough expenses during the year to satisfy the deductible. In that case, the policy owner could carry over any costs during the final three months to the following year to meet the new annual deductible.

Example 12.1 – An insured has a $500 deductible. The individual incurs $100 in the first half of the year, and another $250 during the last quarter, ultimately not reaching the total deductible for the year. The $250 could be carried forward to the following year. The insured would be eligible for claim payments if they incurred an additional $250 in the new year.

Long-term care and disability income policies typically have a time deductible as an elimination period.

Copayment – *Copayments* are arrangements where the insured pays a specific amount for a claim, usually when receiving the service, and the insurer pays the remaining amount. Copayments differ from coinsurance because copayments are generally expressed in set dollar amounts. In contrast, coinsurance is typically expressed as a percentage of the cost.

Gatekeeper Concept – Initially, the member selects a *primary care physician* or *gatekeeper*. If the member requires the attention of a specialist, the primary care physician has to refer the member. This referral process helps prevent the member from seeing the higher-priced specialists unless medically necessary.

Managed Care – A *managed care* program is considered any medical expense plan that attempts to contain costs by controlling participants' behavior. Managed care plans should have the following five essential characteristics:

1. Controlled access to providers;
2. Comprehensive case management;
3. Preventive care;
4. Risk sharing; and
5. High-quality care.

Extension of Benefits – *Extension of benefits* refers to the continuation of coverage under a specified benefit after discontinuing the original coverage to a dependent or employee. This provision protects a disabled individual from becoming uninsured because of a loss of coverage. Basic medical expense benefits will typically be extended for three months, while major medical expense benefits will typically be extended for 12 months. For an extension of benefits to be provided, the insured must have been disabled before the policy was discontinued and has to continue being disabled.

Stop-Loss Provision – Most policies also limit the out-of-pocket expenses the insured can incur during a policy year. A *stop-loss limit* is a stated dollar amount beyond which the insured no longer contributes to sharing costs. The insurer pays 100% of the expenses above the stated stop-loss limit.

Waiting Period – The *waiting period* or *elimination period* stipulates how long an individual must wait to receive benefits for a period of disability. The elimination period starts on the policy's effective date and lasts five months. Benefits are received at the beginning of month six. They cannot be offered retroactively for a period of disability that started during the elimination period.

Waiver of Premium – Insurers typically include the *waiver of premium* provision or rider with guaranteed renewable and noncancelable disability income policies. It specifies that in the event of total and permanent disability, the insurer will waive premiums for the duration of the disability. The insured must be disabled for a specified period, typically six months, to be eligible. The insured must continue paying the policy premium during this 6-month waiting period. However, the waiver is usually retroactive to the date the disability began, and any paid premiums during the waiting period are refunded. This provision or rider usually expires when the insured reaches age 65. As long as the insured becomes disabled before age 65, the insurer will waive premiums for the duration of the disability.

Master Policy – In group insurance, the policy is also referred to as the *master policy* and is issued to the policy owner, which could be an association, employer, union, or trust.

Pre-existing Conditions – *Pre-existing conditions* are those for which the insured has received a diagnosis, advice, treatment, or care during a specific period before the application for health coverage. Until January 2014, health insurance policies could exclude these conditions from coverage. However, the Affordable Care Act eliminated pre-existing conditions restrictions in individual and group health insurance plans. Long-term care insurance and Medicare Supplement policies may have pre-existing condition limitations.

Cancellation and Renewability Features

Cancellable – Sometimes, a person might need health insurance for a specified period. Coverage is then considered a term health policy, which is not renewable. When the term expires, the insured has to purchase another policy. These policies are also known as *period of time* policies as they are only effective for a specific period and will be canceled by the company at the end of the term.

Short-term health plans, travel accident policies, or accident-only policies are examples of term health policies. Other examples include policies that cover specific events, such as summer camps, school functions, or athletic events. Once the event has concluded, coverage is no longer in place.

Noncancelable – The insurer cannot cancel a *noncancelable* policy, nor can the premium be raised beyond what is in the policy. The policy may call for an increase in a particular year, like "age 65," which the insurer must write in the original contract. The insured has the right to renew the policy for the contract's life. The insurance company cannot increase the premium above the amount for which the insurer initially issued the policy. However, the guarantee to renew coverage typically only applies until the insured reaches age 65. At this time, the insured is usually eligible for Medicare. For disability income insurance, the policy will be renewed beyond age 65 only if the insured can prove that they have continued to work a full-time job.

Guaranteed Renewable – The *guaranteed renewable* provision is similar to the noncancelable provision, except that the insurance company can raise the policy premium on the anniversary date. However, the policy owner has the unilateral right to renew the policy for the contract's life. The insurance provider can only raise premiums *on a class basis* and not on an individual policy. As with noncancelable policies, coverage usually is not renewable beyond the insured's age of 65. Insurers must write long-term care and disability insurance policies and Medicare Supplements as guaranteed renewable contracts. The insurance company cannot cancel them when the insured reaches age 65.

Conditionally Renewable – With a *conditionally renewable* policy, the insurer can terminate the contract only at renewal for certain conditions specified in the contract. For example, one condition may be that the insured needs to be employed to collect disability payments. In addition, the policy premiums can be increased. The insurance company *cannot* deny renewal due to claims experience.

Optionally Renewable – *Optional renewability* is similar to conditional renewability, except the insurer can cancel the policy for any reason on certain homogeneous classes. Insurers cannot do this for individuals within a class. Renewability is at the option of the insurance provider. The insurer can only decide not to renew a policy on the policy anniversary or renewal date (premium due date). If the insurance provider elects to renew coverage, it can also increase the policy premium.

Major Kinds of Insurance Mechanisms

Service Type

Blue Cross and Blue Shield – Blue Cross and Blue Shield organizations (Blues) have contractual agreements with hospitals and physicians. The hospitals and physicians are the producers in the cooperative. Blue Plans are voluntary, not-for-profit health care organizations. However, in some states, several Blue plans have recently amended their structure to become for-profit organizations. They are not considered insurance companies.

Blue Plans began as separate associations, with Blue Cross providing payments to hospitals and Blue Shield covering physician charges. Blue Cross still pays hospital charges, and Blue Shield pays physician charges. However, the two associations are now merged as one.

Blue Cross and Blue Shield are operated as local facilities throughout each state; a governing board manages them in each locality. They are considered *prepaid plans* because each subscriber pays a set fee (typically monthly) to receive the services provided under the plan. Blue Cross and Blue Shield is also considered a *service plan* because benefits are paid to the health care providers (hospitals and physicians) instead of to the insured (subscriber).

When dealing with group plans, the Blues and insurance companies utilize *experience rating* to calculate rates to be charged. The rates are based on the overall experience of the group. The Blues, however, still use *community rating* in pricing products for smaller employers and individuals. Community rating involves pooling the experience of all groups in all areas and then setting an average rate that will be adequate to support this experience. This rate then applies to every group insured under a particular plan. Most Blue Shield plans now offer surgical benefits on a reasonable and customary basis.

HMOs – Increasing health care costs during the 1970s and 1980s helped stimulate the rapid growth of *Health Maintenance Organizations (HMOs)*. HMOs were created to manage health care and the associated costs by providing prepaid care that emphasizes preventive care. This concept is quite a departure from traditional health insurance policies that usually do not cover preventive care, covering illness only after it has manifested.

An HMO is regarded as an organized system of health care that delivers a comprehensive array of medical services on a prepaid basis. These services are provided to voluntarily enrolled individuals living within a specified geographic area known as a *service area*. Insureds, also called *subscribers*, pay a premium to the HMO and are provided with a broad range of health care services, including emergency room care and routine doctor visits. The service is provided by physicians and hospitals that contract with the HMO to provide care.

Indemnity Type

An *indemnity plan* pays health insurance benefits to the insured based on a predetermined rate set for medical services. The actual expense amount for those services does not matter. The policy will pay the fixed amount specified in the contract. Generally, an indemnity plan will pay a stated amount for each day the insured is hospitalized as an inpatient. It does not typically pay the cost of specific hospital bills, specific doctor bills, or medical expenses.

Insurers – Commercial insurers like stock, mutual, and life insurers also write health and disability insurance on an indemnity basis. These policies can be written as either individual or group policies and contain benefits for hospital, medical, surgical, and major medical expenses.

MET – A *Multiple-Employer Trust (MET)* comprises two or more employers in similar or related businesses who are not eligible for group insurance on their own. Before HIPAA defined small employers, many small companies could not obtain health insurance at a reasonable cost because there were not enough employees to insure. In situations like this, several small companies banded together to create a large pool of people so that the insurer would provide coverage. This group of employers jointly obtain a single benefit plan to cover employees of each separate employer.

A noninsured plan can operate without the services and funds of an insurer. When the trust fund is established, it can pay for the employee's health care expenses directly (self-funding). The trustee manages the fund, and all financial activity occurs through it. With any self-funded program, the employer bears legal responsibility for providing coverage. Upon leaving the group coverage, the employee has no conversion rights.

PPO – *Preferred Provider Organizations (PPOs)* are the traditional medical systems' answer to HMOs. Under the PPO system, the physicians are paid fees for their services instead of a salary. Nevertheless, the member is encouraged to visit approved member physicians who previously agreed upon the fees to charge. This incentive comes in the form of benefits. Members can utilize any physician they choose. However, the PPO will cover 90% of the cost of a physician on their approved list while only covering 70% of the cost if the member uses a physician not included on the PPO's approved list.

EPO – A type of PPO is an *Exclusive Provider Organization (EPO)*. The members of an EPO do not select health care providers from a list of preferred providers. Instead, insured members under an EPO plan use specific providers who are paid on a fee-for-service basis.

Self-Funding – Self-funded plans are funded by the insured (generally the employer) and administered by a third party. A successful self-funded program will have the following characteristics:

- A group large enough to reasonably predict future loss experience;
- Sound statistical data to support the concept of self-funding;
- A stop-loss contract to assume losses beyond the insured's retention;
- A third-party administrator who handles claims;
- Flexibility in the plan's design and administrative procedures.

Other

Associations – An *association group* (alumni or professional) can purchase group insurance for its members. The group must have been active for at least two years, be organized for reasons other than buying insurance, have at least 100 members, have a constitution and by-laws, and hold at least annual meetings. Examples of these groups include, but are not limited to, college alumni associations, professional associations, trade associations, veteran associations, customers of large retail chains, and saving account depositors. Association group plans can be either contributory or noncontributory.

Franchises – *Franchise* insurance delivers health coverage for small groups whose numbers are too small to qualify for true group insurance. Franchise insurance is not group insurance because individual policies are issued for each participant. Individual underwriting is performed for each person, and every participant submits their application and medical history. The premiums charged are usually less for an individual policy but are more than the premiums for group coverage.

Trusts – Group health insurance policies cover groups of individuals, with or without their dependents, and can be issued to one of the following types of groups:

- An employer insuring at least five employees for the benefit of individuals other than the employer;
- An association or labor union insuring at least 25 members, has a constitution and bylaws, and has been organized and maintained for purposes other than that of purchasing insurance; or
- At the discretion of the state Department of Insurance, any other substantially similar group that is subject to the issuance of group health insurance policies or contracts.

Limited Insurance Policies

Travel Accident – A *travel accident* policy offers coverage for injury or death resulting from accidents while a fare-paying passenger is on a common carrier. The benefits are only paid if the loss occurs while traveling.

Specified and Dread Disease and Critical Illness – A *dread disease* (or limited risk) policy delivers various benefits for a specific disease, like a heart disease policy or cancer policy. Benefits are typically paid as a *scheduled, fixed-dollar* amount of indemnity for specified medical procedures or events, such as chemotherapy or hospital confinement.

Critical illness policies cover multiple illnesses, such as renal failure, heart attack, and stroke. It pays a lump-sum benefit to the insured upon the diagnosis (and survival) of any illnesses the policy covers. The policy typically specifies a minimum number of days the insured must survive after a physician first diagnosed the condition.

Hospital Income or Hospital Confinement Indemnity – A *hospital indemnity* policy offers a stated benefit amount daily, weekly, or monthly for insureds confined in a hospital. Payment under this policy type is unrelated to incurred medical expenses that insurers determine based on the *number of days confined in a hospital*. This policy is also known as a hospital fixed-rate policy.

Accident-Only – *Accident-only* policies are limited policies that offer coverage for disability, death, dismemberment, or hospital and medical care caused by accidents. Because it is a limited medical expense policy, it will only cover losses caused by accidents, not sickness.

Credit Disability – A *credit disability* policy is issued only to those in debt to a particular creditor. In the case of the borrower's disability, insurers will make payments to the creditor on the loan until the disabled borrower can return to work.

Key points to remember about limited policies include:

- *Accidental injury* only pays benefits for injuries from accidents (not from sickness);
- *Specified disease* pays a fixed-dollar amount benefit only for a specified disease;
- *Indemnity policies* pays based on the number of days the service was provided, commonly a fixed dollar amount per day.

Underwriting

Field Underwriting

In *health insurance*, field underwriting is significantly more critical than it is in life insurance. The purpose of health insurance underwriting is to minimize the problem of adverse selection. Adverse selection involves the fact that those most likely to have claims are most likely to obtain insurance. An insurance provider that has sound underwriting guidelines will avoid adverse selection more often than not. It is essential to note that the *specific underwriting requirements will vary according to the insurance company.*

Moral hazard is a substantial factor in health insurance underwriting because of the possibility of malingering. The producer, not the home office underwriter, has personal contact with the applicant. It is the producer's responsibility to ask the applicant questions clearly and precisely and to record the answers accurately.

An agent's role as the field underwriter is to collect credible information from an applicant that would help the underwriter in screening marginal or unacceptable risks before applying for an insurance policy.

Application Procedures – An insurance application begins with a form provided by the insurance company, which the agent completes by asking the applicant questions and recording the applicant's responses. This form is also called the "app." The agent submits the application to the insurance provider for approval or rejection. The application is the applicant's written request to the insurer to issue a policy or contract based on the information found in the application. When insurance providers issue a policy, a copy of the application is stapled to the back, becoming a part of the *entire contract.*

A "notice to the applicant" has to be issued to every applicant for health insurance coverage. This notice informs the applicant that the insurance provider will order a credit report concerning their prior history and previous health insurance applications. The agent is required to leave this notice with the applicant.

Completeness and Accuracy – Agents must take special care with the accuracy of the application in the interest of both the insurance company and the insured. The application is often the primary source of underwriting information. The agent's responsibility is to ensure that they complete the application completely, correctly, and according to the applicant's knowledge.

Signatures – The proposed insured must sign every application for *health insurance* (if they are not the insured) along with the agent who solicits the insurance policy.

Changes in the Application – Most insurance companies require that the applicant fills out the application in ink. The applicant might answer a question incorrectly and want to change it, or the agent may make a mistake when filling out the app. There are two ways to make corrections on an application. The first and best way is to start over with a new application. If that is not practical, the agent may correct an application by drawing a line through the incorrect answer and inserting the correct one. *The applicant must add their initials next to the updated answer.*

Premiums with the Application – Under the terms of the insurability conditional receipt, the insurance coverage becomes effective as of the date of the receipt, on the condition that the application is approved. This receipt is usually provided to the applicant when the initial premium is paid at the time of application.

Disclosure of Information about Individuals – An insurance provider or a producer cannot disclose any personal or privileged information about a person unless any of the following occurs:

- A written authorization by the person dated and signed within the past *12* months has been provided;
- The information is provided to all of the following:
  - A law enforcement agency or an insurance regulatory authority;
  - An affiliate for an audit, but no additional disclosure is to be made;
  - A group policyholder for the purpose of reporting claims experience;
  - To an insurance provider or self-insured plan for coordination of benefits;
  - A mortgagee, lienholder, assignee, or other individuals having a legal or beneficial interest in an insurance policy.

Common Situations for Errors and Omissions – At any time during the sales process, there can be a misrepresentation or misunderstanding that could lead to legal action being taken by the insured. Producers should document everything, including phone conversations, interviews, requests for information, etc. The *sales interview and the policy delivery* are the most common occasions for errors and omissions (E&O) situations that can result in insufficient coverage or failure to maintain and service coverage.

Insurance Company Underwriting

The underwriter's role is to select acceptable risks for the insurer. The selection criteria used in this process, by law, must be only those items that are based on expected experience or sound actuarial principles. The underwriter cannot decline a risk because of deafness or blindness, genetic characteristics, sexual orientation, or marital status.

The primary considerations during underwriting for health insurance policies include gender, age, occupation, moral and morale hazards, physical condition, avocations (hobbies), and the applicant's financial status.

Sources of Underwriting Information

Application – A thorough and accurate application is imperative to the insurer.

Producer Report – Only the producer is involved in completing the producer report, also called the agent's report. It asks questions about the length of time the applicant has been known to the agent. This report also asks about the applicant's net worth and income and whether the producer knows of any reason the contract should not be issued. The producer's report does not become part of the entire contract.

Attending Physician's Statement – If the underwriter determines it is necessary, the insurance provider will send an attending physician's statement (APS) to the applicant's doctor for completion. The APS is the best source for accurate information about the applicant's medical history. The physician can clarify what the applicant was treated for, the necessary treatment, the length of treatment and recovery, and the prognosis.

Suppose an attending physician's report exposes a condition requiring more information for underwriting purposes. In that situation, if this information is unavailable from that physician, the insurance provider can require an examination of the applicant by a physician of the insurer's choice at the insurer's expense.

Investigative Consumer (Inspection) Report – An investigative consumer report includes information obtained through an investigation of an applicant's general reputation, character, personal habits, and mode of living. For example, this report could include interviews with the applicant's friends, associates, and neighbors. These reports cannot be performed unless the applicant is clearly and accurately notified of the report in writing. The consumer report notification is generally part of the application. When an individual completes the application, the producer will separate the notification and give it to the applicant.

Medical Information Bureau (MIB) – The *Medical Information Bureau (MIB)* is a membership corporation owned by member insurers. It is a nonprofit trade organization that gathers adverse medical information from insurers and maintains confidential medical impairment information on individuals. Reports on prior insurance information can be obtained from the Medical Information Bureau. Members of the MIB can get a report on an applicant and receive coded information from any other insurance applications submitted to other MIB members. An insurer cannot use MIB information in and of itself to decline a risk. Still, it can provide the underwriter with additional information crucial to avoiding adverse selection.

Medical Examinations and Lab Tests (Including HIV Consent) – When required by the insurer, medical examinations are conducted by physicians or paramedics at the insurer's expense. Typically, these exams are not necessary for health insurance, thereby emphasizing the importance of the producer in recording medical information on the application. The medical examination requirement is more common in the underwriting process for life insurance. If an insurance provider requests a medical exam, the insurer is responsible for the cost of the exam.

When an insurance provider requires an applicant to take an HIV test, the insurer must first obtain the applicant's written consent for the test. The consent form has to explain the test's purpose and inform the applicant about the confidentiality of the results and procedures for notifying the applicant about the results. Underwriting for HIV or AIDS is allowed as long as it does not unfairly discriminate. An adverse underwriting decision is not allowed if it is solely based on the presence of symptoms. Insurers are required to maintain strict confidentiality regarding HIV-related test results or diagnoses. Test results cannot be provided to the MIB if the patient is identified.

The following are guidelines to help insurance providers avoid unfair underwriting for the risk of HIV/AIDS:

- If tests were performed correctly, insurance companies could decline a potential insured for coverage if their medical sample comes back "positive for HIV/AIDS" after two different tests. An insurer can also decline the applicant if they have already been diagnosed with AIDS/HIV by another medical professional.
- These tests must be paid for by the insurance company, not the insured.
- If an insurance provider tests for HIV, it must first obtain informed, written consent from the insured. This consent often entails a separate disclosure form signed by each insured and the producer. Agents should give a copy of this duplicate form to the client. The disclosure includes written details on the tests performed, their purposes and uses, and how the insurer will provide results to the insured. The form often asks for a doctor's name and address so that the client's physician can get involved should a positive result come back. If the client has no physician, the insurance provider should urge the client to consult a physician or government health agency.
- Informed consent also includes providing the client with information regarding AIDS/HIV counseling from third-party sources.
- The information collected by authorized personnel must be handled correctly and in compliance with confidentially requirements.
- If an insured correctly obtains coverage but later dies from AIDS or AIDS-related conditions, coverage cannot be limited or denied.

From an ethical and nondiscrimination standpoint, no insurance provider or its agents can consider the person's gender, occupation, marital status, sexual orientation, living arrangements, zip code, or other related demographic characteristics in determining whether to take an application, provide coverage, or perform any medical tests. The insurers cannot ask if the insured has been previously tested unless it was for insurance purposes. None of this information should be either on the application or implied. This requirement is so the underwriter can make an unbiased determination and avoid overt or apparent discrimination. The only allowable criterion an insurance company can use to determine whether to test for HIV is the amount of insurance the applicant has applied for at a particular age range.

Negligently disclosing confidential results or underwriting information to an unauthorized third party can result in a civil fine of up to $1,000 plus court costs. The fine can increase to $5,000 plus costs for willful violations. When the violation causes bodily, psychological, or economic harm to the other party, the penalty can include a *misdemeanor* charge, one year in jail, or a fine of up to $10,000.

Additional information that could be required from the applicant for health coverage if the application reveals certain health conditions or other risk exposures is as follows:

- **Department of Motor Vehicles** – Statistically, half of all accidental deaths in the U.S. occur due to traffic collisions. Insurance providers are very interested in the driving records of their applicants. A poor driving record could result in a rated policy.
- **Additional medical testing/Current physical** – The insurance provider can ask for the applicant to be examined by a physician and the results submitted for consideration. It is also common to require examination by a paramedical company and the use of urine, blood, or saliva samples to check for nicotine or other drug use and the presence of HIV. An EKG (electrocardiogram) or a treadmill exam may also be required.
- **Hazardous activity questionnaire** – The insurance provider can also ask the applicant to fill out a separate hazardous activity questionnaire to identify the applicant's risk classification. The questionnaire can include questions regarding scuba diving, hobby aviation, and auto, boat, or motorcycle racing.

Genetic Testing – Genetic characteristics refer to any scientifically or medically identifiable gene or chromosome known to be a cause of a disorder or disease and determined to be associated with a statistically increased risk of development of a disorder or disease. Examples of genetic conditions include sickle cell, Tay-Sachs, and X-linked hemophilia.

Insurance providers cannot require a test of the presence of a genetic characteristic to determine insurability except in policies that are contingent on testing for other medical conditions or diseases. The insurance provider must obtain the applicant's written consent whenever a genetic characteristic test is conducted. The insurance company must also inform the applicant of a test result directly or through a designated physician.

Classification of Risks – Once the underwriters have collected and reviewed all the necessary information on the applicant, they will decide to accept or decline the applicant for insurance. The applicants that have been accepted will fall into one of the three categories of risks, which include preferred, standard, or substandard.

Preferred – *Preferred* risks reflect a reduced risk of loss and are insured at a reduced rate. Nonsmokers would be considered preferred risks.

Standard – *Standard* risks reflect average exposures and can be insured at standard rates and premiums.

Substandard – *Substandard* risks are those that reflect an increased risk of loss. These applicants may be able to obtain health insurance coverage but at a higher premium. An applicant can receive a substandard rating for a poor health history, hazardous vocation, or avocation.

Alternative options available to the underwriter for substandard risks of applicants include:

- Charging a higher premium to reflect the greater exposure to loss; or
- Modify coverage by requiring a longer probationary period.

Rate-Making Components

Morbidity

Morbidity is the incidence or probability of accidents or sicknesses within a given group of people.

Insurer Expenses

The insurance provider collects the mortality charge to pay the policy face amount if an insured dies. Since the insurance company earns interest on the premiums it collects, the expected interest is subtracted from the mortality cost to arrive at the *net premium*.

$$Net\ Premium = Mortality - Interest$$

Then, the insurance provider adds its expected operating costs of underwriting, overhead, and commissions to calculate the *gross premium* that the insured pays.

$$Gross\ Premium = Mortality - Interest + Expenses\ (loading)$$

Another way to look at this formula is net premium plus expenses (loading) equals the gross premium.

$$Gross\ Premium = Net\ Premium + Expenses\ (loading)$$

Example 12.1 – Assume that

$500 Mortality cost		$400 Net premium
- $100 Interest		+ $200 Operating cost
$400 Net Premium	therefore,	$600 Gross Premium

Investment Return

Since premiums are paid before claims are incurred, insurance companies invest the premiums (invested in stocks, bonds, mortgages, etc.) to earn interest on these funds. This interest is the main factor in lowering the premium.

Benefit Duration

Probationary Period – The *probationary period* provision stipulates that a specific time must pass before coverage for specified conditions goes into effect. This provision is generally in disability income policies. The probationary period also applies to new employees who have to wait a specific time before they can enroll in the group plan. This provision intends to prevent unnecessary administrative expenses in cases of employee turnover.

Elimination Period – The *elimination period* is a type of deductible usually found in a disability income policy. It is a specific number of days that have to expire after an accident or onset of an illness before benefits are payable. Longer elimination periods will result in a lower cost of coverage.

Duties of Insureds and Insurers in the Event of Loss

In the event of loss, the following steps have to be taken by the parties to the insurance contract:

1. The insured must inform the company of the loss.
2. The insurer's agent will mail claim forms to the insured.
3. The insured completes the forms and returns them with the proof of loss to the insurance provider.
4. The insurance provider pays all claims as soon as possible or within the policy's specified time limit or the period specified by state law.

The insurance provider must pay death claims immediately upon receipt of written proof of loss. Most states interpret this to be within 30 days. The death proceeds are paid to the insured's estate if no beneficiary is named in the policy. An insurance provider cannot delay the payment of a death claim until the settlement of the insured's estate has been completed.

Chapter Review

This chapter discussed the basic concepts of accident and health or sickness insurance. Let's review the major points:

RIGHTS OF RENEWABILITY	
Noncancelable	• An insurance company cannot cancel or increase premiums beyond the amount stated in the policy
Cancellable	• Insurance providers can cancel the policy at any time or the end of the policy period with proper written notice and a refund of any unearned premiums
Guaranteed Renewable	• Insurance carriers can raise the policy premium (on a class basis only) on the policy anniversary date • The insured has the unilateral right to renew the policy for the life of the contract
INSURANCE MECHANISMS	
Blue Cross and Blue Shield	• Blues have contractual agreements with hospitals and physicians • The hospitals and physicians are the producers in the cooperative • Blue Plans are voluntary, not-for-profit health care organizations • They are considered prepaid plans because each subscriber pays a set fee (typically monthly) to receive the services provided under the plan • Benefits are paid to the health care providers (hospitals and physicians)
Health Maintenance Organizations (HMOs)	• Preventive care • Limited service area • Limited choice of providers • Copayments • Prepaid basis • Primary Care Physician (PCP) acts as a gatekeeper • PCP referral required

INSURANCE MECHANISMS *(Continued)*	
Preferred Provider Organizations (PPOs)	• A group of hospitals and physicians provide services at a reduced fee • Members can use any physician but are encouraged to use approved physicians who have previously agreed upon fees
Other Insurance Mechanisms	• *MET* – A *Multiple-Employer Trust (MET)* is two or more employers in similar or related businesses who are not eligible for group insurance on their own • *EPO* – insured members under an EPO plan use specific providers who are paid on a fee-for-service basis • *Self-funding* – plans that are funded by the insured (generally the employer) and administered by a third party • Associations – an association *group* (alumni or professional) can purchase group insurance for its members
Limited Insurance Policies	• *Travel accident* – offers coverage for injury or death resulting from accidents while a fare-paying passenger is on a common carrier • *Dread disease policy* – provides a variety of benefits for a specific disease such as heart disease policies or cancer policies • *Critical illness* – a lump-sum payment is made to the insured upon the diagnosis and survival of a critical illness • *Hospital indemnity* – provides a specific amount on a daily, weekly, or monthly basis while the insured is hospitalized • *Accident-only* – coverage for a disability, medical care, death or dismemberment resulting from an accident • *Credit disability* – issued only to those in debt to a particular creditor
UNDERWRITING	

Underwriting	• *Application* – completed and signed
	• *Producer's report* – agent's observations about the applicant that can assist in the underwriting process
	• Premiums with application and conditional receipts
	
	• Company Underwriting:
	 - Multiple sources of information: application, consumer reports, MIB
	 - *Risk classification:*
	  ○ Standard
	  ○ Substandard
	  ○ Preferred

Sources of Insurability Information	• *Attending Physician Report* – provides the most accurate information on the applicant's medical history • *MIB report* – helps insurers share adverse medical information on insureds • *Credit Reports* – contain factors related to a risk's potential for loss, including consumer reports (information regarding a consumer's credit, character, reputation, or habits collected from employment records, credit reports, and other public sources) and investigative consumer reports (information obtained through an investigation and interviews with associates, friends, and neighbors of the consumer) • *Medical Exam Report* – conducted by paramedics or physicians

CHAPTER 13:
Medical Expense Insurance

This chapter will teach you about the different types of medical plans available in the market today. As you read this chapter, please focus on the different types of coverage you can offer policy owners and compare them in terms of advantages and disadvantages. One person might find a given type of health insurance more desirable than another based on health status, vocation, and financial status. This chapter has a great deal of essential information to absorb, so be sure to read through it thoroughly.

- Types of Plans
- Managed Care Plans
- Consumer Driven Health Plans
- Optional Coverages
- Contract Issues and Clauses
- Group Health Insurance
- Regulation of Providers
- Patient Protection and Affordable Care Act (PPACA)

Types of Plans

Basic

Insurers commonly group basic hospital, surgical, and medical policies and major medical policies under the banner of *Medical Expense Insurance*. These policies deliver benefits for covering the cost of medical care resulting from sickness or accidents. The three basic coverages (hospital, surgical, and medical) can be purchased separately or as a package. These coverages are known as *first-dollar coverage* because they do not require the insured to pay a deductible. This coverage differs from Major Medical Expense insurance; however, the basic medical coverages generally have more limited coverage than the Major Medical Policies.

Basic hospital expense coverage – Hospital expense policies cover hospital room and board charges and miscellaneous hospital expenses. These expenses can include medicines, lab and x-ray charges, and the use of the operating room and supplies when a hospital admits the insured. The insurer sets the limits on room and board at a specific dollar amount per day up to a maximum number of days, and there is no deductible. These limits may not cover the total hospital room and board costs incurred by the insured. For instance, if the hospital expense benefit was $500 per day, and the hospital charged $600 per day, the insured would be responsible for the additional $100 per day.

Miscellaneous Hospital Expenses – *Miscellaneous hospital expenses* generally have a separate limit. This amount pays for the various costs associated with a hospital stay. This separate limit appears as a multiple of the room and board charges, such as ten times the room and board charges or a flat amount. A policy might specify the maximum limit for certain expenses, such as $100 for drugs or $150 for using the operating room. As with the room and board charges, the miscellaneous hospital expense limits may not cover the total amount needed by the insured during a lengthy hospital stay.

Basic Medical Expense Coverage – *Basic medical expense coverage* is also known as Basic Physicians' Nonsurgical Expense Coverage. It offers coverage for nonsurgical services a physician provides. However, the benefits are typically limited to visits to patients confined in the hospital. Some policies will also cover office visits. There is no deductible, but coverage is usually limited to a certain number of visits per day, a specified limit per visit, or a specific limit per hospital stay.

In addition to nonsurgical physician's expenses, insureds can purchase basic medical expense coverage to cover maternity benefits, emergency accident benefits, mental and nervous disorders, home health care, hospice care, outpatient care, and nurses' expenses. Regardless of the type of plan or coverage purchased, these policies usually offer only limited benefits contingent upon time limitations. The insured must often pay a considerable sum of money and the benefits paid by the medical expense policies.

Basic surgical expense coverage – This coverage is usually written together with Hospital Expense policies. These policies cover the costs of surgeons' services, whether they perform the surgery in or out of the hospital. Coverage includes the surgeons' fees, an anesthesiologist, and the operating room when it is not a miscellaneous medical item. Similar to the other basic medical expense coverage types, there is no deductible, but coverage is limited. All contracts have a *surgical schedule* that lists the types of operations covered and their assigned dollar amounts. If the procedure is not on the schedule, the contract may pay for a similar operation. Special schedules may list a specified amount, express the amount payable as a percentage of the maximum benefit, or assign a relative value multiplied by its conversion factor.

Comprehensive Major Medical

A *comprehensive major medical plan* is a combination of basic expense coverage and major medical coverage in one policy. They cover practically all medical expenses, hospital, surgical, physicians, nursing, laboratory tests, drugs, etc. Comprehensive major medical policies include a deductible and coinsurance, and are usually sold on a group basis. Typically, a single deductible is applied per person and per family, but a corridor deductible could also apply.

Supplemental Major Medical

Supplemental Major Medical Policies can be purchased to supplement the coverage payable under a basic medical expense policy. The supplemental major medical policy covers any expenses not covered by the basic medical expense policy and any costs that exceed the maximum. The supplemental policy will provide coverage moving forward if the time limit has passed in the basic policy.

Managed Care Plans

HMO

General Characteristics – The HMO (Health Maintenance Organization) offers benefits in the form of services rather than reimbursement for a physician's or hospital's services. HMOs are also known as service plans. Usually, the insurance carriers provide the financing, while the doctors and hospitals provide the care. The HMO concept is distinctive in that it offers both patient care and financing for its members.

Combined Health Care Delivery and Financing – Traditionally, the insurers provide the financing while the doctors and hospitals deliver the care. The HMO concept is unique in that it provides patient care and financing for its members.

Limited Service Area – The HMO provides health care services to individuals living within specific geographic boundaries, like city limits or county lines. If a person lives within the boundaries, they are eligible to enroll in the HMO. They are ineligible if they do not live within the service area.

Limited Choice of Providers – The HMO limits costs by only offering care from physicians that meet their standards and are willing to provide care at a pre-negotiated price.

Copayments – A *copayment* or copay is a set dollar amount or a specific part of the cost of care that the member must pay. For example, the member might pay $5, $10, or $25 for each doctor's office visit.

Prepaid Basis – HMOs operate on a *capitation basis*. The HMO receives a flat monthly amount attributed to each member, whether they see a physician. Essentially, it is a prepaid medical plan. As a plan member, you will receive all the necessary services from the member physicians and hospitals.

Preventive Care Services – The primary goal of the HMO Act was to lower the cost of health care by utilizing *preventive care*. While most insurance plans did not provide any benefits for preventive care before 1973, HMOs offer free annual check-ups (routine physicals) for the entire family. Through these visits, the HMOs hope to identify diseases in the earliest stages, when treatment is most likely to succeed. The HMOs also offer members well-baby care and free or low-cost immunizations to prevent certain illnesses.

Primary Care Physician (PCP) – When a person becomes a member of the HMO, they will select their *primary care physician (PCP)* or *gatekeeper*. Once selected, the insurer will pay the primary care physician or

HMO regularly for being responsible for the care of that member, whether or not care is provided. It should be in the best interest of the primary care physician to keep this member healthy to prevent future treatment of disease.

Referral (Specialty) Physician – For the member to see a specialist, the primary care physician (gatekeeper) must refer the member. The referral system prevents the member from seeing higher-priced specialists unless it is essential. Many HMOs impose a financial cost to the primary care physician for referring a patient to a more expensive specialist. Therefore, the primary care physician is incentivized to use an alternative treatment before providing a referral. HMOs must have mechanisms to handle complaints that sometimes result in the delay of a referral or complaints about coverage concerns or other patient care.

Hospital Services and Emergency Care – The HMO offers the member inpatient hospital care, in or out of the service area. The services may be limited when treating mental, emotional, or nervous disorders, including drug or alcohol treatment or rehabilitation.

Emergency care must be provided for the member whether they are in or out of the HMO service area. Suppose a member receives emergency care outside the service area. In that situation, the HMO will be eager to get the member back into the service area so salaried member physicians can provide care.

Other Basic Services – HMOs must have mechanisms to deal with patient care complaints or coverage concerns.

Open Panel or Closed Panel – An *open panel* is when a medical caregiver contracts with a health organization to deliver services to its subscribers or members. The health care provider maintains the right to treat patients who are not subscribers or members. In an open panel arrangement, the physicians are not considered to be employees of the health organization.

A *closed panel* is when the medical caregiver delivers services to only subscribers or members of a health organization and is not allowed to treat other patients contractually. In a closed panel arrangement, the physicians are considered employees of the health organization.

PPO

General Characteristics – A PPO (Preferred Provider Organization) is a group of physicians and hospitals that contract with insurance companies, employers, or third-party organizations to provide medical services at a reduced fee. PPOs differ from HMOs in two ways. First, providers do not offer medical care on a prepaid basis, but physicians are paid a fee for service. Secondly, subscribers do not have to use physicians or facilities that contract with the PPO.

Types of Parties to the Provider Contract – Any qualified physician or hospital that agrees to follow the PPO's standards and charges the appropriate fees that the PPO has established can join the PPO's approved list. Physicians and hospitals can belong to several PPO groups simultaneously.

Primary Care Physician Referral – The insured does not have to choose a primary care physician in a PPO. The insured can select medical providers not found on the preferred list and retain coverage. The insured can receive medical care from any provider. Yet, if the insured chooses a PPO provider, the insured will incur lower out-of-pocket costs. Conversely, if an insured utilizes a non-network provider, the insured's out-of-pocket costs will be higher. In a PPO, all network providers are "preferred." The insured can visit any of them, even specialists, without seeing a primary care physician first. Certain services might require plan pre-certification, which evaluates the medical necessity of inpatient admissions and the number of days needed to treat the condition.

POS

The *Point-Of-Service (POS)* plan is simply a combination of HMO and PPO plans. With the Point-Of-Service plan, employees do not have to be locked into one plan or choose between the two. Employees can make a different selection whenever a need arises for medical services.

Similar to HMOs, PPO plans enter into a contract with health care providers who form a provider network. Plan members do not have to use only in-network providers for their medical care.

In a Point-Of-Service plan, the individuals can visit an in-network provider at their discretion. If they elect to utilize an out-of-network physician, they may do so. However, the member deductibles, copays, and coinsurance could be considerably higher.

With these plans, participants typically have access to a provider network controlled by a primary care physician (gatekeeper). However, plan members can seek care outside the network but at a reduced coverage level. POS plans are also known as open-ended HMOs.

If a participant uses a non-member physician under the POS plan, the attending physician will be paid a fee for service. However, the member patient will have to pay a higher coinsurance amount or percentage for using a non-member physician.

The Point-Of-Service (POS) plan combines the ability to self-refer at increased out-of-pocket costs with gatekeeping arrangements. A patient can acquire higher benefits at a lower cost when care is arranged through or provided by the primary care physician (PCP). Benefits for covered services when self-referring without having a PCP arrange for the service are usually more expensive.

EPO

An *Exclusive Provider Organization (EPO)* is a preferred provider organization (PPO) type. In EPOs, individual members use specific preferred providers rather than having a choice of various preferred providers. An EPO is distinguished by a primary physician who monitors care and refers members to a network of providers.

Consumer Driven Health Plans

Medical Savings Accounts (MSAs)

Medical Savings Accounts (MSAs) are employer-funded accounts linked to a high-deductible medical insurance plan. The employer increases the medical plan deductible and returns all or part of the premium savings to the employees to contribute to an MSA. The employee then utilizes the funds from the MSA to pay for health insurance deductibles during the year. When there is a balance at the end of the year, the employee can leave it in the account and earn interest or withdraw the remaining amount as taxable income. Also, when a distribution is made for a reason other than to cover qualified medical expenses, the withdrawn amount will be subject to an income tax and an additional 20% tax.

Medical savings accounts are only available to a self-employed person or small employers with 50 or fewer employees. Usually, participants in the plan cannot have Medicare or any other health coverage that is not a high deductible health plan (HDHP). The following additional coverages are allowed:

- Specific disease or illness;
- Accidents or disability;

- Workers compensation;
- A fixed amount per day of hospitalization;
- Dental care;
- Vision care; and
- Long-term care.

Contributions to an MSA need to be made in cash or its equivalent. There are two limits on the amount an employer and employee can contribute to an MSA: the annual deductible limit and an income limit. Under the *annual deductible limit* rule, the maximum contribution amount that can be made to an MSA is 65% of the high-deductible plan for individuals or 75% of the family deductible for those with family coverage. Under the *income limit* rule, an individual cannot contribute more than what was earned for the year from the employer through whom the individual has an HDHP.

MSAs were created for ease of use, as they are a cross between a self-funded plan and a traditional Medical Expense Contract. When there is a balance at the end of the year, the employee can let it remain and earn interest or withdraw the amount as taxable income.

Flexible Spending Accounts (FSAs)

A *Flexible Spending Account (FSA)* offers benefits funded by employer contributions and salary reduction. Employees can deposit a certain amount of their income into an account before paying taxes. This account reimburses the employee for eligible health care and dependent care expenses during the year. FSA benefits are subject to "use-it-or-lose-it" and annual contribution rules; this plan does not offer a cumulative benefit beyond the plan year.

The two types of Flexible Spending Accounts include Health Care Accounts for out-of-pocket health care expenses and Dependent Care Accounts (subject to annual contribution limits) to help cover dependents' care expenses. These accounts make it possible for employees and their spouses to continue working.

An FSA is not subject to federal income taxes, Social Security (FICA) taxes, or state income taxes, ultimately saving 1/3 or more in taxes. When the plan favors highly compensated employees, the benefits for these employees are not exempt from federal income taxes.

Child and dependent care expenses have to be for the care of one or more qualifying individuals:

- Dependents under the age of 13 who received care. Employees can claim these individuals as an exemption on their Federal Income Tax return;
- A spouse who was mentally or physically not able to care for themselves; or
- Dependents who are mentally or physically incapable of caring for themselves. They can be claimed as an exemption if the individual earns gross income less than an IRS-specified amount.

Individuals who cannot clean, dress, or feed themselves due to mental or physical problems are unable to care for themselves. Also, individuals who require constant attention to prevent injuring themselves or others cannot care for themselves as well.

The insured can change benefits during open enrollment. After that period, insureds cannot make other changes during the plan year. However, the insured may be able to make a change under one of the following conditions, referred to as qualified life event changes:

1. Marital status;
2. Number of dependents;

3. One of the dependents becomes eligible for or no longer satisfies the coverage requirements under the Medical Reimbursement plan for unmarried dependents because of student status, attained age, or any similar circumstances;
4. The insured, the insured's spouse, or a qualified dependent changes employment status that impacts eligibility under the plan (at least a 31-day gap in employment status is required to qualify);
5. Change in dependent care provider; or
6. Family medical leave.

The IRS limits annual contributions for Dependent Care Accounts to a specified amount adjusted annually for the cost of living. This limit is a family limit. Even if both parents contribute to flexible care accounts, their combined contributions cannot exceed the amount.

Health Reimbursement Accounts (HRAs)

Health Reimbursement Accounts (HRAs) include funds set aside by employers to reimburse their employees for qualified medical expenses, like coinsurance amounts or deductibles. Employers qualify for the preferential tax treatment of funds put in an HRA in the same way they are eligible for tax advantages by funding an insurance plan. Employers may deduct the cost of a health reimbursement account as a business expense.

The following are fundamental characteristics of HRAs:

- They are contribution health care plans rather than defined benefit plans;
- HRAs are not a taxable employee benefit;
- Employer contributions are tax-deductible;
- Employees can roll over their unused balances at the end of the year;
- Employers do not have to advance claims payments to employees or health care providers during the early months of the plan year;
- HRAs are funded with employer dollars, not employee salary reductions;
- They allow the employer to reduce health plan costs by combining the HRA with a high-deductible (and usually lower-cost) health plan; and
- HRAs balance the group purchasing power of larger and smaller employers.

HRAs are available to employees of companies of all sizes. Still, the employer decides eligibility and contribution limits.

An HRA has no statutory limit. However, limits are set by the employer, which can be rolled over at the end of the year based on the employer's discretion. Former employees, including those who have retired, can have continued access to unused HRAs, but only at the employer's discretion. HRAs stay with the originating employer and do not follow an employee to their new employment.

High Deductible Health Plans (HDHPs) and Health Savings Accounts (HSAs)

Individuals frequently use *High Deductible Health Plans (HDHPs)* in coordination with MSAs, HSAs, or HRAs. The high deductible health plan features higher out-of-pocket limits and annual deductibles than traditional health plans, lowering premiums. Except for preventive care, individuals must meet the yearly deductible before the plan pays benefits. Preventive care services are typically first-dollar coverage or paid after copayment. The HDHP credits a part of the monthly health plan premium into the coordinating MSA, HSA, or HRA. Individuals can pay the HDHP deductible with funds from the coordinating account plan.

Health Savings Accounts (HSAs) help individuals save for qualified health expenses incurred by their spouse or dependents. The HDHP can make a tax-deductible contribution to an HSA and use it to pay for out-of-pocket medical expenses. An individual's taxable income does not include employer contributions to a Health Savings Account.

To be eligible for an HSA, a person:

- Must be covered by a high deductible health plan (HDHP);
- Must not have coverage under other health insurance (does not apply to specific injury insurance and accident, disability, long-term care, dental care, vision care); and
- Must not qualify for Medicare and cannot be claimed as a dependent on someone else's Federal Income Tax return.

HSAs are associated with high deductible insurance. Individuals can obtain coverage under a qualified health insurance plan with minimum deductibles.

Each year qualified individuals (or their employers) are allowed to save up to certain limits, regardless of their plan's deductible. A person must be under the Medicare eligibility age when opening an account. For taxpayers age 55 and older, an additional contribution amount of $1,000 is allowed.

HSA holders who use the money for a non-health expenditure will pay tax, plus a 20% penalty. After age 65, withdrawals used for a non-health purpose will be taxed but not penalized.

HSAs are portable; therefore, a person is not dependent on a specific employer to enjoy the advantages of an HSA. Like an individual retirement account (IRA), the individual owns the HSA, not the employer. If the person changes jobs, the HSA follows the individual.

Some high deductible health insurance policies have what is known as an *embedded deductible*. As well as a non-embedded or aggregate deductible that applies to the entire family, an individual deductible (smaller than the aggregate) applies to each covered family member. For example, a family can have a $2,000 aggregate deductible and a $1,000 embedded deductible. When one family member exceeds $1,000 in medical expenses, the insurance provider will pay for additional medical costs for that person, while other family members' medical expenses will apply towards the aggregate deductible.

When a health plan includes both the aggregate deductible and embedded deductibles, the annual contribution limit for an HSA is the lesser of

- The maximum annual contribution limit;
- The aggregate deductible; or
- The embedded deductible multiplied by the number of covered family members.

Consumer Driven Health Plans (CDHPs)

Consumer Driven Plans (also referred to as Consumer Driven Health Plans, CDHP, High-deductible plans, or patient-directed plans) are health care plans controlled by the employer. The member (employee) receives first-dollar coverage from a designated health account (HSA or HRA) until funds are depleted. Before an insurance plan can cover the additional cost, a deductible gap must be met. Other types of plans restrict particular types of coverage. However, members of a consumer driven plan can use funds from the plan to pay for costs related to genetic testing or a special nursery school for a child, for example, without being denied coverage.

The employer determines their employees' eligibility. Consumer driven plans do not have national qualifying requirements.

The employer determines the contribution amount, the growth percentage, and the exit rules. Funds are permitted to be rolled over yearly at the employer's discretion.

Optional Coverages

Dental

Generally, dental insurance distinguishes among several classes of dental costs and provides somewhat different treatments for each.

Routine and preventive maintenance is covered up to an annual maximum without a copayment or deductible. This coverage benefit typically includes regular examinations, teeth cleaning once a year, and perhaps full-mouth X-rays every three years. The absence of a copayment and deductible is intended to encourage preventive maintenance.

Routine and major restorative care includes oral surgery and treatment of cavities, bridges, and dentures. These procedures are covered to a specific maximum, subject to an annual deductible for each insured family member and coinsurance.

If included, *orthodontic care* will have a separate deductible and a maximum, which can differ from the deductible for restorative care.

Under the Affordable Care Act, pediatric dental coverage is an essential health benefit. It *must be available* as part of a health plan or stand-alone plan for children 18 or younger. However, insurance providers are not required to offer adult dental coverage.

Depending on the state, insureds can obtain pediatric dental benefits through any of the following types of plans:

- A qualified health plan which includes dental coverage;
- A stand-alone dental plan purchased with a qualified health plan; or
- A bundled/contracted plan.

Vision

Some employers offer their workers this type of group health insurance to cover eye exams, eyeglasses, and hearing aids on a limited basis. It is essential to know that pediatric vision benefits are mandatory under the Affordable Care Act.

Supplemental Accident

Accidental Death and Dismemberment (AD&D) coverage can be written as a separate policy or as a rider. It is frequently a part of group health and group life plans. AD&D coverage provides a lump-sum benefit payment if the insured dies from an accident or in the event of losing particular body parts resulting from an accident.

Accidental Death and Dismemberment coverage is a pure form of accident insurance and only pays for accidental losses. The *principal sum* is the benefit amount paid for accidental death. This amount is generally equal to the face amount or the amount of coverage under the insurance contract. When a loss of sight or accidental dismemberment occurs, the policy pays a percentage of that principal sum, often referred to as the *capital sum*. The benefit amount will vary according to the severity of the injury.

The policy will typically pay the entire principal for losing two or more limbs or sight in both eyes. However, it might only pay 50% for losing one hand or foot. Also, in cases of accidental death, some policies will pay a double or triple indemnity, which means the policy will pay twice or three times the face amount.

As long as the death results from the accident and occurs within *90 days*, most policies will pay the accidental death benefit.

Contract Issues and Clauses

Family Deductible

The *family deductible* is written for any claim filed by a family member within a year. It applies to the deductible for the whole family. Family deductibles are also typically written with a common accident provision. This provision specifies that if more than one family member is injured in the same accident, only one deductible will apply.

Grace Period

The *grace period* is the time beyond the premium due date. Policyholders can still pay premiums before the policy lapses for nonpayment of the premium. Grace periods may differ according to individual state laws. In most cases, the grace period cannot be less than *seven days for policies with a weekly premium, ten days for policies with a monthly premium, and 31 days for every other mode*. During the grace period, coverage continues in force.

Waiting Periods

The *waiting period* is the time before insurance benefits begin. During the waiting period, the policy is effective, but the insurer has not started paying benefits for covered events.

Elimination Periods

The *elimination period* is identical to the waiting period. Insureds can select elimination periods of 30, 60, 90, 180, or 365 days. Some policies will start paying benefits after only a seven or 14-day elimination period. Longer elimination periods will lower premiums for disability policies. Giving clients a choice of the length of their elimination period allows them to make a value judgment for balancing the premium expense and benefits.

Right to Terminate

Individual health and disability policies have a provision that provides the insurance company the *right to terminate* policies. Right-to-terminate provisions change from policy to policy and affect all insureds covered under a particular type of policy or all insureds in a specific group. These insureds are known as a "class." A class of insureds can be people who live in the same geographical region, are the same age, or perhaps perform the same type of work.

Take-Over Benefits

Coinsurance and Deductible Carryover – The *carry-over provision* lets an insured who incurs medical expenses during the last 90 days of a calendar year apply the expenses toward the new year's deductible.

No Loss, No Gain – When a health policy is replaced for a client with an ongoing claim, the *no-loss/no-gain* law stipulates that the pre-existing condition provision in the new policy will not apply. The new policy must automatically take over payment of the claim immediately.

First Dollar Coverage

Policies designed around a corridor or integrated deductible each provide *first dollar coverage*. With first dollar coverage, up to 100% of covered claims are covered, beginning with the first dollar of the expense incurred by an insured. A *corridor plan* provides basic medical expense coverage of 100% for all covered expenses, but only to a pre-established limit, such as $3500, $5000, $7500, or perhaps as high as $10,000. After the basic benefits are depleted and before the major medical benefits take over, the insured pays the next $3500-$10,000 of covered expenses. Therefore, first dollar coverage provides coverage to a specific limit, followed by 100% insured expense, followed once again by 100% major medical coverage. Plans using an *integrated deductible* also offer first dollar coverage. The insurance provider and the insured will share all covered expenses up to a pre-established limit using an 80-20% coinsurance split, with the stop-loss limit set between $5000 and $25,000. Under this plan, an insured will pay $1000-$5000 of the total first dollar claims expenses.

Restoration of Benefits

The *restoration of benefits* provision lets an insured regain their full lifetime benefit level over a certain period after a significant or catastrophic loss.

Exclusions and Limitations

The purpose of policy exclusions is to protect the insurance provider from claims for losses that were excluded in the initial risk assessment. The insurance provider is entitled to control its risk, and this is possible by excluding certain types of catastrophic, intentional, criminal, or excess losses. The most common types of losses excluded from coverage are those resulting from the following:

- War or acts of war;
- Military service;
- Intentionally self-inflicted injuries;
- Attempted suicide;
- Committing or attempting to commit a felony; and
- Serving as the pilot or crew member of a commercial aircraft. Most insurance policies will cover an insured as a fare-paying passenger on an airline.

Group Health Insurance

Eligible Groups

Eligibility for group coverage requires that the members form the group for a purpose other than obtaining group health insurance. In other words, the coverage needs to be incidental to the group. Usually, two types of groups qualify for group insurance, including employer-sponsored and association-sponsored.

The employer (a sole proprietorship, partnership, or corporation) offers group coverage to employees with an *employer-sponsored group*. Eligible employees typically have to meet specific time of service requirements and work full time. Like group life insurance, group health insurance can be either contributory or noncontributory.

An *association group* (alumni or professional) can purchase group insurance for its members. The group must have been active for at least two years, be organized for reasons other than buying insurance, have at least 100 members, have a constitution and by-laws, and hold at least annual meetings. Examples of these groups include, but are not limited to, college alumni associations, professional associations, trade associations, veteran associations, customers of large retail chains, and saving account depositors. Association group plans can be either contributory or noncontributory.

A *creditor group*, also known as credit life and health insurance, is a specialized use of group life and group health insurance that insures debtors (borrowers). It protects the lender from losing money due to a borrower's disability or death. Usually, the borrower pays the premium, but the lending institution is the policy's beneficiary. The amount of insurance cannot exceed the amount of debt.

Small Employer – A *small employer* is any individual, corporation, firm, partnership, or association engaged in business that, on at least 50% of its working days during the previous calendar year, employed no more than 100 eligible employees. The majority of these individuals must have been employed within the state.

As a condition of conducting business in this state with small employers, every small employer carrier must actively offer to small employers at least *two health benefit plans*:

1. Basic health benefit plan; and
2. Standard health benefit plan.

Basic Care is a managed plan established with the Health Benefits plan committee. The Basic Care Plan is lower in cost than the Standard Benefit Plan. A Standard Benefit Plan is a managed care plan established with the Health Benefits plan committee that delivers better benefits at a higher cost than the Basic Care Plan.

All small employer carriers must provide the small employer health benefit plan on a *guaranteed issue basis* or without regard to related health status factors. Each small employer carrier must issue the plan chosen by the small employer to small employers that choose to be covered under the plan. These small employers must also agree to meet the plan's other requirements.

Qualified Small Employer Health Reimbursement Arrangements (QSEHRA) – Small employers who do not offer group health coverage can assist employees in paying medical expenses through a Qualified Small Employer Health Reimbursement Arrangement (QSEHRA). A QSEHRA is an Affordable Care Act-compliant health plan designed to pay for medical costs and monthly premiums associated with medical plans purchased through the individual market.

In a QSEHRA, the employer is the sole funder of the arrangement. Employee salary reductions are not allowed.

For employers to offer a QSEHRA, the business cannot employ more than 50 full-time employees.

*   Employers can exclude QSEHRA plans to employees who:
    o   Have not met 90 days of service;
    o   Do not reach age 25 before the start of the plan year;
    o   Are seasonal or part-time employees;
    o   Are covered by a collective bargaining agreement; or
    o   Are nonresident aliens with no earned income from references within the United States.

Contributory vs. Noncontributory

Like group life insurance, group health insurance can be either contributory or noncontributory. Under a *contributory* plan, the eligible employees contribute to the premium payment (both the employer and employee pay part of the premium). If a plan is contributory, at least 75% of all eligible employees are required to participate in the plan. If the plan is *noncontributory*, 100% of the eligible employees have to be included, and the participants do not pay part of the premium. The employer pays the whole premium. The reason for these participation requirements is to protect the insurance provider against adverse selection and to lower administrative costs.

Occupational vs. Nonoccupational

Nonoccupational policies exclude coverage of claims that are the result of job-related accidents. Typically, the employer is covered by workers compensation, which is the main coverage for employee disability and medical costs for claims arising out of the performance of a job.

Occupational policies would cover accidents occurring on or off the job.

Coordination of Benefits

The *Coordination of Benefits (COB)* provision (found only in group health plans) avoids over-insurance and duplication of benefit payments for individuals covered under multiple group health plans. This provision limits the total amount of claims paid from all insurance providers covering the patient to no more than the total allowable medical expenses.

The COB provision sets up which plan is the primary or which one is responsible for providing the total benefit amount as specified. Once the primary plan has paid its full benefit, the insured submits the claim to the *secondary*, or *excess*, provider for any additional payable benefits, including deductibles and coinsurance. In no case will the total amount the insured receives surpass the costs incurred or the maximum benefits available under all plans.

Amount covered by Secondary Plan = Loss - Amount covered by Primary Plan

If every policy has a COB provision, the order of payments is determined as follows:

- If a married couple both have group coverage and are each named dependent on the other's policy, the individual's group coverage is considered *primary*. The *secondary* coverage (spouse coverage) will pick up where the first policy's coverage ends.
- If both parents name their children as dependents under their group policies, the *birthday rule* will typically determine the payment order. The coverage of the parent whose birthday falls first in a calendar year will be considered primary). On occasion, the *gender rule* may also apply, according to which the father's coverage is considered primary.
- If the parents are separated or divorced, the policy of the parent who has custody of the children will be considered primary.

Dependents of Insured Employees

Under group insurance policies offering hospital, medical, or surgical expense benefits, coverage can be extended to insure dependents. This type of coverage can be in amounts according to some plan that precludes individual selection. When group disability policies refund premiums or pays dividends, the policyholder must apply the excess premium or dividend for the benefit of insured employees or their dependents.

Like a spouse, group policies must provide equal benefits for the registered domestic partner of an insured, employee, or policyholder. Insurance providers cannot discriminate in coverage between domestic partners or spouses of a different sex and domestic partners or spouses of the same sex.

Blanket Insurance

A *blanket* policy covers members of a particular group participating in a specific activity. Such groups include campers, students, passengers on a common carrier, or sports teams. The covered insureds' names are not often known because they come and go. Unlike group health insurance, the members are covered automatically and do not receive a certificate of insurance. Blanket policies are written and paid on an accident-only basis.

The California Insurance Code allows insurance providers to offer blanket insurance to the following entities:

- Newspapers, magazines, or other similar publications to insure the following individuals:
  - Those who collect payments for the publication or deliver publications;
  - Those who supervise the collections or deliveries;
  - Those who are wholesalers; or
  - Others in the sales, marketing, or distribution process of the publication;
- Charitable, religious, recreational, athletic, educational, or civic organizations;
- Employers who pay the benefits afforded by an unemployment compensation disability plan;
- Employers who offer benefits to any group of workers, dependents, or guests, limited to specified activities or operations of the policy owner;
- An entertainment production company that offers benefits to any group of volunteers, participants, audience members, or contestants.

Blanket life insurance can be issued for a *term not exceeding one year* with premium rates less than the typical rates for such insurance. Blanket policies are renewable.

When the insured pays the policy premiums, the insured can request a copy of the policy in the form of a certificate from the insurance provider.

An individual can elect not to be covered by a blanket insurance plan by submitting a written request to the insurance provider. Suppose more than 10% of the individuals eligible for coverage choose not to participate. In that case, the insurer cannot put the insurance contract into effect, or if it has been in effect, it cannot be renewed.

Eligibility and Rating Factors

When a group applies for medical expense insurance, there are several factors insurance providers will consider when determining the group's eligibility and rating structure.

Demographics (Gender, Age, or Occupation) – The underwriter's role is to select acceptable risks for the insurer. By law, the selection criteria used in the underwriting process must be only those items based on expected experience or sound actuarial principles. The underwriter cannot decline a risk based on genetic characteristics, deafness or blindness, sexual orientation, or marital status.

When underwriting health insurance policies, the prime considerations are gender, age, physical condition, occupation, avocations (hobbies), moral and morale hazards, and the applicant's financial status.

Industry – In determining an applicant's eligibility for insurance, insurance providers will consider the specific duties of the applicant's occupation. Such things as dangerous job duties or high employee turnover can affect an applicant's rating. Insurance providers will consider *the types of industries* applying for group coverage.

Location or Zip Code – Insurance providers will also consider the business's location (city or county). These factors aid insurance companies because they can use information based on industrial classification and the health care costs and demographics in a particular area or zip code to assess risks and possible losses.

Carrier History – Insurance providers will also examine a group's carrier history. Carrier is another term for insurance company or insurer. In looking at a group's carrier history, insurance providers will look at the group's "stability" or how many different insurers a group has used in the past. "Longevity" is another factor an insurance company considers when reviewing a group's carrier history. Longevity refers to the length of time a group has been with a particular carrier. The longer the group has been with an insurer, the lower the group's rates will be.

Medical History – Disability income insurance provides weekly or monthly income payments to replace a portion of a worker's lost salary because of an illness or injury. When an application for a disability income policy is submitted, disability insurers must eliminate those applications that would likely have more severe losses than rates would anticipate. This process is how disability underwriting operates when considering medical history.

Chronic or Ongoing Conditions – When writing medical expense insurance, insurance providers will consider whether the applicant has any *chronic* or *ongoing* conditions, defined as continuing, prolonged, or lingering illness or disability. Issuing health policies to insureds with chronic or ongoing conditions could produce immediate or very high claims within a short period. These claims result in adverse selection and, consequently, higher premiums and overall costs.

Catastrophic Conditions – Catastrophic conditions (e.g., fires, floods, earthquakes, etc.) are also considered when writing medical expense insurance. Vast numbers of catastrophic losses in a very short period from the types of perils typically excluded from coverage and which do not allow for an accurate pattern of predictability will negatively slant the law of large numbers.

Disabled Employees and Dependents (Not Actively at Work, Extended Benefits of a Former Carrier) – Insurance providers will also consider whether the group applying for medical expense insurance provides benefits for disabled employees who are not actively working or disabled dependents of employees. As previously discussed, the extension of benefits provision allows disabled employees to be treated the same as if they were not disabled at the time of termination of the previous group policy from a former carrier.

Contribution (Contributing or Noncontributing Policy) – Insurance companies will use another factor to determine a group's medical expense insurance eligibility. This factor is whether the policy will be *contributing* or *noncontributing*. Contributing means that the employees and the employer share the insurance cost. If the policy is contributing, insurance providers require that at least 75% of all eligible group members choose to participate and be covered by the plan. Insurance companies do this to avoid adverse selection because people with poor health will naturally choose to be in the plan. The "75% requirement" ensures that some good and average risks will also elect to be covered, ultimately balancing out the poorer risks.

Participation (Covered and Eligible Employees and Dependents) – Finally, insurance providers will consider the number of employees participating in the group plan. As discussed in the previous chapter, insurers have a participation percentage requirement. The number of employees and their eligible dependents is also considered. A dependent's disability should not be considered when the group member qualifies for coverage beyond set guidelines that apply to all dependents of those covered. The dependent's insurability does not enter into rating or eligibility.

Benefit Schedule

Some medical expense insurance plans contain a *benefit schedule*, specifically specifying what is covered in the plan and for how much. Other plans can incorporate the term *usual, reasonable, and customary*. Usual, reasonable, and customary means the insurer will pay an amount for a particular procedure based on the average charge in that geographic region.

Regulation of Providers

The California Department of Insurance (CDI) has jurisdiction over entities that provide coverages designed to pay for health care providers' services and expenses. However, CDI does not have jurisdiction if the health care providers are appropriately certified or licensed by other governmental agencies.

The Department of Insurance has primary jurisdiction over regulating the activities of individuals conducting insurance business in the state of California. These individuals include all insurance providers, agents, and others, regardless of whether they are licensed or admitted. However, the Insurance Code also has made a special provision for any individual or entity that provides coverage for various medically-related expenses. Such expenses include hospital, medical, surgical, physical therapy, chiropractic, mental health, speech pathology, audiology, dental, or optometry services.

This special provision places the Department of Insurance in a secondary position as the regulator over these "persons" whenever they can demonstrate that another regulatory agency has primary responsibility for their activities. This other regulator could be an agency of the federal government, another state, or another agency of California. Suppose a provider of such insurance plans cannot show that another agency regulates it. In that case, it will be regulated by the Department of Insurance.

The Insurance Code states explicitly that a *health care services plan*, as defined in the Health and Safety Code, will still fall under the jurisdiction of the Department of Insurance. These types of plans include those operated by the following:

- Nonprofit agencies unless they are both the provider of the insurance and the owner-operator of the facilities providing care under the insurance contract;
- Schools, universities, or colleges;
- Public agencies delivering care or coverage for employees, students, or faculty; and
- Self-funded plans operated by other employers.

It is essential to note that the California Department of Insurance is the primary regulator of issuers of most PPO and EPO plans and other disability insurance providers.

The Department of Managed Health Care is the primary regulator of operations, activities, and management of HMOs and other managed health care services providers, like Point of Service plans and some PPO and EPO plans. This agency has primary responsibility for enforcing the Insurance Code and other laws regarding the managed health care industry. The Department of Insurance exercises only limited oversight over providers in this area.

ERISA

In 1974, the federal *Employee Retirement Income Security Act (ERISA)* was passed. It required those who establish and maintain group health insurance and KEOGH Plans to file annual reports with the IRS and the Department of Labor. The annual reports need to detail the following information:

- Documentation of the trust agreement;
- Claim and benefit denials;
- The method of investment;
- Certificates of Participation;
- Enrollment forms;
- Annual statements; and
- Administrative records.

The goal of ERISA was to increase the national participation rate in pension plans and prevent the loss of benefits by individuals who terminate employment before retirement. It also sought to establish minimum standards for funding and vesting and allow for the overall control of new and existing pension plans.

While the law does not require an employer to establish and maintain a pension plan, if such a plan exists, it must conform to the law's provisions. The law prescribes which employees must be included in a plan. It also specifies the amounts that must be contributed, establishes minimum vesting requirements, and sets forth minimum funding requirements.

In addition to the Internal Revenue Service and the Secretary of Labor, the plan must disclose information regarding its operation and financial condition to individuals covered under the plan and their beneficiaries.

Over the years, many amendments have been added that have attempted to expand the protection to plan participants and beneficiaries regarding health coverage and retirement benefits specifically promised to employees and their dependents.

Employer assistance is available to aid the employer in acting in compliance with the law

COBRA and Cal-COBRA

In 1985, Congress passed the *Consolidated Omnibus Budget Reconciliation Act (COBRA)*. It requires all employers with 20 or more employees to offer group health coverage to terminated employees and their families following a qualifying event. *Qualifying events* include the following:

- Voluntary termination of employment;
- Termination of employment for a cause other than gross misconduct (e.g., company downsizing); and
- A change in employment status from full-time to part-time

Employers extend coverage for up to *18 months* if these qualifying events occur. The terminated employee has to exercise the extension of benefits under COBRA within 60 days of separation from employment. The employer collects a premium of no more than 102% of the individual's group premium rate from the terminated employee. The additional 2% charge covers the employer's administrative costs.

For events such as *death*, *divorce*, or *legal separation*, the coverage period is *36 months* for the terminated employee's dependents.

An important concept to remember is that COBRA benefits apply to group health insurance, not group life insurance. Furthermore, unlike the conversion privilege in which the individual converts coverage to an individual health insurance policy, COBRA continues the same group coverage. The terminated employee pays the group premium that the employer paid (or the employee and the employer paid if the plan was contributory).

Under the Affordable Care Act (ACA), coverage for the insured's children extends until the adult child reaches *age 26*. Under COBRA coverage, the same age limit applies to the insured's eligible children. Also, if "dependent child" status is lost under the group plan, the dependent child qualifies for a maximum of *36 months* of continuation coverage.

There are also several *disqualifying events* under which COBRA benefits can be discontinued. These include becoming covered under another group plan, failure to make a premium payment, becoming eligible for Medicare, or if the employer terminates all group health plans.

In California, two COBRA programs are available, depending on the company's size. *Federal COBRA* regulations apply only to companies with 20 or more employees. However, if the company has 2-19 employees, it falls under a state program called Cal-COBRA.

Cal-COBRA is a state program modeled after the federal program and is directly administrated by the health insurance provider. Individuals who sign up for COBRA or Cal-COBRA are eligible for up to 36 months of continuation coverage.

Cal-COBRA requirements do not apply to the following individuals:

- Eligible for federal COBRA;
- Eligible for Medicare benefits even if it is only Medicare Part A;
- Covered by another medical, hospital, surgical plan, or another group plan;
- Covered or eligible under Chapter 6A of the Public Health Service Act;
- Those who fail to submit the required premium.

Mandated Benefits – FMLA and ADA

Under the *Family Medical Leave Act (FMLA) of 1993*, all eligible employees are entitled to 12 total workweeks of leave during any 12 months for one or more of the following:

- The birth of a child of the employee and to care for the newborn child within the first year of birth;
- The placement of a child for foster care or adoption with the employee within one year of placement;
- To care for the child, spouse, or parent of the employee who has a serious health condition;
- Because of a severe health condition that makes the employee unable to perform the duties of their job; or
- Any qualifying need arising from the fact that the employee's child, spouse, or parent is a covered military member on active duty.

Except if the employee takes leave on an intermittent or reduced-leave schedule, any eligible employee who takes leave under FMLA for the intended purpose of the leave is entitled to the following on return from leave:

- To be restored to the employment position held when the leave began; or
- To be restored to an equivalent position with equivalent benefits, pay, and other terms and conditions of employment.

According to the law, taking leave under FMLA cannot result in the loss of any employment benefit, like group medical expense insurance, earned before the date on which the leave began.

The *Americans With Disabilities Act (ADA)* prohibits employers from rejecting job applicants with disabilities because disabled employees will increase the costs of group health care benefits. Additionally, this law prohibits employers from rejecting applicants for employment whose children, spouses, or dependents are disabled because the group plan would cover them.

Pregnancy Discrimination Act

California's Fair Employment and Housing Act (FEHA) bars employers from discriminating against employees who have become pregnant or who are requesting leave associated with pregnancy.

According to the California Pregnancy Disability Leave Act (PDLL), employers must provide up to four months of leave for an employee whose disability resulted from pregnancy or pregnancy-related conditions.

Mental Health Parity Act

The Mental Health Parity and Addiction Equity Act (MHPAEA) is a federal law passed in 2008. It requires coverage parity for mental health benefits with benefits provided by the insured's medical or surgical coverage.

The following coverage requirements apply to *large group plans* with more than 50 employees that provide mental health benefits and medical or surgical benefits:

- Copayments, deductibles, and treatment limitations for mental health benefits cannot be more restrictive than for any other medical benefit;
- Providers are prohibited from imposing separate cost-sharing requirements for mental health benefits.

The Affordable Care Act enacted rules on how health insurance providers carry out these requirements.

HIPAA

Legislation in July of 1997 ensures the "portability" of group insurance coverage. It includes various required benefits that affect small employers, the self-employed, the mentally ill, and pregnant women. HIPAA (Health Insurance Portability and Accountability Act) regulates protection for group health plans for employers with two or more employees and individual insurance policies sold by insurers.

HIPAA includes the following protection for coverage:

Group Health Plans

- Prohibiting discrimination against employees and their dependents based on health conditions;
- Allowing individuals in special circumstances the opportunity to enroll in a new.

Individual Policies

- Guaranteeing access to individual policies for qualifying individuals;
- Guaranteeing renewability of individual policies.

Eligibility – HIPAA has regulations concerning eligibility for employer-sponsored group health plans. These plans cannot set up eligibility rules for enrollment under the plan that discriminate based on any health factor relating to an eligible individual or their dependents. *Health factors* include any of the following:

- Health status;
- Medical conditions (both physical and mental);
- Receipt of health care;
- Claims experience;
- Genetic information;
- Medical history;
- Disability; or
- Evidence of insurability, including conditions arising from acts of domestic violence and participation in activities such as skiing, snowmobiling, motorcycling, etc.

Employer-sponsored group health plans can apply waiting periods before enrollment as long as they are applied uniformly to all participants.

To be eligible under HIPAA regulations to convert health insurance coverage from a *group plan* to an *individual policy*, a person must meet the following criteria:

- Have been covered under a group plan in the most recent insurance;
- Have 18 continuous months of creditable health coverage;
- Have exhausted any COBRA or state continuation coverage;

- Not be eligible for Medicaid or Medicare;
- Not have any other health insurance;
- Apply for an individual health insurance policy within 63 days of losing prior coverage.

Such HIPAA-eligible individuals have a guaranteed right to obtain individual coverage.

Guaranteed Issue – If the new employee satisfies the requirements, the employer has to offer coverage on a guaranteed issue basis.

Pre-existing Conditions – Under HIPAA, a *pre-existing condition* is a condition for which the employee has pursued medical advice, diagnosis, or treatment within a specified period before the policy issue.

Creditable Coverage – *Creditable coverage* means an insured must be given day-for-day credit for previous health coverage against a pre-existing condition exclusion period when migrating from one group health plan to another or to an individual health plan.

Before enacting the Affordable Care Act (ACA), individual insureds were entitled to receive credit for previous creditable coverage without a break of 63 or more consecutive days.

The ACA has prohibited pre-existing condition exclusions and eliminated waiting periods exceeding 90 days. It also removed the requirement to issue HIPAA group health plan certificates of creditable coverage.

Renewability – At the direction of a plan sponsor, the issuer of group health coverage must renew or continue the current coverage. However, the group health coverage can be discontinued or nonrenewed due to the following: fraud, nonpayment of premium, violation of participation or contribution rules, discontinuation of that particular coverage, association membership cessation, or movement outside the service area.

Patient Protection and Affordable Care Act (PPACA)

Overview

The *Patient Protection and Affordable Care Act (PPACA or ACA, or the Act)* was signed into law on March 23, 2010, as part of the Health Care and Education Reconciliation Act of 2010 (Public Law 111 through 148). The ACA is a comprehensive bill implemented in phases until fully effective in 2018. Since the bill is a federal law, the Act supersedes state regulations and must conform accordingly.

The Act mandates increased educational, preventive, and community-based health care services. To help lower health insurance costs, the ACA intends to do the following:

- Establish a new competitive private health insurance market;
- Hold insurance companies accountable by keeping premiums low, preventing denials of care, and allowing applicants with pre-existing conditions to obtain coverage (the ACA eliminated pre-existing conditions exclusions as of January 2014);
- Help stabilize the economy and the budget by reducing the deficit through cutting government overspending; and
- Extend coverage for dependent children until age 26 in individual and group health plans.

Also, it gives small businesses and nonprofits a tax credit for an employer's contribution to health insurance for employees. It prohibits insurers from rescinding health coverage when an insured becomes ill and eliminates lifetime benefit limits.

Specific health coverage plans, such as stand-alone dental, retiree-only, Medigap, and long-term care insurance, are usually *exempt* from the ACA changes.

These provisions are controversial, and health care laws are constantly being challenged in the courts. Agents should review current laws to ensure they give up-to-date information and advice.

Eligibility – The Health Insurance Marketplace makes health coverage available to uninsured individuals. To be eligible for health coverage through the Marketplace, the person:

- Has to be a U.S. citizen or national or be legally present in the United States;
- Has to live in the United States; and
- Cannot be currently incarcerated.

If a person has Medicare coverage, that person is *not eligible* to use the Marketplace to buy a health or dental plan.

Health status (no discrimination) – A group health plan or insurer offering group or individual health coverage cannot establish eligibility rules based on any of the following health status-related factors linked to insureds or their dependents:

- Claims experience;
- Health status;
- Medical condition (including both physical and mental illnesses);
- Medical history;
- Receipt of health care;
- Genetic information;
- Evidence of insurability (including conditions resulting from acts of domestic violence);
- Disability; or
- Any other health status-related factor.

When health insurance providers set their premium rates, they are only allowed to base those rates on four standards:

1. Location of residence within the state (geographic rating area);
2. Single or family enrollment (family composition);
3. Age; and
4. Tobacco use.

For individual plans, the location refers to the insured's home address; for small group plans, the location relates to the employer's principal place of business.

Essential benefits – Essential benefits include hospitalization, emergency services, wellness, and preventive services, chronic disease management, and maternity care.

It is essential to note that all Health Insurance Marketplace plans are required to cover pregnancy and childbirth, even if pregnancy begins before the coverage becomes effective

Guaranteed issue – Insurers must accept any eligible applicant for individual or group insurance coverage. Enrollment for coverage can be restricted to open or special enrollment periods.

Guaranteed renewability – An insurer that offers either group or individual health coverage must renew or continue the policy at the option of the individual or the plan sponsor.

Pre-existing conditions – Under the ACA, the Pre-Existing Condition Insurance Plan offers coverage to those who private insurers have denied health insurance due to a pre-existing condition.

Appeal rights – When insurers rescind individual or group coverage for fraud or an intentional misrepresentation of material facts, they must provide at least 30 days' advance notice to give the insured time to appeal. All insureds or enrollees have the right to review their files, present evidence and testimony as part of the appeal process, and keep their coverage in force pending the outcome of the appeals process.

Coverage for children of the insured – The Act extends coverage for the insured's children to age 26 irrespective of their residency, marital status, financial dependence on their parents, or eligibility to enroll in their employer's health plan.

Lifetime and annual limits – Health plans are restricted from applying a dollar limit on essential benefits. They cannot establish a dollar limit on the benefits paid during an insured's lifetime.

Emergency care – Emergency services must be covered, even at an out-of-network provider, for amounts that would have been paid to an in-network provider for delivering the same services.

Preventive benefits – The ACA stipulates that 100% of preventative care will be covered without cost sharing. Preventive care includes counseling, screenings, and routine checkups to prevent health problems.

Cost-sharing under Group Health Plans – A group health plan has to ensure that any imposed annual cost-sharing does not exceed provided limitations.

The Act established *insurance exchanges* that administer health insurance subsidies and facilitate enrollment in private health insurance, Medicaid, and the Children's Health Insurance Program (CHIP). An exchange can assist the applicant in doing the following:

- Compare private health plans;
- Obtain information concerning health coverage options to make educated decisions;
- Obtain information concerning eligibility or tax credits for the most affordable coverage;
- Enroll in a health insurance plan that meets the applicant's needs.

Metal Tiers

Under the Affordable Care Act, plans in the Marketplace are classified into five coverage categories, including four "metal level" plans and catastrophic plans.

The metal level plans cover different amounts of an average individual's care costs. The actual percentage the insured will pay per service or in total will depend on the services used during the year. Generally, the metal level plans will pay as follows:

1. Bronze: 60%
2. Silver: 70%
3. Gold: 80%
4. Platinum: 90%

For example, under the bronze plan, the health plan is expected to cover 60% of the cost for an average population, and the participants would cover the remaining 40%. Participants with severe diseases can pay significantly more.

Every insurance provider that offers adult and family coverage under the metal levels must also offer child-only coverage.

Young adults under age 30 and individuals who have a hardship exemption (cannot buy affordable coverage) may be able to obtain individual catastrophic plans that cover essential benefits. These plans have lower monthly premiums and high deductibles (several thousand dollars). The insured is typically required to pay up to a certain amount of medical costs. After the insured satisfies the deductible, the catastrophic plan will cover essential health benefits costs.

Medical Loss Ratio (MLR)

The *Medical Loss Ratio (MLR)* indicates how much of the health coverage premium needs to go toward actual medical care instead of administrative costs and profits. Under the Affordable Care Act, consumers will receive more value for their premium dollar. Insurance companies must spend 80% (individual and small group markets) or 85% (large group markets) of premium dollars on health care and medical care quality improvement rather than administrative costs. Only 15-20% of the premium can be applied to administrative expenses. Insurance providers who fail the MLR test for a calendar year will be required to provide a rebate to their customers and refund excess premiums.

Qualified Health Plan

State insurance exchanges provide coverage through *qualified health plans (QHPs)*. Qualified health plans cannot have pre-existing condition limitations, lifetime maximums, or annual limits on the dollar amount of essential health benefits.

The status of a health plan as a qualified health plan will be based on the following characteristics of the plan:

- Provider networks, including community providers;
- Marketing practices;
- Benefit design;
- Plan activities related to quality improvement; and
- Using standardized formats for consumer information.

Essential Health Benefits

As mandated by the Affordable Care Act, all private health insurance plans offered in the Marketplace must provide the same essential health benefits. Every health care plan must include at least the following *ten essential benefits*:

1. Emergency services;
2. Ambulatory patient services;
3. Hospitalization;
4. Maternity, pregnancy, and newborn care;
5. Services for mental health and substance abuse disorder, including behavioral health treatment;
6. Prescription drugs;
7. Rehabilitative and habilitative services and devices;
8. Laboratory services;
9. Chronic disease management and preventive and wellness services; and
10. Pediatric services, including oral and vision care.

Enrollment

State insurance exchanges must allow an *initial open enrollment* period, *annual open enrollment* periods after the initial period (currently scheduled from November 1 through January 31), and *special enrollment* periods. Enrollees or individuals have 60 days from the date of a triggering event to choose a qualified health plan unless expressly stated otherwise. Triggering or qualifying events include the birth or adoption of a child, marriage, divorce, change in employment, or termination of health coverage.

Enrollees and qualified individuals can enroll in or change from one qualified health plan to another due to the following triggering events:

- A qualified individual or dependent loses their minimum coverage;
- A qualified individual adds a dependent or becomes a dependent through birth, marriage, adoption, or placement for adoption;
- A person who was not previously a citizen or lawfully present individual who gains such status;
- A qualified individual's enrollment or non-enrollment in a qualified health plan is erroneous or unintentional and is the result of the misrepresentation, error, or inaction of an employee, officer, or agent of the exchange;
- An enrollee adequately establishes that the qualified health plan in which they are enrolled substantially violated a material provision of its contract;
- A person is deemed newly eligible or newly ineligible for advance payments of the premium tax credit or has a change in eligibility status for cost-sharing reductions, irrespective of whether the individual is enrolled in a qualified health plan;
- An enrollee or qualified individual gains access to new qualified health plans due to a permanent move;
- A Native American, as defined by the Indian Health Care Improvement Act, can enroll in a qualified plan or change from one qualified health plan to another qualified plan once per month; and
- A qualified individual or enrollee establishes that they meet other exceptional circumstances as the exchange may allow.

Tax Credits

Enrollment in the Health Insurance Marketplace began in October 2013, and tax credits for eligible individuals became available in 2014. After applying for health insurance for a qualified health plan, individuals can take an advance tax credit to lower the cost of their health care coverage if purchased through an exchange. For the premium tax credit, household income refers to the Modified Adjusted Gross Income (MAGI) of the taxpayer, spouse, and dependents. The MAGI calculation includes income sources such as salary, wages, interest, dividends, foreign income, and Social Security.

Legal residents and citizens with incomes between *100% and 400%* of the Federal Poverty Level (FPL) qualify for the tax credits. States can extend Medicaid coverage to people under 138% of the FPL. Individuals who receive public coverage like Medicare or Medicaid do not qualify for tax credits.

Individuals who qualify for a premium tax credit and have household *incomes between 100% and 250% of FPL* qualify for cost-sharing subsidies (reductions). Eligible individuals must purchase a silver-level plan to receive the cost-sharing subsidy.

The tax credit is sent directly to the insurer, reducing the insured's monthly health care premiums. Tax credits are based upon the individual's or family's expected annual income.

Small employers that offer health plans may qualify for federal tax credits, depending on the average wages and size of the employer. These tax credits, available to low-wage employers (under $50,000 average per employee) with 25 or fewer workers, can cover up to 50% of premiums paid for small business employers and 35% of premiums paid for small tax-exempt employers.

To qualify for the credit, a small employer has to pay premiums on behalf of all employees enrolled in a qualified health plan offered through a Small Business Health Options Program (SHOP). This credit is available to eligible employers for two consecutive taxable years.

In California, advance premium tax credits (APTCs) may be available to most households with income not exceeding 400% FPL. The credit is determined by the California Health Benefit Exchange (Covered California) and paid by the Exchange to insurance providers.

California Health Benefit Exchange

Covered California is the state's health benefit Exchange. It provides coverage to households above 138% of FPL, with subsidies available up to 400% FPL. Covered California provides four health plan levels, including platinum, gold, silver, or bronze, ranging from 10% to 40% of the customer's portion of health care costs. Subsidies are available for low-income households, like the Advanced Premium Tax Credit (APTC) for households under 400% FPL and Cost-Sharing Reductions (CSR) for households under 250% FPL.

Covered California for Small Business (CCSB) – Covered California for Small Business (CCSB) is a health insurance marketplace. It is available from Covered California for businesses with 1 to 100 eligible employees. Enrollment in CCBS is available year-round. Employers can select plans from four levels of coverage: Bronze, Silver, Gold, and Platinum, as well as Dual Tier Choice, which lets them choose two adjoining metallic tiers.

Small businesses that purchase health insurance through Covered California can qualify for federal tax credits to offset part of their costs. To be eligible for the federal premium tax credit, employers must have less than 25 full-time equivalent employees. They must also pay employees an average yearly salary of less than $54,000 and contribute at least 50% towards employee premium costs.

Agent Training – All agents interested in selling for the Covered California marketplace must complete Covered California's training and certification program and have a valid license with the California Department of Insurance. Training for initial agent certification is offered entirely online through a computer-based system. It covers a wide range of information and instruction on the following topics:

- The Affordable Care Act;
- Covered California for Small Business;
- Agent roles and responsibilities;
- Eligibility for individuals and families; and
- Privacy requirements.

Upon completion, agents must pass the certification exam. After the initial training, Certified Insurance Agents must be *recertified every five years*.

Chapter Review

This chapter discussed different types of medical expense plans available in the market today. Let's review the key points:

MEDICAL EXPENSE INSURANCE	
Basic Hospital, Medical and Surgical Policies	• *Basic hospital expense coverage* – pays for hospital room and board, and miscellaneous expenses, including medicines and lab and x-ray charges while the insured is confined to a hospital • *Miscellaneous hospital expenses* – covers other miscellaneous expenses associated with a hospital stay; expressed as either a flat amount or a multiple of the room and board charge • *Basic medical expense coverage* – pays for nonsurgical physician's services; it can also be purchased to cover maternity benefits, emergency accident benefits, nurses' expenses, mental and nervous disorders, home health care, hospice care, and outpatient care • *Basic surgical expense coverage* – covers the costs of surgeons' services, regardless of whether the surgery is performed in or out of the hospital
Major Medical Policies	• Supplemental Major Medical Policies • Comprehensive Major Medical Policies • Offer a range of coverage (lifetime benefit per person limit) under one policy, including benefits for prolonged injury or illness, comprehensive coverage for hospital expenses, and catastrophic medical expense protection
Health Maintenance Organizations (HMOs)	• Preventive care • Limited service area • Limited choice of providers • Copayments • Prepaid basis • Primary Care Physician (PCP) acts as a gatekeeper • Referral (Specialty) Physician (PCP referral required)
Preferred Provider Organizations (PPOs)	• A group of hospitals and physicians contract to provide services at a reduced fee • Members can use any physician but are encouraged to use approved physicians who have previously agreed upon fees
Point-of-Service plans	• Combines HMO and PPO plans • Employees are not locked into one plan and are allowed to choose depending on the need for medical services
CONSUMER DRIVEN HEALTH PLANS	
Medical Savings Accounts (MSAs)	• Employer-funded accounts linked to a high-deductible medical insurance plan • MSAs are only available to a self-employed person or small employers with 50 or fewer employees. • There are two limits on the amount an employer and employee can contribute to an MSA: the annual deductible limit and an income limit • *Annual deductible limit* – the maximum contribution amount that can be made to an MSA is 65% of the high- deductible plan for individuals or 75% of the family deductible for those with family coverage • *Income limit* – an individual cannot contribute more than what was earned for the year from the employer through whom the individual has an HDHP • When there is a balance at the end of the year, the employee can let it remain and earn interest or withdraw the amount as taxable income

Flexible Spending Account (FSA)	• Funded by employer contributions and salary reduction • Employees deposit pre-tax funds into an account from which the employee is reimbursed for eligible expenses related to health care and dependent care during the year • FSA benefits are subject to "use-it-or-lose-it" and annual maximum rules
High Deductible Health Plans (HDHPs) and Related Health Savings Accounts (HSAs)	• *High-deductible health plans (HDHPs)* – used in conjunction with MSAs, HSAs, or HRAs. Features higher out-of-pocket limits and annual deductibles than traditional health plans, which result in lower premiums • *Health savings accounts (HSAs)* – individuals with high deductible health plans can make a tax-deductible contribution to an HSA, and use it to cover out-of-pocket medical expenses

GROUP HEALTH INSURANCE

Basics	• Group must be formed for a purpose other than purchasing insurance • Two types of group insurance include employer-sponsored and association-sponsored • *Small employer* – any individual, corporation, firm, partnership, or association engaged in business that, on at least 50% of its working days during the previous calendar year, employed no more than 100 eligible employees • If a plan is contributory, at least 75% of all eligible employees are required to participate in the plan • If the plan is noncontributory, 100% of the eligible employees have to be included, and the participants do not pay part of the premium
Underwriting	• Every eligible member of the group must be covered regardless of age, sex, physical condition, or occupation • Cost varies by the average age of the group and the ratio of males to females • Evidence of insurability is usually not required

REGULATION OF PROVIDERS

ERISA	• *Employee Retirement Income Security Act (ERISA)* – it required those who establish and maintain group health insurance and KEOGH Plans to file annual reports with the IRS and the Department of Labor

COBRA and Cal-COBRA	• *Qualifying Events:*
	  ○ Voluntary termination of employment
	  ○ Termination of employment for other reasons besides gross misconduct (e.g., company downsizing)
	  ○ A change in employment status from full time to part time
	• *Length of coverage:*
	  ○ 18 months – after a qualifying event
	  ○ 36 months – for dependents after events such as divorce, legal separation, or death of the employee
	• Cal-COBRA is a state program modeled after the federal program and is directly administrated by the health insurance provider

FMLA and ADA	• *Family Medical Leave Act (FMLA)* – all eligible employees are entitled to 12 total workweeks of leave during any 12 months for the birth of a child, to care for a child, spouse, or parent, or due to a severe health condition • Taking leave under FMLA cannot result in the loss of any employment benefit

REGULATION OF PROVIDERS *(Continued)*	
FMLA and ADA *(Continued)*	• *Americans With Disabilities Act (ADA)* – prohibits employers from rejecting job applicants with disabilities because disabled employees will increase the costs of group health care benefits
HIPAA	• *Health Insurance Portability and Accountability Act (HIPAA)* – regulates protection for group health plans for employers with two or more employees and individual insurance policies sold by insurers

PATIENT PROTECTION AND AFFORDABLE CARE ACT	
Eligibility	• Must be a U.S. citizen or national or be lawfully present in the U.S. • Must live in the U.S. • Cannot be currently incarcerated
Features and Coverages	• Coverage for the insured's children until age 26 • No pre-existing conditions exclusions • Premium rates can only be based on age, geographic area, family composition, and tobacco use

Insurance Exchanges (Marketplace)	• Federally-facilitated marketplace
	• State exchange
	• Help applicants:
	  - Compare private health insurance plans
	  - Obtain information about health coverage options and eligibility for tax credits
	  - Enroll in an appropriate health plan

Metal Tiers	• Under the Affordable Care Act, there are four metal level plans covering different amounts of an average individual's care cost:
	  o Bronze – 60%
	  o Silver – 70%
	  o Gold – 80%
	  o Platinum – 90%

Essential Benefits	• Ten essential benefits:
	  - Emergency services
	  - Ambulatory patient services
	  - Hospitalization
	  - Pregnancy, maternity, and newborn care
	  - Mental health and substance abuse services
	  - Prescription drugs
	  - Rehabilitative and habilitative services and devices
	  - Laboratory services
	  - Chronic disease management and preventive and wellness services
	  - Pediatric services, including oral and vision care

California Health Benefit Exchange	• Covered California is the state's health benefit Exchange; it provides coverage to households above 138% of FPL, with subsidies available up to 400% FPL • *Covered California for Small Business (CCSB)* – a health insurance marketplace available from Covered California for businesses with 1 to 100 eligible employees

CHAPTER 14:
Disability Insurance

This chapter will take an in-depth look at disability insurance. You will learn about the conditions under which an individual can qualify for disability benefits and what determines the duration and amount of those benefits. You will then learn about different effects taxes have on individual and group participants and sponsors, and read about a variety of riders and provisions available in disability insurance policies.

- Qualifying for Disability Benefits
- Disability Income Insurance Features
- Group Disability Income
- Business Disability Insurance
- Social Security Disability Benefits

Qualifying for Disability Benefits

A significant risk that individuals will face in their lifetime is becoming disabled and unable to perform work-related duties. Recent statistics show a 30% chance of a 25-year-old being disabled for more than 90 days before age 65. It is far less likely that the same 25-year-old will suffer a premature death before age 65.

For most people who cannot work, employment income would end after a brief period. Consequently, most individuals would have to use their savings to pay everyday expenses such as rent, food, and utilities. Each person should ask themselves how long they could survive without an income.

Disability income insurance replaces lost income in the event of this possibility. It is a crucial component of a comprehensive insurance program. It can be purchased individually or through an employer on a group basis.

Disability income benefits are limited to a percentage of an insured's earned income. The insurance provider wants a claimant to have a financial incentive to return to work. An individual becomes eligible for regular disability benefits when they satisfy the insurer's definition of disability because of either sickness or injury. This definition of disability varies from insurer to insurer. The applicant and the agent need to be fully aware of the eligible causes of loss that activate this critical benefit trigger in the disability income policy's insuring clause.

Inability to Perform Duties

A disability income policy requires the insured not to be able to perform the duties of their occupation to pay benefits. The benefits will also depend on the policy's chosen definition of disability.

Own Occupation – An own occupation policy will provide benefits when the insured cannot perform any duties of their own occupation due to a sickness or an accident.

This definition is typically limited to the first 24 months following a loss. It allows insureds (claimants) to receive benefits if they cannot perform the duties of their normal occupation because of disablement. Claimants will receive benefits even though they might be able to earn income from a different occupation. After 24 months, if the insured still cannot perform the duties of their own occupation, the definition of disability narrows to mean the inability to perform *any occupation* for which the insured is reasonably suited by experience, training, or education. This narrow definition dramatically reduces the insurance provider's liability because claimants can likely find something they can do for financial gain. The "own occupation" definition is commonly used for highly trained, skilled occupations like trial attorneys, surgeons, etc.

Any Occupation – A policy containing an "any occupation" provision will provide benefits when the insured cannot perform any of the occupation's duties for which they are suited because of experience, training, or education. "Own occupation" is considered the more liberal definition and provides the insured with a better benefit.

Some insurance companies still use the two-tier approach by combining both definitions in a single disability income policy. It is much easier for an insurer to justify the "any occupation" definition when issuing a policy from an underwriting perspective.

Presumptive Disability

Included in most disability income policies is a *presumptive disability* provision that specifies the conditions which will automatically qualify the insured for full disability benefits. Some disability policies provide a benefit when individuals meet specific qualifications, regardless of their capability to work. The presumptive disability benefit covers dismemberment (the loss of use of any two limbs), permanent and total blindness, or loss of hearing or speech. Some policies will specify a requirement of actual severance of limbs rather than loss of use.

Requirement to be Under Physician Care

Most disability income policies mandate that the insured be under the care of a physician and possibly confined to their house to receive benefits.

Disability Income Insurance Features

Types of Disability

Under some disability income policies, the definition of *total disability* differs. Some policies use a relatively strict definition like the *any occupation* definition, similar to Social Security. This definition of total disability requires the insured to be unable to perform any occupation for which they are reasonably suited because of experience, training, or education. Other insurance providers have adopted a more liberal definition of total disability as the "inability to perform the duties of one's own occupation." As expected, the more liberal *own occupation* definition of disability makes it easier to qualify for disability benefits.

Partial disability covers full-time working insureds and refers to the inability to work full-time or perform some, but not all, of one's regular job duties, resulting in a loss of income. The partial disability benefit covers a partial loss of income when the insured's disability allows them to work; however, they cannot perform their regular job. The partial disability benefit is usually 50% of the total disability benefit and is limited to a specific period, as noted in the policy.

Insurers pay the benefits under a partial disability policy in a flat amount or a residual amount.

Recurrent disability is in a policy provision that specifies the period (typically within six months) during which the recurrence of an illness or injury will be considered a continuation of a previous disability period. The importance of this feature is that the recurrence of a disabling condition will not be treated as a new period of disability so that the insured is not subject to another elimination period.

Residual disability is the disability income policy that will help pay for loss of income when a person returns to work after a total disability. The individual is still unable to work at the same level or as long as they worked before becoming disabled. Many insurance providers have replaced partial disability with residual disability, which will provide benefits for a loss of earnings. When the individual can only work part-time or at a lesser-paying position, residual disability will make up the difference between their current earnings and the earnings before the disability.

The *elimination period* is a waiting period imposed on the insured from the start of disability until benefit payments begin. It is a deductible that measures days instead of dollars. The elimination period eliminates coverage for short-term disabilities; insureds will be able to return to work in a relatively short amount of time. The elimination periods contained in most policies range from 30 days to 180 days. Just as a higher deductible amount translates into lower premiums for medical expense insurance, a longer elimination period results in a lower premium for disability income insurance. An essential consideration in selecting the elimination period is stipulating payment in arrears. In other words, if the insured chooses a 90-day elimination period, the insured will be eligible for benefits on the 91st day; however, payments will not begin until the 121st day. In selecting the duration of the elimination period, the insured needs to determine how long they can go without benefit payments following disability.

Under some disability income policies, a *probationary period* is another waiting period imposed in addition to the elimination period. The probationary period is a waiting period, usually 10 to 30 days from the policy issue date, during which insurers will not pay benefits for disabilities related to illness. This period only applies to sickness, not injury or accidents. The probationary period intends to reduce the chances of adverse selection against the insurance carrier. This period protects insurance companies against individuals who will purchase disability income policies shortly after developing a disease or other health condition requiring immediate medical attention.

Injury can be defined using either the accidental means definition or the accidental bodily injury definition. The accidental means definition indicates that the cause of the accident must be unintended and unexpected. Accidental bodily injury suggests the damage to the body is unintended and unexpected. A policy that uses the accidental bodily injury definition provides broader coverage than a policy that uses the accidental means definition.

Illness or *sickness* is defined as a disease or sickness contracted after the policy has been effective for 30 days. It can also refer to a condition or disorder that manifests after the policy becomes effective (in force).

Benefit Limitations – A percentage of the insured's previous earnings determines the *benefit limitations* on the monthly benefit amount payable under most disability income policies. The benefit limits are the maximum benefits the insurance provider is willing to accept for individual risk. It is common for policies to limit benefits to roughly 66% of the insured's average earnings for two years immediately preceding disability.

An insurance provider rarely writes a disability income policy that reimburses the insured for 100% of lost income. Insurance providers don't pay benefits equal to the insured's previous earnings to reduce the chance of the insured pretending to be injured. If an insurance provider provided insureds benefit payments as much or more than the insured earned, the individual would have no incentive to return to work as quickly as possible. By paying the insured a benefit amount somewhat less than their previous earnings, they are motivated to return to work after recovering from a disability instead of collecting benefits.

Most insurance providers will adjust benefits according to the insured's amounts from workers compensation or Social Security. When the insured receives benefits from these programs, the insurance provider will decrease the benefit amount paid under the policy so that the insured cannot profit from their disability.

Usually, disability income policies do not cover losses arising from the following: military service, war, overseas residence, intentionally self-inflicted injuries, or injuries suffered while committing or attempting to commit a felony.

Occupational and Nonoccupational Coverage

Health insurance, including disability insurance, is written on an *occupational* or *nonoccupational* basis. Occupational coverage provides benefits for injury, illness, or disability resulting from accidents or sicknesses occurring on or off the job. Nonoccupational coverage, on the other hand, only covers claims resulting from accidents or illnesses occurring off the job. Insurers write many individual health policies on an occupational or nonoccupational basis. Most group plans are only nonoccupational; they assume that workers compensation coverage will cover accidents or injuries on the job.

Eligibility and Rating Factors

Age – When applying for disability income insurance, the applicant's age is a significant rating factor. As individuals get older, their chance of mortality (death) increases. The likelihood of individuals becoming ill or having accidents also increases as they age. These older individuals do not recover from an illness or accident as fast as younger individuals. For these reasons, the premium rates usually increase as a person ages.

Gender – A person's gender influences their eligibility and rating factor. Statistically, men have a shorter life expectancy than women, so they are a higher mortality risk. On the other hand, women tend to have more health problems as they mature, making them a higher health risk.

Income Requirement and "Elimination Period" – Insurance providers use two methods to calculate the benefits payable under their disability income policies:

1. Calculate benefits using a percentage of the insured's pre-disability income, and consider other sources of disability income; or
2. A flat-amount approach to the amount of disability income benefits that will be paid in the event of the insured's total disability.

Many factors are underwriting considerations when calculating the amount of disability income that can be offered to an applicant based upon other factors that could create a moral hazard.

Example 14.1 – Suppose that George and Paul each earn $100,000 per year and both apply for disability income. George owns his own home and has no mortgage. He also has $500,000 invested in CDs.

Paul is buying a home, has mortgage payments of $1,500 per month, has to make payments on his car, and is repaying student loans taken out while he was in college.

Suppose George becomes disabled, with the amount of disability income and the interest income from the CDs. In that circumstance, he might not be as anxious to return to work as Paul would be, simply because of the difference in their financial obligations. This difference could cause an underwriter to be reluctant to write as much benefit for George as he would for Paul.

Job Classification – In disability income policies, the *insured's occupation* is a vital underwriting factor. The more hazardous the applicant's occupation, the higher the premium the insurer will charge. Professionals like doctors and attorneys pay the lowest premiums and receive superior definitions of disability. More hazardous occupations, like construction workers, pay higher premiums and receive poorer definitions of disability due to a greater risk of disability.

Avocation – *Avocation* is an individual's interests or hobbies. An insurance provider needs to consider these avocations. Dangerous or high-risk hobbies increase the probability of loss taking place. Also, hazardous hobbies increase the likelihood that a loss will be severe. To determine a person's avocations, the insurance company will have applicants fill out a questionnaire to obtain information regarding their interests and hobbies.

Health (Past and Present) – Insurance providers will evaluate an individual's past and present physical condition to determine eligibility and rating factor. An individual in good health is less likely to have an accidental injury or become ill. A person's height and weight are considered while determining an individual's overall health. Statistics show that people who exceed the recommended weight proportion for a certain height by more than 20% have higher incidences of cancer, heart disease, respiratory problems, and diabetes.

Effect of Taxes on Participants and Sponsors

Individual – In *medical expense* insurance policies, unreimbursed medical expenses paid for the insured, their spouse, and dependents can be claimed as deductions. These expenses must exceed a certain percentage of the insured's adjusted gross income (AGI). The law allows deductions for unreimbursed expenses exceeding 10% of the adjusted gross income. However, suppose either the insured or the insured's spouse was born before January 2, 1952. In that case, they can continue to deduct total medical expenses that exceed 7.5% of their adjusted gross income.

This provision will only apply if the insured itemizes these deductions on their tax return.

Group – Disability income benefits are taxed based on who pays the premium. If an employer covers half the insurance cost, half of the benefit is taxable as income to the employee. Suppose an individual's employer makes payments toward the premium, in whole or in part. In that scenario, the benefit will be taxable for income purposes in the same percentage since the employer will be provided a tax deduction for the employee benefit. The same applies to an individual disability income contract. If the employer covers any part of the premium directly, that same percentage of benefit would be taxable as income compared to the total premium.

Generally, someone else will pay tax on the benefit if a person claims a tax deduction. Disability income premiums are not tax-deductible to individuals. The IRS' treatment of insurance premiums by individuals is commonly understood to mean using "after-tax" dollars. It is similar in theory to "nonqualified" annuities, where the percentage of interest income is always taxable. In disability income, if the income results from someone else's tax deduction, the recipient owes the taxes back.

Employer-paid premiums for disability income insurance for its employees are deductible as a business expense. They are not taxable income to the employee.

Benefits received by an employee are fully taxable to the employee as income if they are attributable to employer contributions.

When the employee and employer share in premium contributions, the employee's contribution is not deductible; however, benefits attributable to their portion of the contribution are not taxable as income. The taxation of income received by the employee will depend on the type of group plan:

- **Noncontributory** – The employer pays the entire premium cost, so the income benefits are included in the employee's gross income and taxed as ordinary income.
- **Fully contributory** – The employee pays the entire cost of the premium. Consequently, the employee receives the income benefits free of federal income tax.
- **Partially contributory** – The cost is paid partially by the employee and the employer. The portion paid by the employee is free of federal income tax. The amount paid by the employer is included in the employee's gross income and taxed as ordinary income.

For example, if an employee funds 40% of the premium and receives a benefit of $1,000, only $600 (60% employer contribution) of the benefit payment will be taxed to the employee as income. In comparison, $400 (40% employee contribution) will be received free of federal income tax.

Short-term disability (STD) group plans typically have a benefit period of fewer than two years. In this type of disability income plan, it is common to place a maximum dollar amount on the benefit that the insurer will pay regardless of earnings. It is also common to have an elimination period except for a disability caused by accidents. *Long-term disability (LTD)* group plans generally pay benefits for two years or longer.

Provisions or Riders

Maximum and Minimum Benefits – Like other policies, disability income insurance policies have minimum and maximum benefits. Typically, the benefits are $50-$100 as a minimum and as high as $10,000 as a maximum. Disability income benefits cannot exceed 50-70% of gross earned income, and the policy must pay those benefits not less frequently than monthly.

Benefit Period – The *benefit period* is when the monthly disability benefit payments will last for each disability after the elimination period has been met. Most policies include benefit periods of one, two, or five years, and to age 65. Some plans offer a lifetime benefit period, and longer benefit periods will have higher premiums.

Notice of Claim – Under a disability income policy, the insured must notify the insurance provider within 20 days or as soon as reasonably possible of the onset of a disability. Suppose the disability is ongoing and benefits are required for two or more years. In that situation, the insurance provider has the right to examine the insured, at its expense, as often as necessary to verify their continuing disability.

Automatic Increase Provision – The *automatic increase* provision increases an insured's monthly benefits every year for five years. Usually, it gives an insured approximately a 25% increase in coverage. The insured's premiums will go up yearly under this provision since the insured is purchasing more disability coverage. The reason for selecting this rider is that the insured's coverage will automatically increase with inflation.

Beneficiary – Contracts for disability income policies require a beneficiary designation because they offer accidental death and dismemberment benefits. Since AD&D pays both life and health benefits, a beneficiary designation provision is needed.

Cost of Living Rider – The purchasing power of disability benefits can be eroded by inflation. The *cost of living adjustment (COLA)* rider will help guard against inflation. Under this rider, the insured's monthly benefit will automatically increase once claim payments begin. Usually, the first increase would be at the end of one year, followed by annual increases for as long as the insured remains on the claim. Some riders allow for compound interest adjustments, while others allow simple interest adjustments.

Social Insurance Riders

Coordination with Social Security Benefits – To avoid over-insurance, the insurance providers have several options to work with Social Security benefits.

Additional Monthly Benefit Rider – Some insurers offer the *Additional Monthly Benefit rider* in the approximate amount that Social Security would pay. The benefit is only provided for one year. It is then anticipated that Social Security benefits would begin at the end of one year.

Social Insurance Supplement Benefit Rider – The insurance provider can offer a *Social Insurance Supplement* rider, which will pay a benefit in the approximate amount that Social Security would pay. Suppose Social Security does pay. In that case, the Social Insurance Supplement benefit is reduced dollar for dollar by the amount of the Social Security benefit payment.

Social Insurance Supplements (SIS) or *Social Security Riders* supplement or replace benefits that might be payable under Social Security Disability. These allow for the payment of income benefits, usually in three different circumstances:

1. When the insured qualifies for Social Security benefits but before the benefits commence (typically, there is a 5-month waiting period for Social Security benefits);
2. If the insured has been denied coverage under Social Security (roughly 75% of individuals who apply for Social Security benefits are denied coverage because of their rigid definition of total disability); or
3. When the amount payable under Social Security is less than the amount payable under the rider (in this situation, the insurer will pay only the difference).

These riders can also supplement or replace benefits payable under a social insurance program like workers compensation.

Benefit Integration – The *integration of benefits* provision is designed to prevent "over-insurance" or duplication of benefits. Therefore, when an insured with an individual disability contract is disabled, the insurance provider will reduce its benefits by an amount equal to the insured's other disability payments.

Residual – When attached to a disability income policy, a *residual rider* provides benefits for loss of income following disability rather than the inability to perform the duties of an occupation. This coverage is essential for a professional whose disability results in a business interruption that causes a loss of clients, even though recovery from the disability is complete.

Rehabilitation – If the insured has been totally disabled, rehabilitation may be needed to help get the insured back to work, either in their old occupation or another occupation. The rehabilitation benefit covers a portion of the cost for the insured to enroll in a formal retraining program to help the insured return to work. This benefit typically offers a specified sum (several times the monthly indemnity) to cover costs not paid by other insurance.

Recurring Disability – A disability that results from the same cause is known as a *recurring disability*. When the insured has been back at work for a certain period, the recurring disability will be considered a new disability. This stipulation results in the insured being exposed to a new elimination period. When the insured has not returned to work for the specified period, the recurring disability will be considered a continuation of the original.

Transplants – Under a disability income policy, donating a body organ will be covered if the transplants are performed in life-threatening situations.

Return of Premium Rider – The *return of premium* rider provides a refund of a percentage of premiums at certain times. For example, at the end of the tenth year, the insurer may offer to refund 80% of the excess premiums paid over claims.

Group Disability Income

Group plans differ from individual plans in a variety of ways. The most common differences between group and individual disability plans are listed below:

- **Group plans** typically specify the benefits based on a percentage of the worker's income. In contrast, individual policies typically specify a flat amount.
- **Short-term group plans** generally include maximum benefit periods of 13 to 26 weeks, with weekly benefits of 50% to 100% of the individual's income. Individual short-term plans include maximum benefit periods of 6 months to 2 years.
- **Group long-term plans** provide maximum benefit periods of more than two years, with monthly benefits typically limited to 60% of the individual's income.
- **Group disability plans** also contain minimum participation requirements. Generally, the employee must have worked for 30 to 90 days before qualifying for coverage.
- Group plans typically make benefits supplemental to any benefits received under workers compensation.
- Some group disability plans only offer benefits for non-occupational disabilities.

There are two major ways of seeking health coverage or disability coverage through group insurance, as opposed to individual plans:

1. Most people obtain health or disability insurance as an employee benefit. The economics of the group approach makes coverage less expensive than individually underwritten coverage because the coverage is underwritten for the group. Also, reduced rates are possible because of the lower potential for adverse selection; and

2. Employer-paid premiums are deductible as a business expense. The premium amount is not taxable as income to the employee. The employee would have to receive more than the premium paid by the employer as additional compensation to purchase the same level of benefits in an individual policy.

There are, however, disadvantages to group insurance. The trend in recent years has moved away from the traditional fee-for-service plans. It has now moved toward several plans involving a more direct relationship between the provider and insurer. These plans include HMOs, PPOs, and point-of-service plans. These plans are known as "managed care" and contain cost containment provisions that many feel leave subscribers with few individual or optional choices for medical care.

Under a self-insured plan, another disadvantage to insureds is that if the plan ends, there is no right of conversion to an individual policy.

The following are *disadvantages* of self-insurance:

- It can leave the organization exposed to catastrophic loss. This disadvantage can be eliminated when the self-insurer purchases reinsurance or stop-loss coverage;
- There may be greater variations in costs from year to year than projected. These variations could result in the loss of tax deductions for the losses occurring in years when there are no profits from which to deduct the losses; and
- Self-insurance can create adverse employee and public relations. The organization determines which loss is rejected or covered instead of having an insurer make the determination.

Business Disability Insurance

Just as an individual obtains disability income insurance to protect their ability to earn a living, a business obtains *business disability insurance* on its key employees to protect itself from loss when they become disabled.

Key Employee (Partner) Disability – An employer can purchase a *key person disability policy* to cover the life of a key employee whose economic value to the business is mission-critical. Employers calculate this value in terms of the potential loss of business income and the cost of hiring and training the key person's replacement. *The business pays the premium, the business owns the contract, and the business is the beneficiary.* The key person is the insured, and the company must have the key person's consent to be insured in writing.

Business Overhead Expense Policy – The *business overhead expense (BOE)* policy is insurance sold to small business owners to meet overhead expenses. Such expenses can include employee salaries, rent, utilities, leased equipment, installment purchases, etc., following a disability. Business overhead expense policies reimburse the business owner for the incurred overhead expenses while the business owner is disabled. This policy does not reimburse the business owner for their compensation, salary, or other forms of income lost due to a disability. There is generally an elimination period of 15 to 30 days, and benefit payments typically last for one or two years. The benefits are usually limited to the maximum monthly amount stated in the policy or the covered expenses incurred. The premiums paid for BOE insurance are tax-deductible to the business as a business expense; however, the benefits received by the company are taxable.

Disability Buy-sell Policy – A *buy-sell agreement* is a legal contract prepared by an attorney. When one of the owners becomes disabled or dies, the buy-sell agreement specifies how the business will pass between owners. It is common for the company to purchase insurance to provide the cash needed to accomplish the buyout when the owner becomes disabled or dies. The policies that fund buy-sell agreements have an extremely long elimination period, possibly one or two years. Typically, policies that fund buy-sell agreements also provide a large lump-sum benefit rather than monthly benefits to buy out the business.

Social Security Disability Benefits

Social Security, also known as *Old Age Survivors Disability Insurance (OASDI)*, is a Federal program enacted in 1935. This program protects eligible workers and dependents against financial loss because of old age, disability, or death. With a few exceptions, Social Security covers almost every individual. In some aspects, Social Security plays a role in federal life and health insurance, which is essential to consider when determining an individual's life insurance needs.

Qualifications for Disability Benefits – Social Security uses the Quarter of Coverage (QC) system to determine whether or not a person qualifies for Social Security benefits. The number of credits or QCs earned by a worker determines the type and amount of benefits. Anyone operating their own business or working in jobs covered by Social Security can earn up to four credits for each year of work.

The term *fully insured* refers to anyone who has earned *40 quarters of coverage* and is entitled to Social Security retirement, Medicare, and survivor benefits. Forty quarters is the equivalent of working for ten years.

Individuals can attain a *currently insured* status (or partially insured) and qualify for certain benefits. They need to have earned six quarters (or credits) of coverage during the 13 quarters ending with the quarter wherein the insured either:

- Dies;
- Qualifies for disability insurance benefits; or
- Qualifies for old-age insurance benefits.

For younger workers, the number of quarters required to be eligible for the benefits differs by age, according to a table established by Social Security.

Definition of Disability – When a person qualifies for Social Security disability benefits by being fully insured or partially insured, they must meet Social Security's definition of disability. Under Social Security, *disability* is the inability to engage in a substantially gainful activity because of a medically determinable impairment (physical or mental). Such impairment has lasted or is expected to last 12 months or resulted in premature death. This definition is not as liberal as most definitions of disability in policies marketed through insurers.

Waiting Period – The waiting period or elimination period for Social Security disability benefits is *five months*. Benefits begin at the beginning of the sixth month and are not retroactive to the start of the disability.

Disability Income Benefits – The amount of Social Security disability benefits is based upon the worker's Primary Insurance Amount (PIA), determined by their Average Indexed Monthly Earnings over their highest 35 years. The lowest five years of earned income can be deleted from the calculation.

Social Security disability benefits will continue for three months when an individual returns to work making more than $850 per month. This amount is an incentive to get people to return to work.

Chapter Review

This chapter discussed different types of disability insurance available to individuals and businesses. Let's review the key points:

DISABILITY INCOME	
Disability Income Insurance	• Replaces lost income if a disability occurs • *Presumptive disability* – specifies the condition that qualifies an insured for full disability benefits • *Recurrent disability* – specifies the period during which the recurrence of an illness or injury will be considered a continuation of a prior disability • *Elimination period* – waiting period that lasts from the onset of disability until benefit payments begin • *Probationary period* – the period after the policy begins during which benefits won't be paid for illness-related disabilities • *Benefit period* – the length of time after the elimination period has been satisfied during which the monthly disability benefit payments will last for each disability • *Benefit limitations* – the maximum benefits an insurer is willing to accept for an individual risk; benefits are based on a percentage of the insured's past earnings • *Social Insurance Supplement (SIS) or Social Security Riders* – supplement or replace benefits payable under Social Security Disability • *Cost of Living* – this rider addresses inflation by automatically increasing the amount of coverage without evidence of insurability; the policy's face value can increase by a cost of living factor tied to the Consumer Price Index (CPI)
Business Overhead Expense Policy	• Pays for a small business owner's overhead expenses incurred while the business owner is totally disabled
Business Disability Buyout Policy	• Specifies who will buy out a partner's interest in a business in the event disability occurs
Key Person Disability	• Covers the potential loss of business income and the expense of hiring and training the replacement for a key person • The business pays the premium, owns the contract, and is the beneficiary
SOCIAL SECURITY DISABILITY BENEFITS	
Qualification for Benefits	• Social Security uses the Quarter of Coverage (QC) system to determine whether or not a person qualifies for Social Security benefits • The number of credits or QCs earned by a worker determines the type and amount of benefits
Insured Status	• *Fully insured* (40 quarters of coverage) – qualify for Social Security retirement, Medicare, and survivor benefits • *Currently insured* (6 quarters of coverage) – qualify for some benefits
Income Benefits	• The amount of Social Security disability benefits is based upon the worker's Primary Insurance Amount (PIA), determined by their Average Indexed Monthly Earnings over their highest 35 years

CHAPTER 15:
Senior Health Products

This chapter discusses senior health products, including the government-sponsored programs of Medicare and Medi-Cal. You will also learn about the Health Insurance Counseling and Advocacy Program (HICAP), how it functions, and who it serves. By the chapter's end, you should be able to explain the differences between senior health products, including basic benefits, eligibility requirements, and services provided.

- Medicare
- Medicare Supplement Policies
- Medi-Cal
- Medicare and Medi-Cal
- Health Insurance and Counseling Advocacy Program

Medicare

Nature, Financing, and Administration

The Center for Medicare and Medicaid Services (CMS), a United States Department of Health and Human Services (HHS) division, manages Medicare which includes the following four parts:

- **Part A (Hospital Insurance)** receives a subsidy through a portion of the payroll tax (FICA);
- **Part B (Medical Insurance)** is funded from monthly premiums paid by insureds and from the general revenues of the federal government;
- **Part C (Medicare Advantage)** allows individuals to receive all of their health care services through available provider organizations; and
- **Part D (Prescription Drugs)** is coverage for prescription drugs.

It is necessary to note that the term *Original Medicare* refers to Part A (Hospital Insurance) and Part B (Medical Insurance) only. It covers health care from any health care provider, doctor, hospital, or facility that accepts Medicare patients. Typically, it does not cover prescription drugs. Original Medicare does not require the patient to choose a primary care provider. It also does not require the patient to obtain a referral to see a specialist, as long as the specialist accepts Medicare.

Eligibility

Medicare is a federal medical expense insurance program for individuals age 65 and older, even if the person continues to work. Medicare benefits are also available to anyone, *regardless of age*, with a permanent kidney failure known as End-Stage Renal Disease (ESRD) or entitled to Social Security disability income benefits for two years.

While a person becomes eligible for Medicare upon turning 65, federal laws extend primary coverage benefits under the employer's plan to active older employees regardless of age. In other words, employer plans typically continue to be *primary* coverage, and Medicare is considered *secondary* coverage.

Medicare is *not part of* the Health Insurance Marketplace. The Marketplace is a critical component of the Affordable Care Act that allows qualified individuals, families, and employees of small businesses to obtain health insurance. When considered eligible for Medicare Part A, an individual will not qualify for Marketplace tax credits to help cover premiums or reductions in cost-sharing. An insured can keep a Marketplace plan after Medicare coverage begins; however, any premium tax credits and reduced cost-sharing through the Marketplace will stop.

Enrollment Periods

The *initial enrollment period (IEP)* is a 7-month period during which a person can enroll in the Medicare Part B program. It begins three months before the month when the individual turns 65 and ends three months after the birthday month.

When an individual enrolls in Medicare after the Initial Enrollment Period ends, the individual might have to pay a late enrollment penalty.

The *general enrollment period*, also known as the *annual enrollment period (AEP)*, runs from January 1 through March 31. The individuals who did not sign up for Medicare Part B when they were first eligible can sign up during this enrollment period. However, the cost of Medicare Part B increases 10% for each entire 12-month period that the individual could have had Medicare Part B but chose not to.

Anyone who qualifies for Medicare can also obtain a Medicare supplement and pay the required premium for those additional benefits. Under OBRA, Medicare supplement insurance cannot discriminate in pricing or be denied based on an applicant's claims experience, health status, medical condition, or receipt of health care. An open enrollment period is a 6-month period that guarantees applicants the right to purchase Medigap once they first enroll in Medicare Part B. To buy a Medigap policy, the applicant must usually have both Medicare Part A and Part B.

A *special enrollment period (SEP)* is available to those eligible for Medicare Part B based on age. These individuals did not enroll because they had group health coverage through their employer or spouse. They can sign up for Part B anytime while the group health plan still covers them. These individuals can also enroll during the eight months following either the termination of the group plan or employment, whichever is first.

Part A – Hospital Insurance

Medicare *Part A* assists with paying for inpatient hospital care, inpatient care in a skilled nursing facility, home health care, and hospice care.

Individual Eligibility Requirements – An individual is eligible for Medicare Part A, Hospital Coverage if they qualify for one of the following conditions:

- A citizen or a legal resident of the United States age 65 or over and eligible for Social Security or Railroad Retirement benefits (Aged);
- Is 65 years old or over and entitled to monthly Social Security benefits based upon the work record of their spouse, and the spouse is at least 62;
- Is younger than 65 years old but has been entitled to Social Security disability benefits for 24 months (Disabled);
- Has End-Stage Renal Disease (ESRD), which is permanent kidney failure requiring dialysis or a transplant;
- Has ALS (Amyotrophic Lateral Sclerosis), or Lou Gehrig's disease, automatically qualifies for Part A during the month disability benefits begin.

Individuals not receiving those specific benefits must sign up for Part A, even if they are eligible for premium-free Part A.

Enrollment – Individuals who want to sign up for Medicare Part A have the following three options:

- **Initial enrollment period** – when a person first becomes eligible for Medicare, starting three months before turning age 65 and ending three months after the 65th birthday;
- **General enrollment period** – between January 1 and March 31 each year;
- **Special enrollment period** – at any time during the year if the person or their spouse is still employed and covered under a group health insurance plan.

Those who do not qualify for premium-free Part A can purchase the coverage for a monthly premium. When a person fails to sign up for Part A when they are first eligible, the monthly premium can go up 10% unless the individual becomes eligible for a special enrollment period.

Inpatient Hospital Care – Hospital insurance helps pay for up to 90 days in a participating hospital during any benefit period, subject to a deductible. The first 60 days are covered at 100% of approved charges after the deductible is satisfied. The insurance provider will pay the next 30 covered days, but they pay with a daily copayment. Each Part A insured has a lifetime reserve of 60 days of hospital care. The lifetime reserve days have a copayment double that of days 61 through 90 and are nonrenewable. Covered services include a semi-private room, meals, regular nursing services, operating and recovery room costs, hospital costs for anesthesia, intensive care and coronary care, X-rays, lab tests, drugs, medical supplies, appliances, rehabilitation services, and preparatory services related to kidney transplant surgery. Blood is also covered, excluding the first 3 pints.

Under the inpatient hospital stay, Part A does not include private duty nursing, a television, or a telephone in the hospital room. It also does not provide a private room unless it is medically necessary. Also, inpatient mental health care in a psychiatric facility is limited to 190 days in a person's lifetime.

Sixty days of non-use of the inpatient hospital care benefit will start a new benefit period and a new deductible.

Skilled Nursing Facility Care – Part A helps pay for up to 100 days in a participating skilled nursing facility during each benefit period, following a 3-day inpatient hospital stay for a related illness. To receive this care, the insured's doctor must certify that daily skilled care is medically necessary. Covered expenses include:

- A semi-private room;
- Meals;
- Regular nursing and rehabilitation services; and
- Other medical supplies.

Home Health Care – For individuals confined to their homes, hospital insurance can pay the total approved costs for home health visits from a participating home health agency. There is no limit to the number of covered visits to a person's home. Covered services include physical therapy, speech therapy, and part-time skilled nursing care. Hospital insurance also covers:

- Occupational therapy;
- Part-time services of home health aides;
- Medical social services; and
- Medical supplies and equipment.

Hospice Care – Under certain conditions, hospital insurance can help pay for the cost of hospice care for terminally ill insureds if a Medicare-certified hospice gives the care. Covered services include doctor services, nursing services, supplies including outpatient drugs for pain relief, medical appliances, home health aides, therapies, homemaker services, medical social services, short-term inpatient care including respite care, and counseling.

The table on the following page is a reference chart for covered hospital services under Medicare Part A.

Medicare Part A: Hospital Insurance Covered Service Reference Chart		
BENEFITS	**MEDICARE PAYS**	**YOU PAY**
HOSPITALIZATION		
First 60 days	All but the deductible	Deductible
Days 61-90	All but daily deductible	Daily deductible
After day 90 (up to 60 days)*	All but daily deductible	Daily deductible
After lifetime reserve days	Nothing	All costs
SKILLED NURSING FACILITY CARE		
First 20 days	100% of approved amount	Nothing
Days 21-100	All but daily deductible	Daily deductible
Beyond 100 days	Nothing	All cost
HOME HEALTH CARE		
For as long as you meet Medicare requirements for home health care benefits.	100% of approved amount; 80% of approved amount for durable medical equipment	Nothing for services; 20% of approved amount for durable medical equipment
HOSPICE CARE		
For as long as doctor certifies need	All but limited costs for outpatient drugs and inpatient respite care	Limited cost sharing for outpatient drugs and inpatient respite care
BLOOD		
Unlimited if medically necessary	All but the first 3 pints per calendar year	For the first 3 pints**

* Sixty lifetime reserve days. For each lifetime reserve day, Medicare will pay for all covered costs except for a daily coinsurance.

** To the extent that 3 pints of blood are replaced or paid for under one part of Medicare during the calendar year. They do not have to be replaced or paid for under the other part.

Part B – Medical Insurance

Medicare *Part B* will pay for doctor's services and various other medical services and supplies that hospital insurance does not cover. Most of the services needed by individuals with permanent kidney failure are covered only by medical insurance.

Individual Eligibility Requirements – Part B is optional and offered to everyone who enrolls in Medicare Part A. Part B is subsidized by monthly premiums and the federal government's general revenues. Most people enrolled in Medicare Part B pay the *standard monthly premium*. However, when an insured's modified adjusted gross income reported on their IRS tax return is above a certain amount, the insured might have to pay a higher premium.

Enrollment – Once a person becomes eligible for Part A, they learn that they will receive and have to pay for Part B unless they decline it. When the person decides they want Part B after initially refusing it, they must wait until the next general enrollment period (January 1 through March 31) to enroll.

Enrollment in Medicare Part B can be delayed when employer coverage is primary because of the individual's active employment at age 65 (or younger if with ESRD), their spouse, or a parent of a disabled dependent.

Coverages and Cost-sharing Amounts – After the annual medical insurance deductible is satisfied, medical insurance will usually pay for 80% of the approved charges for covered expenses for the remainder of the year. There is no maximum out-of-pocket limit on the 20% coinsurance payable for Part B expenses.

Doctor Services – Part B pays for doctor services no matter where a person receives them in the United States. Covered doctor services include:

- Diagnostic tests and X-rays related to the treatment;
- Surgical services;
- Medical supplies furnished by a doctor's office; and
- Services of the office nurse.

Outpatient Hospital Services – Part B pays for outpatient hospital services received for diagnosis and treatment, such as care in a hospital, emergency room, or outpatient clinic.

Home Health Visits – Medicare will cover home health services as long as the insured is eligible, which are recommended by the insured's doctor. Such services limit the number of hours per day and days per week on a part-time basis. The services that Medicare does not fully cover will receive coverage from Medicaid.

Other Medical and Health Services – Under certain conditions or limitations, medical insurance pays for other medical services and supplies. Some examples include periodic support services, ambulance transportation, home dialysis equipment, supplies, independent laboratory tests, outpatient physical therapy, speech pathology services, oral surgery, and X-rays and radiation treatments.

Prescription Drugs (limited coverage) – Only medicines administered in a hospital outpatient department under certain circumstances, such as injected drugs at a doctor's office, medications requiring durable medical equipment (e.g., nebulizer or infusion pump), or some oral cancer drugs, are covered. Other than these examples, insureds under Part B will pay 100% for most prescription drugs unless Part D of Medicare covers them.

Outpatient Treatment of Mental Illness – Medicare pays for outpatient treatment of an approved condition such as anxiety or depression in a doctor's office (or other health care provider's office) or hospital outpatient department. Generally, the enrollee pays 20% of the Medicare-approved amount (coinsurance) and the Part B deductible. It is essential to note that Part A also covers inpatient mental health care.

Yearly "wellness" visit – In addition to a "Welcome to Medicare" preventive visit during the first 12 months, Medicare Part B covers an annual "wellness" visit. During this visit, the provider and the insured can create or update a personalized plan for disease prevention. The insured has no out-of-pocket cost for these visits if the doctor or other qualified health care provider accepts Medicare assignment. Suppose the doctor or the health care provider performs additional services or tests during the same visit that the preventive benefit does not cover. In that situation, the insured might have to pay coinsurance, and the Part B deductible might apply.

Exclusions – Medical insurance under Medicare Part B *does not cover* the following:

- The cost of skilled nursing home care beyond 100 days per benefit period;
- Private duty nursing;
- Intermediate nursing home care;
- Physician charges over Medicare's approved amount;
- Most outpatient prescription drugs;
- Custodial care received in the home;

- Care received outside the United States;
- Dental care, excluding dental expenses resulting from an accident only, cosmetic surgery, hearing aids, eyeglasses, orthopedic shoes, and acupuncture expenses; or
- Expenses incurred because of war or act of war.

Claims Terminology and Other Key Terms – The following are claims terminology and other key terms that apply to Medicare:

- **Actual Charge** – The amount a supplier or physician bills for a particular supply or service.
- **Ambulatory Surgical Services** – Care given at an ambulatory center. Unlike inpatient hospital surgery, these are surgical services provided at a center that do not require a hospital stay.
- **Approved Amount** – The amount Medicare finds reasonable for a service covered under Part B of Medicare.
- **Assignment** – A medical supplier or the physician agrees to accept the Medicare-approved amount as full payment for the covered services.
- **Carriers** – Organizations that process claims submitted by suppliers and doctors under Medicare.
- **Coinsurance** – The portion of Medicare's approved amount the beneficiary must pay.
- **Comprehensive Outpatient Rehabilitation Facility Services** – Outpatient services received from a Medicare-participating facility.
- **Deductible** – The expense a beneficiary must first incur before Medicare begins paying for covered services.
- **Durable Medical Equipment** – Medical equipment such as wheelchairs, oxygen equipment, and other medically necessary equipment that a doctor prescribes for use in the home.
- **Excess Charge** – The difference between the actual charge and the Medicare-approved amount for a supply or service.
- **Intermediaries** – Organizations that process inpatient and outpatient claims on patients by hospitals, home health agencies, skilled nursing facilities, hospices, and certain other providers of health services.
- **Limiting Charge** – The maximum amount a physician can charge a Medicare beneficiary for a covered service if the physician does not accept the assignment.
- **Nonparticipating** – Suppliers or doctors who can choose whether or not to accept assignment on each claim.
- **Outpatient Physical and Occupational Therapy and Speech Pathology Services** – Medically necessary services prescribed by a therapist or doctor.
- **Pap Smear Screening** – Provides a screen for cervical cancer once every two years.
- **Partial Hospitalization for Mental Health Treatment** – An outpatient mental health care program.
- **Participating Doctor or Suppliers** – Doctors and suppliers who have agreed to accept assignment on all Medicare claims.
- **Peer Review Organizations** – Groups of practicing doctors and other health care professionals who the government compensates to review the care received by Medicare patients.

The table on the following page is a reference chart for covered medical services under Medicare Part B.

Medicare Part B: Medical Insurance Covered Services Reference Chart		
BENEFITS	**MEDICARE PAYS**	**YOU PAY**
MEDICAL EXPENSES		
Medicare pays for medical services in or out of the hospital	80% of the approved amount after the deductible	Deductible*, plus 20% of the approved amount and limited charges above the approved amount
CLINICAL LABORATORY SERVICES		
Unlimited if medically necessary	Generally, 100% of the approved amount	Nothing for services
HOME HEALTH CARE		
For as long as the enrollee meets the Medicare requirements for home health care benefits	100% of the approved amount; 80% of the approved amount for durable medical equipment	Nothing for services; 20% of the approved amount for durable medical equipment
OUTPATIENT HOSPITAL TREATMENT		
Unlimited if medically necessary	The Medicare payment to hospital is based on the hospital cost	20% of the billed amount after the deductible
BLOOD		
Unlimited if medically necessary	80% of the approved amount after the deductible, and starting with the 4th pint	First 3 pints plus 20% of the approved amount for additional pints after the deductible**

* Once the Medicare recipient reaches a specified dollar amount in expenses for covered services, the Part B deductible does not apply to any other covered services the enrollee receives for the rest of the year.

** To the extent that any of the 3 pints of blood are replaced or paid for under one part of Medicare during the calendar year. They do not have to be replaced or paid for under the other part.

Part C – Medicare Advantage

In 2003 the Medicare Modernization Act changed the name of *Part C* from Medicare+Choice to *Medicare Advantage*. Medicare Advantage plans must cover all of the services under the Original Medicare, excluding hospice care and some care received in qualifying clinical research studies. It may offer extra coverage, such as dental, vision, hearing, and other health and wellness programs.

Beneficiaries must be enrolled in Medicare Parts A and B to be *eligible* for Medicare Advantage. Medicare Advantage is Medicare provided by approved Health Maintenance Organizations or Preferred Provider Organizations. Many HMOs or PPOs will not charge a premium beyond what Medicare pays. The advantages of an HMO or PPO for a Medicare recipient may be that they cover most medical problems for a set fee allowing insureds to budget for health care costs. Claims forms are not required, and the HMO or PPO pays for services not usually covered by Medicare or Medicare supplement policies. Such services include dental care, eye exams, hearing aids, or prescriptions.

Most Medicare HMOs require beneficiaries to receive medical services through the plan, except in emergencies. A few HMOs allow for greater freedom of choice through point-of-service plans.

A *Medicare Private Fee-for-Service Plan* is a Medicare Advantage Plan offered by a private insurer. Medicare pays a set monthly amount to the private insurer to provide health care coverage. The insurer decides how much enrollees pay for the services they receive.

Another section of Medicare Advantage, known as *Special Needs Plans*, provide more focused and specialized health care for specific groups of individuals. This group includes people with Medicare and Medicaid who live in a nursing home or have certain chronic medical conditions.

Part D – Prescription Drug Benefit

In November 2003, Congress passed the *Medicare Prescription Drug, Improvement, and Modernization Act (MMA)*. This act executed a plan to add Part D, a Prescription Drug Benefit, to the standard Medicare Coverages. This *optional coverage* is provided through private Prescription Drug Plans (PDPs) that contract with Medicare. Beneficiaries must sign up with a plan offering this coverage in their area to receive the benefits provided and enroll in Medicare Part A or Parts A and B. The government will provide a standard plan in areas where private plans are not available. Medicaid recipients are automatically enrolled.

When Medicare beneficiaries do not enroll when they are first eligible, they must pay a 1% penalty for each month they delay enrollment.

Medicare beneficiaries can choose *stand-alone plans* that provide fee-for-service coverage or *integrated plans* that group coverages together, including HMOs and PPOs. These plans are known as Medicare Advantage.

Some standards set by Medicare restrict the plans offered by private insurance companies. However, they still have the freedom to customize their plans. Providers are required to cover drugs for certain classes but do not have to cover every drug in each class.

Those who sign up for Part D will have a monthly premium and a deductible. The monthly premium will vary by plan. After the deductible is satisfied, the plan would provide prescription drug benefits until the insured reaches a benefit limit. Most Medicare drug plans have a coverage gap called a "donut hole." The coverage gap starts after the beneficiary and the drug plan spend a certain amount on covered drugs. In the coverage gap, the beneficiary pays 25% of brand-name prescription drug costs and 25% of the plan's cost for covered generic drugs. It is essential to note that as of 2020, the donut hole for generic drugs has closed.

Once the beneficiary has satisfied the plan's out-of-pocket cost requirements for the year, *catastrophic coverage* starts automatically. Catastrophic coverage covers 95% of prescription drug costs. The beneficiary will pay the greater of the specified amount or 5%. The cost limit for generic drugs would be lower than for name-brand drugs.

Additional assistance is available for those with lower incomes. These beneficiaries will not have a gap in their coverage.

The term *creditable coverage* refers to a person's health coverage that gives them certain rights when applying for new coverage. Creditable coverage includes, but is not limited to, any of the following:

- Coverage provided under any group or individual policy or certificate issued or administered by any health care service plan, insurance provider, or entity;
- Coverage under Medicaid and Medicare Parts A or B;
- Coverage under a state's health benefits risk pool; or
- Health plans under the Federal Employees Health Benefits Program.

Creditable coverage *does not include*:

- Coverage issued to supplement liability insurance;
- Coverage only for accident or disability income insurance;

- Credit-only insurance;
- Workers compensation;
- Other similar insurance in which benefits for medical care are incidental or secondary to other insurance benefits.

Medicare supplemental health insurance provided as a separate policy would not be considered creditable coverage.

Creditable prescription drug coverage must pay at least as much as Medicare's standard prescription drug coverage. When they become eligible for Medicare, individuals with creditable prescription drug coverage can typically keep that coverage without a penalty if they enroll in Medicare Part D later.

Individuals will not have to incur a penalty if they do any of the following:

- Enroll in Medicare Part D when first eligible;
- Have no more than 63 days without a Medicare drug plan or other creditable coverage; or
- Notify the Medicare plan if they have other creditable coverage.

Medicare Claims Payments

If the insured's health care provider accepts Medicare assignments, the insured pays their share of the Medical bill (deductibles, coinsurance). The health care provider will then file a Medicare claim, and Medicare pays its share of the medical bill directly to the provider.

When a health care provider does not accept Medicare assignments, the insured could have to pay most of the medical cost or the entire bill when service is rendered. The provider is still required to file a Medicare claim on behalf of the insured, and Medicare would then pay its portion of the medical bill to the insured.

If a health care provider does not file a claim on the insured's behalf, the insured can take the following steps:

- Call the health provider directly and ask to file a claim;
- If the provider still does not file a Medicare claim after talking to the insured, the insured can call their local Medicare Carrier. The Medicare Carrier will reach out to the health care provider to make them aware of the responsibility for filing a claim.
- An insured should only have to file a Medicare claim in rare situations. To file a Medicare claim, the insured should call their local Medicare Carrier and ask for the correct form for a Medicare beneficiary to file a claim.

Explanation of Medical Benefits – When Medicare handles a claim, the claimant is mailed an Explanation of Medicare Benefits. This document outlines specific services covered and the approved amounts for each and includes the following information:

- Date that the explanation was sent;
- Name and address of the claimant;
- Claimant's Medicare card number;
- Claim number;
- Who to contact with any questions;
- Part B Medical Insurance assigned claims;
- Provider's name and address;
- Amount charged;

- Date of service;
- Medicare-approved amount;
- Medicare paid provider; and
- Amount the claimant can be billed by the provider.

Medicare Assignment and Non-assignment Providers – Suppose a Medicare insured uses a health care provider who does not accept Medicare payments. In that situation, they might be asked to sign a private contract. A private contract is a written agreement between the Medicare insured and the health care provider who has decided not to participate in the Medicare program. The private contract only applies to the services the insured receives from that provider. The insured cannot be asked to sign a private contract in an emergency or when the insured receives urgently needed care.

If the insured signs a private contract with the provider, the following conditions will apply:

- The insured must pay whatever the provider charges for the services. Medicare limiting charges will not apply;
- Claims should not be submitted to Medicare, and Medicare will not pay if one is submitted;
- The insured's Medicare supplement policy (if applicable) will not pay anything for this service;
- Medicare health plans will not cover any amount for the services received from this provider;
- The provider must notify the insured whether Medicare would pay for the service if it were received from another provider who participates in Medicare; and
- The provider must notify the insured if they have opted out of or been excluded from the Medicare program.

Medicare-insured individuals should speak with someone in the State Health Insurance Assistance Program before signing a private contract.

Medicare Summary Notice – The *Medicare Summary Notice (MSN)* is a monthly statement. It lists the insured's health insurance claims, specific services covered, and the approved amounts for each service.

Insured's Right to Appeal – The insured has the right to appeal any decision about their Medicare services. If Medicare does not pay for an item or service an insured has received, the insured can appeal that decision. The insured can also appeal if they do not receive an item or service they think should be given.

Exclusions – Medicare does not cover the following expenses:

- Coinsurance, deductibles, or copayments for health care services;
- Dental care and dentures (in most cases);
- Hearing aids and exams;
- Most chiropractic services;
- Cosmetic surgery;
- Acupuncture;
- Custodial care (help with eating, using the bathroom, bathing, dressing), unless skilled nursing care is provided at the same time, in a nursing home or at home;
- Health care received outside the United States (coverage is limited to Mexico and Canada);
- Most prescription drugs;
- Orthopedic shoes;
- Routine foot care (with a few exceptions);
- Eye care and most eyeglasses (except after undergoing cataract surgery);

- Immunizations (except for pneumonia and flu shots);
- Private duty nursing; and
- The first 3 pints of blood received during a single calendar year.

Medicare Supplement Policies

Medicare supplement plans, also called *Medigap*, are policies issued by private insurers to fill in some of the gaps in Medicare. These plans intend to fill the gap in coverage attributable to Medicare's co-payment requirements, deductibles, and benefit periods. The federal Social Security program does not administer these plans. Instead, they are sold and serviced by private insurance companies and HMOs. These policies must meet specific requirements and receive approval from the state insurance department. Medicare supplement policies pay some or all of Medicare's co-payments and deductibles.

Under the *Omnibus Budget Reconciliation Act (OBRA)* of 1990, Congress passed a law that authorized the NAIC to create a standardized model for Medicare supplement policies. This model requires Medigap plans to meet specific requirements regarding participant eligibility and the benefits provided. This law aimed to eliminate questionable marketing practices and provide consumers with a degree of protection by standardizing the coverage.

Standard Medicare Supplement Plans

The NAIC established standard Medicare supplement benefit plans identified with the letters A through N. They did this to standardize the coverage offered under Medicare supplement plans. *The core benefits found in Plan A must be in every plan*, in addition to the variety of benefits these other plans offer. Any insurer selling Medigap plans must at least provide Plan A, while the other plans are optional.

Once an individual becomes eligible for a Medicare supplement policy, and during the open enrollment period, insurers offer coverage on a guaranteed issue basis. Under these circumstances, an insurance provider must do the following:

- Sell the patient a supplement policy;
- Identify all pre-existing conditions incurred more than six months from the effective date of coverage; and
- Not charge more for a Medicare supplement policy due to past or present health conditions.

It is essential to note that insurance companies offering Medicare Supplement policies must offer Medicare Supplement Plan A and either Plan C or F. The California Insurance Code mandates Medicare Supplement Plan benefits as listed below.

Plan A – Core Package of Benefits

Medicare Supplement Plan A includes only the *core benefits*. The core benefits, also called basic benefits, cover the following:

- Part A coinsurance/copayment (not the Part A deductible);
- Part A hospital costs up to an additional 365 days after Medicare benefits are exhausted;
- Part A hospice care coinsurance/copayment;
- Part B coinsurance/copayment;
- The "blood deductible" for Parts A and B (first 3 pints of blood).

Plans B – N

In addition to Plan A, which includes only the core benefits, most insurance companies offer some or all of the additional plans. Insurance providers are not permitted to change the benefits provided in these supplemental plans, nor can they change the designation letter of any of the following plans:

Plan B – Core benefits plus the Medicare Part A deductible.

Plan D – Core benefits, Medicare Part A deductible, skilled nursing facility coinsurance, and the foreign travel benefit.

Plan G – Core benefits, Medicare Part A deductible, skilled nursing facility coinsurance, 100% of Medicare Part B excess charges, and the foreign travel benefit. This plan has to pay for services of activities of daily living (ADL) that Medicare does not cover.

Plans C, E, F, H, I, and J are no longer available. These plans will remain effective for those insureds who purchased them when they were still available.

Medicare Supplement Plans K and L have lower premiums with higher out-of-pocket costs. The core benefits of these two plans are different as well:

- Approved hospital costs for the copayments for days 61 through 90 during any Medicare benefit period.
- Approved hospital costs for the copayments for lifetime reserve days 91 through 150.
- Approved hospital costs for an additional 365 days after all Medicare benefits are utilized.
- 50% of charges for the first 3 pints of blood in Plan K, 75% of charges for the first 3 pints of blood in Plan L.
- 50% of the Part B coinsurance amount in Plan K, 75% of the Part B coinsurance amount in Plan L.
- 50% of respite care and hospice cost-sharing expenses for Part A in Plan K, 75% of respite care and hospice cost-sharing expenses for Part A in Plan L.

Plan K provides 50% of the Medicare Part A deductible and 50% of skilled nursing facility coinsurance.

Plan L provides 75% of the Medicare Part A deductible and 75% of skilled nursing facility coinsurance.

Plans M and N include benefits similar to Plan D, but the co-pays and deductibles may differ.

The table below outlines the benefits provided under each available Medigap plan.

Medigap Plan	Basic Benefit	Skilled Nursing Coinsurance	Part A Deductible	Part B Excess (100%)	Foreign Travel Emergency
A	•				
B	•		•		
D	•	•	•		•
G	•	•	•	•	•
K	•	50%	50%		
L	•	75%	75%		
M	•	•	50%		•
N	•	•	•		•

Medigap Requirements

Other Requirements – Insurers must use the same format, language, and definitions to describe each Medigap plan's benefits. They must use a standardized outline and chart that summarizes the benefits.

Insurance companies are not permitted to alter the standardized benefits of each plan. They are allowed to offer new, innovative benefits that can be cost-effective and which are not currently available in the marketplace.

Every Medigap policy is *guaranteed renewable*. The insurer may not cancel or nonrenew coverage except for material misrepresentation on the application or because of nonpayment of the premium. Also, although the benefits provided by these plans are identical from one insurer to the next, the premiums vary considerably. Depending on how the insurance provider determines the premium charge, they can usually raise premiums on the policy anniversary date. Medigap policies must also contain a *30-day free look* provision that lets the insured return the policy to the insurance company within 30 days for a full refund of the premium paid.

Medigap policies cannot include a provision limiting coverage for pre-existing conditions for more than six months. Suppose the insured has had a Medigap policy for at least six months and decides to switch to another one. In that scenario, the new policy cannot have a waiting period for pre-existing conditions for the same coverage as the old policy. Also, when the replacement policy offers additional coverage not included in the old policy, the 6-month waiting period is applicable, but only regarding the additional coverages.

Replacement Coverage

Every insurer's application for Medicare Supplement insurance must include a question designed to determine if the applicant has another Medicare Supplement policy. This question must also determine if this policy will replace any other accident and health policy. The applicant must be asked on the application if they are eligible for Medicaid and must be advised that counseling services may be available. It is the responsibility of the agents, brokers, and issuers to ensure that Medicare Supplement policies are not being replaced unnecessarily.

If replacement is involved, the insurer or its agent must provide the applicant with the *Notice Regarding Replacement* before issuing or delivering the policy. The insurer must retain one copy, signed by the applicant and the agent. The Notice Regarding Replacement must notify the applicant of the policy's *30-day free-look* provision.

If a Medicare supplement policy replaces another, the replacing insurer must waive any periods on pre-existing conditions, elimination periods, waiting periods, and probationary periods in the new Medicare supplement policy. Suppose a Medicare Supplement policy replaces another that has been in effect for *six months* or more. In that case, the replacement policy cannot have any time requirement on pre-existing conditions, elimination periods, waiting periods, or probationary periods for benefits similar to those included in the original policy.

To avoid abuses, Medicare supplement policies issued in California must meet the following rules regarding replacement and solicitation:

- No insurer, agent, broker, or another person can cause a policy owner to replace a Medicare supplement policy unnecessarily when it results in a decrease in benefits and an increase in premium;
- Medicare supplement application forms have to include questions that ask whether the applicant has an existing Medicare supplement policy in force or whether the proposed supplement policy intends to replace any other disability policy;
- Each agent must list any other disability policies that the agent or their agency has sold to the applicant, including those still effective and those sold during the past five years that are no longer effective; and

- When a sale does involve replacement, the insurance provider (other than a direct response insurer) must give the applicant a notice regarding the replacement of disability coverage. This notice must be given before the replacement policy is issued or delivered. A copy of the notice, signed by the applicant and agent, needs to be provided to the applicant. The insurer has to keep an additional copy. A direct response insurer, which does not have sales agents, must provide a similar notice regarding replacement upon issuing the policy.

Medicare SELECT

Medicare SELECT policies are Medicare supplement policies that include restricted network provisions. They condition the payment of benefits, in whole or in part, on the use of *network providers*. A SELECT plan negotiates with a provider network of hospitals, doctors, and specialists to charge lower rates for medical services. It virtually operates like an HMO. These lower rates keep costs down for the SELECT plan provider, and members of the plan pay lower premiums.

Every Medicare SELECT policy must be approved by the head of a state's insurance department. Currently, issuers are prohibited from selling new Medicare SELECT policies to individuals whose primary residence is outside the issuer's service area.

Each Medicare SELECT policy must do the following:

- Pay for full coverage under the policy for covered services not available through network providers;
- Not restrict payment for covered services provided by non-network providers on the condition that the services are for symptoms requiring emergency care and obtaining such services through a network provider is not reasonable;
- Provide a complete and fair disclosure in writing of the limitations, restrictions, and provisions of the Medicare SELECT policy to each applicant;
- Make available upon request the opportunity to obtain a Medicare supplement policy offered by the issuer, which has comparable benefits and does not include a restricted network provision. These policies have to be available without requiring evidence of insurability if the Medicare SELECT policy has been in force for six months; and
- Provide for the continuation of coverage if Medicare SELECT policies are discontinued because of the failure of the Medicare SELECT program.

Medicare Disclosure Requirements

Outline of Coverage – The *outline of coverage* included with a Medicare supplement policy must be in at least 12-point type, be in the format and language prescribed by Cal. Ins. Code Section 10192.17(l)(3)(G), and include the following disclosures:

- This policy cannot fully cover all of your medical costs;
- Neither this insurance company nor any of its agents are connected with Medicare;
- This outline of coverage does not provide all the details of Medicare coverage. Contact the local social security office or consult The Medicare Handbook for more information;
- For additional information concerning policy benefits, contact the Health Insurance Counseling and Advocacy Program (HICAP) or your agent (must include their phone number).

Application – *Application* forms used for Medicare supplement policies are required to include questions designed to elicit information as to whether the applicant has a current Medicare supplement, Medicare Advantage, Medi-Cal coverage, or another health insurance policy in force as of the application date or whether a Medicare supplement policy is intended to replace any other disability policy in force.

Replacement – The Notice Regarding Replacement must be provided to the insureds with Medicare supplement policies offered in a replacement transaction. The notice must be in the form specified by the Commissioner using a model notice prepared by the National Association of Insurance Commissioners (NAIC). It must be printed in no less than 12-point type (Cal. Ins. Code Section 10192.18(e)).

Commissioner's Annual Rate Guide – The Commissioner of Insurance prepares an annual consumer rate guide for Medicare supplement insurance and Medicare supplement contracts on or before the fall Medical annual open enrollment. The guide compares policies sold by different insurance providers. The guide must be available through Health Insurance Counseling and Advocacy Program (HICAP) offices. It must also be available by telephone, using the department's consumer toll-free telephone number, and on its website.

Medi-Cal

As people grow older, their need for health care or other services related to aging becomes more demanding. Statistically, most of an individual's health care expenses will be incurred in the last five years of their life. For most people, this means at later ages. In the past 20 years, due mainly to dramatic advances in pharmaceuticals and technology, the cost of medical care, especially later in life, has risen significantly in the United States.

In 2002, there were more than 40 million individuals who had no medical insurance of any kind. One study asserted that some 70 million individuals were without medical insurance for at least one day during the year. For many of these individuals, the federally-funded Medicaid program is available to cover some of their needs. Medicaid is a federal-state partnership in which the federal government pays for most medical claims. At the same time, the states are responsible for covering their own administrative costs. Every state is given the flexibility to determine what will be covered within federal guidelines so that the program is most beneficial for the residents of their state.

The program is known as *Medi-Cal* in California, but it is still primarily funded with federal reimbursements. Medi-Cal is free or low-cost coverage for uninsured adults and children and those with low income and assets.

Eligibility

In various situations, California residents can qualify for benefits from Medi-Cal. However, individuals who receive cash assistance from one of the following programs are automatically eligible for Medi-Cal:

- CalWORKS (CA Work Opportunity and Responsibility to Kids);
- SSI/SSP (Supplemental Security Income/State Supplemental Program);
- Refugee Assistance; and
- Foster Care or Adoption Assistance Program.

Other categories of individuals that could be eligible for Medi-Cal are listed below:

- Children up to age 26 in foster care;
- Individuals over age 65;
- Blind and other disabled individuals of any age; and
- Pregnant women or women diagnosed with cervical or breast cancer.

For most individuals, Medi-Cal operates as, or contracts with, an HMO to deliver services and care for recipients.

Individuals must meet a specific monthly *asset spend-down test* to qualify for long-term care benefits under Medi-Cal. The amounts are readjusted annually, and an individual needing long-term care cannot have countable assets over the specified amount. If married, the individual will still not qualify for Medi-Cal benefits until their spouse's *countable* assets fall below the required annual limit. These rules are in place to prevent individuals from using the state's resources instead of using their assets. The spend-down can result in a surviving spouse living near poverty because of having to dispose of a large share of their assets for their spouse to receive Medi-Cal benefits.

When a person's income exceeds the Medi-Cal limit for their family size, that individual will have to pay a *share of cost (SOC)* in the month when medical expenses occur. Once the SOC has been satisfied, Medi-Cal will cover the rest of the covered medical bills for that month.

Benefits provided by Medi-Cal need to be understood, particularly when it comes to long-term care as a "no interest" loan. When a person dies, the state can exercise its right to pursue asset recovery from a Medi-Cal recipient estate up to the total value of the benefits that were paid for by the state. This stipulation could result, after death, in the seizure of an individual's home or business property, which were not part of their "countable assets," to reimburse the state for its expenditures. Even though these possessions may have been intended to be transferred to children or other heirs, the state may have a priority claim over all others.

Medi-Cal eligibility has been *expanded to include the nonelderly, nondisabled, childless adults up to 138% FPL*. A household's income is calculated using Modified Adjusted Gross Income (MAGI), based on the income tax returns with adjustments. MAGI households are not subject to an asset test.

To qualify for Medi-Cal coverage under the *Adult Expansion Medi-Cal program*, individuals:

- Have to be between the ages of 19 and 64;
- May not be pregnant;
- Do not receive Medicare; and
- Do not have Medi-Cal without a share of cost (SOC).

Medi-Cal coverage may be available to children under age 19 if their household's income is no more than 250% of the FPL.

Medicare and Medi-Cal

Dual eligible beneficiaries are those who qualify for both Medicare and Medi-Cal benefits. Based on the level of benefit received from Medi-Cal, dual eligible enrollees can be categorized as follows:

- Full benefit enrollees who receive full Medi-Cal benefits available in the state;
- Partial benefit enrollees who receive Medi-Cal assistance to pay for Medicare premiums or other cost-sharing obligations.

A Medicare Advantage Dual Eligible Special Needs Plan provides an integrated Medicare/Medi-Cal option for full benefits to an enrollee aged 65 and older living in the plan's service area.

California Insurance Code Requirements

Standardized Plan Benefits – Each standardized plan is required to meet the following requirements for plan benefits:

- The plan cannot exclude or limit benefits for losses incurred more than six months from the effective date of coverage because of a pre-existing condition.
- Losses from sickness have to be indemnified on the same basis as losses from accidents.
- Benefits that pay for cost-sharing amounts under Medicare will automatically be changed to coincide with any changes in the applicable Medicare deductible amount and copayment percentage factors.
- Coverage for a spouse may not be terminated solely because of the event that terminates the insured's coverage except for nonpayment of premium.
- Medicare supplement policies are required to be guaranteed renewable or noncancelable.

Open Enrollment – There are several regulations regarding the open enrollment period for Medicare supplement plans:

- Disabled individuals enrolled in Medicare must be entitled to open enrollment for *six months* following the enrollment date or after the notice of eligibility for Medicare.
- Individuals enrolled in Medicare Part B can also be entitled to open enrollment for *six months* after the events listed below:
  - Receipt of a notice of termination of an employer-sponsored health plan;
  - Receipt of a notice of loss or eligibility for an employer-sponsored health plan because of divorce or a spouse's death;
  - Termination of health care services for a military retiree because of a military base closure or termination of health services coverage.
- An *additional 60-day open enrollment period* is given to an individual whose Medicare Advantage plan coverage was terminated.
- An annual open enrollment period of at least *30 days* (beginning with the individual's birthday), during which the individual can obtain any Medicare supplement policy with benefits of equal or lesser value than those provided by the previous coverage.
- Individuals enrolled in Medicare Part B are entitled to an open enrollment period once they have been advised that they are no longer eligible for benefits under the Medi-Cal program because of an increase in their assets or income.

Guaranteed Issue Periods – Generally, the guaranteed issue period starts on the effective date of disenrollment and ends 63 days after the effective date of disenrollment. In some circumstances involving voluntary disenrollment, coverage will begin 60 days before the effective date of the disenrollment. It will continue for 63 days after the effective date of the disenrollment.

Permitted Commissions – An agent or representative selling Medicare supplement policies can receive commissions as long as the 1st-year commission does not exceed 200% of the commissions paid for selling or servicing the policy in the 2nd year. Commissions in subsequent renewal years must be the same as in the second year. They must be provided for no fewer than five renewal years. The term *commission* refers to monetary and non-monetary compensation, including finders' fees, bonuses, gifts, awards, and prizes.

Appropriate Sales and Replacement – To comply with the California Insurance Code regulations concerning sales and the replacement of Medicare supplement policies, the insurance provider must meet each of the following requirements:

- Establish marketing procedures for fair and accurate comparison of its policies and prevent excessive insurance sales.
- On the first page of a policy, prominently display a notice to the buyer stating that the policy may not cover all of the buyer's medical expenses.

- Make every reasonable attempt to identify whether an applicant already has health insurance.
- Establish auditable procedures for verifying compliance with the Code's regulations.

Insurers cannot participate in unfair trade practices like cold lead advertising, twisting, or high-pressure tactics, which conceal from the customer that marketing is for the solicitation of insurance.

Any agent selling a Medicare Supplement must make reasonable efforts to determine the appropriateness of a recommended purchase or replacement. The application for Medicare Supplement insurance has to include a statement signed by the agent acknowledging that they have reviewed the applicant's current health insurance coverage. This statement must also confirm that additional insurance of the type and amount is appropriate for the applicant.

The sale of any Medicare Supplement policy that would give the insured more than one such policy is prohibited.

Prohibitions on Discrimination – The act of treating any individual or group of individuals unfairly in the sale of or pricing of policies or treating any risk class differently from other risk classes is expressly prohibited by California law.

Health Insurance and Counseling Advocacy Program

The state Department of Aging oversees the *Health Insurance Counseling and Advocacy Program (HICAP)*. In conjunction with local Area Agencies on Aging operated in each county in California, HICAP exists to serve seniors who are already receiving or are about to receive Medicare or Social Security. HICAP provides consumer counseling related to purchasing health insurance, long-term care insurance, Medicare, Medicare Advantage, Medicare supplements, or Medi-Cal insurance.

Funding for HICAP is provided by the state and local governments, mainly with state and local revenue and, to a lesser extent, with federal funds. All services are provided without cost to clients. HICAP agencies do not recommend, sell, or in any other way transact insurance.

HICAP fulfills the following functions:

- **Free assistance** – The program provides free individual counseling regarding Medicare and other health care issues. Counseling is available in every California county. The majority of HICAP counselors are trained and certified volunteers.
- **Education** – Free informational presentations are available to educate groups of Medicare beneficiaries, their families, and providers.
- **Consumer advocacy** – The program handles complaints concerning abusive practices of agents or insurance providers, referring them to state or local enforcement agencies, when appropriate, for investigating crimes such as misrepresentation, twisting, or financial abuse.
- **Legal assistance** – HICAP counselors help with Medicare claims, denials, appeals, or delays of treatment or service. Their responsibility is also to give customers unbiased advice about supplemental insurance, Medicare Advantage plans, and long-term care, among other issues.

How to Locate a Program – A list of local HICAPs for every county in California is provided through www.calmedicare.org. This *Medicare information* website is approved by the Department of Insurance. It gives unbiased and accurate information about Medicare benefits for California residents. Contact information for the local HICAP agencies can also be found at www.aging.ca.gov. The website also provides the *statewide toll-free phone number* available to anyone seeking help or free counseling on Medicare or other health care issues.

Chapter Review

This chapter discussed various senior health products such as Medicare, Medicare supplement policies, Medi-Cal, and HICAP. Let's review the key points:

MEDICARE	

Basics	• Federal medical expense insurance program for individuals who:
	  - Are age 65 or older
	  - Have been qualified to receive Social Security disability income benefits for two years
	  - Have a permanent kidney failure called End-Stage Renal Disease (ESRD)
	• Four parts:
	  - *Part A, Hospital Insurance*, financed through the payroll tax (FICA)
	  - *Part B, Medical Insurance*, financed by insureds and the general revenues
	  - *Part C, Medicare Advantage*, allows for the receipt of health care services through available provider organizations
	  - *Part D, Prescription Drug* coverage

Part A	• Enrollment:
	  - *Initial enrollment period* – when a person first becomes eligible for Medicare (starting three months before turning 65, ending three months after the 65th birthday)
	  - *General enrollment period* – between January 1 and March 31 every year
	  - *Special enrollment period* – at any time during the year if the person or their spouse is still employed and insured under a group health plan
	• Coverage:
	  - Inpatient Hospital Care
	  - Skilled Nursing Facility Care
	  - Home Health Care
	  - Hospice Care

Part B	• Optional; offered to everyone who enrolls in Part A
	• Coverage:
	  - Doctor Services
	  - Outpatient Hospital Services
	  - Home Health Visits
	  - Other Medical and Health Services
	  - Prescription Drugs (limited coverage)
	  - Outpatient Treatment of Mental Illness
	  - Yearly "wellness" visit

Part C	• *Medicare Advantage* – requires enrollment in Parts A and B • Care provided by an approved HMO or PPO

Part D	• Prescription drug benefit • Optional coverage through private prescription drug plans that contract with Medicare
Primary, Secondary Payor	• For individuals eligible for Medicare coverage who continue to work, their employer's health insurance plan would be considered primary coverage while Medicare would be considered secondary coverage
MEDICARE SUPPLEMENT POLICIES	
Basics	• Also referred to as Medigap • Policies issued by private insurance providers to fill in the gaps in Medicare
Coverage	• *Plan A* – includes core benefits, including coinsurance/copayment; additional Part A hospital costs; hospice care coinsurance/copayment; Part B coinsurance/copayment; 3 pints of blood under Parts A and B • *Plans B - N* – includes core benefits plus various additional benefits • Every Medigap policy is guaranteed renewable • Medigap policies must contain a 30-day free look provision
Replacement	• If replacement is involved, the insurer or its agent must provide the applicant with the *Notice Regarding Replacement* before issuing or delivering the policy • The insurer must retain one copy, signed by the applicant and the agent • The Notice Regarding Replacement must notify the applicant of the policy's *30-day free-look* provision
Medicare SELECT	• Medicare SELECT policies are Medicare supplement policies that include restricted network provisions • A SELECT plan negotiates with a provider network of hospitals, doctors, and specialists to charge lower rates for medical services • These lower rates keep costs down for the SELECT plan provider, and members of the plan pay lower premiums
OTHER SENIOR HEALTH PRODUCTS	
Medi-Cal	• Medi-Cal is free or low-cost coverage for adults and children with limited resources and income • Individuals must meet a specific monthly *asset spend-down test* to qualify for long-term care benefits under Medi-Cal • Medi-Cal eligibility has been expanded to include the nonelderly, nondisabled, childless adults up to 138% FPL
Medicare and Medi-Cal	• Dual eligible beneficiaries are those who qualify for Medicare and Medi-Cal benefits • The guaranteed issue period starts on the effective date of disenrollment and ends 63 days after the effective date of disenrollment • An agent or representative selling Medicare supplement policies can receive commissions as long as the 1st-year commission does not exceed 200% of the commissions paid for selling or servicing the policy in the 2nd year
HICAP	• *Health Insurance and Counseling Advocacy Program (HICAP)* – exists to serve seniors who are already receiving or are about to receive Medicare or Social Security • HICAP fulfills the following functions: free assistance, education, consumer advocacy, and legal assistance

CHAPTER 16:
Long-Term Care

In this chapter, you will focus your attention on long-term care insurance. You will learn specific terms and definitions, policy components and features, and how to issue long-term care policies. After completing this chapter, you should know the coverages available in long-term care insurance. You should also be able to explain the major regulations that apply to long-term care policies.

- Long-Term Care
- Places Where Services are Generally Provided
- Triggers for Benefits
- Ways to Issue LTC Contracts
- Daily Benefits and Policy Maximum Limits
- Guaranteed Renewability and Rate Increases
- California Insurance Code Requirements
- Customer Protection Regarding Long-Term Care

Long-Term Care

Long-term care (LTC) insurance includes any insurance policy, certificate, or rider that offers coverage for preventive, diagnostic, therapeutic, maintenance, rehabilitative, or personal care services delivered in another setting beside an acute care unit of a hospital (Cal. Ins. Code Section 10231).

Long-term care insurance includes every product containing any of the following benefit types:

- Institutional care, including care in a nursing home;
- Custodial care facility;
- Convalescent facility;
- Extended care facility;
- Personal care home;
- Skilled nursing facility;
- Home care coverage including home health care;
- Personal care;
- Homemaker services;
- Hospice or respite care; or
- Community-based coverage, including respite care, hospice, or adult day care.

Long-term care insurance includes disability-based LTC policies but does not include insurance intended primarily to provide major medical expense or Medicare supplement coverage.

In California, long-term care insurance contracts can pay for care only in one of the following settings:

- In a facility;
- In an individual's home (or the home of another); or
- In any "community-based" setting, such as adult day care or hospice care.

Long-term care contracts can also be "comprehensive," which means paying for care in a facility, home-based, or community-based care setting.

Although long-term care insurance could be added as a rider to either a Medicare supplement or health insurance policy, it does not pay for any Medicare or other major medical expenses.

The following *standard* levels of care include:

- Skilled nursing care;
- Nonskilled nursing care;
- Intermediate nursing care;
- Personal care;
- Assisted living;
- Home health care; and
- Home care and community-based care

Why this Coverage Might be Needed

Although Medicare and Medicare supplements protect elderly insureds against the cost of medical care, these programs do not provide coverage for long-term custodial or nursing home care. Medicare will cover nursing home care if it is part of the treatment for a covered illness or injury. However, care needed because of aging is not covered by Medicare or Medigap policies. Medicare and Medicare supplements pay for skilled nursing care, but the coverage is limited. Medicaid does pay for nursing home care, but it provides coverage only for those that qualify with low assets and low income.

Medicare does not cover more than 100 days in a skilled nursing facility; even then, it does not pay 100% of the cost. Medi-Cal can pay for skilled or other levels of long-term care in a facility. Still, Medi-Cal has to meet "spend down" tests and "asset recovery" after death.

Individuals could pay for some or all the long-term care expenses from their resources, the resources of family members, or others. However, LTC insurance can be the most cost-effective method of maintaining one's physical and financial independence.

Levels of Care

Usually, long-term care policies will cover three care levels: skilled care, intermediate care, and custodial care. The long-term care policy may also provide additional care levels, all of which the insured receives in their home:

- Home health care;
- Adult daycare;
- Hospice care; or
- Respite care.

Skilled care is daily rehabilitative and nursing care that only medical personnel can give under the direction of a physician. It occurs in an institutional setting and includes changing a sterile dressing or physical therapy provided in a skilled nursing facility. *Care provided by non-professional staff is not skilled care.*

Intermediate care is occasional rehabilitative or nursing care given to insureds with stable conditions that need daily medical assistance less frequently than skilled nursing care. A physician orders it, and skilled medical personnel either monitors or delivers this type of care. Intermediate care could be as simple as providing the medication once daily to a group in physical therapy or changing a bandage. Skilled medical personnel can carry it out in the patient's home, an intermediate care unit, or a nursing home.

Custodial care assists with personal needs such as eating, dressing, or bathing, which nonmedical personnel can give, such as home health care workers or relatives. They can provide custodial care in the patient's home or an institutional setting. In other words, it involves caring for an individual's activities of daily living and not surgical or hospital needs.

Personal Care – *Personal Care* includes hands-on services to help a person with activities of daily living and can be provided by a skilled or unskilled individual.

Places Where Services are Generally Provided

Nursing Home – *Nursing home* care coverage usually pays a specified amount for the time the insured spends in a nursing home or for medical services received in a setting other than a hospital. Nursing home care is usually provided as one of the following:

- **Skilled nursing care** – the highest level of nursing care that demands the greatest expertise from the caretaker;

- **Intermediate nursing care** – similar to skilled nursing care, except the patient does not need continuous attention;
- **Custodial care** – the most basic level of nursing care, which typically requires assistance with the activities of daily living.

Assisted Living – *Assisted Living* delivers help with nonmedical aspects of daily activities in an environment of separate, private living units. In addition to providing meals, activities, rides to medical appointments, and pleasure trips, assisted living can provide:

- Assistance with dressing and bathing;
- Assistance with eating;
- Reminders regarding medication; and
- Linens and personal laundry service.

Residential Care Facilities – *Residential Care* is given while the insured resides in a residential care facility for the elderly (RCFE) or a retirement community. In some arrangements, independence is the same as living in one's home. However, this type of care offers a physical and social environment that contributes to continued intellectual, psychological and physical growth. These facilities are common among the middle and upper classes.

Home Setting – *Home health care* is care given by skilled nursing or other professional services in one's home. Home health care includes occasional visits to the person's home by licensed practical nurses, registered nurses, vocational nurses, or community-based organizations like hospice. Home health care can include occupational therapy, physical therapy, speech therapy, and medical services provided by a social worker.

Home Care – Policies with benefits limited to home care services (including residence and community-based) have to be clearly labeled "Home Care Only" on the first page of the policy and the outline of coverage.

Hospice – *Hospice* is a facility that delivers short-term, continuous care in a home-like setting to terminally-ill individuals with life expectancies of six months or less.

Respite Care – *Respite Care* intends to provide relief to the family caregiver. It can offer a service such as someone coming to the home to allow the caregiver to nap or go out for a while. The caregiver may also receive this relief from an adult daycare center.

Adult Daycare – *Adult daycare* is care given to functionally impaired adults on less than a 24-hour basis by a community center or a neighborhood recreation center. Care includes various health, social, and related activities. Meals and transportation to and from the daycare center typically come with the service.

Triggers for Benefits

Long-term care policies are designed to be federally tax-qualified, meaning benefits received are not taxed. They also provide benefits for care received in a person's home or a community-based setting. LTC policies qualify insureds for benefits, provided they are chronically ill and impaired in at least two *activities of daily living (ADLs)*. Individuals with severe cognitive impairment are also eligible for LTC benefits. An individual's condition must be assessed by a health care practitioner who is not an employee of the insurer to be considered chronically ill or to have a severe cognitive impairment.

The six defined activities of daily living include the following:

1. **Eating** – taking in food and feeding oneself;
2. **Bathing** – bathing without help;
3. **Continence** – bladder and bowel control;
4. **Dressing** – clothing oneself;
5. **Toileting** – personal cleansing and grooming;
6. **Transferring** – mobility, being able to move from one place to another inside the home.

Cognitive impairment is an organic process (or the result of an accident) that results in an individual's inability to understand or appreciate the nature of their surroundings and the danger they represent to themselves or others. *Impaired* means that the individual requires either actual hands-on assistance with their ADLs or substantial supervision (stand-by assistance).

Ways to Issue LTC Contracts

Individual and Group

Long-term care insurance policies can be purchased on an individual basis, similar to other individual health insurance policies. An individual policy provides benefits to a single individual and is issued based upon individual underwriting considerations.

Long-term care insurance can be purchased on a group basis, either at an insured's place of employment or as a member of an association. Group LTC policies must provide the insured, who would otherwise lose their coverage, the right to continue or convert the LTC coverage into an individual policy without proof of insurability.

Tax Qualified and Nonqualified

A long-term care insurance policy fits the definition of a qualified long-term care insurance contract if all of the following are present:

- The only insurance protection provided under the policy is coverage of qualified LTC services;
- The policy does not reimburse or pay expenses incurred for services that are reimbursable under Title XVIII of the Social Security Act;
- The policy is guaranteed renewable;
- All dividends and premium refunds are used to reduce future premiums or increase future benefits to offset inflation;
- The policy satisfies specific consumer protection provisions regarding model regulation and model act provisions, non-forfeitability, and disclosure.

Only products that fit the Qualified LTC definitions are eligible to be marketed as Partnership LTC plans. The table on the following page compares qualified LTC plans with nonqualified LTC plans.

	QUALIFIED	NONQUALIFIED
Premiums	Can be included with other annual uncompensated medical expenses for deductions from income	May or may not be deductible by the insured
Benefits	Generally, will not be counted as income.	May or may not count as income.
Benefit Trigger	Federal law requires an insured be unable to perform two ADLs without substantial assistance	Benefit triggers are not restricted to two ADLs
Medical Necessity	Cannot be used as a trigger for benefits	Can be offered as benefit triggers
Chronic Illness or Disability	Must be expected to last for at least 90 days	No requirement for 90-day period
Cognitive Impairment	A person must require substantial supervision to trigger coverage	No restrictions on coverage

Endorsement to a Life Policy

An alternative to obtaining an LTC insurance policy is an agreement by a life insurance company, known as living benefits, to advance a life insurance policy's benefits rider. Living benefit riders agree to cover a part of the policy's death benefit to insureds to pay for nursing home care or long-term care, should the need arise. The rider will usually stipulate the conditions under which the benefit is triggered (attaining age 65 to 85, etc.). The advance is treated as a lien against the policy's death benefit.

Daily Benefits and Policy Maximum Limits

Under most LTC policies, the benefit amount payable is typically a specific fixed dollar amount per day, regardless of the cost of care. For instance, if an insured has $100 of fixed daily coverage and the care facility only charges $90 per day, the insurer will pay the full amount of $100 per day. Some policies pay the actual charge that was incurred per day. Most LTC policies are also *guaranteed renewable*; however, insurance providers have the right to increase the premiums.

Guaranteed Renewability and Rate Increases

A long-term care policy issued to a person must include a renewability provision prominently appearing on the policy's first page. Renewal provisions cannot be less favorable than guaranteed renewable or noncancelable. The insurance providers who issue LTC policies cannot cancel, nonrenew, or otherwise terminate coverage exclusively due to age or deterioration in the insured's mental or physical health.

The NAIC model regulations for long-term care insurance require that all insurers maintain and make the Long-Term Care Insurance Personal Worksheet available to the applicants. On the premium section of the worksheet, the insurance provider must disclose all rate increases for every policy issued by the insurer or purchased from another insurer. The worksheet must also contain a statement informing consumers of the availability of the rate guide that compares the policies sold by different insurance companies.

California Insurance Code Requirements

Suitability Standards

All insurers marketing long-term care insurance must develop and abide by suitability standards. This requirement determines whether the purchase or replacement of LTC coverage is appropriate for the applicant's needs. A copy of the standards must be available for inspection upon request by the Commissioner of Insurance. It is the insurer's responsibility to train its agents in using suitability standards.

California regulates the sale of long-term care insurance to promote the availability of insurance, encourage the public interest, and protect consumers from deceptive or unfair sales or enrollment practices. However, when obtaining LTC insurance, the consumer needs to be aware of the benefits and limitations to avoid problems in the event of a claim in the future:

- **Benefit limits** – Every LTC policy sets benefit limits regarding how long the benefits are paid or how much the dollar benefit will be for anyone covered by the care service. Maximum coverage periods also vary.
- **Elimination period** – This is the period from the policy's inception during which benefits will not be paid. This period can range from 0 days to 365 days. Longer elimination periods will have a lower premium.
- **Inflation protection** – California insurance providers must offer policy owners the option to obtain inflation protection that increases the policy's benefits to account for anticipated increases in the cost of services. The cost of increased protection can make the policy unaffordable after a while.

Prohibited Provisions

There are several *prohibited provisions* identified in the Insurance Code. LTC contracts cannot be issued under a renewal provision less favorable to insureds than guaranteed renewable for life. They cannot be terminated, nonrenewed, or canceled for any reason other than nonpayment of premium. Also, long-term care contracts are prohibited from establishing a new waiting period for benefits if a policy is replacing or is being converted from another contract from the same insurer. An exception would be for an increase in benefits, which can be temporarily excluded for up to six months.

Other prohibited provisions include:

- Only limiting benefits to skilled nursing facilities;
- Paying considerably different benefits for levels of facility care lower than skilled nursing;
- Defining benefits payable based on a definition of usual and reasonable, usual and customary, or similar language;
- Increasing premiums or terminating coverage for a spouse following divorce from an insured;
- Providing payment for an additional, specific benefit that is less than five times the daily facility benefit; or
- Providing a daily amount for home-care or community-based care benefits less than that required by the Insurance Code (at least $50 per day or 50% of the facility-care benefit, whichever is higher).

California Partnership for Long-Term Care

LTC partnerships permit those who have depleted or at least exhausted some private LTC benefits to apply for Medicaid coverage without satisfying the same means-testing requirements. The partnership between LTC coverage and Medicaid works by disregarding some or all assets of applicants for Medicaid who have exhausted private LTC benefits and by exempting those assets from estate recovery after the insured's death. The partnership program was created to encourage those who would not otherwise do so to obtain LTC insurance. It was also created to reduce the incentives to transfer assets to qualify for Medicaid sooner and to control Medicaid spending on LTC services (22 Cal. Code Regs. Section 58056).

As a condition of issuer participation in California LTC partnerships, issuers must provide written evidence to the Department of Insurance that procedures are in place. This evidence ensures that no agent, broker, or solicitor will be authorized to market, solicit, or sell a Partnership LTC policy or certificate without completing eight hours of education on long-term care and eight hours of training in a live classroom setting regarding the California Partnership for Long-Term Care. Such assurances must be provided in the form of a document signed by the individual, agent, broker, or solicitor and a company representative attesting to completing the required training and submitted to the Department of Insurance.

Marketing Standards and Responsibilities Including HICAP

The Insurance Code defines various marketing standards to which insurance providers and their agents must adhere (Cal. Ins. Code Section 10234.95(c)(3)). Among them are the following:

- Procedures to make sure that excessive insurance will not be sold or issued;
- That agents satisfy the continuing education requirements;
- A notice to applicants and insureds that the Health Insurance Counseling and Advocacy Program (HICAP) exists to assist individuals, free of charge, in understanding and determining whether a particular long-term care insurance policy is in their best interest;
- A current list of Area Agencies on Aging or other HICAP providers in California; and
- Several other publications, like the Department of Aging's long-term care insurance shopper's guide, are required to be given to every applicant or prospect.

A part of this section in the Insurance Code is a discussion of inappropriate practices, like twisting, high-pressure tactics, and the ramifications of cold lead advertising. In any advertisement or other marketing device designed to result in a person inquiring about long-term care insurance, the ad or response card must indicate whether a producer will contact the individual.

Consumer Protection Regarding Long-Term Care

Duties of Honor, Good Faith, and Fair Dealing

Regarding long-term care insurance, all insurance providers, agents, brokers, and others engaged in the insurance business owe their clients a duty of good faith, honesty, and fair dealing. The conduct of insurers, brokers, or agents during the offer and sale of a policy can be counted in any legal action alleging a breach of these duties (Cal. Ins. Code Section 10234.8).

Unnecessary Replacement of LTC Insurance

Insurance providers, agents, and brokers are not allowed unnecessarily to compel policy owners to replace long-term care insurance policies. It is illegal to cause a policy owner to replace a long-term care insurance policy, resulting in a decrease in benefits and a premium increase (Cal. Ins. Code Section 10234.85).

According to the Insurance Code, any *third or additional* policy sold to a policy owner within 12 months is considered unnecessary. However, this rule does not apply to instances in which a policy is replaced exclusively to consolidate policies with a single insurance provider.

Advertisement and Cold Lead Device Disclosure

Every insurer offering long-term care coverage in California must provide a copy of any advertisement to the Commissioner for review at least *30 days* before it is used. The insurance provider must also retain the advertisement for at least *three years* (Cal. Ins. Code Sections 10234.9(c) and 10234.93(b)(3)).

An advertisement intended to generate leads must *prominently* disclose that an insurance agent will contact the consumer if that is the case. A broker, agent, or another individual who contacts a consumer due to receiving information produced by a cold-lead device must immediately reveal that fact to the consumer.

Replacement Coverage

When long-term care coverage is replaced, insurers will calculate the sales commission based on the difference between the yearly premium of the replacement coverage and that of the original coverage. A sales commission represents the percentage of the sale generally paid for first-year sales of long-term care policies or certificates. When the premium on the replacement product is less than or equal to the premium for the product being replaced, the sales commission will be limited to the percentage of sales usually paid for the renewal of long-term care policies or certificates. Replacement is contingent upon the insurance provider's declaration that the replacement policy materially improves the insured's position. This rule does not apply to the replacement of group insurance (Cal. Ins. Code section 10234.97(a) and (b)).

Commission or other compensation includes compensation (monetary or not) relating to the sale or renewal of the policy or certificate, including but not limited to finder's fees, gifts, prizes, awards, and bonuses.

Chapter Review

This chapter discussed long-term care insurance. Let's review the key points:

LONG-TERM CARE	
Policies	<ul><li>Available as an individual policy, group policy, or as a rider to life insurance policies</li><li>Coverage for insureds who require living assistance at home or in a nursing home facility</li><li>Must provide at least 12 months of consecutive coverage in a setting other than a hospital's acute care unit</li><li>Guaranteed renewable, but insurance companies may increase premiums</li></ul>
Levels of Care	<ul><li>*Skilled care* – rehabilitative and daily nursing care provided by licensed medical personnel</li><li>*Intermediate care* – occasional rehabilitative or nursing care for insureds in stable conditions that require daily medical assistance less frequently than skilled nursing care</li><li>*Custodial care* – care for a person's activities of daily living given in an institutional setting or the patient's home</li></ul>

LONG-TERM CARE *(Continued)*	
Levels of Care *(Continued)*	• *Home health care* – provided in one's home by licensed vocational nurses, registered nurses, licensed practical nurses, or community-based organizations like hospice • *Home convalescent care* – given by a long-term care facility, a home health care agency, or a hospital in the insured's home under a planned program established by their attending physician • *Residential care* – given while the insured lives in a retirement community • *Adult daycare* – provides care for functionally impaired adults on less than a 24-hour basis • *Respite care* – provides relief to the family caregiver; adult daycare centers can also provide this type of relief

Triggers for Benefits	• Benefits received are not taxed
	• LTC policies qualify insureds for benefits, provided they are chronically ill and impaired in at least two activities of daily living (ADLs)
	• The six defined activities of daily living include the following:
	    ○ *Eating* – taking in food and feeding oneself;
	    ○ *Bathing* – bathing without help;
	    ○ *Continence* – bladder and bowel control;
	    ○ *Dressing* – clothing oneself;
	    ○ *Toileting* – personal cleansing and grooming;
	    ○ *Transferring* – mobility, being able to move from one place to another inside the home

Daily Benefits and Policy Maximum Limits	• Under most LTC policies, the benefit amount payable is typically a specific fixed dollar amount per day, regardless of the cost of care • Most LTC policies are also guaranteed renewable
Guaranteed Renewability	• A long-term care policy issued to a person must include a renewability provision prominently appearing on the policy's first page
California Insurance Code Requirements	• All insurers marketing long-term care insurance must develop and abide by suitability standard • LTC contracts cannot be issued under a renewal provision less favorable to insureds than guaranteed renewable for life • LTC partnerships permit those who have depleted or at least exhausted some private LTC benefits to apply for Medicaid coverage without satisfying the same means-testing requirements • A part of this section in the Insurance Code is a discussion of inappropriate practices, like twisting, high-pressure tactics, and cold lead advertising
Consumer Protection Regarding Long-Term Care	• Insurers and agents owe clients a duty of good faith, honesty, and fair dealing • Insurance providers, agents, and brokers are not allowed unnecessarily to compel policy owners to replace long-term care insurance policies • Every long-term care insurer in California must provide a copy of any advertisement to the Commissioner for review at least *30 days* before it is used • When long-term care coverage is replaced, insurers will calculate the sales commission based on the difference between the yearly premium of the replacement coverage and that of the original coverage

ADDENDUM

The California Department of Insurance has updated its Accident and Health Educational Objectives. Continue reading for additional information.

The following updates are *content additions* to supplement the existing text.

Medical Expense Insurance (Ch. 13)

Consumer-Driven Health Plans

Individual Coverage HRA (ICHRA)

An employer can offer its employees an Individual Coverage Health Reimbursement Arrangement (ICHRA) to reimburse medical expenses (like copayments, deductibles, and premiums) rather than providing a traditional job-based health plan. It is available to employers of all sizes. It requires an employee to be covered by an individual health insurance plan or Medicare to qualify for reimbursements. The main objective of the ICHRA is to provide for the reimbursement of individual health insurance premiums. However, the ICHRA can also reimburse other out-of-pocket expenses. The employer decides the reimbursement limits, and different rules and restrictions apply.

Senior Health Products (Ch. 15)

CMS Compliance and Regulations

Centers for Medicare and Medicaid Services (CMS) has established regulations and guidelines that producers and brokers must adhere to before helping consumers select and enroll in qualified health plans (QHPs) or Medicare. These guidelines apply to the following:

- Third-Party Marketing Organization (TPMO) disclaimer;
- Permission to contact;
- Call recording;
- Marketing rules;
- Scope of appointment;
- Events and appointments;
- Secret shoppers; and
- Websites.

Third-Party Marketing Organization (TPMO) Disclaimer

CMS considers every insurance producer and broker to be a *Third-Party Marketing Organization (TPMO)*. Producers and brokers must add the TPMO disclaimer to their email communications, website, and all marketing materials, including TV and print ads. When conducting lead-generating activities, producers and brokers must disclose to the beneficiary that they will provide their information to a licensed agent for future contact or that the beneficiary will be transferred to a licensed agent who can complete enrollment in a new plan.

Permission to Contact

While producers can make unsolicited direct contact with prospective enrollees through email, the email must include an opt-out option to remain compliant. Also, the content of an unsolicited email cannot intend to persuade a recipient to pick or keep a plan. Compliant emails would promote the producer's services rather than specific insurance plans. Producers must refrain from making unsolicited phone calls, approaching prospective enrollees in common areas, or going door to door.

Call Recording

Producers must *record calls* (including video calls) with Medicare beneficiaries in their entirety. Examples include introductory calls to educate or inform clients about Medicare Advantage and Prescription Drug plans, follow-up calls when the beneficiary makes a decision about enrollment, and post-enrollment conversations, including retention calls to influence a beneficiary to remain enrolled in their current plan. Producers do not have to record conversations when meeting directly with the beneficiary.

Marketing Rules

CMS regulates marketing and plan presentations, including when producers and brokers can begin conducting marketing efforts and how to proceed.

Producers must wait until October 1 to start marketing the following year's plans to prospective beneficiaries. They can only begin enrolling members on October 15. Producers should never attempt to mislead clients willingly or unwillingly during sales presentations. For instance, producers must avoid using superlatives and absolutes to describe plans and benefits and avoid displaying favoritism between plans or carriers.

Scope of Appointment (SOA)

A *Scope of Appointment (SOA)* outlines what the producer will present to a client during a meeting. The SOA ensures that prospective enrollees will only be pitched plans that they initially requested.

Each Medicare sales appointment requires an SOA, whether the meeting happens remotely or in person. According to CMS, producers must keep SOA forms on file for at least *ten years*, even if the appointment did not result in a sale. SOAs will be valid for *12 months* or until they are used, and the producer will have to obtain a new one if the original form expires.

Producers must wait *48 hours* between obtaining an SOA from a client and conducting an appointment. Exceptions to this rule are when a beneficiary is no more than four days from the end of a valid enrollment period (e.g., Initial Coverage Election Period, Open Enrollment Period, Annual Enrollment Period, Special Enrollment Period) or unscheduled in-person meetings (walk-ins) initiated by a beneficiary.

Events and Appointments

Producers usually host three types of events: sales events, educational events, or individual appointments. A producer must advertise educational events designed to inform Medicare beneficiaries about the parts of Medicare. When conducting an educational event, a producer *can do* the following:

- Disseminate educational materials without including plan-specific information;
- Disseminate educational healthcare materials;
- Answer questions asked by attendees;
- Pass out business cards and contact information to beneficiaries for initiating contact; and
- Have the event in a public venue, which is optional but should not be in-home or in a one-on-one setting).

Producers must never:

- Talk about any carrier-specific plans or benefits or disseminate marketing plan materials;
- Disseminate plan-specific materials or enrollment packets;
- Have a sign-in sheet;
- Request attendees to sign in (signing in must be optional);

- Schedule future marketing appointments;
- Answer questions beyond what attendees ask;
- Request attendees to fill out an SOA or enrollment forms;
- Offer meals;
- Give away cash or other monetary rebates;
- Hold a marketing or sales event within 12 hours of an educational event at the exact location or an adjacent building;
- Guide or attempt to guide attendees toward a particular plan or set of plans;
- Use pressure tactics to sign someone up; or
- Promote or cross-sell non-health-related products.

Secret Shoppers (Enforcement of Consumer Protections)

CMS secret shoppers measure the quality of service and compliance with Medicare regulations to gather specific information regarding products and services. These secret shoppers want to ensure producers are compliant during the annual enrollment period and when they speak with customers.

Websites

Consumer-facing websites promoting a specific insurance company's Medicare Advantage or Medicare Part D products must be presented to CMS for approval.

KEY FACTS

Knowing the key facts can be the difference between passing and failing your exam. Read through each point for a quick review of essential terms and concepts presented in this book.

Basic Insurance Concepts and Principles

- The Cal. Ins. Code defines insurance as a contract in which one person undertakes to indemnify another person against damage, loss, or liability arising from a contingent or unknown event.
- Any individual capable of making a contract can be an insurer, subject to the restrictions imposed by the Cal. Ins. Code.
- Speculative risks are a risk situation that includes a chance of loss and potential for gain. These risks are not insurable.
- A hazard is something that increases the risk of a loss.
- The law of large numbers states that the more similar risks the insurer combines, the better they can approximately guess how many losses they will have in a given period.
- Any situation that presents the likelihood of a loss is called a loss exposure.
- The principle of indemnity is most closely associated with insurable interest.
- The doctrine of utmost good faith states that every party to the contract can rely upon the other party's statements.

Contract Law

- The policy is the written instrument in which a contract of insurance is established.
- Every policy must specify the parties, the insured's interest, the insured's property or life, the risks insured against, the policy period, and the policy premium.
- The following information does not need to be communicated in a contract: known information, information that should be understood, information that is not material to the risk, and information that the other party waives.
- The insurance provider's financial rating is not required to be specified in the insurance policy.
- The premium is the amount the insured pays the insurance company for the coverage provided.
- The rate is the price of insurance for each exposure unit.
- To determine the premium an insured will pay, the insurance provider multiplies the rate by the number of exposure units purchased.
- A policy's express warranty is a statement of fact of a matter relating to the individual or thing insured or to the risk.
- A warranty can be expressed or implied.
- A representation in an insurance contract qualifies as an implied warranty.
- A representation can be oral or written. It can be made at the time of or before the policy issuance.
- A representation can be altered or withdrawn before the policy is issued but not afterward.
- A representation of the future, unless it is purely a statement of an expectation or belief, is considered a promise.
- A representation is false when the facts fail to correspond with its stipulations or assertions.
- If a representation is false in a material point, the injured party is entitled to rescind the contract.
- A false representation on a signed claim form could subject the insured to perjury.
- The materiality of concealment is utilized to determine the importance of a misrepresentation.
- Concealment is when a party fails to communicate what a party knows and ought to share so that the other party can make a sound decision.

- Intentional or unintentional concealment allows the injured party to rescind the insurance.
- Materiality is determined solely by the probable influence of the facts upon the underwriter in forming an opinion of the proposed contract's disadvantages.
- If the insurance provider discovers the insured has violated a material warranty, they can rescind the contract.
- To rescind a policy means to cancel or void the policy by returning all premiums to the insured.
- A nonparticipating policy owner will not receive dividends. Stock insurers issue nonparticipating policies and pay dividends to stockholders, not policyholders.

The Insurance Marketplace

Producers

- An individual cannot transact insurance without a valid license.
- Transacting insurance includes the solicitation, negotiation, or execution of a contract and the business of matters arising out of the contract.
- An individual who transacts insurance without a license is guilty of a misdemeanor.
- Transacting insurance without a license is a misdemeanor punishable by a fine not to exceed $50,000 or up to one year in jail, or both.
- Under federal law, a prohibited person is anyone whose activities affect interstate commerce. These individuals deliberately, with the intent to deceive, make a false material statement or financial report to any insurance regulator to influence that regulator.
- Under federal law, a prohibited person cannot engage in insurance activities in this state without the prior written consent of the Commissioner.
- Under federal law, a convicted prohibited person can be imprisoned for 10 to 15 years and fined up to $50,000 for each violation.
- Insurance agents are authorized by and on behalf of insurance companies to transact all types of insurance other than life, disability, or health insurance.
- Life licensees are authorized to act on behalf of a life or disability insurance provider to transact life, accident and health, or life and accident and health insurance.
- Insurance brokers transact insurance other than life insurance. They do so for compensation and on behalf of another person but not on behalf of an insurance company.
- A licensed life or health agent can submit a life or health insurance application to an insurance company that has not appointed them. If the insurance provider issues the policy, they must appoint the agent within 14 days. This process is known as brokerage.
- An insurer does not appoint an insurance broker.
- A life or health insurance broker license does not exist.
- Property and casualty agents or brokers can offset funds due to an insured for return premiums against amounts due from the same insured for unpaid premiums due on the same or any other policy.
- A life settlement broker is an individual who, on behalf of a policyholder, offers to negotiate the sale of the owner's life insurance policy to a life settlement provider.
- Life settlement brokers only represent the owner. They owe a fiduciary duty to the owner to act according to their instructions.
- Viatical settlements are affected through the use of absolute assignment.
- An insurance solicitor is employed to assist a broker or agent in transacting insurance other than life or health insurance.

- An insurance solicitor can represent more than one broker or agent.
- Errors and omissions insurance protects producers against legal liability resulting from negligence or errors and omissions. It does not cover dishonest, fraudulent, or criminal acts.
- Except when performed by a surplus lines broker, it is a misdemeanor for an individual to act as an agent for a non-admitted insurer.
- A surplus lines broker can place insurance with a non-admitted insurer only if insurance cannot be obtained from admitted insurers in this state.
- Surplus lines coverage cannot be written to obtain a rate lower than the lowest rate an admitted insurer will charge.
- Surplus line brokers must conduct a diligent search among admitted insurers before placing the coverage with a non-admitted insurer.
- Offering free insurance coverage in connection with the sale of services as an inducement to complete the transaction is illegal.
- Agents do not need the Commissioner's approval to use their actual names.
- Licensees have to file with the Commissioner their true names and any fictitious names (DBAs) under which they do business.
- Fictitious names cannot be too similar to a name already on file, cannot mislead the public, or imply the licensee is an insurance provider.
- Licensees must immediately inform the Commissioner of any change in their residence, mailing, principal business, or email address.
- If an agent engages in Internet advertising, they must include their name, license number, and business address, but not their phone number.
- Licensees are required to inform the Commissioner in writing within 30 days of the date they identify a change in their background information.
- Life insurance agents do not have to keep records of printed material that the insurance provider has distributed in general.
- The rules regarding life insurance policy illustrations are not designed to ensure that the illustration states that nonguaranteed elements will continue unchanged for each year shown.
- Life insurance illustrations demonstrating nonguaranteed elements display values, premiums, charges, or credits that are not determined at issue.
- Life insurance illustrations do not have to include a statement that the benefits in the illustration are guaranteed. Benefits can be guaranteed or nonguaranteed.
- If an insurance provider indicates that an illustration will be used, they must submit a summary status report to the policy owner annually.
- The Commissioner can, without a hearing, deny a license application if the applicant has committed a felony as shown by a plea of guilty, no contest (nolo contendere), or by conviction.
- If an applicant has had a professional license revoked in the previous five years, the insurance Commissioner can deny their licensing application without a prior hearing.
- Suppose an insurer knowingly permits one of its agents to mislead a member of the public to induce the individual to change their existing insurance. In that circumstance, the Commissioner can suspend the insurer's certificate of authority for the class of business involved.
- Insurers cannot offer insurance as an inducement to purchase or rent any real or personal property or services without any separate charge to the insured for such insurance.
- Insurance providers must file a notice of appointment with the Commissioner appointing a licensee as the insurer's agent.
- Appointments are effective as of the date they are signed and will continue until the appointee's license expires or until the insurer cancels them.
- To transact insurance, agents must hold at least one insurer appointment.

- If a producer no longer holds any insurer appointments, their license is considered inactive.
- An inactive license can be reactivated before expiration by filing a new appointment.
- A licensee can surrender their license to the Commissioner for cancellation at any time.
- If an employer holds an agent's license and wishes to cancel it, the employer must send a written notice to the Commissioner.
- Upon termination of all appointments, the licensee's permanent license will become inactive.
- Every license issued to a natural person terminates upon that person's death.
- When a corporation ceases to exist, its insurance license is terminated.
- Any licensee who diverts fiduciary funds for personal use is guilty of theft.
- Insurance producers act as fiduciaries when they handle their customers' premiums.
- MGAs (managing general agents) can be any person, partnership, firm, corporation, or association. They handle all or part of an insurance company's business (including a separate department, division, or underwriting office).
- Producers have a fiduciary responsibility when they deal with, handle, supervise, or hold in trust and confidence the affairs of another person, mainly regarding financial matters.
- Licensees who receive fiduciary funds must remit them to the person so entitled or maintain such funds in a trustee bank account in California separate from any other account.
- Licensees can commingle fiduciary funds in their trustee bank account with other funds to establish reserves or advance premiums for the paying of return commissions.
- A written agreement must be obtained from every insurance provider or individual entitled to such funds authorizing the maintenance and retention of any earnings accruing on funds in a trustee bank account.
- Life-only agents or accident and health agents must complete 24 hours of continuing education every 2-year renewal period.
- Agents licensed for all lines of insurance life, health, and property and casualty must complete 24 hours of continuing education every 2-year renewal period, not 48 hours.
- Property and casualty broker-agents must complete 24 hours of continuing education every 2-year renewal period.
- In addition to completing the pre-licensing requirement, life agents, personal lines agents, and property and casualty broker-agents must also complete a 12-hour ethics and code course.
- Third-party administrators often assist employers with administering their self-funded plans.
- The Code of Ethics requires agents to place their customer's interests first.
- When an insurer is guilty of unfair trade practices while issuing, renewing, and servicing a policy, the insurer could be prosecuted for three violations, one for each act.
- When a producer engages in unfair methods of competition, the agent is subject to penalties of no more than $5,000 for each act. If the action is considered willful, the agent is subject to fines of no more than $10,000 for each activity.
- The California Insurance Code (Cal. Ins. Code) and the California Code of Regulations (CCR) identify many unethical or illegal practices. Still, they are not a complete guide to ethical behavior.
- The Cal. Ins. Code includes senior code protections. Individuals aged 60 or older who buy life insurance in California must receive a minimum 30-day free look. Individuals under age 60 who purchase life insurance must receive a minimum 10-day free look period.
- Every insurer offering individual life insurance or annuities to senior citizens using nonguaranteed elements in illustrations must provide a confirmation statement in bold print.
- The free look notice for seniors needs to be printed in no less than 10-point uppercase font on the policy's cover page or certificate and the outline of coverage.
- Agents cannot use or authorize pretext interviews to acquire information about an insurance transaction.

- Term life insurance directed to individuals 55 or older has to prominently disclose any change in premium resulting from the policy duration, aging of the insured, or any other factor. If the insurance provider retains any right to modify premiums in the future, it must also disclose that fact.
- If a senior has obtained an annuity invested in a mutual fund and cancels during the free look period, the CIC requires the senior to be refunded the account's value.

Insurers

- An insurer organized and selling in California is considered to be a domestic insurer in California.
- An insurance company based in another state selling in California is a foreign insurer in California.
- An insurance company based in another country (e.g., Mexico) and doing business in California is an alien insurer.
- A diligent search among admitted insurers is considered to have been made if three admitted insurers have declined the risk.
- In a reinsurance transaction, a primary insurer is the insurance provider who transfers its loss exposure to another insurance provider.
- The insurer that purchases reinsurance is referred to as the primary insurer (a.k.a. ceding insurer).
- The Cal. Ins. Code broadly defines a person to include individuals, partnerships, associations, organizations, corporations, limited liability companies, or business trusts.
- An insurer can be a person, partnership, association, organization, corporation, limited liability company, or business trust.
- Policies issued by mutual insurers pay dividends to policy owners. The dividend option is chosen by the policy owner on the insurance application.
- Policyholders own mutual insurers.
- A stock insurer is an insurance provider owned by individuals who purchase shares of stock in the company. They share the profits in proportion to the number of shares held and vote for a board of directors.
- Dividends received by policy owners of a mutual insurer are not taxable.

General Market Regulation

- The CIC can only be changed when the California state legislature passes a new statute modifying, amending, or repealing an existing one.
- Only the Commissioner can change the CCR according to the State Administrative Procedures Act.
- The Insurance Commissioner is elected by the people in the same manner as the Governor, not to exceed two 4-year terms.
- Under Cal. Ins. Code Section 770, the Commissioner will issue a cease and desist order for a violation of more than one transaction if the violation pertains to loans on the security of real or personal property.
- Pretext interviews can be used to investigate a claim with a reasonable basis for suspecting fraud, material misrepresentation, or criminal activity.
- When new insurance is being sought, the Gramm-Leach-Bliley Act (GLBA) requires a privacy protection notice be provided no later than at the time of policy delivery.
- The California Financial Information Privacy Act gives individuals greater privacy protections than the federal GLBA.
- The purpose of the CA Insurance Information and Privacy Protection Act is to establish standards for collecting, using, and disclosing information gathered during insurance transactions.
- An insurance company is considered insolvent when it cannot meet its financial obligations.
- An insurer cannot escape insolvency by being able to pay for all liabilities and reinsurance of all outstanding risks.

- An insurer with enough reserves to cover all liabilities is considered solvent.
- To remain financially solvent under the CIC, an insurance company must have enough assets to pay for its liabilities, reinsurance of all outstanding risks, and meet minimum requirements equal to their paid-in capital (value of the company if liquidated).
- The State Insurance Guarantee Fund protects policy owners whose insurer becomes insolvent (financially impaired). This fund only covers licensed insurance companies (member insurers).
- The paid-in capital of an insurance provider refers to the amount by which the value of assets exceeds the sum of liabilities.
- Producer records must be made available to the Commissioner at any time.
- It is a misdemeanor to refuse to deliver assets, records, or books to the Commissioner once a seizure order has been executed in an insolvency proceeding.
- Agents who receive a premium financing commission must keep their records for three years.
- If the Insurance Commissioner issues a notice of seizure for documents and the agent fails to produce the documents, the agent would be subject to a $1,000 fine or up to one year in jail.
- The Commissioner can undertake conservation proceedings when an insurance company is in such poor financial condition that its business transactions will be hazardous to policy owners.
- Employer self-funded plans are not covered by the California Life and Health Insurance Guarantee Association (CLHIGA).
- Group stop-loss plans are not covered by the California Life and Health Insurance Guarantee Association (CLHIGA).
- Fraud is an intentional and fraudulent omission on the part of an insured that allows the insurance provider to rescind the contract.
- Each authorized insurer must establish a division to investigate fraudulent claims.
- When an insured is guilty of turning in a fraudulent claim, they can face imprisonment or a $150,000 fine or double the amount of the fraudulent claim, whichever is greater. For example, if an insured turned in a fraudulent claim totaling $55,000, the insured would be fined $110,000.
- If an insured signs a fraudulent claim form, the insured could be guilty of perjury.
- Claims forms must include a statement related to fraudulent claims alerting anyone who knowingly presents a fraudulent or false claim for the payment of a loss is guilty of a crime. It can be subject to fines and imprisonment.
- As used in the CIC, the word "shall" means "mandatory," and the word "may" means "permissive."
- The affidavit of the individual who mails a notice, affirming the facts, is prima facie evidence that the notice was mailed.

Life Insurance – Basics

Uses of Life Insurance

- The applicant for insurance is the person who is applying to purchase insurance.
- Before a sale, an agent should identify the applicant's overall financial objectives.
- Life insurance creates an immediate estate upon the insured's death.
- In life insurance, insurable interest needs to exist at the time of application.
- If an insured increases their insurance policy limits, they are not eliminating their risk; they are transferring more of their risk.
- Businesses use key person life insurance to protect themselves in case a valued employee dies. The business would receive the death benefit to hire and train a replacement.

- The premiums paid for key person life insurance are not tax deductible, and benefits are not taxable.
- If an organization terminates a key employee, it will still be eligible to hold a license, as the organization will be unaffected.
- Obtaining life insurance to fund a buy-sell agreement is a business use of life insurance, not a personal use.
- Under the Cal. Ins. Code, all advertisements, policies, and certificates of term life insurance sold to individuals age 55 and older must include a term life insurance monetary value index, similar to the life insurance surrender cost index.

Individual Underwriting, Pricing, and Claims

- If an adverse underwriting decision occurs, the insurance provider or agent has to provide the individual with the specific reason for the decision in writing and a summary of their rights.
- Preferred risks receive the lowest premium rates as they pose the lowest risk to the insurance company.
- The underwriting division within the insurance provider selects which risks the insurer will take on.
- Members of the Medical Information Bureau (MIB) are required to report medical impairments identified during the underwriting process.
- Life insurance providers are members of the Medical Information Bureau.
- The HIPAA Privacy Rules establish national standards for the disclosure and use of protected health information.
- Life insurance policies do not include a probationary period for pre-existing conditions.
- When an applicant reveals medical conditions that require more information, the insurance provider will typically require an attending physician's report.
- A copy of the signed authorization must accompany the request for an attending physician's report.
- The applicant must sign a consent form to authorize the release of an attending physician's report.
- The agent's commission comes from the portion of the insurance provider's expenses of the premium charged.
- There is no coverage under a conditional receipt until all conditions are met.
- An insurance binder always creates immediate coverage, which is the primary difference between a binder and a conditional receipt. A binding receipt delivers a limited amount of coverage right away.
- Under the Cal. Ins. Code, life insurance agents are prohibited from issuing binders.
- If an agent issues a binder for an insurance company for which they are not appointed, the Commissioner can revoke or suspend the agent's license.
- A written binder is considered a valid insurance policy to prove that the insured has insurance coverage. This binder excludes life insurance. Binders are only allowed in property and casualty insurance.

Types of Life Policies

- There are three types of ordinary life insurance: whole life, endowment, and term.
- Group insurance is not a type of ordinary life insurance.
- Whole life insurance is also called continuous premium whole life insurance.
- When a premium is paid on a universal life policy, the insurer will subtract the mortality and general expenses from it. Then it will add the current interest and deposit it into the cash value.
- The rate of return paid on an indexed whole life policy's cash value will keep up with the inflation rate.
- Variable insurance products are regulated by the state department of insurance and the SEC because they are considered to meet the definition of a securities product.

- A variable life insurance policy allows the owner to self-direct cash values into different subaccounts.
- A variable/universal life policy has no fixed, guaranteed rate of return.
- A family policy provides life insurance for an entire family. It allows the children to convert from term to whole life coverage without requiring a physical exam.
- A family life insurance policy includes whole life for one spouse and level, convertible term for the other spouse and children.
- When a payor benefit rider is added to a juvenile life policy, it waives the premium for the policy until the child turns a certain age (often 21) if the parent dies.
- A joint life policy insures multiple lives and pays out when the first insured dies.
- The following are true concerning survivorship life insurance: it offers premiums that are very low compared to those that would be charged for separate policies. It is well situated to meet the need for cash to cover estate taxes; face amounts are typically more than one million dollars.
- Annually renewable term life insurance has a level face amount but an increasing premium.
- Decreasing term life insurance is often used to pay off an outstanding mortgage upon the borrower's death.
- Employees covered under a group policy receive a certificate of insurance as their proof of coverage.

Individual Life Insurance Contract – Provisions and Options

- An insurance provider or agent must specify those questions on an application designed to obtain information solely for research or marketing purposes.
- The beneficiary is not required to sign the insurance application.
- A nonmedical application allows the insurer to write life insurance without a physical examination.
- The entire contract clause specifies that the application is part of the contract if it is attached when issued.
- The quarterly mode of payment costs a policy owner more than the annual mode of payment.
- The interpretation of policy provisions is not the main objective of insurance regulation.
- The free look on life insurance and annuities is also referred to as the right to return.
- Life insurance companies must give the policy owner a minimum 10-day free look.
- Policyholders aged 60 or older are senior citizens and must receive a 30-day minimum free look.
- An absolute assignment is a permanent transfer of ownership rights.
- The conversion feature allows an employee to go from group coverage to an individual policy.
- Dividends cannot be guaranteed and are declared by the board of directors.
- An insured would name a contingent beneficiary to ensure where the policy proceeds will go if the primary beneficiary dies before the insured.
- The common disaster clause applies when the insured and primary beneficiary dies in the same accident. It states that the primary beneficiary always dies first and protects the contingent beneficiary's interest.
- The spendthrift clause protects the policy proceeds from the beneficiary's creditors. However, this clause will not apply if the proceeds are paid out in a lump sum.
- The insured can change the beneficiary at any time if the beneficiary designation is revocable.
- Automatic premium loan is a provision that can be added to a cash value life insurance policy if the insured forgets to pay the premium. It goes into effect at the end of the grace period.
- A collateral assignment can be used to obtain a loan.
- In California, life insurance premiums are refunded to the beneficiary if death occurs from suicide within the first two years of the effective date of coverage.
- The reduced paid-up nonforfeiture option will provide a new whole life policy with a reduced face amount.

- The misstatement of age clause allows the insurer to adjust the face amount at the time of death to what the premium the insured paid would have purchased had the truth about the insured's age been reported when the policy was purchased.
- Extended term is not a settlement option. An extended term is a nonforfeiture option that offers a new term life policy with the same face amount of coverage as the original insurance policy.
- Extended term is a life insurance nonforfeiture provision, not a rider or a settlement option.
- Extended term insurance is the nonforfeiture option that uses cash surrender values to purchase paid-up term insurance for the entire face amount of the policy.
- A settlement option can be predetermined by the policy owner prior to death but is typically selected by the beneficiary upon the insured's death.
- If a policy loan is outstanding when the insured dies and the beneficiary chooses the fixed period settlement option, the outstanding loan will affect the amount of the payments, not the length for which they are received.
- The interest settlement option only allows the death benefit earnings to be paid to the beneficiary.
- If a beneficiary intends to leave the life insurance proceeds with the insurance provider and receive investment income, the beneficiary should choose the interest option.

Life Policy Riders

- A disability income rider that is added to a life insurance policy will pay a replacement of the insured's lost income in the event the insured becomes disabled.
- The waiver of premium rider will waive the insured's premium should the insured become disabled.
- The accidental death benefit rider will pay double the face amount if the insured dies because of an accident, as defined in the policy.
- If an insured buys a cost of living rider, this rider automatically increases their policy limit tied to the consumer price index. However, if the policy limit increases, the underlying premium also increases.
- The guaranteed insurability rider allows the policy owner to adjust benefits upwards at specified future option dates.

Annuities

- If an annuitant chooses the 10-year period certain annuity payout option, it guarantees that when the annuitant dies within the first 120 payments, the remaining payments will go to the beneficiary. However, the annuitant will be paid on the condition they live, which could be considerably longer than ten years.
- The exclusion allowance is the formula used to calculate the amount of taxable annuity distribution.
- Cash surrender of an annuity before age 59 ½ will result in ordinary income tax and a 10% premature distribution penalty, both of which are applied to the earnings portion.
- A variable annuity is one in which an accumulation unit's value can be multiplied by the number of units owned in a separate account.
- If the owner of a variable annuity returns it during the right-to-return period, they will receive a full refund of all paid premiums.
- Money invested in variable annuities is held in the insurer's separate account.
- An equity-indexed annuity has a fixed minimum interest rate and the opportunity to get a higher rate of return, like that of the stock market.

Life Insurance and Annuities – Replacement and Cancellation

- Both the producer and the applicant must sign the Notice Regarding Replacement.
- When it comes to policy replacement, the agent is not required to send a copy of the replacement notice to the existing insurance provider. The new insurer will provide notice to the existing insurer.
- Replacement is when a producer replaces a customer's current policy with a new one and is not illegal. However, the producer cannot replace the customer's policy if the new policy is worse and the premium is higher. This act would be known as twisting and is illegal.

Group Life, Retirement Plans, and Social Security Disability

- Group coverage usually is less expensive than individual coverage.
- In a group life contract, California requires a minimum of two employees to be covered.
- If an employee wants to enroll without restrictions, the employee would enroll during the open enrollment period (eligibility period).
- In a contributory group policy, the premium payment is shared between the employee and employer. The employee contributes toward the premium.
- A group contract where the employer covers 100% of the premium is a noncontributory group plan.
- All eligible employees have to participate in a noncontributory group life plan.
- In a contributory group insurance plan, the employee pays all or part of the costs.
- A group contract is between the employer and the insurance provider.
- Insurance producers must keep records regarding policies sold in California for a minimum of five years.
- Sole proprietors with no employees are not eligible for group life coverage.
- If a dependent child covered by a group life plan is incapable of self-support, coverage under the plan can continue without any age limitation.
- In a group life plan, a dependent child attending an educational institution can be covered until age 26.
- Group life policies can exclude aviation, suicide, and military action, but not death due to other accidents.
- Most workers pay into Social Security through taxes levied on their earnings. Benefits are based on the contribution amount but are not equal to the contribution amount.
- A widow or widower with no children would be eligible for Social Security survivor benefits at age 60.
- The Social Security blackout period is when surviving family members are not eligible for Social Security survivor benefits. Survivor benefits end during this period.
- When the youngest child reaches age 16, the Social Security blackout period starts.
- When the surviving spouse reaches age 60, the Social Security blackout period ends.
- The Social Security full retirement age is based upon the year in which a person was born.
- Under Social Security, retirement benefits are available only to those workers who are fully insured.
- In Social Security, fully insured status requires 40 quarters of coverage.
- Eligibility for Social Security retirement benefits will depend upon the number of quarters earned.
- An individual that has contributed to Social Security for six of the previous 13 quarters and becomes disabled is insured under the system.

Taxation of Life Insurance and Annuity Premiums and Proceeds

- The death benefits of an annuity are not tax-deductible or tax-free.
- Life insurance death benefits are tax-free.
- In a group life policy with a death benefit of $50,000 or more, the premium cost for insurance above $50,000 is taxable as income to the insured.
- Accidental death in group life insurance is not excluded.
- A modified endowment contract has a 10% IRS premature withdrawal penalty.

Accident and Health Insurance – Basics

- On an accident and health policy with an accidental means clause, the cause, and the result must be accidental for coverage to apply.
- Coinsurance is a feature of medical insurance. It is defined as sharing the loss after the deductible has been met. Coinsurance is typically expressed as a percentage sharing of the loss between the insurance provider and the insured, with the insurance provider paying the larger percentage, such as 90/10.
- A gatekeeper (primary care physician) cannot be a specialist; the gatekeeper needs to be a general practitioner.
- The waiver of premium rider waives the insured's premium should the insured become disabled.
- A guaranteed renewable health insurance policy will have the highest premium.
- Guaranteed renewable health insurance policies have to offer renewal and cannot be changed in any way EXCEPT for rates by class only.
- An insurance provider cannot change a noncancelable health insurance policy.
- A specified disease policy insures only certain dread diseases, like cancer insurance.

Medical Expense Insurance

Individual Insurance

- HMOs and PPOs are known as service providers since the hospitals and doctors get paid directly for those services.
- A capitation fee is a per-head fee paid to doctors treating HMO subscribers.
- An HMO subscriber could receive emergency medical attention without authorization from the primary care physician (gatekeeper).
- Out-of-network coverage from an HMO is only available in emergencies.
- HMOs strive for preventive medicine.
- Health maintenance organizations do not have to provide coverage for prescription drugs.
- Preferred provider organizations (PPOs) consist of various private physicians and hospitals in a given network area. They agree to offer services to the organization's subscribers at a predetermined, discounted fee-for-service rate.
- If a preferred provider performs services, the PPO can cover 100% of the services minus a nominal copayment.

- If non-PPO providers deliver services, the services are still covered, but at a reduced amount, except in emergencies.
- With a PPO, an insured can go out of network. Out-of-network services are available at a reduced amount, except in an emergency.
- An exclusive provider organization (EPO) is a type of PPO that uses a select group of exclusive preferred providers who are compensated on a fee-for-service basis.
- Most EPOs use the gatekeeper concept, where each enrollee is assigned to a primary care physician who refers the enrollee to an exclusive provider.
- EPOs provide an alternative to traditional HMOs and PPOs.

Consumer-Driven Health Plans (CDHPs)

- POS plans, MSAs, and HDPHs are examples of Consumer-driven health plans.
- Consumer-driven models include HSAs, MSAs, FSAs, and HRAs.
- An employer is responsible for establishing FSAs.
- The employer owns an FSA, but the employee can decide which medical expenses to pay using funds from the FSA.
- FSAs can be utilized with most employer-sponsored health plans.
- An HRA (health reimbursement arrangement) is a benefit account established by an employer.
- Each year, the employer contributes to the employee's HRA.
- The employee can use the balance in the HRA toward medical expenses not paid for by the health plan, such as coinsurance and deductibles.
- The employer can only fund an HRA. Employee contributions are not allowed.
- An HSA (health savings account) is considered a retirement account for medical expenses.
- Pre-tax dollars fund FSAs, HRAs and HSAs. They all have tax-free federal income earnings when used for qualified medical expenses. Each of these accounts includes a debit-type card to make withdrawals.
- The employer is the owner of the HRA and the FSA.
- MSAs are similar to HSAs. The critical difference is the medical savings account is only available to small businesses or self-employed individuals. Only individuals or employers can contribute to an MSA, not a mix of the two. HSAs are more common than MSAs.
- (HDHPs) High-deductible health plans are often combined with health savings accounts (HSAs).
- To have an HSA, the insured has to be enrolled in an HSA-compatible insurance plan.
- The employee owns the HSA.
- Only the HSA can invest the money (think of an HSA as a mutual fund account).

Group Medical Expense Insurance

- Generally, group coverage is less expensive than individual coverage.
- The conversion feature lets an employee move from group coverage to an individual policy.
- Employees insured under a group policy receive certificates of insurance as their proof of coverage.
- Employee benefit plans can only self-fund for health benefits, not life insurance.
- If an employee wants to enroll without restrictions, the employee would need to enroll during the open enrollment period (eligibility period).
- In a contributory group policy, the employee and employer share the premium payment. The employee contributes toward the premium.
- In a noncontributory group disability income policy, any paid policy benefits are taxable and included in the employee's gross income.
- A group contract where the employer pays 100% of the premium is a noncontributory group plan.

- The Consolidated Omnibus Reconciliation Act (COBRA) mandates that employers with 20 or more employees provide health insurance continuation to employees and their dependents who become ineligible for coverage due to a qualifying event. If the employee chooses continuation, the employee is responsible for paying the full premium for coverage and can only continue coverage under the group plan for a limited period.
- An employee terminated for cause cannot be eligible for group continuation under COBRA.
- Under COBRA, divorce is a qualifying event that will let the employee apply for continuing coverage under the group plan.
- Under the Americans with Disabilities Act (ADA), wearing eyeglasses is not considered a disability. However, the ADA covers confinement to a wheelchair, deafness, and HIV/AIDs.
- The Family and Medical Leave Act (FMLA) provides eligible employees with up to 12 weeks per year of unpaid, job-protected leave for the following reasons: to care for an immediate family member (e.g., spouse, parent, or child) with a serious health condition, the birth and care of a newborn child, adopting a child; or to take medical leave when the employee cannot work due to a serious health condition.

Patient Protection and Affordable Care Act (PPACA)

- Medical expense policies can no longer include a probationary period.
- Individual and small group medical expense policies can be purchased through the Exchange.
- Health insurance policy premiums cannot be based on gender or health status. Rates can be based on the type of policy or level of tier purchased, and age-banded rates can be used.
- The PPACA correlates with other federal laws, including HIPAA, Medicare, COBRA, and the Children's Health Insurance Program (CHIP).
- Under the PPACA, anyone can receive medical expense insurance, regardless of health.
- An individual who qualifies for the advance premium tax credit can purchase any metal tier of coverage.
- A person offered affordable health coverage through their employer is not eligible for a cost-sharing subsidy or an advance premium tax credit.
- All policies sold through the Exchange must provide coverage for essential health benefits.
- An open enrollment period each year allows new enrollees to buy coverage through the Exchange.
- An individual who has purchased coverage through the Exchange can switch policies during the open enrollment period.
- A special enrollment period allows an individual to enroll in Exchange coverage after a triggering event.
- Triggering events for special enrollment through the Exchange include losing Medicaid coverage due to an increase in income, losing job-based health coverage, marriage, divorce, and the birth or adoption of a child.
- When buying a policy through the Exchange, a person can qualify for premium reductions or cost-sharing subsidies. The Exchange is also designed to qualify individuals for Medi-Cal coverage.
- The PPACA requires insurance providers to offer dependent coverage for children up to age 26 on all group and individual health insurance policies. Children can join or remain on their parent's plan even if they are attending school, married, or not living with them.
- Individuals buying coverage through the Exchange are screened for eligibility for the Medi-Cal (California's Medicaid) program and the Children's Health Insurance Program (CHIP).
- Individuals buying coverage through the Exchange can qualify for advance premium tax credits or cost-sharing subsidies, depending upon their annual income versus the Federal Poverty Level.
- To qualify for the cost-sharing subsidy, an individual must purchase a silver coverage tier.
- Cost-sharing subsidies limit the annual out-of-pocket maximum an individual will be subject to paying.
- Large businesses must offer affordable coverage that satisfies a minimum level of coverage to full-time employees (30 hours or more each week) or face a penalty.

- Medical expense policies sold through the Exchange are offered as standardized plans, called metal tiers, such as platinum, gold, silver, and bronze. Platinum plans are the most expensive and provides the best coverage.

California Health Benefit Exchanges – Individual Exchange and Small Business Health Options Program Exchange (SHOP)

- The California Health Benefit Exchange makes it easier for individuals and small businesses to compare plans and purchase health insurance in the private market.
- The California Health Benefit Exchange was established to enhance competition and provide the same advantages available to large employer groups. It organizes the private insurance market, including greater purchasing power, a more stable risk pool, more competition among insurance providers, and detailed information regarding the quality, price, and services.
- At any time throughout the year, small businesses can obtain coverage through the SHOP program.
- Under the PPACA, small businesses are not required to provide employee coverage.
- Insurance providers have to comply with the medical loss ratio requirement (individual plans 80%, and large group plans 85%).

Disability Insurance

- Disability insurance providers must eliminate applications likely to have losses more frequently or severely than the insurer's anticipated rates. This responsibility belongs to the underwriter.
- A morbidity table includes statistical data on the probability of a sickness or disability. A mortality table provides statistical data relating to the probability of death.
- A probationary period or pre-existing condition exclusion is a period that excludes coverage for prior medical conditions. It begins when a disability income insurance policy is brand new.
- The waiting period found in disability income policies is also known as the elimination period.
- On disability income insurance, the waiting period is like a deductible, except it is stated in terms of time rather than dollars.
- The period (30 days, 60 days, 90 days, or 180 days) the insured is not eligible for benefits after becoming disabled is referred to as the waiting period.
- The disability income coverage under Social Security was established to provide a minimum floor of income in case of total disability. It was not intended to provide a full replacement for lost income.
- An employee would be considered partially disabled when working part-time and receive lost income under a long-term disability benefit.
- Social Security has the most difficult definition of total disability to satisfy.
- Under Social Security, to receive total disability benefits, the disability has to be expected to last at least 12 months or result in death.
- An occupational disability income policy provides coverage on and off the job.
- Premiums are tax-deductible for employers offering a noncontributory group disability income policy, but benefits are taxable to employees.
- If the employee fully pays a group disability income policy's premium, benefits would be excluded from the employee's gross income (not taxable).
- The "any occupation" definition in disability income specifies that the insured must be unable to perform any job the insured is suited to do by prior experience, training, or education.

- If they have the "own occupation" definition of total disability in their policy, a software engineer will be eligible for disability income benefits despite returning to work as a janitor.
- Disability income policies do not provide a benefit period for the insured's lifetime.
- On a disability income policy, the Social Security offset rider will cover the difference between what Social Security pays and the insured's actual loss of earned income.
- In a disability income policy, the purpose of the rehabilitation provision is to encourage a disabled insured to return to their original occupation.
- In a disability income policy, the transplant donor benefit considers the insured disabled if donating a body organ.
- The return of premium rider that can be attached to a disability income policy will deliver a return of a percentage of premiums paid at periodic intervals, on the condition that the insured remains disabled.

Senior Health Products

Social Security

- There is a 5-month waiting period, or elimination period, for Social Security disability benefits.
- The worker's Primary Insurance Amount (PIA) determines the amount of Social Security disability benefits received.
- Benefits are not retroactive to the start of the disability.
- Contributions to Social Security are required for most workers.

Medicare

- Under Part A of Medicare, claims are submitted by the provider.
- Medicare Part A covers hospital services and is free to those eligible individuals once they reach the age of 65.
- Part B of Medicare is optional. If an eligible person enrolls, a monthly premium must be paid for the coverage.
- Coverage for doctors' services provided by Medicare Part B (Medical Insurance) – coinsurance, deductibles, physician services, hospital outpatient, second opinion before surgery, x-rays and diagnostic tests performed on an outpatient basis, mental illness, other covered services, etc.
- Only individuals age 65 or older are eligible for Medicare Part B.
- Insurance providers can offer Medicare supplement insurance plans that only contain the core benefits.
- Medicare Part C is called Medicare Advantage, which is Medicare provided by approved HMOs or PPOs.
- Medicare Part D covers prescription drugs.
- Medicare will send out a quarterly Medicare Summary Notice detailing the services provided under Part A and B if they were covered, and how much coverage they had.
- The Medicare Summary Notice is not a bill for medical services. Money due will be billed by the health care provider who performed the services.

Long-Term Care

- Producers who sell long-term care must complete long-term care-specific continuing education within the core requirement, not in addition to it.

- Skilled nursing care, intermediate nursing care, home health care, custodial care, home care, and community-based care are standard levels of care in a long-term care policy.
- Hospice care is care for the terminally ill and is covered by most LTC policies. Hospice care does not pay for costs associated with rehabilitation.
- A person who requires terminal illness care would find this coverage provided in their LTC policy as hospice care.
- Adult daycare coverage in a long-term care policy will pay for part-time care in a facility for a person who lives at home.
- LTC care policies are underwritten on the ability of the applicant to care for themselves (activities of daily living).
- There are six main activities of daily living (ADLs) that trigger coverage on LTC policies, including eating, dressing, bathing, toileting, continence, and transferring (walking).
- To satisfy the chronically ill trigger of a long-term care policy, an individual has to be unable to perform two activities of daily living at a minimum.
- Convalescence is not a level of care for which benefits are paid on a long-term care policy.
- On the first page of every qualified LTC policy sold in California, insureds must be notified that the LTC insurance contract is federally qualified. It can qualify the insured for federal and state tax benefits.
- An outline of coverage needs to be delivered to an applicant for LTC insurance at the time of solicitation.
- Regarding LTC insurance, every insurance provider, agent, broker, and any other individual engaged in the insurance business owes a policy owner or a prospective policy owner a responsibility of honesty, good faith, and fair dealing.
- On a replacing LTC policy, the commission will be determined based on the difference between the annual premium of the original policy and the replacement policy.

GLOSSARY

Accelerated Benefits – Riders attached to life insurance policies that allow death benefits to be used to pay for nursing or convalescent home expenses.

Accident – An unforeseen, unplanned event that occurs suddenly and at an unspecified place.

Accident Insurance – A type of insurance that protects the insured against loss caused by accidental bodily injury.

Accidental Bodily Injury – An unforeseen, unplanned traumatic injury to the body.

Accidental Death and Dismemberment (AD&D) – An insurance policy that pays a specific amount or a specific multiple of the insured's benefit if the insured dies, loses two limbs, or loses their sight due to an accident.

Accidental Death Benefits – A policy rider specifying that the cause of death will be examined to conclude if it complies with the policy description of accidental death.

Accidental Death Insurance – An insurance policy that provides payment if the insured's death is caused by an accident.

Accumulation Period – The period when the annuitant makes investments or payments in an annuity and when those payments earn tax-deferred interest.

Acquired Immunodeficiency Syndrome (AIDS) – An incurable and infectious disease caused by the human immunodeficiency virus (HIV).

Activities of Daily Living (ADLs) – Activities individuals need to do every day, such as getting dressed, moving about, eating, bathing, etc.

Actual Cash Value (ACV) – The required amount for property loss or to pay damages, which is calculated by subtracting depreciation from the property's current replacement value.

Actual Charge – The amount a supplier or physician bills for a particular supply or service.

Actuary – An individual trained in the technical aspects of insurance and related fields, particularly in the mathematics of insurance; an individual who, on behalf of the insurer, determines the mathematical probability of loss.

Adhesion – An insurance provider offers a contract on a "take-it-or-leave-it" basis. The insured's only option is to accept or reject the agreement. Any ambiguities in the contract will be settled in the insured's favor.

Adjustable Life – Life insurance that allows changes in the premium amount, face amount, protection period, and the duration of the premium payment period.

Adjuster – A representative of an insurance carrier who investigates and acts on the insurer's behalf to obtain agreements for the amount of the insurance claim.

Administrator – A person appointed by a court as a fiduciary to settle a deceased individual's financial affairs and estate.

Admitted (Authorized) Insurer – An insurer authorized to conduct business in a particular state.

Adult Daycare – A program for impaired adults that attempts to meet their functional, social, and health needs in a setting away from their homes.

Adverse Selection – The tendency of risks with a higher probability of loss to buy and maintain insurance more often than the risks that present a lower probability.

Agency – An insurance company or sales office.

Agent – A person with a license to negotiate, sell, or effect insurance contracts on behalf of an insurer.

Agent's Authority – Special powers granted to an agent by their agency contract.

Aleatory – A contract in which the participating parties agree to an exchange of unequal amounts. Insurance contracts are aleatory; the amount the insurance provider will pay in the event of a loss is unequal to the amount the insured will pay in premiums.

Alien Insurer – An insurance provider that is incorporated outside the United States.

Alzheimer's Disease – A disease that causes the victim to become dysfunctional because of the degeneration of brain cells, causing severe memory loss.

Ancillary – Additional, miscellaneous services provided by a hospital, such as lab work, x-rays, and anesthesia, but not hospital room and board expenses.

Annual Statement – An insurer must submit a detailed financial report each year to the Department of Insurance in any state where it conducts business.

Annuity – A contract that provides income for life or a specified period of years.

Apparent Authority – The appearance or assumption of authority based on the principal's words, actions, or deeds or due to circumstances the principal created.

Applicant – A person making an application for themselves or another to be insured under an insurance contract.

Application – A document that gathers information for underwriting purposes. Once a policy is issued, any unanswered questions are considered waived by the insurance company.

Approved Amount – The amount Medicare decides to be reasonable for a service covered under part B of Medicare.

Assignment (Life) – The transfer of a life insurance policy's ownership rights from one person to another.

Assignment (Health) – A claim to a medical supplier or provider to receive payments directly from Medicare.

Attained Age – The age of the insured at a specified date.

Attending Physician's Statement (APS) – A statement commonly obtained from the applicant's doctor.

Authorized (Admitted) Insurer – An insurance provider authorized and licensed to conduct business in a particular state.

Avoidance – A method of dealing with risk by deliberately avoiding it (e.g., if an individual wanted to avoid the risk of being killed in a helicopter crash, they might choose never to fly in a helicopter).

Back-End Load – A fee charged at the time of a sale, transfer, or withdrawal from a life insurance policy or an annuity.

Basic Hospital Expense Insurance – Coverage that provides benefits during a hospital stay for room, board, and other hospital expenses for a certain number of days.

Basic Illustration – A proposal or ledger used to sell a life insurance policy that shows guaranteed and non-guaranteed elements.

Basic Medical Expense Insurance – Coverage for doctor visits, emergency room visits, x-rays, and lab tests; benefits, however, are limited to specified dollar amounts.

Beneficiary – The individual receiving the policy's proceeds when the insured dies.

Benefit Period – The period during which the insurer will pay the insurance benefits for each disability, illness, or hospital stay.

Binder (Binding Receipt) – A temporary contract that binds a policy before the premium is paid (puts an insurance policy into force).

Birthday Rule – The method of determining a dependent child's primary coverage. The plan of the parent whose birthday occurs first in the calendar year will be designated as primary coverage.

Blanket Medical Insurance – A policy covering all medical costs, including hospitalization, doctor visits, and drugs.

Boycott – An unfair trade practice in which one party refuses to do business with another until they agree to certain conditions.

Broker – An individual representing an insured in negotiating and obtaining a contract of insurance.

Buy-Sell Agreement – A legal contract determining what will be done with a business if an owner becomes disabled or dies.

Buyer's Guide – A booklet that describes insurance policies and concepts and provides general information to help applicants make an educated decision.

Cafeteria Plan – A selection of health care benefits from which employees can select the ones they need.

Capital Amount – A percentage of a policy's principal amount paid to the insured if they suffered the loss of an appendage.

Carriers – Entities that process claims and pay benefits in an insurance policy.

Cash Value – The amount to which a policy owner is entitled when the policy is surrendered before maturity.

Cease and Desist Order – A demand of an individual to stop committing an action violating a provision.

Certificate – A statement (or booklet) that confirms that a policy has been written and describes the coverage in general.

Certificate of Authority – A document that authorizes a company to begin conducting business and specifies the kind of insurance a company can transact. It is illegal for an insurer to transact insurance without this certificate.

Certificate of Insurance – A legal document that indicates an insurance policy has been issued. It specifies both the types and amounts of insurance provided.

Claim – A request for the payment of benefits provided by an insurance policy.

Coercion – An unfair trade practice in which an insurance company uses physical or mental force to persuade an applicant to purchase insurance.

Coinsurance – An agreement between insureds and insurers in which both parties are expected to pay a portion of the potential loss and other expenses.

Coinsurance Clause – A provision that specifies the insured and the insurer will share the losses covered by the policy. These proportions are agreed upon in advance.

Commingling – A practice in which individuals in a fiduciary capacity illegally mix their personal funds with funds they hold in trust.

Commission – The payment made by insurers to agents or brokers for the sale and service of policies.

Commissioner (Director, Superintendent) – The chief executive and administrative officer of a state Department of Insurance.

Comprehensive Policy – A plan that provides health care services, including immunization, routine physicals, preventive care, outpatient services, and hospitalization.

Comprehensive Major Medical – A combination of basic coverage and major medical coverage that features high maximum benefits, low deductibles, and coinsurance.

Concealment – The act of intentionally withholding known facts that can void a contract if the facts are material.

Conditional Contract – An agreement in which both parties must perform specific duties and follow rules of conduct to make the contract enforceable.

Consideration – A contract's binding force that requires something of value to be exchanged for the transfer of risk. The insured's consideration is the representations made in the application and the payment of the premium; the promise to pay in the event of a loss is the insurer's consideration.

Consideration Clause – A part of the insurance contract that specifies both parties must give something of value for the transfer of risk and stipulates the conditions of the exchange.

Consolidated Omnibus Budget Reconciliation Act (COBRA) of 1986 – The law allows for the continuation of group health care benefits for insureds for up to 18 months if they terminate employment or are no longer eligible and for dependents of insureds for up to 36 months in cases of the loss of eligibility because of the insured's death, divorce, or attainment of the limiting age.

Consumer Reports – Written or oral statements about a consumer's character, credit, reputation, or habits collected by a reporting agency from credit reports, employment records, and other public sources.

Contract – A legal agreement between two or more parties that is enforceable by law.

Contributory – A group insurance plan that requires the employees to pay a portion of the premium.

Controlled Business – An entity that obtains and possesses a license solely to write business on the owner, relatives, immediate family, employer, and employees.

Convertible – A policy that can be exchanged for another type of policy by a contractual provision, at the option of the policy owner, and without evidence of insurability (e.g., term life converted to a form of permanent life).

Coordination of Benefits – A provision that determines the primary provider in situations where an insured is covered by more than one policy, ultimately avoiding claims overpayments.

Co-pay – An arrangement in which an insured has to pay a specified amount for services "up front," and the insurance provider pays the remainder of the cost.

Countersignature – The act of signing an insurance contract by a licensed agent.

Coverage – The inclusion of perils (causes of loss) covered within a policy's scope.

Credit Life Insurance – A special type of insurance written to pay off a loan balance in the event of the debtor's death.

CSO Table – (The Commissioner's Standard Ordinary Table) A mortality table used in life insurance that mathematically predicts the probability of death.

Custodial Care – Care given to help an insured complete their activities of daily living.

Death Benefit – The amount payable upon the death of the individual whose life is insured.

Decreasing Term – A type of life insurance with a level premium and a death benefit that decreases yearly throughout the policy.

Deductible – The portion of the loss paid by the insured before the insurer can pay any claim benefits.

Defamation – An unfair trade practice in which one agent or insurance provider makes a defamatory statement regarding another with the intent of harming the reputation of the person or company.

Dependent – An individual who relies on another for support and maintenance.

Director (Commissioner, Superintendent) – The head of the state Department of Insurance.

Disability – A mental or physical impairment, either congenital or resulting from a sickness or injury.

Disability Income Insurance – Health insurance that provides periodic payments to replace an insured's income when they are ill or injured.

Disclosure – Identifying the name of the producer, representative, limited insurance representative, firm, or temporary insurance producer on any policy solicitation.

Domestic Insurer – An insurance provider that conducts business in the state of incorporation.

Domicile of Insurer – An insurer's location of incorporation and the legal ability to write business in a state.

Dread (Specified) Disease Policy – A policy with a high maximum limit that covers certain diseases named in the contract (such as meningitis and polio).

Dual Choice – A federal requirement that employers with 25 or more employees, who are within the service area of a qualified HMO, who pay minimum wage and offer a health plan, are required to provide HMO coverage and an indemnity plan.

Earned Premium – The portion of the premium for which the insurer delivers policy protection.

Effective Date – The date an insurance policy begins (also called the inception date).

Eligibility Period – The period in which an employee can enroll in a group health care plan without evidence of insurability.

Elimination Period – A waiting period imposed on the insured from the onset of a disability until benefit payments begin.

Emergency – An injury or disease that occurs suddenly and requires treatment within 24 hours.

Employee Retirement Income Security Act (ERISA) – A law that stipulates federal standards for private pension plans.

Endodontics – An area of dentistry that deals with the prevention, diagnosis, and treatment of the dental pulp within natural teeth at the root canal.

Endorsement – A form that changes the provisions of a life insurance policy (also called a rider).

Endow – To reach the maturity date or time at which the face amount equals the cash value.

Enrollment Period – The time employees have to enroll in a contributory group health plan.

Errors and Omissions Policy (E&O) – A professional liability insurance policy that protects the insurance provider from claims by the insured for mistakes or oversights on the insurer's part.

Estoppel – A legal obstruction to denying a fact or restoring a right that has been previously waived.

Excess Charge – The difference between the amount approved by Medicare for a service or supply and the actual charge.

Excess Insurance – Insurance that pays over and above or in addition to the basic policy limits.

Exclusions – Causes of exposures, loss, conditions, etc., for which insurers will not pay insurance benefits.

Executory Contract – A contract that has not yet been fulfilled by one or both parties that promise action in the event of a specified future event.

Expiration – The date listed in the policy as the date of termination.

Explanation of Benefits (EOB) – A statement outlining the services rendered, insurance company payments, and the insured's billing amounts.

Explanation of Medicare Benefits – A statement to a Medicare patient specifying how the insurer will settle the Medicare claim.

Exposure – A unit of measure used to calculate rates charged for insurance coverage.

Express Authority – The authority granted to an agent due to the agent's written contract.

Extended Care Facility – A facility licensed by the state to provide 24-hour nursing care.

Extension of Benefits – A provision allowing coverage to continue beyond the policy's expiration date for employees who are not at work because of a disability or who have dependents hospitalized on that date. This coverage continues until the employee returns to work or the dependent leaves the hospital.

Face – The policy's first page.

Fair Credit Reporting Act – A federal law that established procedures for consumer-reporting agencies to follow to ensure that records are accurate, confidential, relevant, and properly used.

Fiduciary – An agent or broker handling an insurer's funds in a trust capacity.

Fixed Annuity – An annuity that offers fixed payments and guarantees a minimum interest rate to be credited to the annuity purchase.

Flexible Premium – A policy feature that allows the policy owner to vary the amount and frequency of premium payments.

Flexible Spending Account (FSA) – A salary reduction cafeteria plan that uses employee funds to offer various types of health care benefits.

Foreign Insurer – An insurance provider incorporated in another state.

Fraternal Benefit Societies – Life or health insurance companies formed to provide insurance for members of an affiliated religious organization, lodge, or fraternal organization with a representative form of government.

Fraud – Intentional deceit or misrepresentation to induce an individual to part with something of value.

Free Look – A period during which a policy owner can inspect a newly issued individual life or health insurance policy for a specific number of days and surrender it in exchange for a full refund of the premium.

Front-End Load – A fee or commission charged at the time of purchase of a security or an annuity.

Gatekeeper Model – A model of HMO and PPO organizations that uses the insured's primary care physician, also known as a gatekeeper, as the initial contact for the patient for medical care and referrals.

Grace Period – Time after the premium due date during which policy owners can still pay premiums, and the policy and its riders remain in force.

Group Disability Insurance – A type of insurance covering a group of people against loss of pay due to sickness or an accident.

Group Health Insurance – Health coverage offered to members of a group.

Group Life – Life insurance provided to members of a group.

Hazard – A circumstance that increases the probability of a loss.

Hazard, Moral – The effect of a person's character, reputation, living habits, etc., on their insurability.

Hazard, Morale – The impact a person's indifference regarding loss has on the risk to be insured.

Hazard, Physical – A type of hazard that arises from a person's physical characteristics, such as a physical disability because of either current circumstance or a condition present at birth.

Health Insurance – Protection against loss because of sickness or bodily injury.

Health Maintenance Organization (HMO) – A prepaid medical service plan in which specified providers contract with the HMO to deliver services. Preventive medicine is the focus of the HMO.

Health Reimbursement Accounts (HRAs) – Health plans that allow employers to set aside funds to reimburse employees for qualified medical expenses.

Health Savings Accounts (HSAs) – Health plans intended to help individuals save for qualified health expenses.

Home Health Agency – An agency certified by the insured's health plan that delivers health care services under the contract.

Home Health Care – A type of care in which home health aide or part-time nursing services, speech therapy, occupational or physical therapy services are given in the insured's home.

Home Health Services – A covered expense under Medicare Part A in which a licensed home health agency provides home health care to an insured.

Hospice – A facility for the terminally ill that offers supportive care such as symptom relief and pain management to the patient and their family. Medicare Part A covers hospice care.

Hospital Confinement Rider – An optional disability income rider that waives the elimination period when an insured is admitted to a hospital as an inpatient.

Implied Authority – Authority not expressed or written into the contract. The agent is assumed to transact insurance business on behalf of the principal.

Income Replacement Contracts – Policies that replace a certain percentage of the insured's pure loss of income because of a covered accident or sickness.

Indemnify – To restore the insured to the same condition as before the occurrence of loss with no intent of loss or gain.

Illustration – A proposal or ledger used to sell a life insurance policy that presents guaranteed and non-guaranteed elements.

Insolvent organization – A member organization that cannot pay its financial obligations and is placed under a final order of liquidation or rehabilitation by a court.

Insurability – The acceptability of an applicant who satisfies an insurance company's underwriting requirements.

Insurable Interest – A financial interest in the life of another individual. It involves the possibility of losing something of value if the insured dies. Insurable interest must be specified at the time of policy issue.

Insurance – A contract under which one party (insurer) indemnifies or guarantees another party (insured) against a loss by a specified future peril or contingency in return for a premium payment.

Insured – The individual or organization covered by insurance; the party to be indemnified.

Insurer – An entity that indemnifies against losses, pays benefits, or provides services, also known as an "insurance company" or "insurance provider."

Insuring Clause – A general statement that identifies the basic agreement between the insurer and the insured, generally located on the first page of the policy.

Integrated LTC Rider – A rider attached to a life insurance policy to pay long-term care benefits. The benefits available for LTC depend upon the life insurance benefits available; however, the benefits paid toward LTC will decrease the life insurance policy's benefits.

Intentional Injury – An act that intends to cause an injury. Self-inflicted injuries are not covered, but intentional injuries inflicted on the insured by another person are protected.

Intermediaries – Organizations that process inpatient and outpatient claims on individuals by hospitals, home health agencies, skilled nursing facilities, hospices, and certain other providers of health services.

Intermediate Care – A level of care that is one step down from skilled nursing care; given under the supervision of physicians or registered nurses.

Investigative Consumer Report – Similar to consumer reports in that they also deliver information on the consumer's reputation, character, and habits.

Issue Age – The person's age when a policy is issued.

Joint Life – A single policy that insures two or more lives.

Juvenile Life – A life insurance policy written on the life of a minor child.

Lapse – Terminating a policy because the premium was not paid by the end of the policy grace period.

Law of Large Numbers – A principle that states the larger the number of similar exposure units, the more closely the reported losses will equal the probability of loss.

Legal Reserve – The accounting measurement of an insurance provider's future obligations to pay claims to policy owners.

Level Premium – A policy premium that remains the same during the period premiums are paid.

Life Expectancy – Average number of years remaining for an individual of a given age to live, as displayed on the mortality table.

Limited-Pay Whole Life – A type of whole life insurance that charges a level annual premium and offers a level, guaranteed death benefit to the insured's age of 100. It will endow for the face amount if the insured reaches age 100. Limited-pay life is designed so the policy owner will entirely pay up the premiums for coverage well before age 100.

Limited Policies – Health insurance policies that only cover specific diseases or accidents.

Limiting Charge – The maximum amount a physician can charge a Medicare beneficiary for a covered service if the physician does not accept assignment of the Medicare-approved amount.

Liquidation – Selling assets as a means of raising capital.

Living Benefits Rider – A rider added to a life insurance policy that provides LTC benefits or benefits for the terminally ill.

Lloyd's Associations – Organizations that offer support facilities for underwriters or groups of individuals that accept insurance risk.

Loan Value – The amount of money a policy owner can borrow using the cash value of their life insurance policy as collateral.

Long-Term Care (LTC) – Health and social services provided under the supervision of physicians and medical health professionals for individuals with disabilities or chronic diseases. Care is typically provided in a Long-Term Care Facility, a state-licensed facility that offers such services.

Long-Term Disability Insurance – A type of individual or group insurance that covers illness until the insured reaches age 65 and for life in the event of an accident.

Loss – The decrease, reduction, or disappearance of value to a person or property insured under a policy by a peril insured against.

Loss of Income Insurance – Insurance that pays benefits for the inability to work due to a disability resulting from accidental bodily injury or sickness.

Lump-Sum – A settlement method that pays the beneficiary the proceeds of a life insurance policy in one lump-sum payment rather than in installments.

Major Medical Insurance – A type of health insurance that typically carries a large deductible and pays covered expenses up to a high limit whether the insured is in or out of the hospital.

Maturity Date – When the life insurance policy's face amount becomes payable.

Medicaid – A medical benefits program for individuals whose income and resources are insufficient to cover the cost of necessary medical care jointly administered by the individual states and the federal government.

Medical Expense Insurance – Insurance that provides benefits for medical, hospital, and surgical costs.

Medical Information Bureau (MIB) – An information database that contains the health histories of individuals who have applied for insurance in the past. Most insurers subscribe to this database for underwriting purposes.

Medical Savings Account – An employer-funded account connected to a high deductible medical insurance plan.

Medicare – A United States federal government plan that pays for qualified individuals' specific hospital and medical expenses.

Medicare Supplement Insurance – A type of individual or group insurance that fills the gaps in the level of protection provided by Medicare.

Medigap – Medicare supplement plans issued by private insurers designed to fill in some of the Medicare coverage gaps.

Misrepresentation – A lie or false statement that can render the contract void.

Mode of Payment – The method of premium payment, whether monthly, quarterly, semiannually or annually.

Morbidity Rate – The ratio of incidences of sickness to the number of healthy individuals in a given group over a given period.

Morbidity Table – A table listing the incidence of sickness at specified ages.

Mortality Table – A table listing the probability of death at specified ages.

Multiple-Employer Trust (MET) – A group of small employers who are not eligible for group insurance individually. It is formed to establish a self-funded plan or group health plan.

Multiple Employer Welfare Association (MEWA) – Any organization of at least two employers, other than an admitted insurer, that establishes an employee benefit plan for the purpose of providing accident and sickness or death benefits to employees.

Mutual Companies – Insurance companies that have no capital stock but are owned by the policy owners.

Natural Premium – The amount of premium needed from each group member composed of the same risk, age, and sex that will pay $1,000 for every death that will occur in the group each year.

Non-admitted (Nonauthorized) – An insurer that has not applied for or has been denied a Certificate of Authority and cannot transact insurance business in a particular state.

Nonauthorized (Non-admitted) – An insurer that has not applied for or has applied and been denied a Certificate of Authority and may not transact insurance business in a particular state.

Noncancelable – An insurance policy that the insured has a right to remain effective by paying premiums that stay the same for a substantial period.

Nonforfeiture Values – Those guaranteed values in a life insurance policy that cannot be taken from the policy owner, even if they cease to pay the premiums.

Nonmedical – A life or health insurance policy underwritten based on the insured's statement of health rather than a medical exam.

Non-participating Policies (Non-par) – Insurance policies that do not pay dividends.

Nonqualified Plan – A benefit plan that can discriminate, is not required to be filed with the IRS, and does not offer a tax deduction for contributions.

Nonrenewal – Terminating a policy by an insurance provider on the anniversary or renewal date.

Nonresident Agent – An agent licensed in a state where they are not a resident.

Notice of Claim – A provision specifying an insured's responsibility to provide the insurer with reasonable notice in the event of a loss.

Omnibus Budget Reconciliation Act – A federal law that authorized the NAIC to create a standardized model for Medicare Supplement policies.

Option – A choice of how policy dividends, nonforfeiture values, death benefits, or cash values are received.

Oral Surgery – Operative treatment of the mouth, including extractions of teeth and related surgical treatment.

Orthodontics – A unique field in dentistry that involves the treatment of natural teeth to prevent or correct dental anomalies with appliances or braces.

Out-of-Pocket Costs – Amounts an insured has to pay for deductibles and coinsurance before the insurance provider will pay its portion.

Over-Insurance – An excessive amount of insurance resulting in the insured being overpaid if a loss occurs.

Paid-Up Insurance – Policies where all premiums have been paid but have not yet matured due to death or endowment.

Parol – A legal term that differentiates oral statements from written statements.

Parol Evidence Rule – A rule stipulating a contract cannot be altered without the parties' written consent. In other words, an oral agreement cannot change the contract.

Partial Disability – The ability to perform some but not all duties of the insured's occupation because of sickness or injury.

Participating Policies (Par) – Insurance that pays dividends to policy owners.

Payment of Claims – A provision that states to whom claims payments are to be made.

Payor Benefit – A rider in juvenile policies waives the premiums if the individual paying them (usually the parent) is disabled or dies while the child is a minor.

Peril – The cause of a potential loss.

Periodontics – A specialty of dentistry that involves treatment of the supporting and surrounding tissue of the teeth, such as treatment for gum disease.

Permanent Disability – Disability from which the insured never recovers.

Permanent Life Insurance – A general term used to refer to various forms of whole life insurance policies that remain effective to age 100 so long as the premium is paid.

Persistency – The tendency or likelihood of an insurance policy not lapsing or being replaced with insurance from another insurance provider.

Personal Contract – An agreement between an insurance provider and an individual stating the insurance policy will cover the individual's insurable interest.

Physical Exam and Autopsy – A provision allowing an insurer to have an insured physically examined when a claim is pending at its own expense. Insurers can also have an autopsy performed where not prohibited by law.

Policy Loan – A nonforfeiture value in which an insurance provider loans a part or all of the policy's cash value assigned as security for the loan to the policy owner.

Policyholder – The individual who has possession of the policy, generally the insured.

Policy owner – The individual who is entitled to exercise the owner's rights and privileges in the policy. This person does not have to be the insured.

Pre-Existing Condition – A physical condition that existed before the policy's effective date, which is typically excluded from coverage.

Preferred Provider Organization (PPO) – An organization of medical professionals and hospitals who offer services to an insurer's clients for a set fee.

Preferred Risk – An insurance classification for applicants who have a lower probability of incurring a loss, and who are covered at a reduced rate.

Premium – A periodic insurance payment to keep the policy in force.

Presumptive Disability – A provision found in most disability income policies specifying the conditions that will automatically qualify the insured for full disability benefits.

Primary Beneficiary – The individual who is named as the first to receive benefits from a policy.

Primary Policy – A basic, fundamental insurance policy that pays first with respect to other outstanding policies.

Principal Amount – The entire face value of a policy.

Private Insurance – Insurance provided by nongovernmental insuring organizations.

Pro Rata Cancellation – Termination of an insurance policy, with an adjustment of the premium in proportion to the exact coverage that has been in force.

Probationary Period – The time between the effective date of a health insurance policy and the date coverage begins.

Proceeds – The amount payable by the insurer, typically at the insured's death or when the policy matures.

Producer – An insurance broker or agent.

Proof of Loss – A claim form that a claimant must submit after a loss occurs.

Prosthodontics – A unique area of dentistry that involves the replacement of missing teeth with artificial devices like dentures or bridgework.

Provider – Any individual or group who provides health care services.

Pure Protection – Insurance in which premiums are paid for protection in the event of disability or death, rather than for cash value accumulation.

Qualified Plan – A retirement plan that satisfies the IRS guidelines for receiving favorable tax treatment.

Rate Service Organization – An organization formed by, or on behalf of, a group of insurance providers to develop and file rates with the Department of Insurance. They can also act as a collection point for actuarial data.

Rebating – Any inducement offered in the sale of insurance products not stated in the policy.

Reciprocal Exchange – An unincorporated group of people who mutually insure one another, each separately assuming a share of each risk.

Reciprocity – A situation in which two parties provide each other the same advantages or help. For example, Producer A living in New Jersey can transact business as a nonresident in Virginia if Virginia's resident producers can transact business in New Jersey.

Recurrent Disability – A policy provision that specifies the period during which the recurrence of an illness or injury will be a continuation of a prior period of disability.

Reduction – Decreasing the possibility or severity of a loss.

Reinsurance – A form of insurance in which one insurer (the reinsurer), in consideration of a premium paid to it, indemnifies another insurer (the ceding insurer) for part or all of its liabilities from policies it has issued.

Renewability Clause – A clause that defines the insurance provider's and the insured's right to cancel or renew coverage.

Renewable Term – Insurance that can, at the election of the insured, be renewed at the end of a term without providing evidence of insurability.

Representations – An applicant's statements on the insurance application that are believed to be accurate but are not guaranteed to be true.

Rescission – Terminating an insurance contract due to material misrepresentation by the insured or misrepresentation, fraud, or duress on the agent's or insurer's part.

Reserve – An amount representing actual or potential liabilities kept by an insurance provider in a separate account to cover debts to policy owners.

Residual Disability – A disability income policy that pays benefits for the loss of income when a person returns to work following a total disability but is still unable to perform at the same level as before the disability.

Respite Care – Temporary health or medical care provided by a nursing facility where a patient stays or by paid workers who go to the caregiver's home to provide a short rest.

Restorative Care – An area of dentistry that involves treatments that restore functional use to natural teeth, such as crowns or fillings.

Retention – A method of dealing with risk by intentionally or unintentionally retaining a portion of it for the insured's account. It is the amount of responsibility assumed but not reinsured by the insurance provider.

Rider – A supplemental agreement attached to and made a part of the policy indicating the policy's expansion by additional coverage or a waiver of a condition or coverage.

Right to Return (Free Look) – The period during which a policy owner can inspect a newly issued individual life or health insurance policy for a specified number of days and surrender it for a full refund of premium if they are not satisfied for any reason.

Risk – Uncertainty regarding the outcome of an event when two or more possibilities exist.

Risk, Pure – The uncertainty or chance of a loss taking place in a circumstance that can only result in a loss or no change.

Risk Retention Group – A liability insurance provider owned by its members, which are exposed to similar liability risks by being in the same industry or business.

Risk, Speculative – The uncertainty or opportunity of a loss occurring in a situation involving the chance for either a loss or gain.

Risk, Standard – An insured or applicant who is considered to have an average probability of loss based on their health, vocation, and lifestyle.

Risk, Substandard – An insured or applicant with a higher than average probability of loss and who could be subject to an increased premium.

Rollover – Withdrawing the money from a qualified plan and depositing it into another qualified plan.

Secondary Beneficiary – The individual named to receive benefits upon the insured's death if the (primary) first-named beneficiary is no longer living or does not collect all the benefits because of their death.

Service Plans – Insurance plans where the health care services are the benefits rather than the monetary ones.

Settlement Options – Choices are available to the insured/policy owner to distribute insurance proceeds.

Sharing – A method of dealing with risk for a group of individuals or businesses with the same or similar exposure to loss who share the losses that take place within that group.

Short-Rate Cancellation – Canceling a policy with a less than proportionate return of premium.

Short-Term Disability Insurance – A group or individual policy that covers disabilities of 13 to 26 weeks, and in some cases, for up to two years.

Sickness – A physical disease, illness, or pregnancy, but not a mental illness.

Single Premium Whole Life (SPWL) – A life insurance policy intended to provide a level death benefit to the insured's age 100 for a one-time, lump-sum payment.

Skilled Nursing Care – Daily skilled care or nursing care, such as medication administration, diagnosis, or minor surgery performed by or under the supervision of a skilled professional.

Spendthrift Clause – A clause that prevents the debtors of a beneficiary from collecting the benefits before the beneficiary receives them.

Standard Provisions – Requirements approved by state law that have to appear in every insurance policy.

Standard Risk – An insured or applicant with an average probability of loss based on their health, vocation, and lifestyle.

Stock Companies – Companies owned by stockholders whose investments provide the necessary capital to establish and operate the insurer.

Straight Life – A basic policy that charges a level annual premium for the insured's lifetime and provides a guaranteed, level death benefit.

Subrogation – The legal process by which an insurer seeks recovery of the amount paid to the insured from a third party who may have caused the loss.

Substandard Risk – An insured or applicant who has a higher than normal probability of loss and who may be charged an increased premium.

Superintendent (Director, Commissioner) – The head of a state's insurance department.

Supplemental Illustration – An illustration given in addition to a basic illustration that can be presented in a different format than the basic illustration but can only show a scale of non-guaranteed elements allowed in a basic illustration.

Surrender – An act of giving up a life policy, in which the insurance provider will pay the insured the policy's accumulated cash value.

Term Insurance – Insurance that offers protection for a specified period.

Terminally Ill – A patient who is expected to die within a specified amount of time that is listed in the policy.

Tertiary Beneficiary – The third in line to receive the death benefits of a life insurance policy.

Total Disability – A condition that does not allow a person to perform the duties of any occupation due to sickness or injury.

Transfer – A fundamental principle of insurance under which the risk of financial loss is assigned to another party.

Twisting – A misrepresentation in which an agent persuades an insured/policy owner to lapse, cancel, or switch policies, even when it's to the insured's disadvantage.

Underwriter – An individual who evaluates and classifies risks to accept or reject on behalf of the insurance company.

Underwriting – The process of reviewing, accepting, or rejecting insurance applications.

Unearned Premium – The portion of a premium for which policy protection has not yet been provided.

Unilateral Contract – A contract that legally binds only one party to contractual obligations after the premium is paid.

Universal Life – A combination of adjustable life insurance and a flexible premium.

Utmost Good Faith – The fair and equal bargaining by both parties in forming the contract, where the applicant must disclose risk to the insurer, and the insurer must be fair in underwriting the risk.

Valued Contract – A disability insurance/life insurance contract that pays a specified amount in the event of a loss.

Viatical Settlement – An arrangement that allows a person living with a life-threatening condition to sell their existing life insurance and use the proceeds when they are needed most, before death.

Waiting Period – The time between the start of a disability and the start of disability insurance benefits.

Waiver – The voluntary abandonment of a known advantage or legal right.

Waiver of Cost – A disability rider found in Universal Life Insurance that waives the insurance cost. It does not waive the cost of premiums needed to accumulate cash values.

Waiver of Premium – A continuation of life insurance coverage if the policy owner becomes disabled and cannot pay the premiums.

Warranty – A material stipulation in the policy that, if breached, can void coverage.

Whole Life Insurance – Insurance that is kept in force for the entire life of a person and pays a benefit upon their death, whenever that may be.

Workers Compensation – Benefits required by state law to be paid to an employee by an employer in the event of a disability, injury, or death resulting from an on-the-job hazard.

PRACTICE EXAM:
1

Test your readiness

You are about to take a California Life, Accident and Health or Sickness Practice Exam. This exam consists of *150 Questions (plus five to ten non-scored experimental questions)* and is *3 hours and 15 minutes* long. If you do not have enough time to complete this exam right now, it is better to wait until you can fully devote your attention to completing it in the allotted time.

Any skipped questions will be graded as incorrect. The following chart breaks down the number of questions in each chapter and by topic.

CHAPTER	# OF QUESTIONS
General Insurance	**40**
Basic Insurance Concepts and Principles	16
Contract Law	10
The Insurance Marketplace	14
Life Insurance	**49**
Life Insurance – Basics	8
Types of Life Policies	10
Annuities	8
Life Insurance and Annuities – Policy Replacement/Cancellation	4
The Individual Life Insurance Contract	10
Taxation of Life Insurance and Annuities	3
Group Life Insurance Plans	2
Social Security Disability Program	1
Individual Underwriting, Pricing, and Claims	3
Life Policy Riders	**4**
General Concepts of Medical and Disability Insurance	**4**
Medical Expense Insurance	**45**
Individual Insurance	14
Group Medical Expense Insurance	8
Patient Protection and Affordable Care Act (PPACA)	8
Senior Health Products	15
Disability Income Insurance	**4**
Long-Term Care Insurance	**4**

To calculate your score, subtract the number of incorrectly answered questions from 150. Take this number and divide it by 150. For example, if you incorrectly answered 60 questions, your score would be 60%, the minimum score needed to pass the exam.

#1. A Health Maintenance Organization is regarded as an organized health care system that provides a comprehensive array of medical services on a

a) Per person basis.
b) Limited basis.
c) Prepaid basis.
d) Closed-panel basis.

#2. As insurable interest applies to life insurance, which of the following statements is NOT true?

a) A person has an insurable interest in their own life
b) A debtor has an insurable interest in a lender's life
c) Business partners have an insurable interest in one another
d) A wife or husband has an insurable interest in their spouse's life

#3. An insured's LTC policy is scheduled to pay a fixed coverage amount of $120 per day. The long-term care facility only charged $100 per day. How much will the insurer pay?

a) 20% of the total cost
b) $120 per day
c) $100 per day
d) 80% of the total cost

#4. The most common way to transfer risk is to

a) Purchase insurance.
b) Name a beneficiary.
c) Increase control of claims.
d) Lessen the possibility of loss.

#5. In a credit health policy, who is the beneficiary?

a) The Federal Government
b) The lending institution
c) The insurer
d) The estate of the borrower

#6. Which of these is the most common time for errors and omissions to take place on the part of an insurance provider?

a) Application process
b) Policy delivery
c) Policy renewal
d) Underwriting

#7. The proposed insured makes the premium payment on a new insurance policy. If the insured dies, the insurer will pay the death benefit to the insured's beneficiary if the policy is approved. What kind of contract does this represent?

a) Unilateral
b) Personal
c) Adhesion
d) Conditional

#8. To attain currently insured status under Social Security, a worker must have earned at least how many credits during the last 13 quarters?

a) 4 credits
b) 6 credits
c) 10 credits
d) 40 credits

#9. In a life contract, which of the following is an example of liquidity?

a) The cash value available to the policyholder
b) The death benefit paid to the beneficiary
c) The flexible premium
d) The money in a savings account

#10. In all Medicare supplement plans, which of the following must be present?

a) Outpatient drugs
b) Plan C coinsurance
c) Plan A
d) Foreign travel provisions

#11. Regarding a Key Person Life Insurance policy, who is the owner, and who is the beneficiary?

a) The employer is the owner and the beneficiary
b) The employer is the owner, and the key employee is the beneficiary
c) The key employee is the owner and the beneficiary
d) The key employee is the owner, and the employer is the beneficiary

#12. All of the following needs to be stated in an insurance policy EXCEPT

a) The financial rating of the insurance provider.
b) The parties between whom the contract is made.
c) The risks insured against.
d) The period during which the insurance is effective.

#13. Which of the following would NOT fall into the category of expenses associated with death?

a) Funeral expenses
b) The insured's final medical expenses
c) Day-to-day expenses of maintaining the family
d) The cost of a vacation for surviving family members

#14. Who is responsible for fairly evaluating insurable risks and selecting and distributing to the insurance company those that are profitable to the insurance provider?

a) Underwriter
b) Insured
c) Insurance Commissioner
d) Governor

#15. What risk management technique are they practicing when an individual obtains insurance?

a) Retention
b) Transfer
c) Avoidance
d) Sharing

#16. All of the following are examples of risk retention EXCEPT

a) Premiums.
b) Deductibles.
c) Copayments.
d) Self-insurance.

#17. In level term insurance, "level" refers to the

a) Premium.
b) Cash value.
c) Interest rate.
d) Face amount.

#18. Under a long-term care policy, when can an insured deduct unreimbursed medical expenses?

a) Only if the insured does not itemize the expenses
b) When the expenses exceed a specified percentage of the insured's adjusted gross income (AGI)
c) Only if the insured is age 65 or older
d) All LTC expenses are tax-deductible

#19. Which of the following sets the annual contribution limit of a Dependent Care Flexible Spending Account?

a) The insurer
b) The insured
c) The IRS
d) The employer

#20. Which of these is NOT a characteristic of pure risk?

a) The loss has to be catastrophic
b) The loss has to be due to chance
c) The loss has to be measurable in dollars
d) The loss exposure has to be large

#21. The insured is also the policyholder of a whole life policy. To receive the policy's face amount, what age must the insured reach?

a) 65
b) 70 ½
c) 90
d) 100

#22. An insured has a life policy that requires her only to pay premiums for a certain number of years until the policy is paid up. What type of policy is it?

a) Adjustable Life
b) Graded Premium Life
c) Limited-pay Life
d) Variable Life

#23. The Health Insurance Counseling and Advocacy Program (HICAP) is administered by

a) Medi-Cal.
b) The top ten insurers selling disability policies for seniors.
c) The California Department of Aging.
d) The California Department of Insurance.

#24. What is the purpose of the buyer's guide?

a) To list every policy rider
b) To provide information about the issued policy
c) To let consumers compare the costs of different policies
d) To provide the name and address of the producer issuing the policy

#25. If a prospective insured submits an incomplete application, which is the appropriate action by the insurance provider?

a) Fill in the blanks to the best of the insurance company's knowledge
b) Return the application to the applicant to be completed
c) Issue a policy anyway because the application has been submitted
d) Ask the agent who sold the policy to complete and resign the application

#26. A 40-year-old woman obtains a whole life policy and names her husband as her only beneficiary. Her husband will die ten years later. She never remarries and dies at age 61, leaving two grown-up children. Assuming she never changed the beneficiary, the policy proceeds will go to

a) Both children who share equally on a per-capita basis.
b) The insurance provider.
c) The insured's estate.
d) The insured's firstborn child.

#27. A domestic insurer issuing variable contracts needs to establish one or more

a) Separate accounts.
b) Liability accounts.
c) Annuity accounts.
d) General accounts.

#28. After suffering a back injury, an insured is disabled for a year. Which of the following benefits will he receive if his insurance policy carries a Disability Income Benefit rider?

a) Monthly premium waiver and monthly income
b) Percentage of medical costs paid by the insurance provider
c) Payments for life
d) Yearly premium waiver and income

#29. All of these statements are true regarding health insurance premiums, EXCEPT

a) Substandard risks are always rejected and are not insurable.
b) Standard insurers can issue rated policies.
c) Preferred risks can receive a discounted rate for being a non-drinker or a non-smoker.
d) Standard risks pay the regular premium for their classification.

#30. All of the following losses are covered by a typical Accidental Death & Dismemberment policy EXCEPT

a) Limb.
b) Life.
c) Income.
d) Eyesight.

#31. An insured can reactivate her lapsed life insurance policy if action is taken within a certain period and proof of insurability is provided. Which policy provision allows this?

a) Reinstatement provision
b) Waiver of premium provision
c) Incontestable clause
d) Grace period

#32. Which of the following is NOT usually excluded from life policies?

a) Death because of military service or war
b) Death because of a plane crash for a fare-paying passenger
c) Self-inflicted death
d) Death that occurs while an individual is committing a felony

#33. The automatic premium loan provision is activated at the end of the

a) Policy period.
b) Grace period.
c) Free-look period.
d) Elimination period.

#34. The CEO of a corporation is starting an annuity and decides that her company will be the annuitant. Which of the following statements is true?

a) The contract can be issued without an annuitant
b) The annuitant has to be a natural person
c) A corporation can be an annuitant, provided it is also the owner
d) A corporation can be an annuitant if the beneficiary is a natural person

#35. A man works for Company A, and his wife works for Company B. Health plans insure both spouses through their respective employers that also cover the other spouse. If the husband files a claim,

a) Both plans will cover the full amount of the claim.
b) The coverage through the husband's company is primary.
c) The coverage through the wife's company is primary.
d) The insurance plans will split the coverage evenly.

#36. Under Plan A in Medigap insurance, which of the following is NOT covered?

a) The 20% Part B coinsurance amounts for services approved by Medicare
b) The first three pints of blood every year
c) The Medicare Part A deductible
d) Approved hospital costs for 365 additional days after Medicare benefits end

#37. When the insured purchased his life insurance policy, he added a rider that would allow him to obtain additional insurance in the future without having to prove insurability. This rider is called

a) Cost of living.
b) Guaranteed insurability.
c) Waiver of monthly deductions.
d) Supplemental add-on.

#38. Which of the following describes the annuity period?

a) The period during which funds are accumulated in an annuity
b) The period from the effective date of the contract to its termination date
c) The period during which accumulated funds are converted into income payments
d) The period from the accumulation period to the annuitization period

#39. Equity-indexed annuities

a) Are security instruments.
b) Invest conservatively.
c) Seek higher returns.
d) Are riskier than variable annuities.

#40. Insurers must include which renewal provision(s) in long-term care policies it issues to individuals?

a) Renewable at the option of the insurance provider
b) Noncancelable and guaranteed renewable
c) Renewable and convertible
d) Cancelable and conditionally renewable

#41. The right of the applicant to rescind the policy for a full refund of all premiums

a) Has to be clearly stated in the policy's text.
b) Is implied during the application process.
c) Has to be exercised within three days of the policy issue.
d) Is not a valid right.

#42. The premium for a variable annuity can be invested in all of the following during the free-look period EXCEPT

a) Fixed-income investments.
b) Money-market funds.
c) Mutual funds (only upon the investor's request).
d) Value funds.

#43. The main factor of representation that lets the injured party rescind a contract is

a) When the representation is false in a material point.
b) That any misrepresentation will be considered fraud.
c) Representations are statements believed to be true. They hold no legal consequences.
d) The pledge or assurance of the representation.

#44. An insurance applicant is requesting more information from her agent about a claim that is currently being settled. Within what period must the agent respond?

a) 15 days
b) 21 days
c) 31 days
d) 90 days

#45. Which part(s) is/are taxable as income when a beneficiary receives payments that include both principal and interest?

a) Principal only
b) Interest-only
c) Both principal and interest
d) Neither principal nor interest

#46. What is the penalty for IRA distributions below the required minimum for the year?

a) 10%
b) 25%
c) 50%
d) 60%

#47. An applicant purchases a nonqualified annuity but dies before the starting date. Which of these beneficiaries would receive the annuity's accumulated interest and NOT be taxed?

a) Spouse
b) Charitable organization
c) Dependents
d) Annuitant

#48. An insured had $500 left in her Health Reimbursement Account (HRA) when she quit her job. What happens to that money?

a) The insured can access the $500 at the discretion of her previous employer
b) The previous employer will issue a check for $500 payable to the insured
c) It can be rolled over into a Health Reimbursement Account with her new employer
d) The insured can use up the $500 if she has qualified medical expenses

#49. Concerning installments for a fixed period annuity settlement option, all of the following statements are true EXCEPT

a) The insurance provider determines each payment amount.
b) It is a life contingency option.
c) It pays the benefit only for a designated period.
d) The payments will not be guaranteed for life.

#50. COBRA applies to employers with at least how many employees?

a) 50
b) 20
c) 80
d) 60

#51. Which of the following characteristics does NOT describe managed care?

a) High-quality care
b) Shared risk
c) Preventative care
d) Unlimited access to providers

#52. When immediate annuities are bought with the cash value at surrender or with the face amount at death, this would be a

a) Nonforfeiture option.
b) Rollover.
c) Settlement option.
d) Nontaxable exchange.

#53. Under Social Security, all of the following benefits are available EXCEPT

a) Death benefits.
b) Welfare benefits.
c) Old-age and retirement benefits.
d) Disability benefits.

#54. Regarding a term health policy, which of the following is true?

a) It is guaranteed renewable
b) It is noncancelable
c) It is nonrenewable
d) It is conditionally renewable

#55. What is the size of companies eligible for Health Reimbursement Accounts (HRAs)?

a) Sole proprietors only
b) Companies with at least 100 employees only
c) Companies of all sizes
d) Small employers only

#56. When trying to acquire creditable information about an applicant for health insurance, an agent is acting in what capacity?

a) Field underwriter
b) Office underwriter
c) General agent
d) Consumer report investigator

#57. In insurance, an offer is typically made when

a) The producer hands the policy to the policy owner.
b) A producer explains a policy to a potential applicant.
c) An applicant submits an insurance application to the insurer.
d) The insurance provider approves the application and receives the initial premium.

#58. Who is a third-party owner?

a) An irrevocable beneficiary
b) A policyholder who is not the insured
c) An insurance provider who issues a policy for two people
d) An employee in a group policy

#59. In basic medical insurance, which of the following best describes the principle of first-dollar coverage?

a) The insured is not required to pay a deductible
b) The insured must first pay a deductible
c) The insurer covers the first claim on the policy
d) Deductibles and coinsurance are taxed first

#60. One of the advantages of a family life insurance policy that covers children is that it

a) Can be converted to permanent insurance for the children without requiring evidence of insurability.
b) Covers children for free.
c) Allows the spouse extra coverage for each child covered.
d) Allows children's income to be included in the coverage.

#61. All of the following long-term care coverages would allow an insured to receive care at home EXCEPT

a) Respite care.
b) Home health care.
c) Skilled care.
d) Custodial care in the insured's house.

#62. The purpose of managed care health insurance plans is to

a) Control health insurance claims expenses.
b) Allow for the continuation of coverage when an employee leaves the plan.
c) Give the insured an unlimited choice of care providers.
d) Coordinate benefits.

#63. When an insured incurs medical expenses during the final 90 days of a calendar year, the Carry-Over Provision allows them to

a) Transfer their expenses to the credit of a covered family member if the claim is ongoing from January 1.
b) Waive premium payments for the new year.
c) Apply such expenses to the new year's deductible.
d) Lower their premium for the new year if the claim is finalized before December 31.

#64. A group policy used to provide accident and health insurance to a group of individuals being transported by a common carrier without individually naming the insureds is known as a

a) Blanket policy.
b) Universal policy.
c) Comprehensive policy.
d) Limited benefit policy.

#65. An insured has an HSA and plans to leave his current job for a new one. When the insured leaves his job, what will happen to his HSA?

a) It will be canceled
b) It will revert back to the employer's ownership
c) It will continue because the insured, not his employer, owns it
d) It will stay with the employer for the individual who fills the insured's position

#66. Regarding the COBRA Act of 1985, which of the following statements is NOT correct?

a) It applies only to employers with 20 or more employees that maintain group health insurance for their employees
b) COBRA stands for Consolidated Omnibus Budget Reconciliation Act
c) It mandates all employers, regardless of the number or age of employees, to offer extended group health coverage
d) It covers terminated employees and their dependents for up to 36 months following a qualifying event

#67. The legal definition of "person" would NOT include which of the following?

a) A business entity
b) A corporation
c) A family
d) An individual human being

#68. Group underwriting is beneficial compared to individual underwriting because

a) The cost of coverage is usually lower because of the reduction of risk.
b) Every member is eligible for the entire contract period.
c) There are no enrollment restrictions.
d) Previous claims are never a consideration.

#69. A situation in which an individual can only lose or have no change represents

a) Pure risk.
b) Speculative risk.
c) Adverse selection.
d) Hazard.

#70. The Health Insurance Counseling and Advocacy Program (HICAP) provides services in the following areas EXCEPT

a) Legal assistance.
b) Sales of LTC policies.
c) Consumer counseling.
d) Consumer advocacy.

#71. Underwriting for disability insurance is unique because of the type of risk involved. Which situation demonstrates this?

a) A window washer pays a higher premium and receives a poorer classification of disability
b) A stunt performer pays a low premium and receives a superior classification of disability
c) An accountant pays a higher premium and receives a poorer classification of disability
d) An administrative assistant pays a higher premium and receives a superior classification of disability

#72. Shortly after a replacement transaction on a Medicare supplement policy, the insured decided to cancel the policy but is uncertain whether the free-look provision applies. Where could the insured find that information?

a) Buyer's Guide
b) Certificate of Coverage
c) Notice Regarding Replacement
d) Policy application

#73. According to the metal levels classification of the Affordable Care Act, a health plan is expected to pay 90% of the cost for an average population, and the participants would pay the remaining 10%. What plan is that?

a) Silver
b) Gold
c) Platinum
d) Bronze

#74. An insured is covered under two group health plans – his own and his spouse's. He had incurred a loss of $2,000. After the insured paid a total of $500 in coinsurance and deductibles, the primary insurer paid $1,500 in medical expenses. What amount, if any, would be covered by the secondary insurer?

a) $0
b) $500
c) $1,000
d) $2,000

#75. Which of the following dental insurance categories would cover the filling of cavities?

a) This type of work is not covered
b) Routine and preventative maintenance
c) Routine and major restorative care
d) Orthodontic care

#76. Regarding HMO coverage, which is true?

a) It is divided into geographic territories
b) It is divided based on a family's average tax bracket
c) It is divided by state
d) HMOs offer nationwide coverage

#77. Medicare Advantage is also called

a) Medicare Part A.
b) Medicare Part B.
c) Medicare Part C.
d) Medicare Part D.

#78. An insured is hospitalized with a neck injury. Upon checking her disability income policy, she learns she will not be eligible for benefits for at least 30 days. This period indicates that her policy is written with a 30-day

a) Elimination period.
b) Blackout period.
c) Probationary period.
d) Waiver of benefits period.

#79. What is the typical deductible for basic surgical expense insurance?

a) $0
b) $100
c) $200
d) $500

#80. Which of the following is incorrect regarding a medical savings account (MSA)?

a) It is an employer-funded account linked to a high-deductible medical insurance plan
b) If there is a balance at the end of the year, the employee can withdraw it as taxable income or let it earn interest
c) MSAs are only available to groups with at least 100 employees
d) The employee can use the money from the MSA to pay health insurance deductibles during the year

#81. An insured pays a monthly premium of $100 for her health insurance. What would be the duration of the policy's grace period?

a) 7 days
b) 10 days
c) 31 days
d) 60 days

#82. What limits the amount a policy owner can borrow from a whole life insurance policy?

a) The amount stated in the policy
b) Face amount
c) Cash value
d) Premiums paid

#83. Which of the following groups would most likely be insured under a blanket accident policy?

a) Office workers for a real estate business
b) Factory workers at the electronics assembly plant
c) Independent contractors who perform work for a general contractor
d) Students at a public school

#84. Regarding Accidental Death and Dismemberment coverage, all of the following statements are correct EXCEPT

a) Death benefits are only paid if death occurs within 24 hours of an accident.
b) Accidental death benefits are only paid if death is caused by accidental bodily injury as defined in the policy.
c) Dismemberment benefits are paid for specific disabilities presumed to be total and permanent.
d) Accidental death and dismemberment insurance is considered limited coverage.

#85. How many pints of blood will be covered by Medicare Supplement core benefits?

a) First three
b) None; Medicare pays for it all
c) Everything after the first three
d) One pint

#86. The two types of assignments are

a) Complete and proportionate.
b) Absolute and collateral.
c) Absolute and partial.
d) Complete and partial.

#87. Which of the following terms describes a specific dollar amount of the cost of care that the member must pay?

a) Copayment
b) Cost share
c) Prepayment
d) Contractual cost

#88. Which of the following plans could an individual employed at a manufacturing company qualify for if he decides to fund a retirement plan for himself?

a) Simplified Employee Pension Plan
b) Individual Retirement Account
c) 403(b) TSA
d) HR-10

#89. Which of the following applies to partial disability benefits?

a) Payment is limited to a certain period
b) An insured is entitled to a principal sum benefit for the partial loss of a limb
c) Payment is based on termination of employment
d) Benefits are reduced once an insured is no longer under a doctor's care

#90. Assume that a policy allows the insurance provider to terminate coverage for a "class" of clients under specified circumstances. Which of these classes would it be illegal for the insurance provider to terminate?

a) Every insured living in ZIP code 90210
b) Every insured over age 65
c) Every insured with a sexual preference that increases the risk of HIV infection
d) Every truck driver

#91. Mortality − Interest + Expense =

a) Operating expenses
b) Net premium
c) Gross premium
d) Benefits budget

#92. A 62-year-old woman is planning to be employed until age 68. When will she be eligible for Medicare?

a) Age 65, regardless of her employment status
b) As soon as she retires at age 68
c) Age 70, if still employed
d) Age 69 ½ if no longer employed

#93. A life insurance policy can be delivered by all of the following means, EXCEPT

a) Personal delivery by a trained insurance company employee, with a delivery receipt.
b) Certified mail.
c) Priority mail.
d) First class mail with a delivery receipt.

#94. What is the penalty for excessive contributions to an Individual Retirement Account (IRA)?

a) 4%
b) 6%
c) 10%
d) 15%

#95. Insurance that would pay for hiring and training a replacement for an important employee who becomes disabled is called

a) Business overhead expense disability insurance.
b) Key employee disability insurance.
c) Blanket disability insurance.
d) Long-term disability.

#96. Under long-term care's assisted living care, what services may NOT be provided?

a) Visits by a registered nurse
b) Linens and personal laundry service
c) Assistance with dressing and bathing
d) Reminders regarding medication

#97. All of the following are true concerning key person disability income insurance EXCEPT

a) The employer pays the premiums.
b) The employee is the insured.
c) Premiums are tax-deductible as a business expense.
d) The employer receives the benefits if the key person is disabled.

#98. In a whole life policy, the rider that allows the insurer to forgo collecting the premium if the insured is disabled is called

a) Waiver of monthly deductions.
b) Payor benefit.
c) Waiver of premium.
d) Guaranteed insurability.

#99. Medi-Cal is intended to provide health insurance primarily for people who are

a) Low-income and uninsured.
b) Substandard risks.
c) Between ages 21 and 65.
d) Not offered medical insurance by their employer.

#100. Which of the following is NOT the purpose of HIPAA?

a) To provide immediate coverage to new employees who were covered for the previous 18 months
b) To guarantee the right to obtain individual policies for eligible individuals
c) To prohibit discrimination against employees due to their health status
d) To limit exclusions for pre-existing conditions

#101. A tornado that destroys property is an example of which of the following?

a) A peril
b) A pure risk
c) A loss
d) A physical hazard

#102. An insured has a major medical policy with a $500 deductible and 80/20 coinsurance. He is hospitalized and sustains a $2,500 loss. What is the maximum amount that he will have to pay?

a) $1,000 (deductible + 20% of the entire bill)
b) $2,500 (the entire bill)
c) $900 (deductible + 20% of the bill after the deductible [20% of $2,000])
d) $500 (amount of deductible)

#103. In which distribution system must the potential client take the initiative and respond to an advertisement through a mail or telephone contact with the insurer?

a) Direct agency system
b) Direct response system
c) Managing general agent system
d) Home service system

#104. Which operating division of an insurance company is responsible for promoting, advertising, and distributing the insurer's products to the general public?

a) Underwriting
b) Sales and Marketing
c) Claims
d) Actuarial

#105. Which settlement option provides a single beneficiary with income for the rest of their life?

a) Straight Life
b) Fixed Amount
c) Lump Sum
d) Retained Assets

#106. Which of the following employees insured under a group life plan would be able to convert to individual insurance of the same coverage once the plan is terminated?

a) Employees who have no history of claims
b) Employees who have been insured under the plan for at least five years
c) Employees who have worked in the company for at least three years
d) Employees who have dependents

#107. The minimum rate of interest on an equity-indexed annuity is often based on

a) The annuitant's individual stock portfolio.
b) The insurer's general account investments.
c) An index such as the S&P 500.
d) The returns from the insurer's separate account.

#108. An insured claims to have injured his back at work. He tells the doctor that he cannot lift, bend, or even sit comfortably without pain. Based on the insured's statements, the doctor certifies his disability, and he begins to receive disability benefits. If it can be shown that the insured did not suffer the injury he has claimed or that he is not suffering the effects he is claiming, the insured will be charged with

a) Unfair claims practices.
b) Insurance fraud.
c) Medical misrepresentation.
d) Financial abuse of an insurance provider.

#109. Which of the following does NOT describe hospice care?

a) It delivers care to terminally-ill people
b) It delivers care to people with life expectancies of one to two years
c) It delivers continuous care
d) It delivers care in a home-like setting

#110. What are the tax consequences of a withdrawal during the accumulation period in a nonqualified annuity?

a) Neither interest nor principal is taxed, but penalties can be imposed
b) Taxable interest will be withdrawn first, and the 10% penalty will be assessed if under age 59 ½
c) Nontaxable principal can be withdrawn first, but the 10% penalty will be assessed if under age 59 ½
d) Both interest and principal are taxed; no other penalties are assessed

#111. Units with the same or similar exposure to loss are known as

a) Law of large numbers.
b) Homogeneous.
c) Catastrophic loss exposure.
d) Insurable risks.

#112. Regarding commissions for Medicare supplement policies, which of the following is true?

a) Restrictions only apply to monetary compensation
b) They are not allowed
c) They are allowed up to a certain amount for each policy
d) Restrictions only apply to managing general agents (MGAs)

#113. Regarding the reinstatement provision, which of the following statements is true?

a) It guarantees a policy's reinstatement after it has been surrendered for cash
b) The policyholder must pay any overdue premiums with interest before the policy is reinstated
c) It allows reinstatement within ten years after a policy has lapsed
d) It provides for the reinstatement of a policy regardless of the insured's health

#114. The advantage of qualified plans to employers is

a) They do not have to provide lump-sum payments.
b) Taxable contributions.
c) Tax-deductible contributions.
d) Tax-free earnings.

#115. Creditable coverage includes

a) Workers compensation.
b) Credit-only insurance
c) Coverage only for accident or disability income insurance.
d) Coverage under a state health benefits risk pool.

#116. Insureds are issued certificates of insurance under what kind of policy?

a) Any insurance
b) Group insurance
c) Individual insurance
d) Nonqualified annuity

#117. Under a Dependent Care Flexible Spending Account, all of the following would qualify as a dependent EXCEPT

a) Brian is severely autistic and refuses to take care of his own needs, which are taken care of by his father.
b) James had to amputate both legs but has learned to care for himself and get around in a wheelchair.
c) Sal was paralyzed from the neck down in a car accident and is cared for by his wife.
d) Joe must be constantly watched because of his violent muscle spasms, which often lead to Joe injuring himself.

#118. Using a class designation for beneficiaries means

a) Naming beneficiaries as a group.
b) Not naming beneficiaries.
c) Naming an estate as the beneficiary.
d) Naming every beneficiary by name.

#119. If an individual receives benefits for long-term care from Medi-Cal, when that recipient dies, the state can

a) Pursue asset recovery against the recipient's estate.
b) Pursue asset recovery against the recipient's heirs.
c) Both A and B.
d) Neither A nor B.

#120. Which of the following does NOT describe a competent party in terms of parties to a contract?

a) The individual must be mentally competent to understand the contract
b) The individual must have at least completed secondary education
c) The individual must not be under the influence of alcohol or drugs
d) The individual must be of legal age

#121. The gatekeeper of an HMO helps

a) Prevent double coverage.
b) Determine which doctors can take part in an HMO plan.
c) Control the costs of care from specialists.
d) Determine who will be permitted to enroll in an HMO program.

#122. According to the California Insurance Code, which of the following can be classified as an insurable event?

a) Pure risks
b) Unpredictable losses
c) Speculative risks
d) Extreme levels of loss

#123. A health insurance policy that pays a lump sum if the insured suffers a stroke or heart attack is known as

a) Critical illness.
b) Major medical.
c) AD&D.
d) Medical expense.

#124. All of the following are advantages to personally delivering an insurance policy to a policy owner EXCEPT

a) It is another chance to explain to the policy owner (insured) what they have purchased and why.
b) It reinforces the personal relationship with the agent and the insurance provider that agent represents.
c) It allows the agent to make personal observations regarding the proposed insured.
d) It allows the agent to assess future needs for additional insurance or provide other needed products.

#125. Concerning the standard Medicare Supplement benefit plans, what does the term "standard" mean?

a) Coverage options and conditions are designed for average individuals
b) Every provider will have the same coverage options and conditions for each plan
c) Coverage options and conditions comply with the law but differ from provider to provider
d) All plans must include basic benefits A–N

#126. The paid-up addition option uses the dividend to

a) Accumulate additional savings for retirement.
b) Purchase a smaller amount of the same type of insurance as the original policy.
c) Purchase one-year term insurance in the amount of the cash value.
d) Reduce the following year's premium.

#127. Who is required to sign the notice regarding replacement?

a) Applicant only
b) Agent only
c) Both the agent and applicant
d) Both the insurer and the agent

#128. A policy that covers medical costs related to a specific condition is called a

a) Dread Disease Policy.
b) Condition-Specific Policy.
c) Specific Condition Policy.
d) Limited Coverage Policy.

#129. A life insurance contract has a legal purpose if both of the following elements exist?

a) Policy owners and named beneficiaries
b) Insurable interest and consent
c) Underwriting and reciprocity
d) Offer and counteroffer

#130. An insured pays his Major Medical Insurance premium yearly on the 1st of June. Last June, he forgot to mail his premium to the insurance company. On the 19th of June, he had an accident and broke his arm. The insurer would

a) Pay half of his claim because the insured had an outstanding premium.
b) Pay the claim.
c) Hold the claim in a pending status until the end of the grace period.
d) Deny the claim.

#131. An insured obtained a 15-year level term life insurance policy with a face amount of $100,000. The policy included an accidental death rider, offering a double indemnity benefit. The insured was severely injured in a car accident and, after ten weeks of hospitalization, died from the injuries. What amount would the insured's beneficiary receive as a settlement?

a) $0
b) $100,000
c) $200,000
d) $100,000 plus the total of any premiums paid

#132. A signature is required on a health insurance application from all of the following individuals EXCEPT

a) The policy owner.
b) The agent.
c) The spouse of the policy owner.
d) The proposed insured.

#133. For an insured group's reported losses to become more likely to equal the statistical probability of loss for that particular class, the insured group needs to become

a) More active.
b) Larger.
c) Smaller.
d) Older.

#134. Which policy would contain an IRS-required corridor or gap between the death benefit and the cash value?

a) Universal Life – Option A
b) Universal Life – Option B
c) Equity-Indexed Universal Life
d) Variable Universal Life

#135. An insured has a disability that prevents him from doing certain kinds of work. Due to his qualifications, he responds to a recruitment ad and is hired for the job. What federal act allows him to apply for the position?

a) Social Security Act
b) Equal Opportunity Employment Act
c) Americans With Disabilities Act
d) No federal law exists; he can apply for any job

#136. Events in which an individual has both the opportunity to win or lose are classified as

a) Retained risk.
b) Speculative risk.
c) Insurable.
d) Pure risk.

#137. Health coverage becomes effective when the

a) Medical examination has been completed and the premium paid.
b) Initial premium has been received in the insurer's home office.
c) Initial premium has been paid, and the application has been approved.
d) Agent delivers the policy to the insured.

#138. Regarding group health insurance, COBRA stipulates that

a) Group coverage has to be extended for terminated employees up to a specific time at the expense of the former employee.
b) Retiring employees must be allowed to convert their group coverage to individual policies.
c) Terminated employees must be allowed to convert their group coverage to individual policies.
d) Group coverage has to be extended for terminated employees up to a specific time at the employer's expense.

#139. All of these are features of a group life insurance plan EXCEPT

a) To underwrite the plan, a minimum number of participants is required.
b) The average age of the group determines the plan's cost.
c) Participants are required to prove insurability.
d) The participants receive a Certificate of Insurance as their proof of coverage.

#140. Which of the following terms describes the specified dollar amount beyond which the insured no longer participates in sharing expenses?

a) Stop-loss limit
b) Out-of-pocket limit
c) First-dollar coverage
d) Corridor deductible

#141. Under an extended term nonforfeiture option, the policy cash value is converted to

a) A smaller face amount than the whole life policy.
b) A higher face amount than the whole life policy.
c) The same face amount as the whole life policy.
d) The face amount equal to the cash value.

#142. The types of perils that are typically excluded from coverage and that do not allow for an accurate pattern of predictability and will adversely slant the law of large numbers are known as

a) Catastrophic Losses.
b) Moral Hazards.
c) Morale Hazards.
d) Insurable Interests.

#143. Employers can lower health plan costs by combining a Health Reimbursement Account (HRA) with

a) Nothing; HRAs cannot be combined with any other health plan.
b) A high deductible health plan (HDHP).
c) A low deductible health plan.
d) An Individual Retirement Account (IRA).

#144. Your client wants to purchase a par policy to supplement her retirement savings program. What does your client need to know about insurance policy dividends?

a) Dividends require the purchase of additional insurance
b) Dividends are guaranteed
c) Dividends are considered a refund of unused premiums
d) Dividends are written into the contract

#145. Which premium mode would have the highest yearly cost for an insurance policy?

a) Monthly
b) Quarterly
c) Semi-annual
d) Annual

#146. Who can provide skilled nursing care?

a) Doctor
b) Spouse
c) Family member
d) Community volunteer

#147. What will happen if a producer submits an insurance application to an insurer to which she is not appointed?

a) The insurance company will not accept the policy
b) The producer will be found guilty of a misdemeanor
c) The insurance company must appoint the agent if it accepts the policy
d) The application will not have to be approved by an underwriter

#148. An insured obtained a noncancelable health insurance policy one year ago. Which of the following situations would NOT be why the insurance provider cancels the policy?

a) The insured suffers an accident and sustains a large claim
b) The insured does not pay the policy premium
c) The insured reaches the maximum age limit stated in the policy
d) The insurance provider discovers a misrepresentation within two years of the policy's issue date

#149. When is the Restoration of Benefits most beneficial to the insured?

a) When they sustain a significant loss
b) When they become uninsurable during the policy period
c) When they do not pay their premium
d) When they forget to file a claim before the statute of limitations expires

#150. If a Medicare insured uses a health care provider who does not accept Medicare payments, which of the following will be true?

a) The insured may need to sign a private contract with the provider
b) Medicare insureds cannot use non-participating providers
c) The provider may need to sign a private contract with Medicare
d) The insured needs to notify their Medicare agency

Practice Exam 1 Answers

#1. **c) Prepaid basis.**

An HMO is an organized health care system that offers an array of medical services on a prepaid basis to voluntarily enrolled individuals living within a specified service area. (pp. 155, 167)

#2. **b) A debtor has an insurable interest in a lender's life**

A lender has an insurable interest in a debtor's life, but only to the extent of the debt. (p. 6)

#3. **b) $120 per day**

Most long-term care policies will pay the benefit amount in a specific fixed dollar amount per day, irrespective of the cost of care. (p. 232)

#4. **a) Purchase insurance.**

The most effective way to handle risk is to transfer it. Insurance is the most common way to transfer risk from a person or group to an insurer. (pp. 2, 4)

#5. **b) The lending institution**

Creditor group, also known as credit life and credit health insurance, is a specialized use of group life and group health insurance. It protects the creditor (lending institution) from losing money due to a borrower's disability or death. (p. 91)

#6. **b) Policy delivery**

Insurers are encouraged to document all conversations and correspondence with an insured if crucial errors and omissions happen. The most common times for these errors are during the sales interview and policy delivery processes. (p. 159)

#7. **d) Conditional**

A conditional contract requires both the insurance provider and policyholder to meet certain conditions before the agreement can be executed, unlike other policies, which put the burden of the condition on either the insurance provider or the policyholder. (p. 11)

#8. **b) 6 credits**

To be considered currently (or partially) insured, an individual must earn six credits during the last 13-quarter period. (p. 139)

#9. **a) The cash value available to the policyholder**

Liquidity in life insurance refers to the availability of cash to the insured. Certain life insurance policies offer cash values that can be borrowed at any time and utilized for immediate needs. (p. 63)

#10. **c) Plan A**

To standardize the coverage offered under a Medicare supplement policy, the NAIC has established standard Medicare supplement benefit plans, which are identified with the letters A through N. The benefits in Plan A are considered core benefits and must be included in the other plans. (p. 216)

#11. **a) The employer is the owner and the beneficiary**

Under key-person insurance, the business (the employer) is the applicant, owner, premium payer, and beneficiary. (p. 64)

#12. **a) The financial rating of the insurance provider.**

The insurer's financial rating is not required to be specified in the policy. (p. 13)

#13. **d) The cost of a vacation for surviving family members**

These costs would consider the insured's final medical expenses, funeral expenses, and day-to-day expenses of maintaining the family, including mortgage or rent payments, utilities, car payments, groceries, etc. (p. 62)

#14. **a) Underwriter**

The underwriter's role is to equitably evaluate insurable risks and select and distribute to the insurance company those that are profitable to the insurer. (p. 67)

#15. **b) Transfer**

Insurance is a transfer of the risk of financial loss from a covered peril from the insured to the insurer. (pp. 2, 4)

#16. **a) Premiums.**

Retention is an intended assumption of risk or plan to accept responsibility for the loss by an insured through the use of self-insurance, copayments, or deductibles. (p. 5)

#17. **d) Face amount.**

Level term policies maintain a level death benefit (or face amount) over the policy's term. In level term insurance, the premium stays consistent throughout the years, unlike the premiums of many policies, which increase as the policy owner ages. (p. 82)

#18. **b) When the expenses exceed a specified percentage of the insured's adjusted gross income (AGI)**

In either medical expense insurance policies or long-term care insurance policies, unreimbursed medical expenses paid for the insured, the insured's spouse, and dependents can be claimed as deductions if the expenses exceed a certain percentage of the insured's AGI. (pp. 197-198)

#19. **c) The IRS**

The IRS establishes limits for the annual contribution for Dependent Care Accounts. (p. 171)

#20. **a) The loss has to be catastrophic**

To be characterized as a pure risk, the loss must be due to chance, measurable, definite, and predictable, but not catastrophic. (pp. 2, 5)

#21. **d) 100**

Whole life insurance policies mature when the insured reaches 100 years of age. The cash value at that time is scheduled to equal the face amount; therefore, when the insurer pays the face amount, it also, in effect, pays the cash value. (p. 84)

#22. **c) Limited-pay Life**

In limited-pay policies, the premiums for coverage will be completely paid up well before the insured reaches age 100, generally after a specified number of years. (p. 84)

#23. **c) The California Department of Aging.**

The Department of Aging is responsible for managing the operations of all local HICAP agencies in California. (p. 223)

#24. **c) To let consumers compare the costs of different policies**

The buyer's guide offers generic information regarding life insurance policies and lets consumers compare the costs of different policies. (p. 66)

#25. **b) Return the application to the applicant to be completed**

All questions must be answered before the policy is issued. If the insurer receives an incomplete application, it must be returned to the applicant for completion. (p. 68)

#26. **c) The insured's estate.**

Since there is no viable beneficiary at the time of death, proceeds are paid to the insured's estate. (p. 98)

#27. **a) Separate accounts.**

Any domestic insurer that issues variable contracts must set up one or more separate accounts. These insurers must maintain assets with a value at least equal to the reserves and other liabilities associated with the account. (p. 90)

#28. **a) Monthly premium waiver and monthly income**

The Disability Income Benefit rider waives the policy premiums, similar to the Waiver of Premium rider. Unlike the Waiver of Premium rider, the insured is allowed to receive a monthly or weekly income during the disability period. (p. 108)

#29. **a) Substandard risks are always rejected and are not insurable.**

Substandard risks can be insured and charged a higher premium rate for the additional risk they pose for the insurance provider. (p. 161)

#30. **c) Income.**

Accidental Death and Dismemberment (AD&D) policies cover the loss of body parts or only the loss of life. (p. 173)

#31. **a) Reinstatement provision**

Policy owners can reinstate a lapsed policy within three years by paying back the premiums, with interest, and proving insurability. (pp. 14, 96)

#32. **b) Death because of a plane crash for a fare-paying passenger**

Typically, policies do not exclude conditions where an insured is a fare-paying passenger on a commercial airline. (p. 97)

#33. **b) Grace period.**

Provided the policy has sufficient cash value, this provision triggers a loan at the end of the grace period, so the policy remains in force. (p. 100)

#34. **b) The annuitant has to be a natural person**

Annuity owners can be individuals or entities like corporations and trusts. Still, the annuitant has to be a natural person whose life expectancy is considered for the annuity. (p. 114)

#35. **b) The coverage through the husband's company is primary.**

The policy covering the individual filing the claim will be considered the primary policy. (p. 177)

#36. **c) The Medicare Part A deductible**

Medicare Supplement Plan A provides the core or basic benefits established by law. All of the above are part of the basic benefits, except for the Medicare Part A deductible, a benefit provided through the other supplement plans. (pp. 216-217)

#37. **b) Guaranteed insurability.**

Guaranteed insurability is a rider that is included at the time of application (or can be added later), which lets the insured increase the amount of insurance without proving evidence of insurability. (p. 109)

#38. **c) The period during which accumulated funds are converted into income payments**

The annuity period is when accumulated funds are converted into an income stream. (p. 114)

#39. **c) Seek higher returns.**

Equity-Indexed Annuities are not securities, but they invest fairly aggressively to aim for higher returns. The Equity-Indexed Annuity has a guaranteed minimum interest rate like a fixed annuity. The current rate of interest that is credited is often tied to a familiar index such as the S&P 500. (p. 116)

#40. **b) Noncancelable and guaranteed renewable**

No long-term care policy issued to a person can contain renewal provisions other than noncancelable or guaranteed renewable. (p. 232)

#41. **a) Has to be clearly stated in the policy's text.**

Suppose the policy is returned within the specified timeframe. In that case, insurers must specify the right of the applicant to rescind the policy for a full refund of all premiums paid in the policy's text (outlined on the title page and described in the text). (p. 126)

#42. **d) Value funds.**

During the 30-day free-look (cancellation) period, the premium for a variable annuity can only be invested in money-market funds and fixed-income investments unless the investor explicitly requests that the premiums be invested in the mutual funds. (p. 121)

#43. **a) When the representation is false in a material point.**

Suppose a representation is false in a material point. In that circumstance, the injured party can rescind the contract when the representation becomes false. (pp. 12-13)

#44. **a) 15 days**

Upon receiving any communication from a claimant (about a claim) that reasonably suggests that a response is expected, all licensees must furnish the claimant with a complete response within 15 days. (p. 58)

#45. **b) Interest-only**

If a beneficiary receives payments that include both principal and interest portions, only the interest is taxable as income. (p. 145)

#46. **c) 50%**

If the distributions are not large enough, or if there are no distributions at the required age, the penalty is 50% of the deficit from the required annual amount. (p. 147)

#47. **a) Spouse**

Suppose an annuity owner dies before the effective starting date. In that situation, the contract's interest continues to be taxable unless the beneficiary is a spouse. This tax can be deferred. (p. 148)

#48. **a) The insured can access the $500 at the discretion of her previous employer**

Former employees, including retirees, can have continued access to unused HRAs, but this is at the employer's discretion. (p. 171)

#49. **b) It is a life contingency option.**

Under the fixed period installments annuity settlement option, the annuitant chooses the period for the benefits; the insurance provider determines how much each payment will be. This option only pays for a certain amount of time, and there are no life contingencies. (p. 118)

#50. b) 20

Under COBRA (the Consolidated Omnibus Budget Reconciliation Act of 1985), any employer with 20 or more employees is required to extend group health coverage to terminated employees and their families. (p. 181)

#51. d) Unlimited access to providers

There are five distinguishing characteristics of managed care: high-quality care, preventive care, comprehensive case management, controlled access to providers, and risk sharing. (p. 153)

#52. c) Settlement option.

A settlement option is exercised when an immediate annuity is obtained with the cash value at surrender or the face amount at death. (pp. 115, 118)

#53. b) Welfare benefits.

Social Security is not a welfare program. It is an entitlement program. (pp. 139, 202)

#54. c) It is nonrenewable

In a term health policy, the owner has no rights of renewal. (p. 154)

#55. c) Companies of all sizes

HRAs are available to employees of companies of all sizes. (p. 171)

#56. a) Field underwriter

An agent's role as the field underwriter is to collect creditable information from an applicant that would aid the agent in screening unacceptable or marginal risks before applying for an insurance policy. (pp. 67, 158)

#57. c) An applicant submits an insurance application to the insurer.

In insurance, the offer is typically made by the applicant in the form of an application. Acceptance occurs when an insurance provider's underwriter approves the application and issues a policy. (p. 10)

#58. b) A policyholder who is not the insured

Third-party owner is a legal term used to identify a person or entity that is not an insured under the contract but has a legally enforceable right. (p. 132)

#59. a) The insured is not required to pay a deductible

The three basic types of coverage (hospital, medical, and surgical) are often referred to as first-dollar coverage. They typically do not require the insured to pay a deductible. (p. 166)

#60. a) Can be converted to permanent insurance for the children without requiring evidence of insurability.

Children covered by a family policy can convert their term coverage to permanent coverage without providing evidence of insurability. (p. 86)

#61. c) Skilled care.

Adult daycare, respite care, home health care, and custodial care are all coverages used to reduce the need to be admitted into a care facility. Skilled care is almost always given in an institutional setting. (p. 229)

#62. a) Control health insurance claims expenses.

Managed care is characterized by programs of ongoing quality control, arrangements with selected providers, utilization review, and financial incentives for members to use procedures and providers covered by the plan. (pp. 167-169, 201)

#63. **c) Apply such expenses to the new year's deductible.**

The Carry-Over Provision allows insureds to apply medical expenses incurred in the final 90 days of a calendar year to the following year's deductible. (p. 153)

#64. **a) Blanket policy.**

A single policy covering several certificate holders without individually naming the insureds is called a blanket policy. (pp. 177-178)

#65. **c) It will continue because the insured, not his employer, owns it**

HSAs, like IRAs, are portable and belong to the person, not the employer. When the insured moves to his new job, his HSA moves with him. (p. 172)

#66. **c) It mandates all employers, regardless of the number or age of employees, to offer extended group health coverage**

COBRA is only applicable to employers with 20 or more employees. (p. 181)

#67. **c) A family**

A person is a legal entity that acts on behalf of itself and makes contracts in its own name. The term "person" refers to an individual human being, partnership, organization, corporation, association, and trust. (p. 2)

#68. **a) The cost of coverage is usually lower because of the reduction of risk.**

The cost is usually lower for group underwriting in comparison to individual underwriting. (p. 132)

#69. **a) Pure risk.**

Pure risk applies to situations that can only result in a loss or no change. Insurers are only willing to insure pure risks. (p. 2)

#70. **b) Sales of LTC policies.**

The HICAP agencies do not recommend or sell products. (p. 223)

#71. **a) A window washer pays a higher premium and receives a poorer classification of disability**

The more hazardous the applicant's occupation, the higher the premium the insurer will charge. (p. 197)

#72. **c) Notice Regarding Replacement**

The Notice Regarding Replacement has to inform the applicant of the replacement policy's 30-day free-look provision. (p. 218)

#73. **c) Platinum**

Bronze benefit plans cover 60% of expected health care costs; silver plans cover 70%; gold plans cover 80%, and platinum plans cover 90%. (p. 186)

#74. **b) $500**

Once the primary insurer has paid the full benefit, the secondary insurer will pay what the first insurer will not cover, like coinsurance and deductibles. The insured is then reimbursed for out-of-pocket costs. (p. 177)

#75. **c) Routine and major restorative care**

Routine and major restorative care covers dental work, like oral surgery, cavity treatment bridges, and dentures. Routine and preventative maintenance only covers routine dental check-ups. (p. 173)

#76. **a) It is divided into geographic territories**

HMOs offer services to those living within specific geographic regions. If one lives within the region, they are eligible to join the HMO. However, they are ineligible if they do not live within the region. (pp. 155, 167)

#77. **c) Medicare Part C.**

Medicare consists of Part A (Hospital Insurance protection), Part B (Medical Insurance protection), and Part C (Medicare Advantage, formerly Medicare+Choice). Medicare Part D is a stand-alone drug plan for individuals who need the coverage and are eligible for Medicare Part A and Part B. (pp. 206, 212-213)

#78. **a) Elimination period.**

The elimination period is the time immediately after the start of a disability when benefits are not payable. This period reduces the cost of providing coverage and eliminates filing many claims. (pp. 153, 162, 174)

#79. **a) $0**

Similar to the other types of basic medical expense coverage, there is no deductible, but coverage is limited. (p. 166)

#80. **c) MSAs are only available to groups with at least 100 employees**

Medical savings accounts (MSAs) are available only to groups of 50 or fewer employees. The remaining statements are correct. (pp. 169-170)

#81. **b) 10 days**

If the premium is paid weekly, the grace period is seven days. If paid monthly, the grace period is ten days and 31 days for all other modes. (p. 174)

#82. **c) Cash value**

The amount available to the policy owner for a loan is the policy's cash value. If there are any outstanding loans, the insurer will deduct that amount from the amount of the unpaid loans and interest. (p. 84)

#83. **d) Students at a public school**

Blanket insurance is issued to groups whose members are constantly changing. (p. 177)

#84. **a) Death benefits are only paid if death occurs within 24 hours of an accident.**

Under an Accidental Death and Dismemberment insurance policy, the death benefit will be paid if the accidental death takes place within 90 days of the accident, not 24 hours. (pp. 173, 174)

#85. **a) First three**

Since Medicare will not pay for the first three pints of blood, a Medicare Supplement plan will pay for that. (p. 216)

#86. **b) Absolute and collateral.**

Absolute assigns the entire policy. Collateral assigns a part or all of the benefits. (p. 95)

#87. **a) Copayment**

A copayment is a specific dollar amount of the cost of care that the member pays. (pp. 153, 167)

#88. **b) Individual Retirement Account**

Individuals with earned income can fund an Individual Retirement Account (IRA). (pp. 136-137)

#89. **a) Payment is limited to a certain period**

The partial disability benefit is generally 50% of the total disability benefit and is limited to a specified period. (p. 195)

#90. **c) Every insured with a sexual preference that increases the risk of HIV infection**

Answers A, B, and D are legally acceptable "classes." Sexual preference is not a legal classification. (pp. 51, 53)

#91. c) Gross premium

If "mortality" is the cost of insured mortality, "interest" is the interest earned by an insurer, and "expense" (or loading) represents company operating costs. The interest is deducted from the mortality cost, producing the net premium. The loading is added to the net premium to produce the gross premium. (p. 162)

#92. a) Age 65, regardless of her employment status

The person will still be eligible for Medicare at age 65. However, suppose she is still insured under her employer's group health plan. In that situation, the group plan will be her primary coverage, and Medicare will be her secondary coverage. (p. 206)

#93. c) Priority mail.

Acceptable delivery methods include Personal Delivery with a signed delivery receipt, Certified or Registered Mail, 1st Class Mail with a signed delivery receipt, or any other reasonable method determined by the Commissioner. (p. 76)

#94. b) 6%

Individuals can contribute 100% of their earned income to a specified amount. The penalty for excess contribution to a traditional IRA is 6%. (p. 119)

#95. b) Key employee disability insurance.

Under key employee (partner) disability insurance, the business is the contract holder and will receive benefits if a specified key employee becomes disabled. (p. 201)

#96. a) Visits by a registered nurse

The following services can be provided: Assistance with eating, dressing, and bathing, linens and personal laundry service, and reminders regarding medication. Assisted living offers nonmedical assistance. (p. 230)

#97. c) Premiums are tax-deductible as a business expense.

In key person disability insurance, the business owns the contract, pays the premium, and is the beneficiary. The key person is the insured, and the company must have the consent of the key person to be insured in writing. (p. 201)

#98. c) Waiver of premium.

The waiver of premium rider waives the premium if the insured owner has been totally disabled for a predetermined period. (p. 108)

#99. a) Low-income and uninsured.

Medi-Cal exists to offer coverage to low-income or uninsured individuals in California. (pp. 220-221)

#100. a) To provide immediate coverage to new employees who were covered for the previous 18 months

HIPAA does not restrict employers or providers from establishing pre-existing conditions exclusions or waiting periods, so the coverage to new employees would not be immediate. (pp. 73, 183-184)

#101. a) A peril

In an insurance policy, a peril is the cause of loss that insurers will cover. (p. 2)

#102. c) $900 (deductible + 20% of the bill after the deductible [20% of $2,000])

The insured would first pay the $500 deductible; out of the remaining $2,000, the insurance provider will cover 80% ($1,600), and the insured will cover 20% ($400). (pp. 152, 167)

#103. **b) Direct response system**

The potential client has to take the initiative and respond to the advertisement through a mail or telephone contact with the insurance company as directed in the ad under the direct response system. (p. 18)

#104. **b) Sales and Marketing**

The marketing department is responsible for promoting, advertising, and distributing an insurer's products to the general public. (p. 40)

#105. **a) Straight Life**

The Straight Life option provides a single beneficiary with an income stream for the remainder of their life. (p. 103)

#106. **b) Employees who have been insured under the plan for at least five years**

If the master contract is terminated, all individuals on the plan for at least five years will be allowed to convert to individual insurance of the same coverage. (p. 136)

#107. **c) An index such as the S&P 500.**

A guaranteed minimum interest rate on an equity-indexed annuity is often tied to a familiar index, like the S&P 500. (p. 116)

#108. **b) Insurance fraud.**

Unlawful insurance fraud includes false statements or omissions of material fact, false information and statements made on an insurance application, and malicious statements regarding the financial condition of an insurance company. (pp. 20, 57)

#109. **b) It delivers care to people with life expectancies of one to two years**

Hospice provides continuous, short-term care in a home-like setting to terminally-ill individuals with life expectancies of six months or less. (pp. 208, 230)

#110. **b) Taxable interest will be withdrawn first and the 10% penalty will be assessed if under age 59 ½**

During the accumulation phase of an annuity, any withdrawn funds are taxed on a last-in-first-out basis (LIFO). (pp. 115, 146)

#111. **b) Homogeneous.**

The cornerstone of insurance is sharing risk between a large homogeneous group with a similar loss exposure. (p. 3)

#112. **c) They are allowed up to a certain amount for each policy**

A producer or other representative engaged in the sale of Medicare supplement policies can receive commissions if the first-year commission does not exceed 200% of the commissions paid for selling or servicing the policy in year two. (p. 222)

#113. **b) The policyholder must pay any overdue premiums with interest before the policy is reinstated**

Upon policy reinstatement, the policyholder must pay all back premiums plus interest and is required to repay any outstanding loans and interest. (p. 96)

#114. **c) Tax-deductible contributions.**

Qualified plans have these tax advantages: The earnings in the plan accumulate tax deferred; employer contributions are tax-deductible and are not taxed as income to the employee; lump-sum distributions to employees are eligible for favorable tax treatment. (pp. 119, 146)

#115. **d) Coverage under a state health benefits risk pool.**

Creditable coverage includes, but is not limited to, coverage under Medicare Parts A or B and Medicaid, coverage provided under any individual or group policy, or health plans under the Federal Employees Health Benefits Program. (p. 184)

#116. **b) Group insurance**

Individuals covered by group life insurance receive a certificate of insurance from the master policy. They do not receive a policy. (pp. 132-133)

#117. **b) James had to amputate both legs but has learned to care for himself and get around in a wheelchair.**

Individuals who cannot feed, clean, or dress due to physical or mental problems are considered unable to care for themselves. (p. 170)

#118. **a) Naming beneficiaries as a group.**

Class designations are used when an insured chooses to distribute benefits among the living beneficiaries and their heirs without naming each person individually, like "all my children." (p. 98)

#119. **a) Pursue asset recovery against the recipient's estate.**

Asset recovery will only begin if there is no surviving spouse. (p. 221)

#120. **b) The individual must have at least completed secondary education**

The parties to a contract must be mentally competent to understand the contract, of legal age, and not under the influence of alcohol or drugs. (p. 10)

#121. **c) Control the costs of care from specialists.**

Initially, the member selects a primary care physician or gatekeeper. If the member requires the attention of a specialist, the primary care physician must refer the member. This process helps keep the member away from a higher-priced specialist unless absolutely necessary. (pp. 153, 167-168)

#122. **a) Pure risks**

As a loss becomes more predictable, it becomes more insurable. Only pure risks are insurable. Speculative losses are uninsurable. (p. 2)

#123. **a) Critical illness.**

A critical illness policy covers multiple illnesses, like stroke, heart attack, and renal failure. It pays a lump-sum benefit to the insured upon the diagnosis (and survival) of any illnesses covered by the policy. (p. 157)

#124. **c) It allows the agent to make personal observations regarding the proposed insured.**

Answers A, B, and D are all advantages of personally delivering a policy with a signed and dated written delivery receipt. (p. 76)

#125. **b) Every provider will have the same coverage options and conditions for each plan**

The term "standard" implies that every provider will have the same coverage options and conditions for each plan. (p. 216)

#126. **b) Purchase a smaller amount of the same type of insurance as the original policy.**

The dividends are used to obtain a single premium policy in addition to the face amount of the permanent policy. (p. 102)

#127. **c) Both the agent and applicant**

Before issuing a replacement policy, the insurance provider must furnish the applicant with a notice regarding replacement, which must be signed by both the agent and the applicant. (p. 127)

#128. **a) Dread Disease Policy.**

Dread Disease policies cover medical conditions like heart disease or cancer. (p. 157)

#129. **b) Insurable interest and consent**

To ensure the legal purpose of a life insurance policy, it must contain both insurable interest and consent. (p. 10)

#130. **b) Pay the claim.**

Since the accident occurred during the grace period, the insurer will pay the claim. (p. 174)

#131. **c) $200,000**

In this case, the beneficiary would most likely receive twice the face value of the policy. The reason for this is that the insured's fatal injuries resulted from an accident, and died within the 90-day benefit limit stipulated in most policies. (p. 108)

#132. **c) The spouse of the policy owner.**

Every health insurance application requires the signature of the proposed insured, the policy owner (if different than the insured), and the agent who sells the insurance. (p. 158)

#133. **b) Larger.**

Based on the law of large numbers, the larger a group becomes, the easier it is to predict losses. Insurance providers use this law to predict specific losses and establish appropriate premiums. (p. 3)

#134. **a) Universal Life – Option A**

As required by the IRS, a Universal Life Level Death Benefit option (Option A) policy has to maintain a specified gap or "corridor" between the death benefit and the cash value. (p. 89)

#135. **c) Americans With Disabilities Act**

The existence or consequence of the insured's disability cannot be excluded from recruitment, selection, training, compensation, and all terms, conditions, and privileges of employment. (p. 182)

#136. **b) Speculative risk.**

Speculative risk involves the opportunity for gain or loss and is not insurable. (p. 2)

#137. **c) Initial premium has been paid, and the application has been approved.**

If the premium was paid, coverage becomes effective on the conditional receipt date, provided the underwriter approves the application. (p. 158)

#138. **a) Group coverage has to be extended for terminated employees up to a specific time at the expense of the former employee.**

COBRA ensures employers with 20 or more employees continue group medical insurance for terminated workers and dependents for 18 to 36 months. (p. 181)

#139. **c) Participants are required to prove insurability.**

Group life insurance does not involve individual underwriting. (p. 91)

#140. **a) Stop-loss limit**

A "stop-loss limit" is a specified dollar amount beyond which the insured no longer has to participate in the sharing of expenses. (p. 154)

#141. **c) The same face amount as the whole life policy.**

Under this option, the insurance provider uses the policy's cash value to convert to term insurance for the same face amount as the previous permanent policy. (p. 100)

#142. **a) Catastrophic Losses.**

A peril is an immediate danger or specific event causing the loss, ultimately creating the risk. Catastrophic losses are unusually large numbers of losses in a very short period (e.g., fires, earthquakes, floods, etc.). (p. 5)

#143. **b) A high deductible health plan (HDHP).**

HRAs allow employers to lower health plan costs by combining the HRA with a high-deductible health plan (HDHP). (p. 171)

#144. **c) Dividends are considered a refund of unused premiums**

Policy dividends are the underwriting income of mutual insurers. They are not income or profit; they are refunds and are not guaranteed. (p. 40)

#145. **a) Monthly**

Suppose the policy owner chooses to pay the premium more frequently than annually. In that circumstance, there will be an additional charge (loading) because the insurer will not have the premium to invest for an entire year. The insurer will have additional expenses in billing the premium. (p. 95)

#146. **a) Doctor**

Skilled nursing care encompasses daily nursing and rehabilitative care that medical professionals can only give under the direction of a physician. Skilled care is usually provided in an institutional setting. (pp. 208, 229)

#147. **c) The insurance company must appoint the agent if it accepts the policy**

Suppose an insurer approves an application submitted by an agent without an appointment. In that scenario, the insurer must forward a notice of appointment of the agent to the Commissioner within 14 days after the agent submits the insurance application. (p. 33)

#148. **a) The insured suffers an accident and sustains a large claim**

The insurer cannot cancel coverage because of covered claims. All the rest are allowable reasons for an insurance company to terminate the contract. (pp. 154-155)

#149. **a) When they sustain a significant loss**

Restoration of Benefits lets the insured regain their full lifetime benefit level over a period following a significant or catastrophic loss. (p. 175)

#150. **a) The insured may need to sign a private contract with the provider**

When a Medicare insured uses a healthcare provider who doesn't accept Medicare payments, they could be asked to sign a private contract. A private contract is a written agreement between the health care provider and the Medicare insured who has decided not to participate in the Medicare program. It only applies to the services the insured receives from that provider. (p. 215)

PRACTICE EXAM:
2

Your preparation is paying off

You are about to take another California Life, Accident and Health or Sickness Practice Exam. This exam consists of *150 Questions (plus five to ten non-scored experimental questions)* and is *3 hours and 15 minutes* long. If you do not have enough time to complete this exam right now, it is better to wait until you can fully devote your attention to completing it in the allotted time.

Any skipped questions will be graded as incorrect. The following chart breaks down the number of questions in each chapter and by topic.

CHAPTER	# OF QUESTIONS
General Insurance	**40**
Basic Insurance Concepts and Principles	16
Contract Law	10
The Insurance Marketplace	14
Life Insurance	**49**
Life Insurance – Basics	8
Types of Life Policies	10
Annuities	8
Life Insurance and Annuities – Policy Replacement/Cancellation	4
The Individual Life Insurance Contract	10
Taxation of Life Insurance and Annuities	3
Group Life Insurance Plans	2
Social Security Disability Program	1
Individual Underwriting, Pricing, and Claims	3
Life Policy Riders	**4**
General Concepts of Medical and Disability Insurance	**4**
Medical Expense Insurance	**45**
Individual Insurance	14
Group Medical Expense Insurance	8
Patient Protection and Affordable Care Act (PPACA)	8
Senior Health Products	15
Disability Income Insurance	**4**
Long-Term Care Insurance	**4**

To calculate your score, subtract the number of incorrectly answered questions from 150. Take this number and divide it by 150. For example, if you incorrectly answered 60 questions, your score would be 60%, the minimum score needed to pass the exam.

#1. Regarding the Medical Information Bureau (MIB), all of the following are true EXCEPT

a) MIB reports include previous insurance information.
b) Insurance providers cannot refuse to accept an application solely because of information in a MIB report.
c) MIB reports are gathered from information doctors and hospitals supplied.
d) MIB information is reported to underwriters in coded form.

#2. A Medicare supplement plan needs to have at least which of the following renewal provisions?

a) Conditionally renewable
b) Nonrenewable
c) Noncancelable
d) Guaranteed renewable

#3. Who has to sign the notice regarding replacement?

a) Applicant only
b) Agent only
c) Both the agent and the applicant
d) Both the insurer and the agent

#4. An insured has both a primary group health plan and an excess plan, each paying for losses up to $10,000. The insured incurred a loss of $15,000. Disregarding any deductibles or copayments, how much will the excess plan cover?

a) $10,000
b) $7,500
c) $5,000
d) $0

#5. Events or conditions that increase the likelihood of an insured loss occurring are referred to as

a) Hazards.
b) Exposures.
c) Risks.
d) Perils.

#6. An insured has a disabled grown-up child who chiefly depends upon him for support and maintenance. How will that affect the insured's insurability in the group plan?

a) The insured will receive full benefits, but his dependent will not be covered
b) The insured's dependent's condition will not affect his eligibility or rating
c) The insured will not qualify for group benefits because of his dependent's physical condition
d) The insured can qualify for partial benefits along with government subsistence

#7. How often must all insurance companies in California report their financial condition to the Commissioner?

a) January 1 of odd-numbered years
b) Every year, on or before March 1
c) March 1 of even-numbered years
d) Every year, on or before January 1

#8. Which of these terms is used for an applicant's written request to an insurance provider for the insurer to issue a contract based on the information given?

a) Insurance Request Form
b) Request for Insurance
c) Application
d) Policy Request

#9. Regarding the guaranteed insurability rider, all of the following are true EXCEPT

a) The insured can purchase additional coverage at the attained age.
b) The insured can purchase additional insurance up to the amount stated in the base policy.
c) It lets the insured obtain additional insurance amounts without proving insurability only at specified events or dates.
d) This rider is available to every insured with no additional premium.

#10. Which of the following is NOT a feature of pure risk?

a) The loss exposure has to be large
b) The loss has to be catastrophic
c) The loss has to be due to chance
d) The loss has to be measurable in dollars

#11. Vinnie owns a home and has no mortgage payments. He makes $100,000 a year and has $500,000 invested in CDs. His brother Darrell has a mortgage payment of $1,500 and a car payment of $300 every month. He makes $50,000 a year. Both Vinnie and Darrell become disabled and apply for disability income. Which of these would most likely be true, all other things equal?

a) Vinnie and Darrell will receive equal benefits
b) Vinnie will receive no benefits since he has no financial obligations
c) Vinnie will more likely receive a larger benefit since his net worth is higher
d) Darrell will be more likely to receive a larger benefit since he has more financial obligations

#12. A guaranteed renewable health insurance policy allows the

a) Policy to be renewed at the time of expiration, but the policy can be canceled for cause during the policy term.
b) Insurance provider to renew the policy to a specified age.
c) Policy owner to renew the policy to a stated age, with the insurer having the right to raise premiums on the entire class.
d) Policy owner to renew the policy to a stated age and guarantees the premium for the same period.

#13. The Health Insurance Counseling and Advocacy Program (HICAP) counselors are primarily

a) Trained and certified volunteers.
b) Licensed Life Agents.
c) Licensed Life and Disability Analysts.
d) Any of the above.

#14. Under the Affordable Care Act (ACA), which classification applies to health plans based on the amount of covered costs?

a) Grandfathered and non-grandfathered
b) Risk classification
c) Metal level classification
d) Guaranteed and nonguaranteed

#15. Which of the following is NOT true concerning Blue Cross and Blue Shield organizations?

a) They are typically not-for-profit
b) They are insurers
c) They are service organizations
d) They establish contractual agreements with hospitals and physicians

#16. An applicant for health insurance has not had a medical claim in five years. She does not smoke or drink and exercises daily. What classification do you assume the applicant would receive from her insurer?

a) Standard
b) Superior
c) Preferred
d) Low-risk

#17. Profitable distribution of exposure serves the purpose of

a) Protecting the insurance provider against adverse selection.
b) Helping the insurance provider select only the ideally insurable risks.
c) Preventing the insurance provider from being estopped.
d) Helping the insurance provider determine payable benefits.

#18. All of the following LTC coverages would permit an insured to receive care at home EXCEPT

a) Home health care.
b) Skilled care.
c) Custodial care in the house of an insured.
d) Respite care.

#19. Regarding the annuity period, which of the following is TRUE?

a) It can last for the annuitant's lifetime
b) During this period, the annuity payments grow interest tax-deferred
c) It is also called the accumulation period
d) It is the period during which the annuitant pays premiums into the annuity

#20. Which of the following is accomplished by having an elimination period in a policy?

a) To ensure that claims are not paid until an investigation can be done to verify that the claim is valid and covered by the policy
b) To give the client some flexibility in determining their own premium
c) To give the insured time to save up the initial premium charged when they receive a premium rating
d) To allow the insurance provider to do an in-depth background check on ethnic groups that pose an enhanced risk before issuing a policy

#21. A policyholder owns a policy in which he is insured as the breadwinner with permanent insurance and decreasing term insurance in the form of a rider. What type of policy does this insured own?

a) Family Protection Policy
b) Family Income Policy
c) Family Policy
d) Family Maintenance Policy

#22. Which statement is INCORRECT concerning Medicare Part B?

a) It provides limited prescription drug coverage
b) It offers partial coverage for medical expenses not fully covered by Part A
c) It is fully funded by FICA (Social Security taxes)
d) It is referred to as medical insurance

#23. The practicing providers are compensated on a fee-for-service basis under which of the following organizations?

a) Blue Cross/Blue Shield
b) Open panel
c) PPO
d) HMO

#24. What is the main difference between coinsurance and copayments?

a) With coinsurance, the insurance provider pays the entire cost
b) Coinsurance is a set dollar amount
c) Copayment is a set dollar amount
d) With copayments, the insured pays the entire cost

#25. The sole beneficiary of a life insurance policy predeceases the insured. If the policy owner does not change the beneficiary before the insured's death, the proceeds of the policy will go to

a) Probate.
b) The state.
c) The beneficiary's estate.
d) The insured's estate.

#26. Where in the long-term care policy must the insurance company state the renewal provision?

a) In the policy appendix
b) Anywhere the insurance company deems appropriate
c) On the first page
d) In the Provisions and Exclusions section

#27. When a person obtains insurance, what risk management technique are they practicing?

a) Sharing
b) Retention
c) Transfer
d) Avoidance

#28. The Accelerated Benefit provision would have which of the following effects on the benefits paid to the beneficiary?

a) It would decrease the benefits by 70%
b) It would increase the benefits paid to the beneficiary
c) It would reduce the benefits paid to the beneficiary
d) It would not affect the benefits paid to the beneficiary

#29. An applicant is denied insurance due to information found on a consumer report. Which of the following stipulates that the insurer must provide the applicant with the consumer reporting company's name and address?

a) Conditional receipt
b) Disclosure rule
c) Fair Credit Reporting Act
d) Consumer Privacy Act

#30. All long-term care insurers in California must submit to the Commissioner a list of every agent or other insurer representative authorized to solicit individual consumers for the sale of LTC insurance. These submitted agent lists need to be updated at least

a) Monthly.
b) Quarterly.
c) Annually.
d) Semiannually.

#31. An applicant obtained a $70,000 annuity with a single premium and started receiving payments two months later. What type of annuity is it?

a) Flexible
b) Deferred
c) Variable
d) Immediate

#32. The patient is required to pay which of the following under Medicare Part B?

a) 20% of covered charges over and above the deductible
b) 80% of covered charges over and above the deductible
c) All reasonable charges over and above the deductible according to Medicare standards
d) A per-benefit deductible

#33. In employee benefit plans, the selection of coverage refers to

a) The employee selecting benefits.
b) The employer selecting providers.
c) The employer selects the benefits for employees.
d) None of the above.

#34. Which of the following determines a variable life policy's cash value?

a) The policy's guarantees
b) The premium mode
c) The performance of the policy portfolio
d) The company's general account

#35. Insurance is a contract where one party seeks to protect another party from

a) Hazards.
b) Loss.
c) Exposure.
d) Uncertainty.

#36. Under HIPAA, which of the following is INCORRECT regarding eligibility requirements for conversion to an individual policy?

a) The coverage gap for eligibility is 63 or fewer days
b) A person previously covered by group health insurance for six months is eligible
c) A person who has used up COBRA continuation coverage is eligible
d) A person who doesn't qualify for Medicare may be eligible

#37. Business overhead insurance will pay for which of the following in the event of a loss?

a) Medical bills of the business owner
b) Rent
c) Loss of profits
d) Salary of the business owner

#38. The causes of loss covered by an insurance policy are known as

a) Losses.
b) Risks.
c) Hazards.
d) Perils.

#39. In life insurance, liquidity refers to

a) The insured receiving payments every month in retirement.
b) Cash values that can be borrowed at any time.
c) The death benefit supplanting the assets that would have built up if the insured had not died.
d) The policy owner receiving yearly dividend checks.

#40. The automatic premium loan provision is activated at the end of the

a) Free-look period
b) Elimination period.
c) Policy period.
d) Grace period.

#41. In which of the following situations is it illegal for an insurance provider to disclose privileged information about an insured?

a) A researcher for marketing purposes
b) The Department of Insurance to determine legal compliance
c) Law enforcement authorities for law-oriented purposes
d) An auditor for auditing purposes

#42. In a Health Maintenance Organization (HMO), which of the following is another name for a primary care physician?

a) Tracking physician
b) Router
c) Gatekeeper
d) Screener

#43. The section of a disability income policy that specifies the eligible causes of loss under which an insured is presumed to be disabled is the

a) Consideration clause.
b) Probationary period.
c) Insuring clause.
d) Incontestability clause.

#44. Which of these is known as a second-to-die policy?

a) Juvenile life
b) Joint life
c) Survivorship life
d) Family income

#45. What are restricted network provisions concerning Medicare SELECT policies?

a) They decide who can be insured
b) They decide on premium rates
c) They help avoid adverse selection
d) They condition the payment of benefits

#46. An Individual Retirement Account owner is almost 75 years old when she chooses to collect distributions. What is the penalty the IRA owner would pay?

a) 50% tax on the amount that was not distributed as required
b) No penalties since the IRA owner is older than 59 ½
c) 10% for early withdrawal
d) 15% for early withdrawal

#47. Employees will be taxed on the cost of group life coverage paid by the employer if the amount of insurance exceeds

a) $10,000.
b) $15,000.
c) $25,000.
d) $50,000.

#48. Which of the following laws is the basis of the statistical prediction of loss upon which insurance rates are calculated?

a) Law of large numbers
b) Law of masses
c) Law of averages
d) Law of group evaluation

#49. A licensed insurance producer overhears a conversation that leads him to believe an individual is committing fraud. The individual is investigated if the producer submits a written report to law enforcement. However, it turns out that it was an erroneous accusation. What charge will the agent face?

a) No charges; the Insurance Code gives the agent legal immunity
b) Libel, a written untruth
c) A misrepresentation
d) Slander

#50. Which of the following would cause an "any occupation" disability income policy to pay out benefits?

a) The insured begins a new job and is injured due to a more hazardous occupation
b) The insured cannot perform the duties of their specific occupation
c) The insured is unable to perform any jobs in the field related to the insured's experience and education
d) The insured's family has unexpected expenses because of the insured's disability

#51. What percentage of eligible employees must participate in a non-contributory health insurance plan before the plan can become effective?

a) 100%
b) 75%
c) 50%
d) 25%

#52. A couple is about to retire, and they are planning for their golden years. They want to ensure that their retirement annuity will pay monthly benefits for the remainder of their lives. If one person dies, the other would still like to continue receiving benefits. Which settlement option should they select?

a) Joint and Survivor
b) Joint life
c) Life with period certain
d) Straight life

#53. Graded-Premium Whole Life policy premiums are usually lower initially but steadily increase over five to ten years. When the period of increase ends, the premiums will

a) Return to the initial premium amount.
b) Decrease again.
c) Be level after that.
d) Continue to increase.

#54. Which of the following will be TRUE if an insurance provider issues a policy based on an application with unanswered questions?

a) The policy will be void
b) The insurance provider can deny coverage later due to the missing information on the application
c) The policy will be viewed as if the insurance provider waived its right to have an answer on the application
d) The policy will be interpreted as if the insured did not have an answer to the question

#55. Which amount would be taxable yearly if $100,000 of life insurance proceeds were used in a settlement option that paid $13,000 annually for ten years?

a) $3,000
b) $13,000
c) $10,000
d) $7,000

#56. Which of these is NOT covered by a Health Maintenance Organization (HMO)?

a) Well-baby care
b) Elective services
c) Immunizations
d) Routine physicals

#57. Which provision gives the policy owner a period, while coverage is effective, to review a health insurance policy and decide whether or not to keep it?

a) Elimination Period
b) Probationary Period
c) Free Look Period
d) Grace Period

#58. Under which annuity option does the annuitant choose the period for benefits, and the insurance provider determines how much each payment will be?

a) Installment refund
b) Cash refund
c) Installments for a fixed period
d) Installments for a fixed amount

#59. Which of the following is NOT true concerning Equity-Indexed Annuities?

a) The insurer keeps a percentage of the returns
b) They have guaranteed minimum interest rates
c) They are not as risky as variable annuities
d) Compared to fixed annuities, they earn lower interest rates

#60. Which of the following would give the underwriter information regarding an applicant's health history?

a) A medical examination
b) The agent's report
c) The inspection report
d) The Medical Information Bureau

#61. Regarding taxation, how are contributions to a tax-sheltered annuity treated?

a) They are taxed as income to the employee
b) They are taxed as income to the employee but are tax-free once withdrawn
c) They are not included as income for the employee but are taxable upon distribution
d) They are not taxed

#62. Which of the following terms best describes the arrangement in which an insured receives an annual life insurance dividend check?

a) Cash option
b) Reduction of Premium
c) Annual Dividend Provision
d) Accumulation at Interest

#63. Which of the following types of long-term care is NOT provided in an institutional setting?

a) Home health care
b) Custodial care
c) Skilled nursing care
d) Intermediate care

#64. An individual that DOES NOT work on behalf of the insurer for which they do business but rather represents the prospect, client, or insured is called

a) An insurance broker.
b) An insurance solicitor.
c) An insurer's agent.
d) A fiduciary trustee.

#65. Which describes the characteristics of a comprehensive major medical policy?

a) Basic expense and major medical coverage are offered in a single policy
b) The deductible is always expressed as a deferred amount
c) It is identical to major medical insurance
d) There is no coinsurance

#66. In a fixed annuity, who bears all of the investment risk?

a) The beneficiary
b) The annuitant
c) The insurer
d) The owner

#67. Which of the following factors are NOT used by an insurance company to determine the eligibility and rating of applicants for disability income insurance policies?

a) The applicant's age and gender
b) Income requirement and elimination period
c) The number of catastrophic losses in a given period
d) Job classification, avocation, and the applicant's past and present health

#68. Skilled care would more than likely be provided in which of the following locations?

a) At a doctor's office
b) In an institutional setting
c) At the patient's home
d) In an outpatient setting

#69. Under a group insurance policy, when an employee's coverage is terminated, the coverage remains in force

a) Until the employee can secure coverage under a new group plan.
b) Until the employee notifies the group insurance provider that a coverage conversion policy is issued.
c) For 31 days.
d) For 60 days.

#70. What type of care is provided with intermediate care in LTC insurance?

a) Nonmedical daily care
b) Daily care, but not nursing care
c) Intensive care
d) Occasional nursing or rehabilitative care

#71. Which of the following is an eligibility requirement for all Social Security Disability Income benefits?

a) Be at least age 50
b) Have attained fully insured status
c) Be disabled for at least one year
d) Have permanent kidney failure

#72. A long stretch of national economic hardship results in a 7% inflation rate. A policyholder notices that the face value of his life insurance policy increased by 7% because of this. Which policy rider caused this change?

a) Cost of Living Rider
b) Value Adjustment Rider
c) Return of Premium Rider
d) Inflation Rider

#73. If an annuity or retirement plan is qualified, this means

a) It has an early withdrawal penalty.
b) It accepts after-tax contributions.
c) It is noncancelable.
d) The IRS approves it.

#74. An individual who does not lock the doors to their house or does not repair broken windows demonstrates an indifferent attitude. This individual presents what type of hazard?

a) Legal
b) Physical
c) Morale
d) Moral

#75. An applicant properly notifies her insurance provider of a straightforward claim. However, the insurance company waits an immensely long time to process it. Which of the following terms best describes the insurer's behavior?

a) Misrepresentation
b) Fraud
c) Unfair claims settlement practice
d) There is nothing wrong with this incident; there is no specified deadline for insurance providers to process a claim

#76. Which of the following would be exempt from the California Department of Insurance's jurisdiction?

a) An insurance provider that offers coverage for chiropractic services
b) A producer who transacts insurance in the state of California
c) Health care service plan
d) An admitted insurer subject to jurisdiction in Nevada

#77. Which foundational principle of insurance states that if a policy allows for greater compensation than the financial loss sustained, the insured can only receive benefits for the amount lost?

a) Indemnity
b) Stop-loss
c) Consideration
d) Reasonable expectations

#78. The Small Employer classification means any individual actively engaged in a business that, on at least 50% of its working days during the previous year, employed

a) No more than 50 employees.
b) At least ten and not more than 100 employees.
c) No more than 25 employees.
d) At least three and not more than 25 employees.

#79. Which of the following is true of the distributions when contributions are made to an immediate annuity with before-tax dollars?

a) Distributions are taxable
b) Distributions are not taxable
c) Distributions cannot begin before age 72
d) There are no distributions

#80. Employer contributions made to a qualified plan

a) Are taxed annually as salary.
b) Are subject to vesting requirements.
c) Can discriminate in favor of highly paid employees.
d) Are after-tax contributions.

#81. Under the Accidental Death and Dismemberment (AD&D) coverage, what type of benefit will be paid to the beneficiary in the event of the insured's accidental death?

a) Capital sum
b) Double the amount of the death benefit
c) Refund of premiums
d) Principal sum

#82. What amount can a supplier or physician bill for a particular supply or service?

a) Assignment
b) Coinsurance
c) Approved amount
d) Actual charge

#83. At age 35, an applicant wants to obtain insurance. She realizes that her insurance needs will likely change and wants a policy that can be modified to accommodate those changes as they take place throughout her life. Which of the following policies would most likely fit her needs?

a) Single Premium Whole Life
b) Interest-sensitive Whole Life
c) Decreasing Term
d) Adjustable Life

#84. If an insurer offers Medicare supplement policies, it has to offer which of the following plans?

a) A-N
b) A
c) A and B
d) A-J

#85. The following individuals are covered by a High Deductible Health Plan (HDHP). Also, they are not claimed as dependents on another person's tax returns. Which would NOT be eligible for a Health Savings Account (HSA)?

a) Sophia is 67 and is covered by a basic medical expense policy
b) Blanche is 55 and is covered under a dental care policy
c) Rose is 60 and also has a long-term care insurance plan
d) Dorothy is 40 and is not covered by any other health insurance

#86. In an insurance policy, which of the following does NOT have to be identified?

a) The first named insured
b) The insurance company's financial rating
c) The stated periodic premium
d) A statement of insurable interest

#87. What type of health care plan has features of an HMO and PPO?

a) FSA
b) POS
c) HIPPA
d) MET

#88. Employer-paid group disability income insurance premiums are

a) Tax-deductible by the employee.
b) Tax-deferred to the employer.
c) Deductible by the employer as a business expense.
d) Taxable to the employee.

#89. What is the benefit of selecting extended term as a nonforfeiture option?

a) It matures at age 100
b) It allows for coverage to continue past the maturity date
c) It can be converted to a fixed annuity
d) It has the highest insurance protection amount

#90. When the insured chooses the extended term nonforfeiture option, the cash value will be used to obtain term insurance with what face amount?

a) In lesser amounts for the policy's remaining term of age 100
b) The same amount as the cash value from the surrendered policy
c) An amount equal to the original policy minus the cash value
d) An amount equal to the original policy for as long as the cash values will obtain

#91. Under a long-term care policy, what is the elimination period?

a) The number of consecutive days during which benefits are paid
b) The period that benefits are received tax-free
c) The period during which no benefits are paid
d) The period the insured will have to review the policy and return it for a full refund

#92. An applicant for insurance receives a conditional receipt but dies before the policy can be issued. The insurance provider will

a) Pay the proceeds of the policy up to an established limit.
b) Not pay the proceeds of the policy in any event.
c) Automatically pay the proceeds of the policy.
d) Pay the policy's proceeds only if it would have issued the policy.

#93. In an HMO, who selects a primary care physician?

a) The individual member
b) Subscribers of an HMO do not have a primary care physician
c) The insurance provider
d) A referral physician

#94. An agent selling variable annuities is required to be registered with

a) The Guaranty Association.
b) SEC.
c) FINRA.
d) Department of Insurance.

#95. Which of the following is NOT a service or a characteristic of an HMO plan?

a) Contracting with insurance companies
b) Providing free annual checkups
c) Encouraging early treatment
d) Providing care on an outpatient basis

#96. On a guaranteed renewable health insurance policy, insurance providers can change which of the following?

a) Coverage
b) Individual rates
c) No changes are permitted
d) Rates by class

#97. An insurer wants to obtain an applicant's insurance history. Which source provides coded information to insurers about the information included in prior applications for insurance?

a) Federal Bureau of Investigation
b) Medical Information Bureau
c) Insurer's Protection Guild
d) Integrated Insurer's Support

#98. Compared with that of a joint life policy, the premium of a survivorship life policy would be

a) As high.
b) Half the amount.
c) Lower.
d) Higher.

#99. In decreasing term insurance, which policy component decreases?

a) Dividend
b) Premium
c) Face amount
d) Cash value

#100. An insured obtained a life insurance policy on his life. He names his wife as the primary beneficiary and his son as the contingent beneficiary. Under what circumstances could the son collect the death benefit?

a) If the insured died from accidental means
b) If the primary beneficiary dies before the insured
c) Both the primary and contingent beneficiaries will share death benefits equally
d) With the written consent of the primary beneficiary

#101. Which of the following is true regarding a policy with a face value of less than $10,000?

a) If it is returned during the free-look period, the policy will be canceled, and the insurance provider will retain the premium paid
b) The policy can be canceled at any time with a full premium refund
c) The policy will be void if it is returned during the free-look period
d) An insured cannot return the policy

#102. Workers compensation benefits are regulated by which entity?

a) Insurer
b) Federal government
c) State government
d) Employer

#103. When a policy contains an automatic premium loan provision, what will happen if the insured dies before the loan is paid back?

a) The beneficiary of the policy will take over the loan payments
b) The policy becomes null and void
c) The loan balance will be deducted from the death benefit
d) The policy beneficiary receives the full death benefit

#104. What are the consequences of a failure to comply with the Commissioner's office while executing a seizure order?

a) It can become grounds for license termination and revocation of all agency contracts
b) It is a felony and is punishable by five years in prison and restitution to victims proportionate to damages claimed
c) It would be considered obstruction of justice and subject to a fine of $5,000 per day
d) It is a misdemeanor punishable by one year in prison, a fine of $1,000, or both

#105. The agent is referred to as the "Field Underwriter" due to the information they collect for the insurance company. This helps the insurer to

a) Reduce the number of underwriters.
b) Avoid adverse selection.
c) Comply with State law.
d) Learn about the underwriting process.

#106. Which of these following occupations will have the lowest disability insurance premiums?

a) Firefighter
b) Personal Trainer
c) Construction worker
d) Stunt performer

#107. An insured wants to ensure that upon his death, the life insurance policy will pay a portion of the proceeds each year to his spouse. He also wants to ensure that their children receive the principal when they reach a certain age. Which settlement option should the insured choose?

a) Fixed amount option
b) Interest-only option
c) Life income with period certain
d) Joint and survivor

#108. The individual, not the employer, owns Health Savings Accounts (HSAs), which means the individual is not dependent on a specific employer to enjoy the advantages of an HSA. What term best describes this?

a) Attached
b) Stationary
c) Portable
d) Mobile

#109. Partners in a company enter into a buy-sell agreement to obtain life insurance. The policy specifies that if one partner dies prematurely, the other would be financially able to buy the deceased partner's interest. What type of policy can be used to fund this agreement?

a) Term insurance only
b) Permanent insurance only
c) Universal life insurance only
d) Any form of life insurance

#110. The mode of premium payment

a) Is the method used to calculate the policy's cash surrender value.
b) Does not affect the amount of premium paid.
c) Is defined as the amount and the frequency of the premium payment.
d) Is the factor that determines a policy's dividend amount.

#111. Medical expense insurance consists of which of the following three basic coverages?

a) Basic, Major, Overhead
b) Medical, Dental, Vision
c) Reimbursement, Preventive, Service
d) Hospital, Surgical, Medical

#112. According to the California Insurance Code, any producer caught violating the regulations concerning misrepresentation will be charged with a

a) Misdemeanor, a possible 1-year imprisonment, and a fine not to exceed $500.
b) Felony, a possible 2 - 5-year imprisonment, and a fine not to exceed $2,000.
c) Felony, a possible 2-year imprisonment, and a fine not to exceed $5,000.
d) Misdemeanor, a fine not to exceed $25,000, and a possible 1-year imprisonment.

#113. How does a member of an HMO see a specialist?

a) HMOs do not cover specialists
b) The member is allowed to select their own specialist
c) The primary care physician refers the HMO member
d) The insurance provider chooses the specialist

#114. When a client replaces an existing Medicare Supplement or LTC insurance policy with another from the same insurer, California law requires that

a) The agent has to advise the client about HICAP and its related services.
b) A copy of the replacement notice must be submitted to the local HICAP office within three business days.
c) Replacement by the same insurer is illegal.
d) None of the above

#115. Which is usually true concerning insureds who have been classified as preferred risks?

a) They can choose when to pay their monthly premiums
b) They keep a higher percentage of their policies' earned interest
c) Their premiums are lower
d) They can borrow a higher amount from their policies

#116. When a whole life policy is surrendered before it matures, the cash value can be used to

a) Pay back all past-due premiums plus interest.
b) Receive payments for a fixed amount.
c) Obtain a single premium policy for a reduced face amount.
d) Obtain a term rider to attach to the policy.

#117. An insured obtained a 10-year level term life policy guaranteed renewable and convertible. What occurs at the end of the 10-year term?

a) The insured has to provide evidence of insurability to renew the policy
b) The insured can only convert the policy to another term policy
c) The insured can renew the policy for another ten years at the same premium
d) The insured can renew the policy for another ten years but at a higher premium

#118. Which of the following people would automatically qualify for Medi-Cal benefits?

a) An individual with low income under the age of 65
b) An individual receiving Social Security payments
c) An individual receiving Supplemental Security Income assistance
d) A child under the age of 21

#119. Which of the following is NOT a disadvantage of self-insurance?

a) It can leave the organization exposed to catastrophic loss
b) Self-insurance allows insureds to finance losses that cannot be insured
c) There may be greater variations in costs from year to year than projected
d) Self-insurance can create adverse employee and public relations

#120. Which of the following determines the interest rates paid to the owner of a fixed annuity?

a) The insured's investment performance
b) A statewide pre-determined annual interest rate
c) An insurance provider's guaranteed minimum interest rate
d) The investment performance of the insurance provider

#121. A whole life insurance policy has premiums adjusted so that during the policy's first few years, the premiums are lower than those of a straight whole life policy. In the ensuing years, the premiums are higher than those of a straight whole life policy. What type of whole life policy is this?

a) Indeterminate premium
b) Enhanced life
c) Modified life
d) Indexed life

#122. All of these are personal uses of life insurance EXCEPT

a) Buy-sell agreement.
b) Survivor protection.
c) Estate creation.
d) Cash accumulation.

#123. Who will be affected by the share of cost requirement for Medi-Cal?

a) A nonresident insured
b) Individuals under the age of 65
c) Individuals who receive money from other assistance programs
d) Individuals whose income exceeds the limit for Medi-Cal

#124. The Waiver of Monthly Deductions (Waiver of Cost of Insurance) rider is found in what type of insurance?

a) Joint and Survivor
b) Juvenile Life
c) Universal Life
d) Whole Life

#125. Which of the following insurance types covers the entire family in a single policy?

a) Family Income Policy
b) Survivorship Policy
c) Whole Life Policy
d) Family Policy

#126. Which of the following is true regarding elimination periods and the cost of coverage?

a) A longer elimination period has a higher cost of coverage
b) Elimination periods do not affect the cost of coverage
c) A longer elimination period has a lower cost of coverage
d) A shorter elimination period has a lower cost of coverage

#127. Why is it necessary for an insurance company to document all correspondence with an insured?

a) State law
b) Federal law
c) Errors and omissions
d) Statistics gathering

#128. The insured's health policy only covers medical costs related to accidents. Which of the following policy types does the insured have?

a) Restrictive
b) Accidental Death
c) Comprehensive
d) Accident-only

#129. A producer solicited a policy for a client who originally qualified for standard premiums. The applicant was rated as a substandard risk during the underwriting process and charged a higher premium. Upon policy delivery, the producer failed to mention that the premiums would be higher, and the client filed a lawsuit against the insurer. This scenario is an example of

a) Concealment, which an Errors and Omissions (E&O) policy will not cover.
b) An unfair claim settlement.
c) An omission, which an Errors and Omissions (E&O) policy will cover.
d) A misrepresentation and is unlawful.

#130. What is a share of cost (SOC)?

a) An insured's annual copayment for covered medical services
b) The amount an individual has to cover for medical expenses before Medi-Cal pays the rest
c) A monthly payment to Medi-Cal by the insured
d) The amount covered by Medi-Cal for medical bills

#131. Under an individual disability policy, the MINIMUM period in which claim payments have to be made to an insured is

a) Within 45 days.
b) Weekly.
c) Biweekly.
d) Monthly.

#132. A person was involved in a head-on collision while driving home one day. Her injuries were not serious, and she recovered. However, she decided never to be involved in another accident, and she would not drive or ride in a car ever again. Which risk management method does this describe?

a) Avoidance
b) Reduction
c) Sharing
d) Retention

#133. Under a disability policy, a small business owner is the insured that funds a buy-sell agreement. If the owner becomes disabled or dies, the policy would provide which of the following?

a) Disability insurance for the owner
b) Cash to the business partner of the owner to accomplish a buyout
c) The rent money for the building
d) The salary of the business manager

#134. If an insured continually uses the automatic premium loan option to pay the policy premium,

a) The cash value will continue to increase.
b) The insurance provider will increase the amount of the premium.
c) The policy is terminated when the cash value is decreased to nothing.
d) The face amount of the policy will be decreased by the amount of the automatic premium loan.

#135. Which of the following is NOT provided by an HMO?

a) Services
b) Financing
c) Patient care
d) Reimbursement

#136. On what kind of premium is Variable Life insurance based?

a) Decreasing
b) Graded
c) Level, fixed
d) Increasing

#137. Any insurance producer who conducts insurance business and is guilty of violating the Code with respect to insurance replacement shall on the first violation be

a) Fined a sum of $10,000.
b) Suspended from licensing for 180 days.
c) Fined a sum of $5,000.
d) Fined a sum of $1,000.

#138. Most long-term care plans have which of the following characteristics?

a) Variable premiums
b) Open enrollment
c) Guaranteed renewability
d) No elimination period

#139. An employee pays a $50 monthly premium for her group health coverage. The employer has been contributing $150 for the total monthly cost of $200. What would be her maximum monthly premium for COBRA coverage if the employee leaves the company?

a) $50.50
b) $150
c) $204
d) $50

#140. Qualified LTC policies covering home care have to provide benefits if the insured is impaired in at least two of the six activities of daily living (ADLs). The term "impaired" means

a) Unable to perform any of the ADLs.
b) Has Parkinson's disease.
c) Needs occasional assistance with ADLs.
d) Needs substantial hands-on or standby assistance with ADLs.

#141. Which of the following terms is the closest to an authorized insurer?

a) Certified
b) Licensed
c) Legal
d) Admitted

#142. The coverage provided by a disability income policy that does not pay benefits for losses occurring due to the insured's employment is called

a) Occupational coverage.
b) Workers compensation.
c) Nonoccupational coverage.
d) Unemployment coverage.

#143. Medi-Cal is intended to provide health insurance primarily for individuals who are

a) Substandard risks.
b) Between the ages of 21 and 65.
c) Not extended medical insurance by their employer.
d) Low-income and uninsured.

#144. Under the Affordable Care Act (ACA), health insurance can no longer be underwritten based on which of the following factors?

a) The applicant's health condition
b) The applicant's family composition
c) The applicant's age
d) The applicant's tobacco use

#145. During policy delivery, which of the following is an agent's responsibility?

a) Issue the policy to the applicant if they are present
b) Decline or approve the risk
c) Collect a medical statement from the physician
d) Collect payment at the time of policy delivery

#146. The party affected by unintentional or intentional concealment is entitled to which of the following?

a) Estoppel
b) Waiver of concealed conditions
c) Subrogation of a contract
d) Rescission of a contract

#147. What is the classification of a business that has 30 employees who engage in business on at least 50% of its working days during the previous calendar year?

a) Partnership
b) Participating plan
c) Association
d) Small employer

#148. Attempting to determine how much insurance a person would need based on their financial goals is known as

a) Needs approach.
b) Human life value approach.
c) Estate planning.
d) Viatical approach.

#149. What describes the specific information about a policy?

a) Illustrations
b) Buyer's guide
c) Producer's report
d) Policy summary

#150. The part of Medicare that helps pay for inpatient hospital care, inpatient care in a skilled nursing facility, home health care, and hospice care is called

a) Part A.
b) Part B.
c) Part C.
d) Part D.

Practice Exam 2 Answers

#1. **c) MIB reports are gathered from information doctors and hospitals supplied.**

The information in MIB reports comes from the underwriting disclosures of applicants to MIB member insurance companies on past insurance applications. (pp. 70, 72, 159-160)

#2. **d) Guaranteed renewable**

Medicare supplements need to be at least guaranteed renewable. (p. 218)

#3. **c) Both the agent and the applicant**

Before issuing a replacement policy, the insurance provider must give the applicant a notice regarding replacement. It must be signed by both the agent and the applicant. (p. 127)

#4. **c) $5,000**

When the primary plan has paid its full benefit, the insured submits the claim to the secondary, or excess, provider for any additional benefits that may be payable. (p. 177)

#5. **a) Hazards.**

Conditions like existing health and lifestyle or activities such as scuba diving are hazards. They can increase the likelihood of a loss occurring. (pp. 2-3)

#6. **b) The insured's dependent's condition will not affect his eligibility or rating**

There should be no consideration of the dependent's disability when the group member qualifies for coverage beyond set guidelines that will apply to all dependents of those covered. (pp. 177, 179)

#7. **b) Every year, on or before March 1**

Every year, on or before March 1, each insurance company doing business in California must report its financial condition to the Commissioner. (p. 48)

#8. **c) Application**

A person can submit an application to an insurance provider requesting that the insurer review the information and issue an insurance contract. (p. 14)

#9. **d) This rider is available to every insured with no additional premium.**

The guaranteed insurability rider can be set up to allow for specific additional amounts of insurance to be obtained at specific dates, ages, and events without providing evidence of insurability. However, the coverage is obtained at the insured's attained age, and the maximum allowable purchase is specified in the base policy. This rider typically expires at the insured's age of 40. (p. 109)

#10. **b) The loss has to be catastrophic**

To be characterized as a pure risk, the loss has to be definite, measurable, predictable, and due to chance, but not catastrophic. (p. 2)

#11. **d) Darrell will be more likely to receive a larger benefit since he has more financial obligations**

The insurance provider will be reluctant to write as much benefit for Vinnie as it would for Darrell. Suppose Vinnie becomes disabled, with the amount of disability income and the interest income from the investments. In that case, he might not be anxious to return to work as Darrell would be, simply due to the differences in their financial obligations. (p. 196)

#12. **c) Policy owner to renew the policy to a stated age, with the insurer having the right to raise premiums on the entire class.**

Coverage is guaranteed; however, the insurer can adjust rates for the entire class. (pp. 154-155)

#13. **a) Trained and certified volunteers.**

Although there are paid staff supervisors, counselors are volunteers who receive thorough training and registration. (p. 223)

#14. **c) Metal level classification**

Besides self-insured plans, other plans are categorized into four levels determined by how much of a person's expected health care costs are covered. The four plans include bronze, silver, gold, and platinum, referred to as the metal level classification. (pp. 186-187)

#15. **b) They are insurers**

Blue Cross and Blue Shield organizations have contractual agreements with hospitals and physicians. Blue Plans are voluntary, not-for-profit health care organizations. Some states have recently amended their structure to become for-profit entities. Still, they are not insurers. (p. 155)

#16. **c) Preferred**

A preferred status means an insured is in excellent physical condition and employs healthy habits and lifestyles. These individuals are eligible for lower premiums than those in the lower categories. (p. 74)

#17. **a) Protecting the insurance provider against adverse selection.**

A profitable distribution of exposures exists when preferred risks are balanced with poor risks, with the standard risks in the "middle." Distributing risks this way protects the insurance provider from adverse selection. (p. 3)

#18. **b) Skilled care.**

Skilled care is generally provided in an institutional setting. Respite care, custodial care, adult day care, and home health care are all coverages used to reduce the need to be admitted into a care facility. (pp. 229-230)

#19. **a) It can last for the annuitant's lifetime**

In the annuity period, accumulated funds are converted into a stream of income that can last for the annuitant's lifetime. (p. 114)

#20. **b) To give the client some flexibility in determining their own premium**

The clients' choice of elimination period allows them to balance premium expenses and benefits. (pp. 162, 174)

#21. **b) Family Income Policy**

Under a family income policy, if the insured dies during the income period, monthly benefits are paid to the survivors for the remainder of the income phase. The beneficiary is then paid the death benefit. (p. 86)

#22. **c) It is fully funded by FICA (Social Security taxes)**

Part B is subsidized by monthly premiums and funded from the federal government's general revenues. (pp. 209-212)

#23. **c) PPO**

PPOs contract on a fee-for-service basis. (pp. 156, 168)

#24. **c) Copayment is a set dollar amount**

With coinsurance and copayment provisions, the insured shares part of the cost for services with the insurance provider. Unlike coinsurance, a copayment has a set dollar amount that the insured will pay every time particular medical services are used. (pp. 153, 167)

#25. **d) The insured's estate.**

Without a living beneficiary, proceeds will be paid to the insured's estate. (p. 96)

#26. **c) On the first page**

A renewal provision must be captioned on the policy's first page. (p. 232)

#27. **c) Transfer**

Insurance is a transfer of the risk of financial loss from a covered peril from the insured to the insurer. (p. 4)

#28. **c) It will reduce the benefits paid to the beneficiary**

The Accelerated Benefit provision allows the early payment of some portion of the death benefit if the insured is confined to a long-term care facility or becomes terminally ill. (pp. 109, 110, 145)

#29. **c) Fair Credit Reporting Act**

The Fair Credit Reporting Act stipulates what information can be collected and how it can be used. (p. 71)

#30. **d) Semiannually.**

The insurance provider must submit an updated list semiannually of every agent authorized to solicit long-term care insurance. (p. 110)

#31. **d) Immediate**

With an immediate annuity, distribution starts within one year of purchase. (p. 115)

#32. **a) 20% of covered charges over and above the deductible**

As mandated by Medicare, the patient has to pay 20% of covered charges above the deductible. (pp. 209-212)

#33. **a) The employee selecting benefits.**

The selection of coverage lets the employee select benefits that best suit their needs. There might also be a choice of providers for coverage. (p. 133)

#34. **c) The performance of the policy portfolio**

A variable life policy's cash value is not guaranteed. It fluctuates with the portfolio's performance in which the insurance company has invested the premiums. (p. 90)

#35. **b) Loss.**

Insurance will protect an individual, business, or entity from loss. (p. 2)

#36. **b) A person previously covered by group health insurance for six months is eligible**

All of these eligibility requirements are correct, except for a person previously covered for at least six months. HIPAA requires that the person have continuous creditable health coverage for at least 18 months. (pp. 73, 183-184)

#37. **b) Rent**

Business overhead insurance will provide the funds needed to pay the salary of employees other than the owners and their other ongoing business expenses, such as rent. (p. 64)

#38. **d) Perils.**

In an insurance policy, perils are the causes of loss covered by the insurer. (p. 2)

#39. **b) Cash values that can be borrowed at any time.**

In life insurance, liquidity refers to the insured's availability of cash through cash values. (p. 63)

#40. **d) Grace period.**

Provided the policy has sufficient cash value, this provision triggers a loan at the end of the grace period to keep a policy in force. (p. 100)

#41. **a) A researcher for marketing purposes**

There are specific circumstances in which it is legal for an insurance provider to disclose privileged information about an insured, including law enforcement, auditing, and legal purposes. (pp. 158-159)

#42. **c) Gatekeeper**

Initially, the member selects a primary care physician or "gatekeeper." If the member requires the attention of a specialist, the primary care physician must refer the member. This process helps keep the member from seeing the higher-priced specialists unless absolutely necessary. (pp. 167-168)

#43. **c) Insuring clause.**

The insuring clause is a provision on the first page of the disability income policy that specifies the coverage and when it applies. (pp. 94, 194)

#44. **c) Survivorship life**

Survivorship life (also called last survivor or second-to-die) is similar to joint life. It insures two or more lives for a premium determined by a joint age. (p. 87)

#45. **d) They condition the payment of benefits**

A Medicare SELECT policy includes restricted network provisions that condition the payment of benefits on the use of network providers. (p. 219)

#46. **a) 50% tax on the amount that was not distributed as required**

Distributions must begin no later than age 72 (previously 70 ½) for the annuitant to avoid a 50% penalty of the shortfall from the required annual amount. (pp. 137, 147)

#47. **d) $50,000**

The employee is taxed for the cost of coverage paid by the employer exceeding $50,000. (p. 91)

#48. **a) Law of large numbers**

The law of large numbers is the foundation for the statistical prediction of loss upon which rates for insurance are calculated. (p. 3)

#49. **a) No charges; the Insurance Code gives the agent legal immunity**

Insurance providers, agents, and brokers have legal immunity from civil suits claiming slander or libel. These claims could result from filing reports, giving statements, or furnishing any other information, provided the information is offered in good faith. (p. 57)

#50. **c) The insured is unable to perform any jobs in the field related to the insured's experience and education**

A policy containing an "any occupation" provision will only provide benefits when the insured cannot perform any of the duties of the occupation for which they are suited because of experience, training, or education. (pp. 194, 195)

#51. **a) 100%**

If the plan is noncontributory, 100% of the eligible employees have to be included before the plan becomes effective, and the participants do not pay part of the premium. The employer pays the whole premium. (p. 133)

#52. **a) Joint and Survivor**

The Joint and Survivor option guarantees an income for two or more recipients that neither can outlive. (p. 103)

#53. **c) Be level after that.**

The premium amounts for a Graded-Premium Whole Life policy are typically 50% lower than premiums for straight life policies. The premium increases incrementally for five or ten years and then remains level. (p. 85)

#54. **c) The policy will be viewed as if the insurance provider waived its right to have an answer on the application**

When a policy is issued with questions left unanswered, the contract will be interpreted as if the insurer waived its right to have an answer to the question. It will not be able to deny coverage later due to unanswered questions. (p. 68)

#55. **a) $3,000**

Suppose $100,000 of life insurance proceeds was used in a settlement option paying $13,000 yearly over ten years. In that circumstance, $10,000 per year would be tax-free (as principal), and $3,000 per year would be taxed as interest. (p. 145)

#56. **b) Elective services**

HMOs emphasize preventive health care as a way to decrease medical costs through the early detection of health problems before they require more costly treatment. (pp. 155, 167-168)

#57. **c) Free Look Period**

The Free Look provision gives a policyholder ten days after the policy is delivered to decide whether or not they want the policy. If the policyholder chooses to return the policy within this period, they receive a full refund of all paid premiums. (pp. 96, 126)

#58. **c) Installments for a fixed period**

Under the Installments for a Fixed Period option, the annuitant chooses the period for the benefits, and the insurance provider determines how much each payment will be. This option only pays for a specified period, and there are no life contingencies. (p. 118)

#59. **d) Compared to fixed annuities, they earn lower interest rates**

Equity-indexed annuities are not as risky as variable annuities or mutual funds. They are expected to earn a higher interest rate than a fixed annuity. (p. 116)

#60. **d) The Medical Information Bureau**

Only the MIB will provide information about the medical history of an applicant. (pp. 70, 72, 159-160)

#61. **c) They are not included as income for the employee but are taxable upon distribution**

Funds contributed are excluded from the employee's current taxable income until withdrawn. (pp. 119, 138, 146-148)

#62. **a) Cash option**

The cash option lets an insurer send the policy owner an annual, nontaxable dividend check. (pp. 102, 144)

#63. **a) Home health care**

Home health care is administered in the home. Skilled nursing, intermediate, and custodial care can all be administered in an institutional setting. (p. 230)

#64. **a) An insurance broker.**

An individual who does not work on behalf of the company for which they do business but rather represents the prospect, insured, or client is called an insurance broker. (p. 21)

#65. **a) Basic expense and major medical coverage are offered in a single policy**

A comprehensive major medical plan combines basic expense and major medical coverage, sold as a single policy. (p. 167)

#66. **c) The insurer**

Fixed annuities guarantee a minimum interest amount to be credited to the purchase payment. Income payments are the same from one payment to the next. The insurer can afford to make guarantees because the money of a fixed annuity is placed in the insurer's general account, which is part of its investment portfolio. The insurer makes conservative enough investments to ensure a guaranteed rate to the annuity owners. (p. 116)

#67. **c) The number of catastrophic losses in a given period**

Catastrophic conditions (e.g., fires, floods, earthquakes, etc.) are considered when writing medical expense insurance. (pp. 178-179, 196-197)

#68. **b) In an institutional setting.**

Skilled care is performed under the supervision of a physician, generally in an institutional setting. (p. 229)

#69. **c) For 31 days**

Under the conversion privilege, an employee has 31 days to convert to an individual policy. (p. 136)

#70. **d) Occasional nursing or rehabilitative care**

Intermediate care in LTC insurance is nursing and rehabilitative care given by medical professionals for stable conditions requiring less frequent assistance than skilled care. (p. 229)

#71. **b) Have attained fully insured status**

Although Social Security offers many benefits, like retirement, survivors, and Medicare, only those who have attained fully insured status are eligible for Disability Income benefits. Contributing to Social Security for ten years (40 quarters) attains fully insured status. (p. 139)

#72. **a) Cost of Living Rider**

The Cost of Living rider adjusts the policy's face value annually according to the national rate of inflation or deflation. This rider adjusts the policy's face amount to correspond with the inflation rate, keeping the policy's initial value constant over time. (p. 109)

#73. **d) The IRS approves it.**

The IRS approves qualified retirement plans, giving the employee and employer benefits like tax-deferred growth and deductible contributions. (pp. 119, 136-137)

#74. **c) Morale**

A morale hazard is someone who has an indifferent attitude towards an insurer. They are irresponsible or careless because they know their loss will be covered. (p. 3)

#75. **c) Unfair claims settlement practice**

When an insurance provider knowingly or frequently commits an act that deceives or neglects an insured, its behavior is an unfair claim settlement practice. In this circumstance, there is no reason why the insurance provider was warranted in waiting to process the claim. (pp. 51-52)

#76. **d) An admitted insurer subject to jurisdiction in Nevada**

All entities that offer coverage intended to pay for the services and expenses of health care providers must be under the jurisdiction of the California Department of Insurance (CDI). (pp. 179-180)

#77. **a) Indemnity**

The principle of indemnity stipulates that the insured can only be compensated for the amount of the loss, even if the policy is written with larger benefit limits. (p. 6)

#78. **a) No more than 50 employees.**

The insurance code's classification rules stipulate that a Small Employer is any individual involved in a business that, on at least 50% of its working days during the previous year, employed not more than 50 eligible employees. (p. 176)

#79. **a) Distributions are taxable**

If contributions are made with pre-tax dollars, contributions are fully taxable. Distributions must begin no later than age 72 (previously 70 ½) for the annuitant to avoid a penalty, which is 50% of the shortfall from the required annual amount. (pp. 115, 146-148)

#80. **b) Are subject to vesting requirements.**

Qualified plans need to have a vesting requirement. (p. 137)

#81. **d) Principal sum**

Accidental Death and Dismemberment (AD&D) insurance only covers accidental losses and is considered a pure form of accident coverage. The principal sum is the type of benefit that is paid for accidental death. In case of accidental dismemberment or the loss of sight, a percentage of that principal sum will be paid by the policy, often called the capital sum. (p. 173)

#82. **d) Actual charge**

Actual charge is the amount a supplier or physician bills for a particular supply or service. (p. 211)

#83. **d) Adjustable Life**

Adjustable Life policies allow for increases or decreases in the premium or face amount, provided that the premium is sufficient to pay for the mortality. Any increase in the face amount requires proof of insurability. (p. 88)

#84. **b) A**

An insurer needs to make available to every applicant a policy form offering the basic core benefits (Plan A) if it provides any Medicare supplement policies. An insurer does not have to issue all or any of the plans B through N. (p. 216)

#85. **a) Sophia is 67 and is covered by a basic medical expense policy**

A person must have a High Deductible Health Plan (HDHP) to be eligible for a Health Savings Account (HSA). They cannot be covered by other health insurance except for accident, disability, specific injury, dental care, vision care, or long-term care insurance. The individual also cannot be eligible for Medicare (usually age 65), and cannot be claimed as a dependent on someone else's tax return. (pp. 171-172)

#86. **b) The insurance company's financial rating**

The financial rating of an insurance provider does not have to be stated in a policy. (p. 13)

#87. **b) POS**

With the Point-Of-Service (POS) plan, the employees do not have to be locked into one plan or decide between the two plans. Each time a need for medical services arises, a different choice can be made. (p. 169)

#88. **c) Deductible by the employer as a business expense.**

Group disability income premiums paid by the employer are tax-deductible to the business as a business expense. The premium payments are neither tax-deductible nor taxable to the employee. (p. 201)

#89. **d) It has the highest insurance protection amount**

Under this option, the insurance provider uses the policy's cash value to convert to term insurance for the same face amount as the previous permanent policy. The length of the new term coverage lasts for as long of a duration as the amount of cash value will purchase. (p. 100)

#90. **d) An amount equal to the original policy for as long as the cash values will obtain**

With this option, the cash value is used as a single premium to obtain the same face amount as the original policy for as long as the cash will purchase at the insured's current age. (p. 100)

#91. **c) The period during which no benefits are paid**

The elimination period begins on the day that the policy becomes effective. This period is the amount of time (typically 0-365 days) that no benefits will be paid. LTC policies usually have a 30-day elimination period. (p. 233)

#92. **d) Pay the policy's proceeds only if it would have issued the policy.**

The conditional receipt states that coverage will be effective either on the date of the medical exam or the date of the application, whichever occurs last. The applicant must be found to be insurable as a standard risk. The policy is issued as the applicant applied for it. (p. 68)

#93. **a) The individual member**

When a person becomes a member of the HMO, they pick a primary care physician. Once selected, the primary care physician will be regularly compensated for the responsibility of caring for that member. (pp. 167-168)

#94. **c) FINRA.**

Since variable annuities are considered securities, an individual must be registered with FINRA (formerly NASD) and possess a securities license in addition to a life agent's license to sell variable annuities. (p.117)

#95. **a) Contracting with insurance companies**

HMOs identify medical issues early by providing preventive care. They encourage early treatment and, whenever possible, provide care on an outpatient basis rather than admitting the insured into the hospital. Contracts are between the member and the HMO, not an insurer. (pp. 167-168)

#96. **d) Rates by class**

Concerning a guaranteed renewable health insurance policy, the insurance provider can only increase premiums on a class, not an individual policy. (pp. 154-155)

#97. **b) Medical Information Bureau**

The Medical Information Bureau receives information provided by an applicant on insurance applications and issues it in a coded format to insurers who ask for these reports. MIB information alone cannot be used to decline a risk, but it can help provide insurers with critical information. (pp. 70, 72, 159-160)

#98. **c) Lower.**

Because the death benefit is not paid out until the last death, the survivorship life policy results in a lower premium than that usually charged for joint life. (p. 87)

#99. **c) Face amount**

Decreasing term policies have a level premium and a death benefit that decreases yearly over the policy term. (pp. 82, 83)

#100. **b) If the primary beneficiary dies before the insured**

As the contingent beneficiary, the son would have to outlive the insured and primary beneficiary. (pp. 98-99)

#101. **c) The policy will be void if it is returned during the free look period**

If the owner returns the policy within the free-look period, the contract will be void from its beginning. All paid premiums and any policy fees will be refunded to the owner. (pp. 126-127)

#102. **c) State government**

The state government offers and regulates workers compensation benefits, which will differ slightly from state to state. (p. 56)

#103. **c) The loan balance will be deducted from the death benefit**

If the loan and interest are not repaid, and the insured dies, it will be deducted from the death benefit. (p. 100)

#104. **d) It is a misdemeanor punishable by one year in prison, a fine of $1,000, or both**

Failure to comply with a seizure order is a misdemeanor crime punishable by one year in prison, a fine of $1,000, or both. (p. 42)

#105. **b) Avoid adverse selection.**

The writing agent is typically the only insurance company representative that sees the applicant in person. (pp. 40, 67)

#106. **b) Personal Trainer**

More hazardous jobs will have higher insurance premiums. Therefore, because working as a personal trainer poses the least amount of risk, the premiums for this occupation would be the lowest. (p. 197)

#107. **b) Interest-only option**

The policy owner can specify that interest will only be paid annually to the surviving spouse, with the principal paid to their children when they reach a certain age or when the surviving spouse dies. (p. 103)

#108. **c) Portable**

HSAs are portable, so the individual is not dependent on a certain employer to enjoy the advantages of an HSA because the individual owns it. (p. 172)

#109. **d) Any form of life insurance**

Any life insurance can serve business owners and their survivors and protect the business. (p. 64)

#110. **c) Is defined as the amount and the frequency of the premium payment.**

The mode refers to the policy owner's premium payment frequency: monthly, quarterly, semiannually, or annually. The premium amount changes accordingly. (p. 74)

#111. **d) Hospital, Surgical, Medical**

Basic medical policies and major medical policies are usually grouped into medical expense insurance. The three basic coverages are hospital, surgical, and medical, and they can be purchased separately or as a package. (p. 166)

#112. **d) Misdemeanor, a fine not to exceed $25,000, and a possible 1-year imprisonment.**

Any agent or producer violating the misrepresentation provisions is guilty of a misdemeanor and punishable by a fine not exceeding $25,000 (for losses less than $10,000) and imprisonment not exceeding one year. Also, the Commissioner can suspend the producer's license for a maximum period of three years. (p. 12)

#113. **c) The primary care physician refers the HMO member**

For the HMO member to visit a specialist, the gatekeeper (primary care physician) must refer the member. In some HMOs, the primary care physician absorbs financial costs for referring patients to a more expensive specialist. (p. 168)

#114. **a) The agent has to advise the client about HICAP and its services.**

As required by California law, the agent has to advise the client about HICAP. (pp. 2219, 223-233, 242)

#115. **c) Their premiums are lower**

A preferred risk classification means an insured is in excellent physical condition and employs healthy habits and lifestyles. These insureds pay lower premiums than other risk categories. (p. 74)

#116. **c) Obtain a single premium policy for a reduced face amount.**

Suppose a whole life policy lapses or is surrendered before maturity. In that circumstance, the cash value can be used as a single premium to obtain a paid-up permanent policy with a reduced face amount. (p. 100)

#117. **d) The insured can renew the policy for another ten years but at a higher premium**

Policies that are guaranteed renewable and convertible can be renewed, without providing evidence of insurability, for another similar term. They can also be converted to permanent insurance without providing evidence of insurability. (p. 82)

#118. **c) An individual receiving Supplemental Security Income assistance**

California residents in various circumstances can qualify for benefits from Medi-Cal. However, individuals who receive cash assistance from one of the following programs are automatically eligible for Medi-Cal: SSI/SSP, CalWORKS, Foster Care or Adoption Assistance Program, and Refugee Assistance. (p. 220)

#119. **b) Self-insurance allows insureds to finance losses that cannot be insured**

Answers A, C, and D are all disadvantages of self-insurance. (pp. 5, 201)

#120. **c) An insurance provider's guaranteed minimum interest rate**

With fixed annuities, the insurer must pay the owners at least a guaranteed minimum interest rate. If the insurer's investments perform well, the insurer will pay a higher interest rate. However, since the interest rate can never fall below the guaranteed minimum, that determines what the insurer will pay. (p. 116)

#121. **c) Modified life**

Modified life is a permanent policy, but in the early years, the premium rates are the same as a term policy. In the later years, premium rates increase to build cash values and cause the policy to endow. (p. 85)

#122. **a) Buy-sell agreement.**

A common use of life insurance by businesses is a Buy-Sell Agreement. (p. 64)

#123. **d) Individuals whose income exceeds the limit for Medi-Cal**

Suppose a person's income exceeds the Medi-Cal limit for their family size. In that case, the person will have to pay a certain amount, known as a share of cost (SOC), in the month when medical expenses occur. (p. 221)

#124. **c) Universal Life**

The Waiver of Monthly Deductions rider is included in Universal Life policies. It will pay all monthly deductions while the insured is disabled, following a 6-month waiting period. This rider only pays monthly deductions, not the total premium amount necessary to accumulate cash value. (p. 266)

#125. **d) Family Policy**

A family policy offers permanent life insurance for the breadwinner and term riders for other family members. Regarding a family income policy, the principal wage earner is the only insured family member. (p. 86)

#126. **c) A longer elimination period has a lower cost of coverage**

The elimination period is a period that needs to expire after the onset of an illness or occurrence of an accident before benefits are payable. A longer elimination period will have a lower cost of coverage. (pp. 153, 154, 162)

#127. **c) Errors and omissions**

Insurers are motivated to document all correspondence and conversations with an insured if critical errors and omissions occur. (pp. 25-26)

#128. **d) Accident-only**

Accident-only policies pay medical benefits related to an accident. Medical conditions regarding sickness are not covered. (p. 157)

#129. **c) An omission, which an Errors and Omissions (E&O) policy will cover.**

Although the producer could have been guilty of malicious intent, such omissions are possible. They are covered by Errors and Omissions (E&O) policies. (pp. 25-26)

#130. **b) The amount an individual has to cover for medical expenses before Medi-Cal pays the rest**

When a person's income exceeds the Medi-Cal limit for their family size, that person will have to pay a certain amount, called a share of cost (SOC), during the month when medical expenses were incurred. (p. 221)

#131. **d) Monthly.**

If a claim involves disability income benefits, the policy must pay those benefits not less frequently than monthly. (p. 198)

#132. **a) Avoidance**

Avoidance is a method of risk management by which a person tries to eliminate the risk of loss by avoiding any exposure to an event that could result in a loss. (p. 4)

#133. **b) Cash to the business partner of the owner to accomplish a buyout**

If an owner dies or becomes disabled, the disability policy under the buy-sell agreement would provide enough cash for a buyout of the company. (pp. 201-202)

#134.   **c) The policy is terminated when the cash value is decreased to nothing.**

This option stipulates that in case of a possible policy lapse, the premium will be automatically paid from the contract's guaranteed cash value. Once the cash value is depleted, the policy will terminate. (p. 100)

#135.   **d) Reimbursement**

The HMO concept is unique in that it provides patient care and financing for its members. The HMO delivers benefits in the form of services rather than reimbursement for the hospital's or physician's services. (pp. 167-168)

#136.   **c) Level, fixed**

Variable life insurance (sometimes called variable whole life insurance) is a level, fixed premium, investment-based product. (p. 90)

#137.   **d) Fined a sum of $1,000.**

A producer guilty of violating the replacement provision of the Insurance Code will be fined $1,000 for the first offense. (pp. 128-129)

#138.   **c) Guaranteed renewability**

The benefit amount payable under most LTC policies is generally a specific amount per day, and some policies pay the actual charge incurred per day. Most LTC policies are also guaranteed renewable; however, insurance providers have the right to increase the premiums. (p. 232)

#139.   **c) $204**

The employer is allowed to collect a premium from the terminated employee at a rate of no more than 102% of the individual's group premium rate (in this example, 102% of a $200 total premium is $204). The 2% charge is to cover the employer's administrative costs. (p. 181)

#140.   **d) Needs substantial hands on or standby assistance with ADLs.**

The requirement to qualify for benefits is for the individual to need human assistance (hands-on) or continual substantial supervision (standby) when performing the ADLs. (p. 110)

#141.   **d) Admitted**

Insurers who meet the state's financial requirements and are approved to do business in the state are authorized or admitted into the state as legal insurers. (p. 38)

#142.   **c) Nonoccupational coverage.**

Most group disability income insurance is nonoccupational coverage, covering insureds only off the job. The employer carries workers compensation for on-the-job sickness or injuries. (p. 196)

#143.   **d) Low-income and uninsured.**

Medi-Cal exists to provide health coverage to low-income or uninsured individuals in California. (p. 220)

#144.   **a) The applicant's health condition**

When health insurers establish their premium rates, they can only base them on four standards: age, geographic rating area, family composition, and tobacco use. (p. 185)

#145.   **d) Collect payment at the time of policy delivery**

The agent is responsible for delivering the policy to the insured and collecting any premium that might be due at the time of delivery. (p. 67)

#146.   **d) Rescission of a contract**

Intentional or unintentional concealment entitles the affected party to rescind the contract. (pp. 11-12)

#147. **d) Small employer**

Small employer refers to any individual actively engaged in a business that, on at least 50% of its working days during the previous year, employed not more than 50 eligible employees. (p. 176)

#148. **a) Needs approach.**

The needs approach determines how much of a benefit would be needed to replace a lost income and additional expenses if the insured dies prematurely. (p. 64)

#149. **d) Policy summary**

A policy summary explains the elements and features of the specific policy. (p. 66)

#150. **a) Part A.**

Medicare Part A pays for these services, contingent upon copayments and limitations on the number of days of care. (pp. 207-209)

FINAL EXAM

This last test will ensure you are ready to pass the licensing exam

You are about to take a California Life, Accident and Health or Sickness Final Practice Exam. This exam consists of *150 Questions (plus five to ten non-scored experimental questions)* and is *3 hours and 15 minutes* long. If you do not have enough time to complete this exam right now, it is better to wait until you can fully devote your attention to completing it in the allotted time.

If you score well answering the Final Exam, you can be reasonably certain that you have the knowledge necessary to perform well on the actual test.

Any skipped questions will be graded as incorrect. The following chart breaks down the number of questions in each chapter and by topic.

CHAPTER	# OF QUESTIONS
General Insurance	**40**
Basic Insurance Concepts and Principles	16
Contract Law	10
The Insurance Marketplace	14
Life Insurance	**49**
Life Insurance – Basics	8
Types of Life Policies	10
Annuities	8
Life Insurance and Annuities – Policy Replacement/Cancellation	4
The Individual Life Insurance Contract	10
Taxation of Life Insurance and Annuities	3
Group Life Insurance Plans	2
Social Security Disability Program	1
Individual Underwriting, Pricing, and Claims	3
Life Policy Riders	**4**
General Concepts of Medical and Disability Insurance	**4**
Medical Expense Insurance	**45**
Individual Insurance	14
Group Medical Expense Insurance	8
Patient Protection and Affordable Care Act (PPACA)	8
Senior Health Products	15
Disability Income Insurance	**4**
Long-Term Care Insurance	**4**

To calculate your score, subtract the number of incorrectly answered questions from 150. Take this number and divide it by 150. For example, if you incorrectly answered 60 questions, your score would be 60%, the minimum score needed to pass the exam.

#1. Regarding a 10-year level premium policy, which of the following is TRUE?

a) The premium will stay the same at renewal
b) The premium will be reduced at the end of the term
c) The premium will be level for the first few years of the policy but will increase by the 10th year
d) The premium will stay level for ten years

#2. Which of the following documents could an insured submit to an insurance provider to communicate the severity of a loss?

a) Petition for remittance
b) Proof of claim
c) Notification of loss
d) Notarized loss report

#3. The "stop-loss" feature on a major medical policy is designed to

a) Establish the number of claims that can be filed on a policy during a calendar year.
b) Establish a maximum out-of-pocket expense amount an insured must pay for medical expenses during a calendar year.
c) Establish a maximum out-of-pocket expense amount an insured must pay for medical expenses during the policy's life.
d) Discourage insureds from making unnecessary appointments with doctors.

#4. A Medicare supplement policy needs to have a free-look period of at least

a) 10 days.
b) 15 days.
c) 30 days.
d) 45 days.

#5. What is it called when a doctor accepts the Medicare-approved amount?

a) Assignment
b) Consent
c) Verification
d) Acceptance

#6. When can HIV-related test results be submitted to the MIB?

a) When the patient gives the authorization
b) Only when a patient has negative test results
c) Only if the person's identity is not revealed
d) Under all circumstances

#7. A policy owner returns the policy to the insurance company a week after it is delivered. How much of the premium will be returned to the applicant?

a) 80%
b) 50%
c) None
d) 100%

#8. If a policyholder dies, and it is identified that the insured misstated their gender or age, the life insurance provider will

a) Adjust the death benefit to what the premium would have obtained at the actual gender or age.
b) Pay the face amount specified at the time of policy issue.
c) Deny all claims due to the misrepresentation.
d) Adjust the back premiums for the proper gender or age.

#9. Which of the following terms best describes the care a Health Maintenance Organization (HMO) provides?

a) Major medical
b) Fee-for-service
c) Preventive
d) Elective

#10. Restoring an insured financially after a claim is called

a) Reasonable expectations.
b) Indemnity.
c) Adhesion.
d) Restoration.

#11. How does insurance distribute the financial consequences of individual losses?

a) It transfers the risk to the insured's associates
b) It transfers the risk to a small number of insured individuals
c) It transfers the risk to all insured individuals
d) It retains the financial consequences

#12. A dentist is off work for five months because of a disability. The dental assistant's salary would be covered by

a) Disability Income.
b) Key Employee Disability.
c) Partnership Disability.
d) Business Overhead Insurance.

#13. What is the reason for a benefit schedule?

a) To provide the average charges for procedures
b) To include the dates for the payment of benefits
c) To list the insured's deductibles and copayments
d) To specify what and how much is covered in the plan

#14. An insured recently had a new house built and decided to install smoke detectors in multiple places throughout the home. What method of handling risk is being used by the insured?

a) Retention
b) Avoidance
c) Sharing
d) Reduction

#15. The premiums for a conditionally renewable policy are more likely to be

a) Decreased.
b) Variable.
c) Flexible.
d) Increased.

#16. All of the following statements about producers are true EXCEPT

a) A producer must first establish a licensing relationship with the state or states where they wish to conduct business.
b) Exclusive agents work for themselves.
c) Producers can be natural persons or corporations.
d) The independent producer has contracts to transact insurance with more than one insurer.

#17. A core Medicare supplement policy (Plan A) will pay for the following expenses EXCEPT

a) The Part A deductible.
b) The first three pints of blood.
c) 20% of the Part B coinsurance amounts for Medicare-approved services.
d) Part A coinsurance.

#18. Who is responsible for ensuring the health insurance application is complete and accurate?

a) The agent's
b) The policy owner's
c) The underwriter's
d) The applicant's

#19. Key person insurance can offer protection for all of the following economic losses sustained by a business EXCEPT

a) Funding the cost of training a current employee to perform the duties of a deceased employee.
b) Paying the death benefit to the insured's estate.
c) Providing deferred compensation retirement benefits if the insured key person lives until retirement.
d) Funding the expense of finding a suitable replacement after the death of an employee.

#20. In California, how long is the grace period for an individual life insurance policy?

a) 3 months
b) 60 days
c) 1 month
d) 7 to 10 business days

#21. In a variable life insurance policy, all of the following assets are held in the insurer's general account EXCEPT

a) Face amount reserves.
b) Incidental benefit amounts.
c) Cash surrender values.
d) Mortality reserves.

#22. HMOs are known as what type of plans?

a) Service
b) Health savings
c) Consumer driven
d) Reimbursement

#23. Which of these can be described as a flexible premium adjustable life policy?

a) Whole Life
b) Term Life
c) Credit Life
d) Universal Life

#24. Which of the following indicates how much of the health coverage premium is required to go toward actual medical care?

a) Medical Loss Ratio (MLR)
b) Minimum Value (MV) calculator
c) Modified Adjusted Gross Income (MAGI)
d) Metal tiers

#25. Which of the following services will NOT be provided by an HMO?

a) Emergency care
b) Inpatient hospital care received outside the service area
c) Unlimited coverage for drug rehabilitation
d) Treatment for mental disorders

#26. Concerning disability income insurance, which of the following defines "own occupation" disability?

a) A disability that causes the insured to be unable to work at their regular job even though they might be able to perform the duties of another occupation
b) Any disability that requires home confinement
c) A disability resulting from an infectious disease that, should the insured return to work, would cause the disease to spread
d) A disability resulting from an accident that occurred while on the job

#27. Which of the following consists of daily nursing and rehabilitative care that a medical professional can only administer under the direction of a doctor?

a) Assisted living
b) Skilled care
c) Intermediate care
d) Custodial care

#28. An employee is covered under COBRA. Her previous monthly premium payment was $100, but her employer now collects $102 monthly. What is the reason why the employer collects an extra $2?

a) Premiums go up each year regardless of health conditions
b) To cover other employees who are eligible to bypass premium payment
c) To cover the employer's administration costs
d) Penalty for termination

#29. To be acceptable to insurance companies, what percentage of eligible employees must be enrolled under a contributory group health insurance plan?

a) 65%
b) 75%
c) 100%
d) 50%

#30. A coffee shop owner is insured by a business overhead expense policy that pays a maximum monthly benefit of $2,500. The shop's actual monthly expenses are $3,000. If the owner becomes disabled, the monthly benefit payable under her policy will be

a) $2,100.
b) $2,500.
c) $3,000.
d) $2,000.

#31. Which dividend option will increase the death benefit?

a) Extended term
b) Reduced paid up
c) Paid-up additions
d) Accumulation

#32. How is the beneficiary affected once the initial benefit limit in Medicare Part D is reached?

a) The beneficiary must pay for 75% of prescription drug costs
b) The beneficiary no longer has to pay prescription drug costs
c) Medicare Part A will cover all costs
d) The beneficiary must pay for a portion of prescription drug costs

#33. An individual has a history of DUIs. To his insurance provider, this presents what type of hazard?

a) Legal
b) Physical
c) Moral
d) Morale

#34. An annuitant pays the annuity premium on the 13th of every month. Which of the following best describes this arrangement?

a) Single
b) Level
c) Flexible
d) Lump sum

#35. According to the Affordable Care Act (ACA), when is pregnancy considered a pre-existing condition?

a) Always
b) Never
c) Only if excluded explicitly by the insurer
d) If it begins before the coverage becomes effective

#36. Under Social Security, to attain fully insured status, an individual must have earned how many credits?

a) 6
b) 10
c) 20
d) 40

#37. Which of these is NOT a personal use of life insurance?

a) A person obtains insurance to help the family pay off the mortgage in case of premature death.
b) A person obtains insurance to fund a buy-sell agreement.
c) A person obtains insurance to provide future income to a surviving spouse.
d) A person obtains cash value insurance to fund his children's college education.

#38. Amy obtained a life insurance policy and listed her parents as the beneficiaries. She can change beneficiaries at any time. What type of beneficiary designation does this policy owner have?

a) Irrevocable
b) Contingent
c) Primary
d) Revocable

#39. All of the following could qualify as a group to obtain group health insurance EXCEPT

a) A multiple employer trust.
b) A single employer with 14 employees.
c) An association of 35 people.
d) A labor union.

#40. Under which of the following conditions would the proceeds of a life insurance policy be taxable by the federal government?

a) If they are paid to the policy owner
b) If there is a transfer for value
c) If they are collaterally assigned to a lender
d) If they are received as a lump sum

#41. Regarding the selection of a Commissioner of Insurance in California, which of the following is true?

a) The Senate elects the Commissioner for one 2-year term
b) The people elect the Commissioner for a 4-year term
c) The Governor appoints the Commissioner permanently
d) The House nominates the Commissioner for two 5-year terms

#42. The owner of a whole life policy with an accidental death rider intentionally kills himself after owning the policy for 18 months. What is the insurer's course of action?

a) Pay double the face amount
b) Deny payment of the death benefit
c) Deny payment of only the face amount but pay the rider because suicide is considered an accident
d) Only pay the face amount because suicide is not considered an accident

#43. An insured receives $50,000 from a $100,000 Accidental Death and Dismemberment policy. This payment is due to the loss of his left arm in an accident. The insured has received the

a) Principal Amount.
b) Capital Amount.
c) Contributory Amount.
d) Primary Amount.

#44. In business disability insurance, who is the insured?

a) Key employees
b) All employees
c) The insurer
d) The employer

#45. Under the Affordable Care Act (ACA), pregnancy, maternity, and preventive care services are considered

a) Essential benefits.
b) Elective benefits.
c) Limited benefits.
d) Optional benefits.

#46. What does Basic Medical Expense cover?

a) X-ray charges
b) All office visits, under any circumstance
c) Surgery
d) Nonsurgical services a doctor provides

#47. An employee that becomes ineligible for group coverage due to a change in status or termination of employment must exercise an extension of benefits under COBRA

a) Within 60 days.
b) Within 30 days.
c) Before termination is complete.
d) Within 10 days.

#48. Under what circumstances will the contingent beneficiary receive the death benefit?

a) If the primary beneficiary's death occurs before the insured's death
b) If the tertiary beneficiary predeceases the insured
c) If it is designated by the insured
d) If it is designated by the primary beneficiary

#49. What type of risk is wagering on a sporting event?

a) Calculated
b) Simple
c) Pure
d) Speculative

#50. The exclusion ratio is used to calculate

a) The amount of premiums that must be included in taxes.
b) The interest base and the payout base.
c) The benefit amounts to be paid to the annuitant.
d) The annuity benefit to be excluded from taxes.

#51. Core benefits are included in every Medicare supplement policy. What is the required Part B percentage of coinsurance?

a) 15%
b) 20%
c) 35%
d) 10%

#52. Which of these describes the relationship between a principal sum and a capital sum?

a) A principal sum varies, while a capital sum does not
b) A capital sum varies, while a principal sum does not
c) A principal sum is a percentage of a capital sum
d) A capital sum is a percentage of a principal sum

#53. All of the following are true of credit life EXCEPT

a) The policy owner is the creditor.
b) The insured names the beneficiary.
c) The death benefit cannot exceed the loan amount.
d) The premium payment is included in the loan payment.

#54. Which of the following periods is the general enrollment period for Medicare Part B?

a) March 1 through March 31 every year
b) January 1 through March 31 every year
c) March 1 through May 31 every year
d) January 1 through January 31 every year

#55. A policy owner dies six months after the policy issue date. Upon the policy owner's death, it is determined that the insured made a material misstatement on the application. What is the most probable course of action for the insurance provider?

a) A hearing by a court of law to determine the appropriate actions
b) No course of action will be permitted since the policy has already been issued
c) Rescind the policy
d) An administrative hearing by the Department of Insurance

#56. When will benefits begin if a person qualifies for Social Security disability benefits after the 5-month elimination period?

a) Benefits start at the beginning of the 6th month and are retroactive to the start of the disability
b) Benefits will begin after the 6th month and are retroactive to the start of the disability
c) A lump sum of benefits will be paid at the beginning of the 6th month, which is retroactive to the start of the disability
d) Benefits start at the beginning of the 6th month and are not retroactive to the start of the disability

#57. Medicare Part A does NOT include which of the following services?

a) Private Duty Nursing
b) Post hospital Skilled Nursing Facility Care
c) Hospitalization
d) Hospice Care

#58. In an HMO, what is the purpose of the gatekeeper?

a) Ensuring that patients do not go to doctors outside of the HMO's region
b) Establishing strong preventive care
c) Ensuring that services are properly prepaid
d) Controlling costs

#59. What does it mean when insurance contracts are unilateral?

a) The insured is required to make a promise to pay the premium
b) Each party to the contract must exchange something of value
c) A promise is only made at the time of policy application
d) Only one party makes a promise

#60. Which type of deductible do a husband and wife have in their policy if both incur expenses attributed to a single major medical insurance deductible?

a) Per occurrence
b) Family
c) Flat
d) Annual

#61. Which of these is the best definition of indemnification?

a) The act of one individual who agrees to restore an injured person to the condition they enjoyed before the loss
b) A legal entity that acts on behalf of itself, accepting civil and legal responsibility for its actions and making contracts in its own name
c) A contract in which the two parties to the contract agree to what things of value will be exchanged
d) A contract in which one person undertakes to indemnify another person against damage, loss, or liability resulting from a contingent or unknown event

#62. Which of the following is provided by skilled medical professionals to those who require occasional medical assistance or rehabilitative care?

a) Home health care
b) Skilled care
c) Intermediate care
d) Custodial care

#63. Benefits for a Disability Income policy are based on which of the following?

a) Minimum wages
b) Typical wages for a similar profession
c) The insured's earnings
d) Average US wages

#64. In California, medical claims covered by Medi-Cal are paid for by

a) Workers compensation insurance.
b) Health Maintenance Organizations.
c) The state of California, primarily through federal reimbursements.
d) Assessments on insurance providers offering medical insurance based on market share.

#65. An insured's Basic Hospital Expense policy has a $500 per day limit for room and board in a hospital for a maximum of five days. The insured got sick and spent three days in the hospital at $650 per day. How much will the insured have to pay to cover the balance of the room and board charges?

a) $0
b) $150
c) $350
d) $450

#66. Group coverage CANNOT be discontinued for which of the following reasons?

a) Movement outside of the service area
b) Fraud
c) The insurer's stock value lowers
d) Nonpayment of premium

#67. Regarding an optionally renewable policy, which of the following is NOT true?

a) Renewability is at the option of the insurance provider
b) Nonrenewal can happen on the anniversary date of the policy
c) Policy premiums can increase at renewal
d) The insurance provider can only cancel the policy for reasons specified in the contract

#68. Which of the following is NOT a type of hazard?

a) Moral
b) Morale
c) Exposure
d) Physical

#69. Insurance provides a way to

a) Eliminate a loss.
b) Transfer a loss.
c) Retain a loss.
d) Avoid a loss.

#70. In health insurance, the length of the grace period will vary according to

a) The length of the benefit period.
b) The age of the insured.
c) The mode of premium payment.
d) The length of the waiting period.

#71. What type of insurance would an individual select as the most efficient way of paying the outstanding debt on their home in the event of death?

a) Family maintenance
b) Mortgage redemption
c) Joint life (first-to-die)
d) Level term

#72. The policy owner in a group policy can be all of the following EXCEPT

a) An association.
b) The insurer.
c) A union.
d) The employer.

#73. Under a disability income policy, what advantage does the Recurrent Disability provision provide to the insured?

a) It imposes an elimination period for the disability
b) It eliminates a second elimination period for the same disability
c) It gives the insured a lifetime of disability benefits
d) It eliminates the imposition of an elimination period for a separate disability

#74. An organization will stop being an entity that is eligible to hold a license for all of the following reasons EXCEPT

a) An association's termination.
b) A corporation's dissolution.
c) A partnership's dissolution.
d) A key employee's termination.

#75. Under an Accidental Death and Dismemberment (AD&D) policy, the death benefit payable is known as the

a) Policy limit.
b) Principal sum.
c) Face amount.
d) Capital sum.

#76. Which of the following riders allows for payment of part of the policy's death benefit if the insured is diagnosed with a terminal disease that will result in death within two years?

a) Living Needs Rider
b) Long-Term Care Rider
c) Cost of Living Rider
d) Accidental Death Rider

#77. An annuity has built up a cash value of $70,000, of which $30,000 comes from premium payments. In the event the annuitant dies during the accumulation phase, the beneficiary will receive

a) $30,000.
b) $70,000.
c) $100,000 (a combination of the cash value and the premiums paid).
d) Survivor benefits determined by the insurance provider.

#78. According to the Common Disaster clause, if the insured and the primary beneficiary die in the same accident and it cannot be determined who died first, which of the following will be presumed?

a) The primary beneficiary's estate and the contingent beneficiary will split benefits equally
b) The insured predeceases the primary beneficiary
c) The primary beneficiary predeceases the insured
d) The deaths happened at the same time

#79. The agent's contract includes which type of authority?

a) Assumed
b) Express
c) Apparent
d) Implied

#80. What is the primary difference between franchise and group insurance?

a) Franchise insurance delivers coverage for large groups
b) Franchise insurance has lower premiums than group insurance
c) Participants do not have to submit their applications for franchise insurance
d) Underwriting is done for each person in franchise insurance

#81. Which of these is NOT a typical type of Long-Term Care coverage?

a) Residential care
b) Home health care
c) Child daycare
d) Skilled nursing care

#82. Concerning the Health Insurance Counseling and Advocacy Program (HICAP), which of the following is NOT true?

a) The State Department of Aging manages it
b) It offers consumer counseling
c) It works cooperatively with local area agencies on aging
d) It exists to help seniors who are not eligible to receive Medicare or Social Security

#83. According to the metal level classification of health plans, a bronze plan will cover what percentage of health care costs?

a) 60%
b) 70%
c) 80%
d) 90%

#84. During policy solicitation, an insurance provider exaggerates a competitor's financial condition. This scenario is an example of

a) Controlled business.
b) Defamation.
c) Twisting.
d) False advertising.

#85. The policy summary for a life insurance policy is not provided when the application is taken. When does the policy summary have to be given to the policy owner?

a) When the policy is issued
b) When the policy is delivered
c) Within 15 days of the application date
d) Within 30 days of the policy issue date

#86. In insurance, which of the following terms describes the cause of a loss?

a) Material fact
b) Hazard
c) Peril
d) Causative factor

#87. To be financially solvent, an insurance provider must accomplish all of the following EXCEPT

a) Possess enough assets to cover its liabilities.
b) Maintain an amount at least equal to its required minimum paid-in capital.
c) Contribute a specified amount of capital reserves to the state.
d) Reinsure any risk exceeding the state's retention limits.

#88. With Adjustable Life, all of the following can be changed by the policy owner EXCEPT

a) The premium.
b) The period coverage will last.
c) The insured.
d) The death benefit.

#89. Which of the following parts of Medicare provides prescription drug benefits?

a) Part C
b) Part D
c) Part A
d) Part B

#90. The annuity income amount is determined by the life of which individual?

a) Owner
b) Insured
c) Annuitant
d) Beneficiary

#91. According to the presumptive disability provision, the insured is presumed totally disabled upon the loss of all of the following EXCEPT

a) Hearing.
b) Two limbs.
c) Feeling.
d) Sight.

#92. Upon the surrender of a life insurance policy, any built-up cash value that exceeds the premium payments is

a) Not taxed.
b) Taxed as income on 50% of the excess.
c) Assessed a fine of 10% of the excess.
d) Taxed as ordinary income.

#93. A community center could provide which of the following types of care?

a) Skilled care
b) Adult daycare
c) Respite care
d) Intermediate care

#94. Health insurance premium rates can be based upon all of the following EXCEPT

a) Age
b) Medical history
c) Religion
d) Gender

#95. If an applicant for insurance submits the initial premium with an application, which action constitutes acceptance?

a) The underwriters approve the application
b) The applicant provides a statement of good health
c) The agent delivers the policy
d) The insurer receives the application and the initial premium

#96. The Affordable Care Act (ACA) stipulates that insurance companies provide coverage for the insured's adult children up to the age of

a) 21.
b) 26.
c) 28.
d) 30.

#97. When the benefits of a basic medical insurance plan are exhausted, what type of plan will then start covering those losses?

a) Social security
b) Supplemental major medical
c) Supplementary basic medical
d) None; once benefits are exhausted for a benefit period, the insurance provider is responsible for covering the remainder of the expenses

#98. Which of the following statements is INCORRECT?

a) Medicare and Medigap policies provide coverage for nursing home or long-term custodial care
b) Medicare and Medicare supplements do not cover skilled nursing care
c) Medicaid does not pay for nursing home care in any circumstance
d) Medicare and Medigap policies do not provide coverage for nursing homes or long-term custodial care

#99. A person is approaching retirement and is worried about having the right coverage should she have to be placed in a long-term care facility. Her agent mentions that LTC policies would offer the necessary coverage at all of the following levels EXCEPT

a) Intermediate.
b) Skilled.
c) Acute.
d) Custodial.

#100. Who is the owner of an annuity?

a) The individual who receives the benefits
b) The individual on whose life the annuity is written
c) The insurance provider
d) The individual who purchases the annuity

#101. An underwriter is reviewing an applicant with an extensive medical history. Which of the following would give the underwriter a better understanding of how the applicant was treated for various illnesses?

a) MIB Report
b) Policy application
c) Medical exam
d) Attending Physician's Statement

#102. A subscriber was treated for a medical condition by her primary care physician for three months with an experimental remedy without a major health improvement before being referred to a specialist. Which of the following types of health plans does this subscriber have?

a) A limited benefit plan
b) A fully-paid indemnity plan that covers his condition only at a specified provider
c) Major medical insurance with a low deductible and low coinsurance
d) A gatekeeper HMO plan to control the costs

#103. The Guaranteed Insurability Rider permits the policy owner to obtain additional amounts of life insurance without proof of insurability at all of the following EXCEPT

a) The birth of a child.
b) Marriage.
c) The purchase of a new home.
d) Every three years from age 25 to 40.

#104. What is the penalty for each month of delayed enrollment when Medicare beneficiaries do not enroll when they are first eligible?

a) 1%
b) 2%
c) 3%
d) 4%

#105. In health insurance, what does coinsurance refer to?

a) The amount the insurer pays for the insured's treatment
b) A percentage of the cost of service that the insured and the insurance company share
c) A portion of the deductible the insured has to pay for treatment
d) The amount an insured pays for treatment

#106. The notice about policy cancellation that is provided to senior consumers has to include all of the following information EXCEPT

a) An explanation of where the premiums have been invested.
b) The time limit for cancellation.
c) To whom to return the policy.
d) A possible surrender charge.

#107. An annuity would typically be purchased by an individual who wants to

a) Provide income for retirement.
b) Provide a death benefit to the surviving family.
c) Earn a higher interest rate.
d) Create an estate.

#108. An illustration used in the sale of a life insurance policy is required to include a label specifying

a) "Life insurance illustration."
b) "Guaranteed items."
c) "Subject to change."
d) "Representation of insurance."

#109. A person's retirement plan meets all federal requirements and entitles her to certain tax benefits. What term best describes the owner's retirement plan?

a) Unqualified
b) Variable
c) Deferred
d) Qualified

#110. All of the following are ways to handle risk EXCEPT

a) Reduction.
b) Transfer.
c) Elimination.
d) Avoidance.

#111. An insured was seriously injured in a snowboarding accident that sent him to the hospital for six weeks. Her medical expense policy covered all of the following EXCEPT

a) Loss of income while hospitalized.
b) Necessary medical supplies and medicine.
c) Surgical expense.
d) Hospital room and board.

#112. Concerning Modified Endowment Contracts (MECs), which of the following statements is INCORRECT?

a) A life insurance policy that fails the 7-pay test is classified as a Modified Endowment Contract
b) The main reason for the regulations governing Modified Endowment Contracts was to decrease incentives for using life insurance as a short-term investment vehicle
c) A distribution from a Modified Endowment Contract can be subject to a 10% penalty if withdrawn before age 59 ½
d) Modified Endowment Contracts must always pass the 7-pay test

#113. In a whole life policy, Cash Value guarantees are called

a) Dividends.
b) Nonforfeiture values.
c) Living Benefits.
d) Cash Loans.

#114. Regarding the waiver of monthly deductions rider, all of the following are true EXCEPT

a) The rider will pay all monthly deductions while the insured is disabled.
b) The rider waives insurance premiums if the insured is disabled.
c) The rider is only applicable to universal life policies.
d) The rider cannot waive the cost of premiums that build up cash value.

#115. An applicant for a disability insurance policy has a heart condition of which they are unaware and therefore they answer "no" to the question about heart problems on their application. The applicant's answer is a

a) Fraudulent answer.
b) Representation.
c) Warranty.
d) Concealment.

#116. Which of the following is the written document in which insurance coverage is set forth?

a) The Certificate of Authority
b) The contract
c) The California Insurance Code
d) The covenant of insurance

#117. Which of these would be considered a peril?

a) Driving too fast for the conditions
b) Playing golf during a thunderstorm
c) Fire
d) Smoking

#118. An insured's hospital policy specifies that it will pay a flat fee of $75 per day for every day of hospitalization. On what basis will the policy pay benefits?

a) Indemnity
b) Reimbursement
c) Expense
d) Service

#119. When a producer delivered an insurance policy to the insured, they collected the initial premium and a document verifying that the insured had no injuries or illness since the application date. What is the name of this document?

a) Statement of Insurability
b) Insuring Agreement
c) Insurability Clause
d) Statement of Good Health

#120. For which of the following reasons could an insurance provider terminate a long-term care insurance policy?

a) The insured's deterioration in physical health
b) The insured's deterioration in mental health
c) Nonpayment of premium
d) The insured's advanced age

#121. When insurance is obtained, which method of dealing with risk is applied?

a) Transfer
b) Sharing
c) Avoidance
d) Reduction

#122. Which of the following is a physical hazard?

a) Carelessness
b) Lying
c) Bankruptcy
d) Diabetes

#123. Which of these best describes a pure life annuity?

a) It provides the highest monthly benefits
b) It continues payments to the beneficiary when the annuitant dies
c) It is also called a refund life annuity
d) It guarantees to pay out all the proceeds

#124. Decreasing Term insurance is often used to

a) Cover a mortgage.
b) Liquidate an estate.
c) Accumulate cash value for retirement.
d) Pay estate taxes.

#125. During the Social Security blackout period, the surviving spouse does not receive benefits until the age of

a) 59 ½.
b) 60.
c) 65.
d) 70 ½.

#126. An insured receives fixed amount benefit payments from his late wife's insurance policy. The insured's agent informed him that if he dies before all of the benefits are paid, the remaining amount will go to the contingent beneficiary. Which settlement option did the insured choose?

a) Fixed Period
b) Interest-Only
c) Joint and Survivor
d) Fixed Amount

#127. A 25-year-old full-time student is living off a trust fund. Why would she NOT qualify for an IRA?

a) She does not have earned income
b) Because of her full-time student status
c) She does not have enough income for qualified contributions
d) She does not meet the age requirements

#128. Under HIPAA portability, which of the following do NOT receive protection under required benefits?

a) Pregnant women
b) Mentally ill
c) Groups of one or more
d) Self-employed

#129. Which of the following is the cause of loss?

a) Hazard
b) Exposures
c) Risk
d) Peril

#130. All of the following are characteristics of catastrophic plans EXCEPT

a) Essential benefits.
b) High premiums.
c) Out-of-pocket costs.
d) High deductibles

#131. In life insurance, which of the following individuals is NOT required to have an insurable interest in the insured?

a) The beneficiary
b) The policy owner
c) The insured
d) The applicant

#132. Which of the following is correct concerning the Medical Information Bureau (MIB)?

a) Information found in the MIB report is available to all physicians
b) The MIB helps underwriters to evaluate and classify risks
c) The MIB report must be attached to every life insurance policy
d) Each life insurance applicant receives a copy of the life insurance medical exam findings

#133. What does it mean if an annuity or retirement plan is qualified?

a) It satisfies IRS requirements for favorable tax treatment
b) It has unlimited uses
c) Dividends will be paid until payments are distributed
d) It is not allowed by the IRS

#134. Which of the following used to be known as Medicare + Choice Plans?

a) Medical Insurance
b) Medicare Supplement Plans
c) Original Medicare Plan
d) Medicare Advantage Plans

#135. Under the Accidental Death rider, which of the following losses would be covered?

a) A mountain-climbing accident
b) Death resulting from a long-term disability
c) Death caused by a head-on collision
d) Suicide

#136. How long would the grace period be under the policy if an insured pays a monthly health insurance premium?

a) 7 days
b) 10 days
c) 14 days
d) 25 days

#137. Your client wants to provide his elderly parents with a retirement income if something happens to him. He wants to ensure that both beneficiaries are guaranteed an income for life. Which settlement option should this policy owner select?

a) Fixed-period installments
b) Life income
c) Joint and Survivor
d) Fixed-amount installments

#138. Which of the following premium modes would result in the lowest overall premium, all other factors being equal?

a) Annual
b) Quarterly
c) Semi-Annual
d) Monthly

#139. Which of the following is provided by nonmedical personnel and meets the insured's personal needs?

a) Intermediate care
b) Custodial care
c) Skilled care
d) Assisted living

#140. What specific type of insurance is often written in conjunction with a hospital expense policy and includes fees for anesthesiologists and surgeons?

a) Practitioner's insurance
b) Basic surgical expense insurance
c) Basic medical insurance
d) Personnel insurance

#141. As it relates to insurance contracts, which statement best describes an agreement?

a) Each party has to offer something of value
b) The contract's intent must be legally acceptable to both parties
c) The one party accepts the exact terms of the other party's offer
d) All parties have to be capable of entering into a contract

#142. Due to an injury, an insured has been unable to work for eight months. When her life insurance premium came due, she could not pay, yet the policy remained in force. The policy includes

a) Nonforfeiture options.
b) A waiver of premium rider.
c) Guaranteed insurability benefits.
d) A facility of payment clause.

#143. All of the following are required to sign an application for health insurance EXCEPT the

a) Producer.
b) Insurer.
c) Proposed insured (if they are not the insured).
d) Applicant.

#144. Which terms refer to the nontaxable portion of all annuity benefit payments?

a) Interest
b) Principal
c) Cost base
d) Tax base

#145. Medicare is a health insurance program for all of the following EXCEPT

a) Individuals with permanent kidney failure.
b) Individuals who have been on Social Security Disability for two years.
c) Individuals with low assets and low income.
d) Individuals 65 or over.

#146. All of the following are covered by Medicare Part B EXCEPT

a) Home health visits.
b) Outpatient hospital services.
c) Long-term care services.
d) Doctor's services.

#147. Which of the following best demonstrates the law of large numbers?

a) The larger the pool of risks, the more accurate the predictions will be
b) Larger groups produce healthier applicants
c) Large groups offer less opportunity for loss
d) The larger the group, the more likely it will be to receive a good choice

#148. All Social Security Medicare program parts are available to a qualifying retiree. Which of these requires the insured to pay a monthly premium?

a) Medi-Cal
b) Medicare Part A
c) Medicare Part B
d) Medicaid

#149. In group health policies, which of the following best describes the Probationary Period?

a) A specified period that an individual joining a group has to wait before becoming eligible for coverage
b) The number of days the insured has to determine if they will accept the policy as received
c) The specified amount of time when benefits can be reduced under certain conditions
d) The number of days that have to expire after the onset of an illness before benefits will be earned

#150. Policies written on a third-party ownership basis are typically written to cover which of the following?

a) Policy owners who are not insureds
b) The estate of an insured
c) Policy owner's estate
d) Minor children or business associates of the policy owner

Final Exam Answers

#1. **d) The premium will stay level for ten years**

During the policy term, level premium term insurance provides a level death benefit and a level premium. (p. 82)

#2. **b) Proof of claim**

An insured can submit a proof of claim to the insurance provider after a loss has occurred to notify the insurer and provide information on how severe or large the loss was. (p. 58)

#3. **b) Establish a maximum out-of-pocket expense amount an insured must pay for medical expenses during a calendar year.**

A stop-loss feature is a provision that gives the insured financial security by limiting the maximum amount that would have to be paid in copayments and deductibles during a calendar year. (p. 154)

#4. **c) 30 days.**

The free-look period for Medicare supplement policies has to be at least 30 days. (p. 218)

#5. **a) Assignment**

Assignment is when a doctor agrees to accept the Medicare-approved amount. (p. 211)

#6. **c) Only if the person's identity is not revealed**

Insurers have to maintain strict confidentiality regarding HIV-related test results or diagnoses. Test results cannot be provided to the MIB if the patient is identified. (pp. 72, 160)

#7. **d) 100%**

When a policy owner is dissatisfied with a policy, they can return it for a full refund of all premiums paid. (p. 96)

#8. **a) Adjust the death benefit to what the premium would have obtained at the actual gender or age.**

Suppose the applicant has misstated their gender or age on the application. If a claim occurs, the insurance provider can adjust the claim benefits to an amount that the premium at the correct age or gender would have obtained. (p. 97)

#9. **c) Preventive**

HMOs emphasize preventive health care as a method of reducing medical expenses by early detection of health issues before they may need significant and more costly treatment. (p. 155)

#10. **b) Indemnity.**

Under the principle of indemnity, an insured or a beneficiary can collect only to the extent of the financial loss. (p. 6)

#11. **c) It transfers the risk to all insured individuals**

Insurance is the transfer of the possibility of a loss (risk) to an insurer, which spreads the costs of unexpected losses to many individuals. In most situations, only a small number of insureds will suffer a loss. Insurance redistributes the financial consequences of individual losses to all insured individuals. (p. 2)

#12. **d) Business Overhead Insurance.**

Business overhead insurance is intended to pay the ongoing business expenses of small business owners when they are disabled and unable to work. It will provide the funds required to pay the salary of employees other than the owners and their other ongoing business expenses, like rent. (pp. 64-65, 201)

#13. **d) To specify what and how much is covered in the plan**

Certain medical expense insurance plans include a benefit schedule that explicitly states what is covered in the plan and for how much. (p. 179)

#14. **d) Reduction**

Since risk typically cannot be avoided entirely, people often attempt to reduce the possibility or severity of a loss. Reduction would include actions like installing smoke detectors in their home, having a yearly physical to detect health issues early, or making lifestyle changes. (p. 5)

#15. **d) Increased.**

With a conditionally renewable policy, the insurance provider can terminate the contract only for certain conditions specified in the contract. Also, the policy premiums can be increased. (p. 155)

#16. **b) Exclusive agents work for themselves.**

Exclusive or captive agents work for or represent one insurance company at a time. Independent agents work for themselves and can be appointed by multiple insurance providers. (p. 18)

#17. **a) The Part A deductible.**

Plan A only includes the core benefits and does not include coverage for the Part A deductible. (p. 216)

#18. **a) The agent's**

As a field underwriter, the agent has to ensure that the applications are complete and accurate. (p. 158)

#19. **b) Paying the death benefit to the insured's estate.**

The business, not the family or the insured's estate, is the policy owner, premium payor, and beneficiary. (p. 64)

#20. **b) 60 days**

An individual life insurance policy will not lapse for up to 60 days after the premium due date. (p. 96)

#21. **c) Cash surrender values.**

The insurance provider does not guarantee or participate in the investment risk of a variable life insurance policy. Since all underlying assets have to be kept in a separate account, variable life insurance policies cannot provide a guaranteed cash surrender value. (p. 90)

#22. **a) Service**

The Health Maintenance Organization (HMO) provides benefits in the form of services rather than reimbursement for hospital or physician services. (p. 167)

#23. **d) Universal Life**

Universal life is referred to by the generic name of flexible premium adjustable life. The policy owner has the flexibility to raise the amount of premium going into the policy and to reduce it later again. (pp. 88-90)

#24. **a) Medical Loss Ratio (MLR)**

The Medical Loss Ratio (MLR) indicates how much of the health coverage premium has to go toward actual medical care, as opposed to administrative costs and profits. (p. 187)

#25. **c) Unlimited coverage for drug rehabilitation**

Emergency care must be provided for the member in or out of the HMO's service area. The HMO member is also provided inpatient hospital care, in or out of the service area. The services can be limited for treating emotional, mental, or nervous disorders, including drug or alcohol rehabilitation. (pp. 167-168)

#26. **a) A disability that causes the insured to be unable to work at their regular job even though they might be able to perform the duties of another occupation**

The definition of "own occupation" means the insured cannot perform their regular job but could be retrained for other jobs. (p. 194)

#27. **b) Skilled care**

Skilled nursing care is daily nursing and rehabilitative care that medical professionals can only give under the direction of a physician. (p. 229)

#28. **c) To cover the employer's administration costs**

The 2% charge is to cover the employer's administrative costs. (p. 181)

#29. **b) 75%**

State laws establish the minimum number of individuals that constitute a group. Insurance companies can have a larger number required for certain plans. (p. 133)

#30. **b) $2,500.**

Business overhead expense insurance reimburses the insured for the covered expenses incurred or the maximum specified in the policy, whichever is less. (pp. 64, 201)

#31. **c) Paid-up additions**

The paid-up additions option uses the dividend to buy small amounts of the same type of insurance as the original policy. The dividend pays up the additional insurance that was purchased. (p. 102)

#32. **d) The beneficiary must pay for a portion of prescription drug costs**

Once the initial benefit limit is reached, a gap called a "donut hole" occurs. The beneficiary is responsible for paying a portion of prescription drug costs. (pp. 213-214)

#33. **d) Morale**

Morale hazards, like DUIs, result from a state of mind that causes indifference to loss, like carelessness. Actions taken without forethought could cause physical injuries. (p. 3)

#34. **b) Level**

The main ways to pay an annuity premium are with a single premium, which is a single lump-sum payment, and a periodic premium, in which the premium is paid in multiple installments. Periodic premium payments can be level (the amount is the same for each payment) or flexible (the amount varies from one payment to the next). (p. 115)

#35. **b) Never**

All health insurance Marketplace plans cover pregnancy and childbirth, even if pregnancy begins before the coverage becomes effective. (pp. 185, 187)

#36. **d) 40**

Under Social Security, a person must have worked and contributed to Social Security for at least 40 calendar quarters, which is ten years, to attain fully insured status. (p. 139)

#37. **b) A person obtains insurance to fund a buy-sell agreement.**

Partners typically purchase buy-sell agreements in a business as a personnel or business use of insurance. Answers A, C, and D are examples of personal or family uses of insurance. (pp. 62-65)

#38. **d) Revocable**

A policy owner can change revocable beneficiaries at any time. (p. 99)

#39. **c) An association of 35 people.**

Group insurance can be issued to an employer, employee, or group formed for a purpose other than obtaining insurance. An association group (alumni or professional) can purchase group insurance for its members. The group must have been active for at least two years, be organized for reasons other than buying insurance, and have at least 100 members. (p. 156)

#40. **b) If there is a transfer for value**

If life insurance proceeds are collected in a lump-sum payment, they are usually not subject to federal taxation. If the benefit payment results in a transfer for value (if the policy is sold to another individual), it cannot be exempt from taxation. Transfer for value rules do not apply when a policy is collaterally assigned to a lender. (p. 145)

#41. **b) The people elect the Commissioner for a 4-year term**

The Commissioner is elected by the people and serves a 4-year term but can serve no more than two terms. (p. 43)

#42. **b) Deny payment of the death benefit**

The insurance company's liability is limited to a premium refund when the insured commits suicide within two years after the policy's effective date. (p. 87)

#43. **b) Capital Amount.**

The Capital Amount, or Capital Sum, is usually 50% of the principal and pays for the loss of a single body part. (pp. 173-174)

#44. **a) Key employees**

A business obtains business disability insurance for its key employees to protect it from loss in the event the employee becomes disabled. (p. 201)

#45. **a) Essential benefits.**

Essential benefits include hospitalization, emergency services, wellness, and preventive services, chronic disease management, and maternity care. (p. 187)

#46. **d) Nonsurgical services a doctor provides**

Basic Medical Expense Coverage pays for nonsurgical services a physician provides. (p. 166)

#47. **a) Within 60 days.**

The terminated employee needs to exercise an extension of benefits under COBRA within 60 days of being separated from employment. (p. 181)

#48. **a) If the primary beneficiary's death occurs before the insured's death**

The contingent beneficiary, also called a secondary or tertiary beneficiary, has a second claim if the primary beneficiary dies before the insured. (p. 99)

#49. **d) Speculative**

With speculative risk, there is both a chance to win and a chance to lose. Speculative risks are not insurable. (p. 2)

#50. **d) The annuity benefit to be excluded from taxes.**

The exclusion ratio is used to compute the annuity amounts to be excluded from taxes. (p. 147)

#51. **b) 20%**

A 20% coinsurance rate is a core benefit in Part B of Medicare supplement policies. (p. 210)

#52. **d) A capital sum is a percentage of a principal sum**

The accidental death and dismemberment rider (AD&D) pays the face amount (principal) for accidental death. It pays a percentage of that amount, or a capital sum, for accidental dismemberment. (p. 108)

#53. **b) The insured names the beneficiary.**

With Credit Life, the lending institution is the owner and names the policy's beneficiary. (pp. 91-92)

#54. **b) January 1 through March 31 every year**

The general enrollment period for Medicare Part B is annually from January 1 through March 31. (pp. 206, 207)

#55. **c) Rescind the policy**

Since the contestability period is still in force, the company can rescind the policy for material misrepresentation on the application. (pp. 12, 97)

#56. **d) Benefits start at the beginning of the 6th month and are not retroactive to the start of the disability**

Five months is the elimination period for Social Security disability benefits. Benefits begin at the beginning of the 6th month and are not retroactive to the start of the disability. (p. 202)

#57. **a) Private Duty Nursing**

Under Medicare Part A, private duty nursing is not covered. (pp. 207-209)

#58. **d) Controlling costs**

Initially, the HMO member selects a primary care physician or gatekeeper. If the member requires the attention of a specialist, the primary care physician must refer the member. This requirement helps keep the member away from higher-priced specialists unless it is essential. (pp. 153, 167-168)

#59. **d) Only one party makes a promise**

Only one of the parties to the contract is legally bound to do anything in a unilateral contract. (p. 11)

#60. **b) Family**

With a family deductible, expenses for two or more family members can satisfy a yearly common deductible. (p. 153)

#61. **a) The act of one individual who agrees to restore an injured person to the condition they enjoyed before the loss**

After a loss, the act of one person who agrees to restore the injured person to the condition they enjoyed before the loss is called indemnification. (p. 6)

#62. **c) Intermediate care**

Intermediate care is occasional nursing and rehabilitative care ordered by a physician and provided by skilled medical professionals for such things as administering medications or changing a bandage. (p. 229)

#63. **c) The insured's earnings**

Disability income benefits are limited to a percentage of the insured's earned income. Insurers want claimants to have a financial incentive to return to work. (p. 194)

#64. **c) The state of California, primarily through federal reimbursements.**

Medi-Cal is California's version of Medicaid, a federal-state partnership for providing medical coverage to medically-indigent individuals. Claims are paid for mainly with funds from the federal government. However, the states are responsible for the majority of their administrative expenses. (p. 220)

#65. **d) $450**

In this scenario, if the hospital expense benefit was $500 per day, and the hospital charged $650 per day, the insured would be responsible for the additional $150 per day. (p. 166)

#66. **c) The insurer's stock value lowers**

Group health coverage may not be renewed or discontinued due to fraud, nonpayment of premiums, or movement outside the service area. (p. 184)

#67. **d) The insurance provider can only cancel the policy for reasons specified in the contract**

The insurance provider can cancel optionally renewable policies for any reason whatsoever. A, B, and C are true. (p. 155)

#68. **c) Exposure**

Physical hazards result from the risk's structural, material, or operational features, apart from the individuals owning or managing it. Moral hazards refer to those applicants that might lie on an insurance application or, in the past, have submitted fraudulent claims against an insurer. Morale hazards refer to an increase in the hazard presented by a risk resulting from the insured's indifference to loss because of the existence of insurance. (pp. 2-3)

#69. **b) Transfer a loss.**

Insurance allows individuals to transfer a risk from themselves to a large group. (pp. 2, 4)

#70. **c) The mode of premium payment.**

The grace period can be 7, 10, or 30/31 days, depending upon whether the premium is paid weekly, monthly, quarterly, semi-annually, or annually. (p. 174)

#71. **b) Mortgage redemption**

Mortgage redemption insurance, structured as decreasing term life insurance, is intended to pay off debt as it amortizes. The decreasing death benefit pays just enough to cover the balance if a premature death occurs. (p. 87)

#72. **b) The insurer.**

In group insurance, the policy is known as the master policy. It is issued to the policy owner, who can be the employer, a trust, a union, or an association. (p. 134)

#73. **b) It eliminates a second elimination period for the same disability**

When the insured is readmitted to the hospital for the same injury, it is treated as a continuation of the first injury. (p. 195)

#74. **d) A key employee's termination.**

An organization can survive the loss of a key employee, but it would not survive any other scenarios. (p. 32)

#75. **b) Principal sum.**

Under Accidental Death and Dismemberment insurance, the principal sum is paid for accidental death. (p. 173)

#76. **a) Living Needs Rider**

The Living Needs Rider allows for the partial payment of policy death benefits if the insured is diagnosed with a terminal illness that will result in death within two years. (p. 109)

#77. **b) $70,000.**

Suppose the annuitant's death takes place during the accumulation period. In that circumstance, the beneficiary will receive the cash value or the amount of premiums paid into the plan, whichever is greater. In this example, the beneficiary will receive $70,000. (p. 115)

#78. **c) The primary beneficiary predeceases the insured**

According to the Common Disaster clause, if it cannot be determined who died first, it will be assumed the primary beneficiary died first. Therefore, the proceeds go to the contingent beneficiary. Proceeds will go to the insured's estate only if no contingent beneficiary is designated. (p. 99)

#79. **b) Express**

The agent's contract gives the agent express authority. (p. 19)

#80. **d) Underwriting is done for each person in franchise insurance**

Franchise insurance is not group insurance because individual policies are issued for every participant. Individual underwriting is completed for each person, and each participant submits their own application and medical history. (p. 157)

#81. **c) Child daycare**

LTC services are intended for senior citizens. It provides coverage for individuals who can no longer live independently and require living assistance in a nursing home facility or at home. (pp. 229-230)

#82. **d) It exists to help seniors who are not eligible to receive Medicare or Social Security**

HICAP helps seniors who are already receiving or are about to receive Medicare or Social Security. (p. 223)

#83. **a) 60%**

According to the metal level classification of health plans, the bronze plan will pay for 60% of the cost for an average population, and the participants would pay for the remaining 40%. (p. 186)

#84. **b) Defamation.**

It is against the law to make, publish, or circulate any written or oral statement or literature that is false, maliciously critical of, or significantly misrepresents the financial condition of any insurer and intends to injure anyone engaged in the insurance business. (p. 53)

#85. **b) When the policy is delivered**

The policy summary has to be provided when the policy is delivered to the policy owner. (p. 66)

#86. **c) Peril**

A peril is the cause of a loss. (p. 2)

#87. **c) Contribute a specified amount of capital reserves to the state.**

The insurance provider retains reserves to pay future claims; they are not paid to the state. (p. 42)

#88. **c) The insured.**

The policy owner, not the insured, controls the premium, coverage period, or benefit. (p. 88)

#89. **b) Part D**

Part D was added to Medicare to provide prescription drug benefits. (pp. 213-214)

#90. **c) Annuitant**

The annuitant is the individual whose life expectancy determines the annuity income amount. (p. 114)

#91. **c) Feeling.**

Should an insured suffer the loss of A, B, or D, the insurance company will assume that the insured is totally disabled. (pp. 194-195)

#92. **d) Taxed as ordinary income.**

Upon surrender or endowment, any cash value exceeding the premium payments (cost basis) is taxable as ordinary income. (pp. 100-101)

#93. **b) Adult daycare**

Adult daycare can be provided at a community or recreation center. (p. 230)

#94. **c) Religion**

When underwriting health insurance policies, the prime considerations are gender, age, occupation, avocations (hobbies), physical condition, moral and morale hazards, and the applicant's financial status. (p. 185)

#95. **a) The underwriters approve the application**

Acceptance occurs when an insurance provider's underwriter approves the application and issues a policy. (p. 10)

#96. **b) 26.**

The law extends coverage for the insured's children to age 26, regardless of their residency, marital status, financial dependence on their parents, or eligibility to enroll in their employer's plan. (p. 184)

#97. **b) Supplemental major medical**

A supplemental major medical plan will cover expenses not paid for by the basic policy and expenses exceeding the maximum. (p. 167)

#98. **a) Medicare and Medigap policies provide coverage for nursing home or long-term custodial care**

Although Medicare and Medicare supplements protect elderly insureds against the cost of medical care, these programs do not provide coverage for long-term custodial or nursing home care. Answers B, C, and D are correct. (pp. 228-229)

#99. **c) Acute.**

Long-term care services are provided in a setting other than a hospital's acute care unit. (p. 228)

#100. **d) The individual who purchases the annuity**

The annuity owner is the individual who purchases the contract but does not have to be the one who receives the benefits. (p. 114)

#101. **d) Attending Physician's Statement**

An Attending Physician's Statement (APS) includes past diagnoses, treatments, recovery times, and prognoses. (p. 149)

#102. **d) A gatekeeper HMO plan to control the costs**

Subscribers are participants in an HMO. In some HMOs, the primary care physician incurs a cost to refer patients to a more expensive specialist and, as a result, can try alternative treatments before referring a patient. (pp. 155, 167-168)

#103. **c) The purchase of a new home.**

The Guaranteed Insurability Rider lets the owner obtain additional insurance without providing proof of insurability at marriage, the birth of a child, or every three years between the ages of 25 to 40. (p. 109)

#104. **a) 1%**

If Medicare beneficiaries do not enroll when they are first eligible, they must pay a 1% penalty for each month they delay enrollment. (p. 213)

#105. **b) A percentage of the cost of service that the insured and the insurance company share**

After an insured satisfies the deductible required by the policy, the insured and the insurance company split the cost of additional expenses up to a specific limit. This coinsurance amount is presented as a percentage. (p. 152)

#106. **a) An explanation of where the premiums have been invested.**

The notice of a right to cancel the policy includes information regarding the time limit, to whom to return the policy, and possible surrender charges and penalties. (pp. 121-122, 126)

#107. **a) Provide income for retirement.**

The primary purpose of an annuity is to liquidate an estate and provide income for retirement. Life insurance creates an estate and provides a death benefit to the policy's beneficiaries. (p. 114)

#108. **a) "Life insurance illustration."**

An illustration used in the sale of a life insurance policy needs to be clearly labeled "life insurance illustration." (p. 30)

#109. **d) Qualified**

A qualified retirement plan entitles the owner to tax benefits. For a retirement plan to be qualified, certain federal requirements must be met. (pp. 119, 136-139)

#110. **c) Elimination.**

Risk cannot be eliminated. Answers A, B, and D are techniques used to manage risk. (pp. 4-5)

#111. **a) Loss of income while hospitalized.**

Answers B, C, and D would be covered by medical expense insurance. The insured would need disability income insurance to cover lost wages. (pp. 166-167, 194)

#112. **d) Modified Endowment Contracts must always pass the 7-pay test**

Life insurance contracts are required to pass the 7-pay test; otherwise, they are classified as Modified Endowment Contracts (MECs). (pp. 149-150)

#113. **b) Nonforfeiture values.**

Because permanent life insurance policies have cash values, certain guarantees, called nonforfeiture values, are built into the policy that the policy owner cannot forfeit. (p. 84)

#114. **b) The rider waives insurance premiums if the insured is disabled.**

The waiver of monthly deductions rider waives the cost of insurance and other expenses should the insured become disabled. The waiver of premium rider waives the policy premium if the insured becomes disabled (p. 108)

#115. **b) Representation.**

Regarding insurance applications, representations are statements believed to be true to the best of one's knowledge. They are not guaranteed to be true. (p. 12)

#116. **b) The contract**

The policy is the written agreement that puts the insurance coverage into effect. (pp. 11, 14)

#117. **c) Fire**

Fire is a peril, which is a cause of loss. Hazards increase the likelihood that a peril could occur. (p. 2)

#118. **a) Indemnity**

Indemnity policies do not pay bills or expenses; they provide the insured with a stated benefit amount for each day they are confined in a hospital. (p. 157)

#119. **d) Statement of Good Health**

Suppose the premium was not collected with the application. In that case, the producer may be required to obtain a Statement of Good Health at the time of policy delivery. This document confirms the insured has not suffered injury or illness since the application date. (p. 76)

#120. **c) Nonpayment of premium**

An insurance provider that issues a long-term care policy cannot cancel or decline to renew a policy based exclusively on the insured's age or mental or physical deterioration. (pp. 232, 233)

#121. **a) Transfer**

Transfer is a fundamental principle of insurance, where the risk of financial loss is assigned to another party. Insurance is the most common method of transferring risk from a person or group to an insurer. (pp. 2, 4)

#122. **d) Diabetes**

Physical hazards are individual characteristics that increase the chances of the cause of loss and exist due to a physical condition, prior medical history, or a condition at birth, like blindness. (p. 2)

#123. **a) It provides the highest monthly benefits**

Under pure life, also known as life-only or straight life, this payment ends at the annuitant's death. This option offers the highest monthly benefits for an individual annuitant. With this option, while the annuity payments are guaranteed for the annuitant's lifetime, there is no guarantee that all the proceeds will be fully paid out. (p. 117)

#124. **a) Cover a mortgage.**

Decreasing term coverage is generally obtained to insure the payment of a mortgage or other debts if the insured dies prematurely. (p. 83)

#125. **b) 60.**

The time between the day when a family's youngest child turns 16 and before the surviving spouse turns age 60 is referred to as a blackout period. (p. 140)

#126. **d) Fixed Amount**

The fixed amount option pays a fixed, specified amount in installments until the principal and interest (proceeds) are exhausted. The recipient chooses a specified fixed dollar amount to be paid until it is gone. (p. 104)

#127. **a) She does not have earned income**

Earned income refers to wages, salary, and commissions. It would not include income from investments, trust funds, unemployment benefits, and any other unearned payment forms. (p. 119)

#128. c) Groups of one or more

HIPAA ensures the portability of group insurance coverage and includes various required benefits that affect the self-employed, small employers, pregnant women, and the mentally ill. HIPAA applies to groups of two or more. (p. 183)

#129. d) Peril

Perils are causes of loss. (p. 2)

#130. b) High premiums.

Catastrophic plans offer lower monthly premiums but also feature high deductibles. The insured is typically required to pay up to a certain amount of medical costs. After the insured satisfies the deductible, the catastrophic plan will cover essential health benefit costs. (p. 187)

#131. a) The beneficiary

The beneficiary is not required to have an insurable interest in the insured's life. (p. 6)

#132. b) The MIB helps underwriters to evaluate and classify risks

The Medical Information Bureau (MIB) is an information source for underwriting that specifically focuses on an applicant's medical history. (pp. 70, 72, 159-160)

#133. a) It satisfies IRS requirements for favorable tax treatment

A qualified annuity allows the employer or individual to use contributions to the plan as a tax deduction. Also, while in the plan, the income earned by the contribution builds income tax-free. The money is not taxed until it is withdrawn from the plan and then is taxed at the current tax rate. (pp. 119, 136-139)

#134. d) Medicare Advantage Plans

A Medicare Advantage Plan is a Medicare program that offers the patient more choices among health plans. Everyone with Medicare Parts A and B is eligible, except those with End-Stage Renal Disease. Medicare Advantage Plans used to be called Medicare + Choice Plans. (pp. 212-213)

#135. c) Death caused by a head-on collision

The Accidental Death rider pays some multiple of the face amount as long as death is the result of an accident as defined in the policy. It would not include death caused by any disability or health problem, self-inflicted injuries, war, or dangerous hobbies or avocations. (p. 108)

#136. b) 10 days

If the premium is paid on a monthly basis, a policy's grace period needs to be at least ten days. (p. 174)

#137. c) Joint and Survivor

The life income joint and survivor option will guarantee an income for two or more individuals for as long as they are alive. Most contracts allow the surviving recipient to receive a reduced payment after the first recipient dies. (p. 103)

#138. a) Annual

Paying the premium once per year would be the least expensive payment mode because of fewer billing and loading charges. (p. 74)

#139. b) Custodial care

Custodial care is care for meeting the personal needs of an insured, such as assistance in dressing, bathing, or eating, provided by nonmedical personnel under a physician's orders. (pp. 229, 230)

#140. **b) Basic surgical expense insurance**

Basic surgical expense coverage is usually written in conjunction with hospital expense policies. Coverage includes anesthesiologists, surgeons' fees, and the operating room when it is not covered as a miscellaneous medical item. (p. 166)

#141. **c) The one party accepts the exact terms of the other party's offer**

In insurance contracts, there needs to be a definite offer by one party, and this offer has to be accepted in its exact terms by the other party. Both an offer and its acceptance are included in an agreement. (p. 10)

#142. **b) A waiver of premium rider.**

The Waiver of Premium rider causes the insurance provider to waive future premiums if the premium payor is disabled for six months or more. (p. 108)

#143. **b) Insurer.**

Health insurance applications require the signatures of the proposed insured, the policy owner (if different than the insured), and the agent or producer. (p. 158)

#144. **c) Cost base**

The cost base is the nontaxable portion; this is the anticipated return of the paid-in principal. The interest earned on the principal is the taxable portion. This portion is known as the tax base. (p. 146)

#145. **c) Individuals with low assets and low income.**

Medicare is a federal program for individuals over 65, individuals on Social Security for two years, and individuals with permanent kidney failure. Income and assets have nothing to do with Medicare eligibility. (p. 206)

#146. **c) Long-term care services.**

The Medicare program does not cover long-term care services. (pp. 209-212)

#147. **a) The larger the pool of risks, the more accurate the predictions will be**

It is more likely for similar results to occur if a larger group is studied. (p. 3)

#148. **c) Medicare Part B**

Medicaid (called Medi-Cal in California) is a program that offers health benefits for uninsured or low-income individuals; therefore, no premiums are charged. Part A of Medicare is provided at no cost to retirees; Part B requires a monthly payment from the insured. (pp. 209-212)

#149. **a) A specified period that an individual joining a group has to wait before becoming eligible for coverage**

The Probationary Period is the waiting period that new employees would typically have to meet before becoming eligible for benefits. (p. 162)

#150. **d) Minor children or business associates of the policy owner**

Most third-party ownership policies are written in business situations or for minors in which the parent owns the policy. (p. 132)

INDEX

A NOTE FROM LELAND

What did you think of *California Life and Health Insurance License Exam Prep*?

First of all, thank you for purchasing this study guide. I know you could have picked any resource to help prepare for your Life and Health exam, but you chose this book, and I am incredibly grateful.

I hope that it added value and provided the confidence to pass the exam on your first attempt. If you feel this book adequately prepared you and helped you pass the exam, I'd like to hear from you. I hope you can take some time to post a review on Amazon and include a screenshot of your passing score. Your feedback and support will help this author improve this book and his writing craft for future projects.

Thank you again, and I wish you all the best in your future success!

Leland Chant

Made in United States
Orlando, FL
20 March 2024

44990671R00207